A Larger Hope?

A Larger Hope? Universal Salvation from Christian Beginnings to Julian of Norwich, by Ilaria L. E. Ramelli

A Larger Hope? Universal Salvation from the Reformation to the Nineteenth Century, by Robin A. Parry, with Ilaria L. E. Ramelli

A Larger Hope?

Universal Salvation from Christian Beginnings
to Julian of Norwich

A Larger Hope?

Universal Salvation from Christian Beginnings
to Julian of Norwich

by

ILARIA L. E. RAMELLI

With a foreword by
Richard Bauckham

CASCADE *Books* · Eugene, Oregon

A LARGER HOPE? UNIVERSAL SALVATION FROM CHRISTIAN
BEGINNINGS TO JULIAN OF NORWICH

Cascade Books
An Imprint of Wipf and Stock Publishers
199 W. 8th Ave., Suite 3
Eugene, OR 97401

www.wipfandstock.com

PAPERBACK ISBN: 978-1-61097-884-2
HARDCOVER ISBN: 978-1-4982-8798-2
EBOOK ISBN: 978-1-5326-4300-2

Cataloguing-in-Publication data:

Names: Ramelli, Ilaria, 1973–, author | Bauckham, Richard, foreword writer

Title: A larger hope? Universal salvation from Christian beginnings to Julian of
    Norwich / Ilaria L. E. Ramelli, with a foreword by Richard Bauckham

Description: Eugene, OR: Cascade Books, 2019 | Series: A Larger Hope, vol. 1 |
    Includes bibliographical references and index.

Identifiers: ISBN 978-1-61097-884-2 (paperback) | ISBN 978-1-4982-8798-2 (hard-
    cover) | ISBN 978-1-5326-4300-2 (ebook)

Subjects: LCSH: Universalism | Origen | Restorationism—History of doctrines |
    Universal salvation—Biblical teaching | Hell—Christianity | Salvation—Chris-
    tianity

Classification: BT263 R36 2019 (print) | BT263 (ebook)

Manufactured in the U.S.A.

Cover image: "Origen Teaching the Saints" by Eileen McGuckin, used with
permission.

Ad maiorem Dei gloriam
May this contribute to the glory of God

Table of Contents

Foreword

The extent to which a belief in universal salvation was held and taught in the early centuries of the Christian church has often been under-estimated. As Professor Ramelli shows, this belief did not originate with Origen, the best known patristic proponent of it, but most of those who subsequently held to it were influenced by Origen and the particular shape that he gave to this hope of the final "restoration" of all God's rational creatures, including the importance of free will, which God will not suppress, and the purifying and restorative character of post-mortem punishment. Professor Ramelli shows that this hope cannot be dismissed as no more than an intrusion into the Christian tradition from Platonic philosophy. These theologians rooted their teaching in exegesis of Scripture and embraced a Christocentric vision of the universe and God's purpose for it.

Here we are taken on an enlightening tour of the relevant writings of the major figures and also some minor figures. Some are well known, others very little known. Some are surprising. Ramelli is thoroughly acquainted with all of the texts and the relevant secondary literature. A very valuable feature is the extensive quotations from all the writers in question, given in her own translations. Moreover, Professor Ramelli provides for us in each case with a full profile of the various factors that contribute to each writer's understanding of the doctrine of universal restoration. Given the extent and diversity of the literature this is a major achievement—and a unique one too—for which anyone with an interest in this important subject will be heartily grateful. At a time when the popularity of belief in universal salvation seems to be increasing, this book will be an important resource both for learning about the form that belief actually took in a major theological tradition of the early centuries and for engaging with the arguments of the key theologians who taught it.

Richard Bauckham
Emeritus Professor of New Testament Studies, University of St Andrews
Senior Scholar, Ridley Hall, Cambridge

Preface

No being will remain outside the number of the saved.
(St. Gregory of Nyssa, *On 1 Cor 15:28*, Downing, 21)

Laudetur Iesus Christus,
semper laudetur.
May Jesus Christ be praised,
May He always be praised.

The present book addresses a general learned readership, pastors, students (graduates and undergraduates), and other interested Christians. For all references to original texts, often in extensive quotations, and to scholarship regarding the sections from the New Testament to John the Scot Eriugena (approximately the first Christian millennium), as well as a much more detailed treatment, I refer to my *The Christian Doctrine of Apokatastasis: A Critical Assessment from the New Testament to Eriugena*,[1] a very substantial, thousand-page scientific monograph aimed at scholars, academic specialists, and postgraduate students, which—much to my comfort, after an intense labor of sixteen years—has received excellent reviews, e.g., by Anthony Meredith in the *International Journal of the Platonic Tradition*; Mark Edwards in *Journal of Theological Studies*; Johannes van Oort in *Vigiliae Christianae*; Steven Nemes (Fuller Theological

---

1. Leiden: Brill, 2013. https://brill.com/view/title/16787. Online edition: http://booksandjournals.brillonline.com/content/books/9789004245709. https://www.amazon.co.uk/Ilaria-L.-E.-Ramelli/e/B01M2WJKVL; https://www.amazon.com/Christian-Doctrine-Apokatastasis-Supplements-Christianae/dp/900424509X.

Seminary) in the *Journal of Analytic Theology*;[2] Robin A. Parry in the *International Journal of Systematic Theology*, and Chris L. De Wet in the *Journal of Early Christian History*. Abstracts of all these reviews are available at www.brill.com/christian-doctrine-apokatastasis and https://brill.com/view/title/16787. Many scholars have referenced this monograph and endorsed its conclusions.[3]

2. http://journalofanalytictheology.com/jat/index.php/jat/article/view/jat.2015-3.181913130418a/271.

3. For example, George Karamanolis, *The Philosophy of Early Christianity* (Durham: Acumen, 2013), 307; Lautaro Roig Lanzillotta, "Greek Philosophy and the Problem of Evil in Clement of Alexandria and Origen," CFC(g) 23 (2013) 207-23, esp. n. 44; George Van Kooten, Oda Wischmeyer and N. T. Wright, "How Greek was Paul's Eschatology?," *New Testament Studies* 61.2 (2015) 239-53; Thomas McGlothlin, "Raised to Newness of Life: Resurrection and Moral Transformation in Second- and Third-Century Christian Theology" (PhD diss. Duke University, 2015, advisors J. Warren Smith, Elizabeth Clark, Joel Markus, Zlatko Plese); Nikolai Kiel, *Ps-Athenagoras De Resurrectione* (Leiden: Brill, 2015), 322, 330, 596, 606, n. 508, 771, etc.; Thomas Allin, *Christ Triumphant*, annotated edition, ed. Robin Parry (Eugene, OR, Wipf & Stock, 2015), 109, 113, 115, 117, 118, 119, 123, 124, 125, 127, 130, 134, 140, 145, 149, 150, 151, 154, 158, 164, 170, 172, 173, 174, 177, 345. István Perczel, "St. Maximus on the Lord's Prayer: An Inquiry into His Relationship to the Origenist Tradition," in *The Architecture of the Cosmos: St. Maximus the Confessor: New Perspectives*, eds. Antoine Lévy, Pauli Annala, Olli Hallamaa, and Tuomo Lankila (Helsinki: Luther-Agricola-Society, 2015), 221-78: 230; Steven Nemes, "Christian Apokatastasis: Two Paradigmatic Objections," *Journal of Analytic Theology* 4 (2016) 67-86; Daniel Heide, "Apokatastasis: The Resolution of Good and Evil in Origen and Eriugena," *Dionysius* 3 (2015) 195-213: 195, 196, 197, 199, 201, 203, 204, 205, 206, 212; James Gould, *Practicing Prayer for the Dead* (Eugene, OR: Wipf and Stock, 2016), 107, 108, 109, 110, 111, 112, 117, 123, 125, 126, 131, 132, 134, 138, 139, 142, 144, 146, 209, 244, 269, etc. Ryan Fowler, *Imperial Plato: Albinus, Maximus, Apuleius* (Las Vegas: Parmenides, 2016), 307; Aleksandar Dakovac, "Apocatastasis and Predestination: Ontological Assumptions of Origen's and Augustine's Soteriologies," *Bogoslovska smotra* 86.4 (2016) 813-826: 814; Elena Ene-D Vasilescu, "Love Never Fails: Gregory of Nyssa on Theosis," in *Visions of God and Ideas on Deification in Patristic Thought*, eds Mark Edwards, Elena Ene D-Vasilescu (Oxford: Routledge, 2016), Ch. 3, n. 58; 59; Maged S. A. Mikhail, *The Legacy of Demetrius of Alexandria 189-232 CE: The Form and Function of Hagiography in Late Antique and Islamic Egypt* (London: Routledge/Taylor & Francis, 2016), 34; Martin Wenzel, "The Omnipotence of God as a Challenge for Theology in Origen and Gregory of Nyssa," in *Theology in Evagrius, the Cappadocians, and Neoplatonism*, ed. Ilaria Ramelli, with the collaboration of Kevin Corrigan, Giulio Maspero, and Monica Tobon (Leuven: Peeters, 2017), 23-38; Daniel J. Crosby, "The Tyranny of Authority: Eternal Damnation in the Fragments of Clement of Alexandria?" in *Scholarship, Research, and Creative Work at Bryn Mawr College* (2017), 1-15: 3-5 (http://repository.brynmawr.edu/gsas_pubs/42017); Ken Parry, review of *The Architecture of the Cosmos: St. Maximus the Confessor: Bryn Mawr Classical Review* 2017.10.48 (http://bmcr.brynmawr.edu/2017/2017-10-48.html); Giulio Malavasi, "The Greek Version(s) of

It will be followed in due course, God willing, by two other scholarly monographs: one on non-Christian and pre-Christian philosophical concepts of *apokatastasis*, from ancient philosophy to late antique Platonism (Proclus, Damascius), and another on the political, theological, pastoral, ecclesiastical, social, historical, and even linguistic causes for the rejection of the doctrine of *apokatastasis* or universal restoration, in late antiquity, by the "Church of the Empire"—mainly under the influence of Justinian in the East and of Augustine in the West.

In addition to my monograph on apokatastasis, see Brian Daley, *The Hope of the Early Church: A Handbook of Patristic Eschatology*,[4] and Brian Daley, "Eschatology in the Early Church Fathers," in *The Oxford Handbook of Eschatology*.[5] On p. 7 of the online edition, Daley remarked: "few general studies exist of the broader shape and development of early Christian hope concerning the end of this present history and the beginning of God's kingdom." My monograph, *The Christian Doctrine of Apokatastasis*, and the present book contribute to filling this persistent scholarly gap. It is helpful to read this monograph and the present book together with my invited response to Michael McClymond's critique, in *Theological Studies* 76.4 (2015) 827–35.[6]

Augustine's *De gestis Pelagii*," Zeitschrift für Antikes Christentum 21,3 (2017), 559–72; *Women and Knowledge in Early Christianity*, ed. Ulla Tervahauta, Ismo Dunderberg et alii (Leiden: Brill, 2017), 352 etc.; David Konstan, "A New Subjectivity? Teaching Eros through the Greek Novel and Early Christian Texts," in *Reading and Teaching Ancient Fiction: Jewish, Christian, and Greco-Roman Narratives*, eds. Sara Johnson, Rubén René Dupertuis, and Chris Shea (Atlanta: SBL Press, 2018), 251–60: 260; Johannes Zachhuber, Oxford papers (http://www.academia.edu/36548030/Philosophy_and_Theology_in_Late_Antiquity_Some_reflections_on_concepts_and_terminologies); Nathan Eubank, "Prison, Penance or Purgatory: The Interpretation of Matthew 5.25–6 and Parallels," *New Testament Studies* 64.2 (2018) 162–77; Valeriu Gherghel, *Origen and The Paradox of Literalist Reading*, http://hermeneia.ro/wp-content/uploads/2016/08/13_VARIA_Gherghel-V.pdf; George Karamanolis, "Gregory of Nyssa," in *Brill Encyclopedia of Early Christianity* (Leiden: Brill, forthcoming), etc.

4. Cambridge: Cambridge University Press, 1991; rev. ed., Peabody, MA: Hendrickson, 2003.

5. Oxford: Oxford University Press, 2007, online ed. 2009 DOI: 10.1093/oxfordhb/9780195170498.003.0006.

6. DOI: 10.1177/0040563915605265. tsj.sagepub.com. Available online at: http://tsj.sagepub.com/cgi/reprint/76/4/827.pdf ; http://connection.ebscohost.com/c/articles/111306962/reply-professor-michael-mcclymond; http://www.thefreelibrary.com/Reply+to+professor+Michael+McClymond.-a0434320574 ; http://www.docfoc.com/ilaria-ramelli-theological-studies; https://www.scribd.com/doc/260021087/Ilaria-Ramelli-Theological-Studies; https://www.scribd.com/document/298849526/

For the Christian doctrine of universal salvation in more recent times, besides the present volume, which addresses also the span of time from Eriugena to Meister Eckhart and Julian of Norwich (absent from *The Christian Doctrine of Apokatastasis*), I refer readers to Robin Parry and Christopher Partridge (eds.), *Universal Salvation? The Current Debate*,[7] and Gregory MacDonald (ed.), *All Shall be Well: Explorations in Universal Salvation and Christian Theology, from Origen to Moltmann*.[8] A concise but rigorous handbook of patristic eschatology is offered by Brian Daley, *The Hope of the Early Church*, mentioned above. A short survey on patristic universalism was provided by Thomas Allin in 1885; see now the annotated edition: Thomas Allin, *Christ Triumphant: Universalism Asserted as the Hope of the Gospel on the Authority of Reason, the Fathers, and Holy Scripture*.[9] I look forward to David Bentley Hart's constructive book on universalism (Yale, 2019).

In the present book I do not merely summarize the content of *The Christian Doctrine of Apokatastasis*, but also add many new sections that were absent from the larger volume, e.g., on annihilationism, some apocrypha, Hilary of Poitiers, Basil of Caesarea, Macarius of Magnesia, Aphrahat, Barsanuphius, Theophylact, Meister Eckhart, the appendix on the terminology of eternity, and all the last section from Eriugena to Julian of Norwich. Furthermore, I have added various new texts, proofs, and arguments concerning a number of theologians—from Clement and Eusebius to Basil of Caesarea, from Ambrose and Marius Victorinus to Maximus the Confessor, from Gregory of Nazianzus and Diodore of Tarsus to Titus of Basra and Eriugena, and more—which were not included in the 2013 monograph. So I hope that even those who have read *The Christian Doctrine of Apokatastasis* will find new material here that will be of interest.

In collaboration with David Konstan, I wrote a monograph some ten years ago about the Greek words *aiōnios* and *aidios*, entitled *Terms for Eternity*.[10] Given the significance of the word *aiōnios* in discussions about

Reply-to-Professor-Michael-McClymond;   http://encyclopedia2.thefreedictionary. com/Origen; http://encyclopedia2.thefreedictionary.com/Origen under Reply to Professor Michael McClymond;http://mahoundsparadise.blogspot.com/2017/07/pope-francis-appoints-universalist-all.html, etc. See here an updated version in Appendix 2.

7. Carlisle, UK: Paternoster, 2003. Grand Rapids: Eerdmans, 2004.

8. Eugene, OR: Cascade, 2011.

9. Edited with an introductory essay and notes by Robin A. Parry, with a foreword by Thomas Talbott (Eugene, OR: Wipf and Stock, 2015), 83–136.

10. Piscataway, NJ: Gorgias, 2007, with new editions in 2011 and 2013, reviewed

universal salvation in the Bible and in the early church that earlier study has predictably proven important in the preparation of my *Apokatastasis* monograph. Given this importance, the main findings of that extensive research are briefly summarized in an Appendix at the end of this book.

This book is the first of a projected series of three books on the doctrine of universal salvation. In the second volume, *A Larger Hope? From the Reformation to the Nineteenth Century*, Robin Parry, with some contributions from me, will pick up the story in its mainly Protestant streams. The third volume, which will be co-authored, shall trace the significant developments in the shape and fortunes of the idea in the twentieth and twenty-first centuries. We hope that these books taken together will provide a helpful and reliable resource for those wishing to explore an often-forgotten stream in the history of the Christian tradition.

by Carl O'Brien in *The Classical Review* 60.2 (2010), 390-391; in *International Review of Biblical Studies*, ed. Bernhard Lang, 54 (2007/2008), Leiden: Brill, 2009, 444, 1901; Danilo Ghira in *Maia* 61 (2009), 732-734; Shawn Keough in *EThL* 84.4 (2008) 601; in *Biblical Scholarship* (2016): https://biblicalscholarship.wordpress.com/2016/02/20/summary-terms-for-eternity-aionios-and-aidios-in-classical-and-christian-texts/ Referred to by Joel Kalvesmaki, ed., *Guide to Evagrius Ponticus*, summer 2014 edition (Washington, DC, 2014, evagriusponticus.net); *The Cambridge Companion to Socrates*, ed. D. R. Morrison (Cambridge: CUP, 2011), p. x; Steven Nemes, "Christian Apokatastasis: Two Paradigmatic Objections," *Journal of Analytic Theology* 4 (2016), 67-86: philpapers.org/rec/NEMCA; http://gcu.academia.edu/StevenNemes; Gregory MacDonald, *The Evangelical Universalist*, 2nd ed. (Eugene, OR: Cascade Books, 2012), p. xv James Gould, *Practicing Prayer for the Dead* (Eugene, OR: Wipf and Stock, 2016), 107, 269; John Behr, *Origen: On First Principles*, vol. 1 (Oxford: OUP, 2017), lxxviii; Tera Harmon, "Motion (κίνησις) and Anthropology in the Writings of Gregory of Nyssa" (PhD diss. University of Notre Dame, 2016, advisors Susan Wessel, Robin Darling Young, William Mccarthy); Réka Valentin, "Immortality in the Book of Wisdom in the Context of the Overlapping World," *Studia Universitatis Babes-Bolyai, Theologia Catholica Latina* 55,2 (2010) 85-99: 86; Thomas Axeland, "Origen's Commentary on John: Spiritual Interpretation, Polemics, and Transformation" (PhD diss. University of British Columbia, Regent College, 2013), 146; David Sielaff, "Modern Recognition of Universal Salvation," *Association for Scriptural Knowledge* 8.10 (2010), 1-15, etc.

Acknowledgments

A tribute of special gratitude goes to Robin Parry, who invited me to write this book many years ago, and without whom this work would definitely not be here. He also added the beginnings of several sections, to offer a survey of the dates and biography of theologians (and was patient enough during the two years of a partial blindness owing to vitreous and incipient retinal detachment, which is ongoing and we hope will subside soon!).

I am also deeply grateful to Richard Bauckham, who graciously accepted to honor me by writing the foreword to this work, to the colleagues who wrote honouring endorsements, and to all friends and colleagues with whom I have discussed the topic of universal salvation in Christianity over many years on a number of occasions. They are too many to be named and I would easily risk forgetting some, which would be too unfair.

I would like to thank heartily, as ever, all the intelligent, upright, and affectionate friends and colleagues, all of them great scholars and wonderful persons, who, around the world, gladden me in my research and academic engagement, and have continued to do so for over twenty years of scientific work at the academic level by now. Also, I must profoundly thank all those who assist me in all ways, at home, at University, and everywhere, and have done so for many years. Without them I simply couldn't manage to live and work.

Finally, not last, but first and foremost, in awe I thank the admirable and incredible help of Heaven, on which all of my professional work and my very life has entirely depended.

Abbreviations

Adv. eos qui cast. aegre fer.	Gregory of Nyssa, *Adversus eos qui castigationes aegre ferunt* / *Against Those Who Cannot Bear Reproaches*
AH	Irenaeus of Lyons, *Adversus Haereses* / *Against Heresies*
Amb.	Maximus the Confessor, *Ambigua* / *Ambiguous Points*
Ant.	Josephus, *Antiquitates Iudaicae* / *Jewish Antiquities*
Apol. c. Hier.	Rufinus, *Apologia contra Hieronymum* / *Apology against Jerome*
Aut.	Theophilus of Antioch, *Ad Autolycum* / *To Autolycus*
Bibl.	Photius, *Bibliotheca* / *Library*
Car.	Maximus the Confessor, *Capita de Caritate* / *Chapters on Love*
Carm.	Gregory Nazianzen, *Carmina* / *Poems*
C. Aster.	Marcellus of Ancyra, *Contra Asterium* / *Against Asterius*
CC	Origen, *Contra Celsum* / *Against Celsus*
CCG	Corpus Christianorum, series Graeca
CD	Augustine, *De Civitate Dei* / *The City of God*
C. Eun. Or. Prod.	Gregory Nazianzen, *Contra Eunomium Oratio Prodialexis* / *Oration against Eunomius*

C. Iul.	Augustine, *Contra Iulianum* / *Against Julian*
C. Marc.	Eusebius, *Contra Marcellum* / *Against Marcellus of Ancyra*
Comm. in Eccl.	Didymus of Alexandria, *Commentarii in Ecclesiasten* / *Commentary on Ecclesiastes*
Comm. in Eph.	Jerome, *Commentarii in Epistulam ad Ephesios* / *Commentary on Ephesians*
Comm. in Gal.	Theodore of Mopsuestia, *Commentarii in Epistulam ad Galatas* / *Commentary on Galatians*
Comm. in I-II Cor.	Didymus of Alexandria, *Commentarii in Epistulas I–II ad Corinthios* / *Commentary on 1–2 Corinthians*
Comm. in Io.	Origen, *Commentarii in Ioannem* / *Commentary on John*
Comm. in Iob	Didymus of Alexandria, *Commentarii in Iob* / *Commentary on Job*
Comm. in Is.	Eusebius of Caesarea / Basil of Caesarea, *Commentarii in Isaiam* / *Commentary on Isaiah*
Comm. in Matt.	Origen, *Commentarii in Matthaeum* / *Commentary on Matthew*
Comm. in Ps.	Eusebius or Origen (or another author, indicated in the text), *Commentarii in Psalmos* / *Commentary on Psalms*
Comm. in Ps. 20–21; 35–39	Didymus of Alexandria, *Commentarii in Psalmos XX–XXI; XXXV–XXXIX* / *Commentary on Psalms 20–21; 35–39*
Comm. in Rom.	Origen, *Commentarii in Epistulam ad Romanos* / *Commentary on Romans*
Comm. in Rom. Fr.	Origen, *Commentariorum in Epistulam ad Romanos Fragmenta* / *Fragments from the Commentary on Romans*
Comm. in Zach.	Didymus of Alexandria, *Commentarii in Zachariam* / *Commentary on Zachary*

C. Ruf.	Jerome, *Contra Rufinum* / *Against Rufinus*
C. usur.	Gregory of Nyssa, *Contra Usurarios* / *Against Usurers*
DE	Eusebius of Caesarea, *Demonstratio Evangelica* / *Demonstration of the Gospel*
De an.	Gregory of Nyssa, *De Anima et Resurrectione* / *On the Soul and the Resurrection*
De beat.	Gregory of Nyssa, *De Beatitudinibus* / *On the Beatitudes*
De benef.	Gregory of Nyssa, *De beneficentia* / *On Doing Good*
Decal.	Philo of Alexandria, *De Decalogo* / *On the Decalogue*
Decr.	Athanasius, *De decretis Nicaenae Synodi* / *On the Decisions of the Council of Nicaea*
De gest. Pel.	Augustine, *De gestis Pelagii* / *On Pelagius' Deeds*
De haer.	Augustine, *De haeresibus* / *On heresies*
De hom. op.	Gregory of Nyssa, *De hominis opificio* / *On the Creation of the Human Being*
De Incarn.	Athanasius / Marcellus of Ancyra (?), *De Incarnatione et contra Arianos* / *On the Incarnation, Against the Arians*
De mor.	Augustine, *De moribus Ecclesiae Catholicae et de moribus Manichaeorum* / *On the Customs of the Catholic Church and on the Customs of the Manichaeans*
De mort.	Gregory of Nyssa, *De mortuis* / *On the Dead*
De orat.	Origen, *De oratione* / *On Prayer*
De or. dom.	Gregory of Nyssa, *De oratione dominica* / *On the Lord's Prayer*
De perf.	Gregory of Nyssa, *De perfectione* / *On Christian Perfection*

De praed.	John the Scot Eriugena, *De praedestinatione* / *On Predestination*
De praed. adv. Joh. Erig.	Prudentius of Troyes, *De praedestinatione adversus Johannem Erigenam* / *On Predestination against John Eriugena*
De res.	Methodius, *De resurrectione* / *On the Resurrection*
De Spir. S.	Basil, *De Spiritu Sancto* / *On the Holy Spirit*
De trid. sp.	Gregory of Nyssa, *De tridui spatio* / *On the Three-Day Interval between Christ's Death and Resurrection*
De v. Mos.	Gregory of Nyssa, *De Vita Mosis* / *On the Life of Moses*
De virg.	Gregory of Nyssa, *De virginitate* / *On Virginity*
Dial. cum Her.	Origen, *Dialogus cum Heraclide*; *Dialogue with Heraclides*
DN	Ps. Dionysius the Areopagite, *De divinis nominibus* / *On the Names of God*
Eccl. theol.	Eusebius, *Ecclesiastica theologia* / *The Theology of the Church*
Ecl. Proph.	Clement of Alexandria, *Eclogae Propheticae* / *Prophetic Excerpts*
Ench.	Augustine, *Enchiridion* / *Handbook*
EH	Pseudo-Dionysius, *De ecclesiastica hierarchia* / *On the Hierarchy of the Church*
Ep.	Basil of Caesarea (or another author specified in the text), *Epistulae* / *Letters*
Ep. ad Anat.	Evagrius Ponticus, *Epistula ad Anatolium* / *Letter to Anatolius*
Ep. ad Mel.	Evagrius Ponticus, *Epistula ad Melaniam* / *Letter to Melania* or *Great Letter*
Ep. ad Sm.	Ignatius of Antioch, *Epistula ad Smyrnaeos* / *Letter to Christians in Smyrnae*

Ep. fidei	Evagrius, *Epistula fidei* / *Letter on Faith*
Exp. in Prov.	Origen, *Expositio in Proverbios* / *Explanation of Proverbs*
Exh. ad Mart.	Origen, *Exhortatio ad Martyrium* / *Exhortation to Martyrdom*
Fr. in Iob	Origen, *Fragmenta in Iob* / *Fragments on Job*
Fr. in Matt.	Origen, *Fragmenta in Matthaeum* / *Fragments on Matthew*
Fr. in Prov.	Origen, *Fragmenta in Proverbios* / *Fragments on Proverbs*
Fr. in Ps.	Didymus of Alexandria, *Fragmenta in Psalmos* / *Fragments on Psalms*
GNO	*Gregorii Nysseni Opera*. Leiden: Brill
HE	Eusebius, *Historia Ecclesiastica* / *Church History*
Her.	Philo of Alexandria, *Quis heres rerum divinarum sit* / *Who is the Heir of the Divine Goods?*
HL	Palladius, *Historia Lausiaca* / *Lausiac History*
Hom. in Cant.	Gregory of Nyssa, *Homiliae in Canticum Canticorum* / *Homilies on the Song of Songs*
Hom. in Ex.	Origen, *Homiliae in Exodum* / *Homilies on Exodus*
Hom. in Ier.	Origen, *Homiliae in Ieremiam* / *Homilies on Jeremiah*
Hom. in Ies. Nav.	Origen, *Homiliae in librum Iesu Nave* / *Homilies on Joshua*
Hom. in Lev.	Origen, *Homiliae in Leviticum* / *Homilies on Leviticus*
Hom. in Luc.	Origen, *Homiliae in Lucam* / *Homilies on Luke*
Hom. in Ps. 36–8	Origen, *Homiliae in Psalmos XXXVI–XXXVIII* / *Homilies on Psalms 36–38.*
Hom. in Reg.	Origen, *Homiliae in Reges* / *Homilies on Kings*

In d. nat. Salv.	Gregory of Nyssa, *In diem natalem Salvatoris* / *On the Day of the Birth of the Savior*
In ep. can. br. enarr.	Didymus of Alexandria, *In Epistulas Canonicas brevis enarratio* / *Short Explanation of the Canonical Epistles*
In Inscr. Ps.	Gregory of Nyssa, *In Inscriptiones Psalmorum* / *On the Titles of the Psalms*
In Luc.	Eusebius of Caesarea, *In Lucam* / *Exegesis of Luke*
In Or. Dom.	Gregory of Nyssa or Maximus the Confessor, *In Orationem Dominicam* / *Comments on the Lord's Prayer*
In sex. Ps.	Gregory of Nyssa, *In Sextum Psalmum* / *On the Sixth Psalm*
In Theoph.	Gregory Nazianzen, *In Theophaniam* / *On the Theophany (Manifestation of the Divinity)*
KG	Evagrius Ponticus, *Kephalaia Gnostica* / *Chapters on Knowledge*
Lib. Ascet.	Maximus the Confessor, *Liber Asceticus* / *Book on Asceticism*
LS	Liddell-Scott: *A Greek-English Lexicon*, compiled by Henry-George Liddell and George Scott, revised and augmented throughout by Sir Henry Stuart Jones, with a revised supplement. Oxford: Clarendon, 1996.
Opusc.	Maximus the Confessor, *Opuscula* / *Minor Works*
Or.	Basil of Caesarea, Gregory Nazianzen, *Orationes* / *Orations*
Or. cat.	Gregory of Nyssa, *Oratio catechetica magna* / *Great Catechetical Oration*
Pan.	Gregory the Wonderworker, *Panegyricus* / *Thanksgiving Oration*
Periph.	John the Scot Eriugena, *Periphyseon* / *On Natures*

PG	*Patrologia Graeca / Greek Patrology*
Princ.	Origen, *De Principiis / On First Principles*
Prom.	Dionysius of Alexandria, *De promissionibus / On God's Promises*
Protr.	Clement of Alexandria, *Protrepticus / Exhortation*
Q. ad Thal.	Maximus the Confessor, *Quaestiones ad Thalassium / Problems, to Thalassius*
Q. et dub.	Maximus the Confessor, *Quaestiones et dubia / Problems and Dubious Issues*
Sel. in Ps.	Origen, *Selecta in Psalmos / Selected Passages that Comment on the Psalms*
Sent.	Evagrius Ponticus, *Sententiae / Sayings*
Strom.	Clement of Alexandria, *Stromateis / Books of Miscellany*
Symp.	Methodius of Olympus, *Symposium*
TLG	*Thesaurus Linguae Graecae*
TM	Ps. Dionysius, *Theologia Mystica / Mystical Theology*
Vir. Ill.	Jerome, *De viris illustribus / On Illustrious Men*

By Way of Introduction

I do not think that the reign of death is eternal as that of Life
and Justice is, especially as I hear from the Apostle that the last
enemy, death, must be destroyed [1 Cor 15:24]. For should one
suppose that death is eternal as Life is, death will no longer be
the contradictory of Life, but equal to it. For "eternal" is not the
contradictory of "eternal," but the same thing. Now, it is certain
that death is the contradictory of Life; therefore, it is certain that,
if Life is eternal, *death cannot possibly be eternal*. . . . Once the
death of the soul, which is "the last enemy," has been destroyed,
the kingdom of death, together with death itself, will finally be
wiped away.

(Origen of Alexandria, *Commentary on Romans* 5:7)

UNIVERSAL SALVATION AND GREEK RESTORATION
(*APOKATASTASIS*)

Origen of Alexandria († c.255), the greatest Christian philosopher, theologian, and exegete of the patristic era, is regarded as the founder of the
doctrine of universal salvation. He embedded it in his theory of *apokatastasis* (ἀποκατάστασις) or restoration of all rational creatures to the
Good (i.e., God their Creator). However, as I will show, he had important
antecedents, such as Bardaisan of Edessa and Clement of Alexandria, as
well as some "apocryphal" writings, and especially the Bible, of which
Origen was the utmost Christian exegete. He himself declares that there
was a tradition behind him when he refers *apokatastasis* to the universal
restoration: "The end [*telos*] is the so-called *apokatastasis*, because then

1

no enemy will remain, if it is the case that Christ 'must reign until he has put all his enemies under his feet; but the last enemy will be destroyed: death."[1] The words "the so-called *apokatastasis*" indicate that Origen is referring to an *already existent* tradition. And this was not a tradition that only possessed the concept of universal salvation, but not the word *apokatastasis* (such as the *Apocalypse of Peter*),[2] but rather texts that contained *both* the concept *and* the very term *apokatastasis*, such as those of Clement,[3] which Origen knew, but also a biblical passage: Acts 3:21.[4]

The Greek term *apokatastasis* basically indicates a "restoration, reconstitution, return" to an original condition. It is attested in classical and Hellenistic Greek literature long before Christianity, and also has technical meanings. For instance, in a medical sense, it designates the recovery of health; in a political sense, the return of a hostage to his homeland, or a political restoration; in a military sense, an inversion of maneuver; in a physical sense, the reestablishment of atoms after a collision. In astronomy, the *apokatastasis* of a heavenly body was its return to its original position, or a zodiacal revolution, or the return of the sun and the moon to visibility after an eclipse.

Apokatastasis was also a philosophical term, especially in Stoic cosmology. There, it indicated the periodical return of the universe to its original condition, in a cosmic cycle.[5] Stoic cosmology was articulated in aeons (αἰῶνες) or "great years" that succeed one another; each of these aeons is identical, or almost identical, to all others, with the same events, the same people, and their same behaviors. The sequence of aeons continues *forever*. The end of an aeon is determined by a conflagration in which everything is resolved into the fire–aether–Logos (reason)–*pneuma* (breath, wind) that coincides with the supreme divinity (Zeus, Jupiter). The latter each time initiates a new expansion into a cosmos.

Origen knew the Stoic doctrine of aeons and *apokatastasis* very well. But the Stoic aeons are different from those of Origen. Indeed, Origen explicitly criticized the Stoic conception[6] for two main reasons:

---

1. 1 Cor 15:24–28. Origen's passage is in his *Commentary on John* 1:16:91. See Ramelli, "1 Cor 15:24–26," 241–58.

2. On which, see below, Chapter 1.

3. See my "Origen, Bardaisan, and the Origin of Universal Salvation."

4. On which, see below, Chapter 1.

5. *Stoicorum Veterum Fragmenta* 2:599; 2:625.

6. E.g., *CC* 4:12; 4:67–68; 5:20; *Princ.* 2:3.

1) it destroyed human free will by maintaining that everything that happens is repeated again and again and again *by necessity*;

2) by positing an *infinity* of the sequence of aeons, it did not imply an end or *telos* to which all of history points (and which for Origen is universal salvation), but a senseless eternal repetition.

Origen himself explains the basic meaning of *apokatastasis*: someone's return or restoration to a condition that is proper and original to him or her (*ta oikeia*). He illustrates this general meaning by means of some specific examples: the medical-therapeutic meaning of the resetting of a limb into its place after a displacement, the political meaning of the reintegration of an exile, or the military meaning of the readmission of a soldier into a unit from which he had been chased away.[7] All of these meanings can metaphorically be applied to the final restoration of all human beings or all rational creatures to God.

APOKATASTASIS IN HELLENISTIC JUDAISM AND THE GREEK BIBLE

Hellenistic Judaism and Philo

The term *apokatastasis* is attested in Hellenistic Judaism, especially in Alexandria, in works that were well known to Clement of Alexandria and Origen. The correlate verb (ἀποκαθίστημι, ἀποκαθιστάνω, "to restore") is found in the Septuagint, the Hellenistic Greek translation of the Hebrew Bible, and both the verb and the noun (*apokatastasis*) are attested in the New Testament. The *Letter of Aristeas* 123:4 attests to the political meaning of *apokatastasis*. Philo of Alexandria, the main representative of Hellenistic Judaism, at the end of the first century B.C. and the beginning of the first A.D., uses *apokatastasis* to indicate the periodical restitution of land to its owners.[8] A similar sense is attested, in the late first century A.D., by Flavius Josephus, in reference to the restoration of the Hebrews to their land.[9] Philo refers *apokatastasis* to the liberation of the Hebrews from Egypt as an allegory of the restoration of the soul.[10]

---

7. *Hom. in Ier.* 14:18.

8. *Decal.* 164.3.

9. *Ant.* 11.63. In *Ant.* 11.98 *apokatastasis* is used for the restoration of Jerusalem.

10. *Her.* 293; see my "Philo's Doctrine of Apokatastasis."

Genesis 15:16, "at the fourth generation they will return here," was said "not only to indicate the time in which they will inhabit the Holy Land, but also to present the perfect restoration [*apokatastasis*] of the soul." This is the return of the soul to its original condition, without sin. The same meaning of *apokatastasis* is found in Clement of Alexandria, who was well acquainted with Philo's thought, and in some "gnostic" texts.[11] But, unlike Clement and Origen, neither Philo nor most of the "gnostics" had a notion of apokatastasis that entailed a belief in universal salvation or bodily resurrection.

The Septuagint (LXX)

In the Septuagint, the Greek translation of the Hebrew Bible that stems from a Jewish Hellenistic context, the noun *apokatastasis* ("restoration") is lacking. However, the correspondent verb ("to restore") is present, and its subject is always God.[12] It is *God* who "restores." In Exodus 14:26–27, God restores the water, having it flow again so as to submerge the Egyptians. In Leviticus 13:16, the meaning is therapeutic, as it will be in the Gospels: in a theological passive, God restores the skin of a leper to health. In Job 5:18 God is said to have a person suffer, but then to restore her again. Origen will take this statement as a reference to the eventual universal restoration and the end of purifying sufferings for sinners.[13]

God will *restore* the life of the righteous who suffers (Job 8:6 and 22:28; cf. 33:25). In Psalm 34:17 God *restores* the life of a person in anguish, saving her from evil. In Isaiah 23:17 God will *reconstitute* Tyre to its ancient state of prosperity.[14] In Jeremiah 15:19 God will *restore* Israel if Israel returns to God and repents; Origen will see here, too, a reference to the eventual apokatastasis. In Jeremiah 16:15, 23:8, and 27:19, God will *restore* Israel to the land of its forefathers. In Ezekiel 16:55 God will *restore* Sodom and Gomorrah to their original condition prior to their

---

11. See below, Chapter 2.

12. Apart from trivial meanings such as the restitution of money, possessions, an earthly kingdom, and the like (Gen 23:16; 29:3; 40:13 and 21; 41:13; 2 Kgs 9:7; 1 Esd 1:29 and 33; 5:2; 6:25; 1 Macc 15:3; 2 Macc 12:25; 12:39).

13. See Ramelli, "Origen's Exegesis of Jeremiah," 59–78.

14. In Greek: ἀποκαταστήσεται εἰς τὸ ἀρχαῖον, "he will restore to the ancient (state)," a phrase that will return in St. Gregory of Nyssa in reference to the universal restoration.

destruction; this too was read by patristic exegetes as a reference to the mystery of universal restoration and salvation.[15]

The Greek New Testament

In the New Testament—apart from Matthew 17:11, Mark 9:12, and Acts 3:21, to which I shall return below in Chapter 1—there are several occurrences of the verb "to restore" related to *apokatastasis*, and these are all rendered in the Latin translation of the Vulgate with *restituo*. It is notable that, consistently with the Old Testament use, the subject of the action of restoration is *always God or Christ*. In four cases, in the Gospels, it is Jesus who restores someone to health (Matt 12:13; Mark 3:5; 8:25; Luke 6:10). Jesus, by performing these healing acts, shows God's therapeutic and restoring power. This power works both on the body and on the soul, as St. Gregory of Nyssa will especially point out in his holistic conception of resurrection–restoration (*anastasis–apokatastasis*): both body and soul will be restored by God to their original, prelapsarian integrity.

In the rest of the New Testament, the verb "to restore" related to *apokatastasis* appears in Acts 1:16 and Hebrews 13:19, the subject of the action of restoration being again God. In Acts 1:16 the disciples ask the risen Lord when he will *restore* the kingdom to Israel; Jesus replies that this restoration is an eschatological event.[16] In Hebrews 13:19, the author hopes to be *restored or returned* by God to his addressees. God *restored* Jesus from death to life; all the more God will be able to *return* the author to his addressees.

FROM GREEK PHILOSOPHY AND SCRIPTURE TO CHRISTIAN AUTHORS

As we have seen, the term *apokatastasis* was used in Greek in various senses related to the concept of "restoration, restitution, reconstitution, reintegration, return," and in philosophy it was a Stoic cosmological

---

15. In Daniel 4:36(A) God restores Nebuchadnezzar's kingdom; in Os 2:5 God will restore Israel to the condition of its birth; in Tob(BA) 10:13, God will restore Tobit, having him return home safe and sound.

16. The Vulgate uses a future: *Domine si in tempore hoc restitues regnum Israhel*, "Lord, will you restore the kingdom of/to Israel in this time?" This passage must be connected to Acts 3:20–21, where "universal restoration" (*apokatastasis*) is foreseen. See here below, Chapter 1.

theory, which Origen knew and criticized. In the Greek Bible, which is the main source of inspiration for Origen and the other fathers who supported the doctrine of universal salvation, the noun *apokatastasis* and the relevant verb are found in the Old and in the New Testament.

As I set out to show now, in the Bible there are many, not only lexical, but also *conceptual* bases for the Christian doctrine of universal restoration and salvation. This view was supported by a number of patristic, mediaeval, modern, and contemporary authors, including many who are venerated as saints and recognized as "orthodox," and also including many women. After Bardaisan and Clement, who both fought "Gnosticism" and Marcionism, let me just mention, for instance, St. Anthony, St. Pamphilus Martyr, Methodius of Olympus, Eusebius of Caesarea, Didymus of Alexandria, St. Macrina Junior, St. Gregory of Nyssa, St. Gregory Nazianzen, St. Evagrius Ponticus, Diodore of Tarsus, Theodore of Mopsuestia, St. John of Jerusalem, the "Tall Brothers," St. Melania, Rufinus of Aquileia, St. Jerome and St. Augustine for many years of their lives, Cassian (according to some to be distinguished: St. John Cassian and Cassian the Sabaite), St. Isaac of Nineveh, St. John of Dalyatha, Joseph Hazzaya, Stephen Bar Sudhaili, Pseudo-Dionysius the Areopagite, St. Maximus the Confessor, John the Scot Eriugena, St. Julian of Norwich, Lady Ann Conway, Jane Lead, and many others, up to St. Thérèse of Lisieux, St. John Paul II, and those engaged in the contemporary debate. Most of these believers based their hope for universal salvation on the Bible. The doctrine of universal salvation in its Christian form, as I thoroughly argued elsewhere,[17] entirely depends on Christ's work.

So Scripture and Christian beliefs about Jesus are both core to the development of the theology of apokatastasis in the early church, but the role of *philosophical* notions of apokatastasis cannot be dismissed either, with respect not only to the Stoic doctrine (whose necessitarianism and infinite cyclicality Origen expressly criticized, as mentioned above), but also to Platonism (for while Plato himself did not believe in universal salvation, later Neoplatonists, such as Macrobius, did).[18] Platonism, in its Christianized form, was indeed embraced by most of the fathers who

---

17. In my *The Christian Doctrine of Apokatastasis*.

18. "Pagan" philosophical notions of apokatastasis, especially Stoic and, even more, Platonic will be the object of a specific scholarly monograph I am currently writing. On Macrobius, see my "The Debate on Apokatastasis in Pagan and Christian Platonists," 197–230.

supported universal salvation, first of all Origen,[19] and provided them with a number of tenets to support it, including the critical idea of the ontological non-subsistence of evil—which entails evil's ultimate vanishing—and ethical intellectualism. For, if wrong moral choices come from a clouding-over of intellectual sight, its illumination on the part of the Logos will not fail to bring about restoration. We shall explain and explore these ideas later in the book.

Two main and interrelated tenets are also shared by the Christian supporters of universal salvation:

1. A continuity between the present and the future life, in an uninterrupted process of education. God is the Teacher and Father, who may use even drastic means to educate, but only in the interest of the pupil or child.

2. Any punishment inflicted by God is therapeutic and cathartic, not retributive, and therefore not eternal.

Having introduced some of the key terminology and ideas, we are now in a position to begin our journey. We will do that by turning to the texts accepted by the church as Holy Scripture, for it was here that many believers in the early church found the basis for a larger hope, the hope that God will one day restore the *whole* creation through Christ to the good destiny for which he created it.

---

19. It is even possible that Origen the Neoplatonist and Origen the Christian were one and the same person: see Ramelli, "Origen, Patristic Philosophy," 217–63; Ramelli, "Origen the Christian Middle/Neoplatonist," 98–130; Ramelli, "Origen and the Platonic Tradition"; Ramelli, *Origen of Alexandria.*

I

Some Biblical Roots of the Hope
for Universal Salvation?

An Origenian Reading of Scripture

Many passages in the Bible can be taken to support a doctrine of universal salvation and were understood by many in the early church to do precisely that.[1] In this chapter, I shall very briefly cite some examples of biblical texts that were understood by some of the church fathers in universalist ways. There is no time to give any of them more than a passing glance, for our focus will be on subsequent developments, but the brief survey here will give a flavor of some of the passages that laid a foundation for what was to come.

THE HEBREW BIBLE

In the Old Testament, in Isaiah 42:1–4, the Servant of YHWH, whom Luke 3:18–21, followed by patristic authors, identifies with Christ, will bring justice to the nations. This justice is salvific, not retributive: it restores sight to the blind and liberates the prisoners from darkness and oppression. In Isaiah 49:6 God declares he wants his "salvation to reach the boundaries of the earth," and in Isaiah 49:15, God uses a comparison: "Can a mother forget her baby and have no compassion on the little one she has given birth to? But even if she could, I *shall not forget you.*" Isaiah

---

1. See also Beauchemin, *Hope beyond Hell*, 19ff.

51:4–5 announces the justification (i.e., making people righteous) and salvation given by God, so that the peoples "will hope in his arm," God's saving power. All nations of all tongues will come and see God's glory (Isa 66:18); all peoples will see the salvation brought about by the Lord; "all will come and worship me" (Isa 66:23). Even the Egyptians and the Assyrians, the worst idolaters, will worship God, and God will bless them together with Israel (Isa 19:23–25).[2] The global extent of God's salvific plans is clear from such passages.

In Ezekiel 33:11, the Lord makes clear that he wants none to perish: "As I live, I do not rejoice in the death of the sinners, but I want them to repent and live," and Ezekiel 16:54–55 he even announces the restoration of Sodom and Samaria with Jerusalem, as "sisters." Given Sodom's role as the paradigm of the destruction of sinners by divine fire (Matt 10:34; 11:24; 2 Pet 2:6; Jude 7), this restoration is noteworthy.

Lamentations 3:22 and 31–33 lay some theological groundwork for a wider hope: "The faithful love of the LORD never ceases, *his acts of mercy never end.* . . . the LORD *will not reject forever.* Even if he causes pain, *he will have compassion,* thanks to the abundance of his faithful love, because he does not want to afflict or hurt anybody." Wisdom 11:23 and 26 in the Apocrypha insists on God's mercy, which is the counterpart of God's omnipotence: "You have *mercy upon all,* because you can do everything; you do not look at the sins of humans, in view of their *repentance.* . . . You *spare all beings* because all are yours, o Lord, who love life." Consider too Wisdom 15:1: "You are good and faithful, patient, and govern all according to *mercy.*" The possibility of repentance and forgiveness thanks to God's mercy is also the focus of Sirach 17:19 and 24: "God offers the return to those who *repent.* . . . How great is the LORD's *mercy,* his forgiveness to those who convert to him!" (cf. Wis 12:2–19). These passages and others like them were picked up by some of the church fathers and interpreted in terms of a vision for the restoration of all things.

THE NEW TESTAMENT

Gospels

In the New Testament there are very few passages that might be taken to indicate an *eternal* damnation: the most obvious candidates are those that speak of "αἰώνιον fire" and "αἰώνιος punishment," and of the worm

2. See also Isa 45:20–25 and MacDonald, *The Evangelical Universalist,* 64.

"that does not die" and the fire "that cannot be quenched" (e.g., Matt 18:8–9; 25:41). However, while all of these phrases indicate otherworldly suffering, none of these indicates its *eternity*. They have not a quantitative, but a *qualitative* meaning; they denote that this fire, punishment, and worm are not similar to those of this world/age, but belong to the other world/age. For fire in this world can be quenched and worms in this world die, but in the world to come it will not be so. As for the adjective αἰώνιος (*aiōnios*), it *never* means "eternal" in Scripture unless it refers to God; when it refers to life, death, and other things such as "fire," it means "belonging to the world to come," "otherworldly," "divine." In the Bible, only life in the other world is called "eternal" proper (ἀΐδιος/ *aïdios*), whereas death, punishment, and fire are never called ἀΐδια, but only αἰώνια, "otherworldly."[3] The mistranslation and misinterpretation of αἰώνιος as "eternal" (already in Latin, where both αἰώνιος and ἀΐδιος are rendered *aeternus* and their fundamental semantic difference is blurred) certainly contributed a great deal to the rise of the doctrine of "eternal damnation" and of the "eternity of hell." (For more detail on the meaning of the word αἰώνιος/*aiōnios*, see the first Appendix to this book.)

What is more, soon after speaking of the worm and the fire (with a reminiscence of Isaiah 66:24, also echoed in Matthew 18:8–9), Mark 9:49 offers a further explanatory comment on the flames of Gehenna, characterizing the fire as *purifying*, and insisting that all will be purified by it—". . . for everyone will be *salted* with fire."

But how can God save all people? Given the depths of our sin and our free will, which God is not controlling, can God ensure that all will be saved? In Matthew 19:25 Jesus declares that salvation is "impossible for human beings, but everything is possible for God." Origen, as I shall show, will echo this argument when he will ground his doctrine of universal salvation in the claim that "nothing is impossible for the Omnipotent; no being is incurable for the One who created it." God will find a way. In Luke 16:16, Jesus even proclaims that after John the Baptist, the last prophet, "the good news of the kingdom of God is announced, and everyone is *forced in*" by God.[4]

As for John, I will briefly address the Gospel and Letters together. In 1 John 4:8 and 16, God is described as Love (ἀγάπη/*agape*; Latin *caritas*), in his very being. In John 1:29, Christ is the one who takes upon himself

---

3. See Ramelli and Konstan, *Terms for Eternity*, new edition (2013).

4. For an argument for this interpretation, with a theological passive, see my "Luke 16:16," 747–68.

the sins of *the world*, thus purifying the world. God, out of love, sent Christ to save the *world* (John 3:17; 12:47; 1 John 4:14); his sacrifice expiates the sins of *the whole world* (1 John 2:2; 1 John 4:10). Referring to his crucifixion, Jesus declares: "Now the ruler of this world [i.e., the devil] will be thrown out. And when I am lifted up from earth, I will drag *all people* to myself" (John 12:31–32). Jesus has been entrusted with all humans, and wants to bestow eternal life on all them: "Father . . . glorify your Son, that your Son may glorify you, because you have entrusted him with *every human being*, that he may give eternal life to *every being that you have given him*. Eternal life is that they know you" (John 17:1–2). This corresponds to 1 Timothy 2:4–6: "God wants all humans to be saved and to reach the knowledge of the truth," that is, God. Martha already believed in the (bodily) resurrection of the dead, when Jesus replied to her: "*I am* the Resurrection and Life. Whoever believes in me, even if she dies, will continue to live, and whoever lives and believes in me will absolutely not die in the world to come [εἰς τὸν αἰῶνα]" (John 11:24–26). Many Johannine passages declare that eternal life, or life in the world to come, is Christ and is guaranteed to those who believe in Christ.

Acts

Acts 3:20–21 includes the only occurrence of the noun *apokatastasis* in Scripture. Peter, who is delivering a speech to "the Jews" in Jerusalem, at Pentecost, announces the eschatological "times of *universal* restoration":

> Repent/convert, that your sins may be cancelled, and the times
> of consolation may come, coming from the face of the Lord,
> and he may send Jesus Christ, who was handed for you. Heaven
> must keep him until the times of *the restoration of all beings*
> [ἀποκαταστάσεως πάντων], of which God has spoken by means
> of his holy prophets from time immemorial.[5]

The eschatological consolation and universal restoration will come when all have repented and their sins have thus been forgiven by God. Then will God's promise to Abraham be fulfilled: "All the families of the

---

5. Méhat, "Apocatastase," 196–214, understands *apokatastasis* here as the realization of the promises of God and not the restoration of all beings; *contra* LS 201, s.v. *apokatastasis*, and a systematic investigation in the TLG. *Apokatastasis* in Greek, from the beginning to the New Testament, does not mean "realization" or "accomplishment," but "restoration," "reintegration," "reconstitution" to an original state.

earth will be blessed in your offspring" (Gen 12:3; Acts 3:25). Universal restoration parallels the eschatological consolation. Both come from the Lord; God will console and restore all beings.[6] The same is suggested in Matthew 17:11: after the Transfiguration Jesus recommends that his disciples do not speak of this until his resurrection. They ask him whether Elijah will come before the Messiah at the end of time; Jesus replies that Elijah will come and God will restore all beings.[7]

Peter's discourse to the crowd in the temple courts, which Origen will interpret as a clear announcement of the future universal restoration and salvation, is to be contextualized within the Jewish eschatological expectations of that time (the restoration of Israel, the entering of the nations, and the forgiveness of sins).[8] The same is the case with Acts 1:6: the disciples asked the risen Jesus when he would restore the kingdom to Israel. Both passages are Lukan, but the connection between Peter's speech and the announcement of universal apokatastasis is nevertheless interesting, not least because four other texts belonging to the Petrine tradition support restoration.[9] Origen in *Princ.* 2:3:5 interprets the "universal restoration" announced in Acts 3:21 as the "perfect end [*telos*]" and "the perfection of all beings" at the end of all aeons: "What will take place at the universal restoration [*in restitutione omnium*], when all beings will achieve their perfect end, must be understood as something beyond all aeons. Then there will be the perfect accomplishment of all, when all

6. See my "Matt 17:11," 107–26. Acts 3:21 is considered to refer to the eschatological restoration also by Doering, "Urzeit–Endzeit Correlations," esp. 20.

7. For this rendering, or the alternative "all beings will be restored," see Ramelli, "Matt 17:11." Cf. Mark 9:12.

8. On the restoration of Israel, besides my *Apokatastasis* monograph, see my "Philo's Doctrine of Apokatastasis": reviewed by Matthew Kraus, *Bryn Mawr Classical Review* Sept 5, 2015 and by Johannes van Oort, *Vigiliae Christianae* 69.5 (2015) 577; Eskola, *A Narrative Theology of the New Testament.* The restoration of Israel was perceived as foretold in Scripture, e.g., Joel 2:28—3:1: "And it shall come to pass afterward, that I will pour out my spirit on all flesh; your sons and your daughters shall prophesy, your old men shall dream dreams, and your young men shall see visions. Even upon the menservants and maidservants in those days, I will pour out my spirit. For behold, in those days and at that time, I restore the fortunes of Judah and Jerusalem" (RSV).

9. 1) In 1 Peter the announcement of Christ's descent to hell to save those who were condemned at the time of the universal flood and are also the allegory of those unbaptized; 2) the announcement of Christ's descent to hell in the Gospel of Peter; 3) the announcement of the salvation of those damned to hell in the *Apocalypse of Peter*; 4) the promise of universal apokatastasis in the "Ps. Clementines" that form the frame of the Ethiopic *Apocalypse of Peter.* See below on these texts.

beings will be no longer in any aeon, but God will be 'all in all.'" (Note the quotation of 1 Corinthians 15:28, Origen's and Gregory of Nyssa's favorite passage in support of their doctrine of apokatastasis.[10]) Likewise, Origen interprets Acts 3:21 in reference to the eventual universal apokatastasis in *Comm. in Matt.* 17:19, where, echoing St. Paul, he remarks that now we do not see God as God is, but we shall do so in the end, and this end will be the universal restoration: "In the end, when there will be 'the restoration of all beings, of which God has spoken by means of his holy prophets from time immemorial,' we shall see God not as now, when we see what God is not, but as it becomes that future state, when we shall see what God is." In *Hom. in Ier.* 14:18, Origen connects Jeremiah 15:19 to Acts 3:21: "If we return, God will restore us: the end of this promise is the same as is written in the Acts of the Apostles: 'until the times of universal restoration, of which God has spoken from time immemorial by means of his holy prophets' in Jesus Christ."

Paul

10. See my "Christian Soteriology," 313–56.

Paul represents Origen's and Gregory of Nyssa's favorite scriptural pillar for their universalistic soteriology.[11] In Romans 1:16–17 Paul describes the gospel as the power of God for the salvation of all those who believe. In Romans 3:23–24 he declares that "all" have sinned, but they are gratuitously justified thanks to Christ. Jesus "was put to death because of our sins and resurrected for our justification" (Rom 4:25); "while we were still sinners, Christ died for us. Much more now that we are justified by means of his blood, *we will be saved from God's wrath thanks to him*" (Rom 5:8–9). The Christian doctrine of apokatastasis was never a way of ignoring sin, or bypassing the salvation wrought by Christ in his death and resurrection or the importance of faith in Christ, but it held fast to all of these teachings from the book of Romans. It simply maintained that just as sin applies universally so too justification will extend universally.

The most universalistic passages—which in turn will inspire the fathers in their wider hope—are the following. In Romans 5:18–19 Paul states: "because of one human being [Adam] condemnation has spread to *all humans*. Likewise, thanks to the work of justice of one human being [Christ] *life-giving justification pours upon all humans*. By virtue of the obedience of one human, *all will be made just*."[12] In a similar vein, in Romans 11:11–32 Paul proclaims the final restoration and salvation of all gentiles and all Israel:

> Did they [the people of Israel] stumble so as to lie fallen forever? Surely not, but thanks to their fall salvation has reached pagans. . . . Therefore, if their failure has been the richness of the pagans, how much more will their total participation be. . . . If their refusal has marked the reconciliation of the world, what will their admission ever be but a resurrection from the dead? . . . The hardening of a part of Israel is taking place until *the totality* [πλήρωμα/*plērōma*] *of the nations/'pagans' has entered*, and then *all* [πᾶς/*pas*] *of Israel will be saved*. . . . You have obtained mercy on account of their disobedience, so they too, now, have become disobedient in view of the mercy to be bestowed on you, that they too may obtain mercy. For God has the power to graft

---

11. The church fathers did not distinguish authentic, deutero-Pauline, and pseudo-Pauline letters in the Pauline corpus in the way that modern scholars do.

12. On the universality of the effects of both Adam's and Christ's acts, Bell, "Rom 5.18–19 and Universal Salvation," DeBoer, *The Defeat of Death*, 175, and MacDonald, *The Evangelical Universalist*, 79–84, among many other exegetes and theologians, concur with me.

them anew [back into the olive tree]. . . . God closed *all* [πάντας/
pantas] in disobedience so as to have mercy upon *all*.

The totality [πλήρωμα/*plērōma*] of the nations added to the whole [πᾶς/
pas] of Israel amounts to *all humanity*. (Πλήρωμα/*plērōma*, which is
sometimes translated "fullness," in many places in the Septuagint means
"totality." For instance, in Psalm 23:1, it parallels "all people" [πάντες/
pantes], so it means the totality of people; see also Psalm 49:12; 88:12;
95:11, in which *plērōma* parallels "all beings," [πάντα/*panta*], so as to
mean "all beings". See also Psalm 97:7; Jeremiah 8:16; 29:2; Ezekiel 12:19,
in which *plērōma* parallels again πάντες/*pantes*, so as to mean the totality of all beings [see again Ezek 19:7; 30:12].) Origen read in Romans
11:11–32 the announcement of universal salvation and the fulfillment of
God's promise to Abraham that he would inherit all the world through
faith (Gen 12:3). This fulfillment will occur "when in the end, after *the
totality of the gentiles* has entered, *all of Israel will be saved . . .* when the
totality of the gentiles will have entered and *all of Israel* will be saved . . .
The words, 'all the families of the earth will be blessed in you,' mean that
Abraham will inherit the whole world; . . . he will inherit it thanks to the
justification brought about by faith" (*Comm. in Rom.* 4:2–3). Note here
how Origen repeats the point that he wants to emphasize.

The beautiful and eloquent promise in Romans 8:35–39 will also be
remembered by the fathers: "*nothing* will be able to separate us from the
love of God," not even the evil powers, not even death (either physical or
spiritual death, in Origen's view). This is an *undefeatable* love.

Another text that caught the eye of Origen was Romans 14:11,
where Paul announces the eventual universal submission to Christ and
God that Origen and Gregory will interpret as spontaneous and as coin-
ciding with universal salvation: in the end "the Lord says, *every knee* will
bow before Me, *every tongue* will praise God." Enemies who are forced
to submit and are crushed do not praise their oppressor, but if all will
submit spontaneously and willingly, all will praise God and be saved.

God's own faithfulness is opposed to human incredulity and insta-
bility in Romans 3:3–4: "If some have not believed, can their incredulity
ever cancel God's own faithfulness (*tēn pistin tou Theou*)? Impossible."[13]
Humans in their sin and faithlessness cannot cause God to abandon
them. The same phrase can be used of Jesus, such that Paul speaks of

---

13. This passage will be echoed in 2 Tim 2:13: "If we lack faith, God, for his part,
remains faithful."

"the faith(fulness) of Christ" (*pistis Christou*) in several passages.[14] Since Paul declares this "faith *of* Christ" to be salvific, the salvation of humans does not rest only upon their own faith or confidence (*pistis*), but also *on Christ's and God's faithfulness*, which is a much more solid foundation.

In 1 Corinthians 15:22–23 Paul is clear in his universalism: "As *all humans* die in Adam, so will *all humans be made alive* in Christ." Those who die because of Adam are not some subgroup of the human race, but *all* human beings; therefore, those who are vivified by Christ are the same all humans without exception. What is more, this vivification is not simply the resurrection of the body, but justification and thereby salvation. We can see this from Romans 5:18–19: "Because of one human being, condemnation has spread to *all humans*; so also, thanks to one human's work of justice, *life-giving justification spreads to all humans. . . . All will be made just.*"

Another strong universalistic hint comes from the same letter (1 Cor 15:24–28): Christ will reign until he has subjected all enemies— the last is death, which will rather be destroyed, since it is no creature of God. Then he will hand the kingdom to the Father, and God will be "all *in all*." This is Origen's and Gregory of Nyssa's favorite passage in support of universal salvation; they interpreted the submission of all as the salvation of all. Paul expresses himself in similar terms in 1 Corinthians 9:22: "I have made myself all to all, in order to *save all* [*pantas*]."[15]

Indeed, God has reconciled all to himself by means of Christ (2 Cor 5:19),[16] and the final universal submission of every creature to Christ is likewise proclaimed by Paul in Philippians 2:10–11: "in the name of Christ every knee will bend, in heaven, *on earth, and in the underworld,* and *every tongue will proclaim* that Jesus Christ is the Lord." The verb "proclaim" in Greek (ὁμολογέω/*homologeō*, ἐξομολογέω/*exomologeō*), like other closely related terms, in the Septuagint and the New Testament

---

14. Rom 3:22 and 26; Gal 2:16 and 20; 3:22; Phil 3:9; 1 Thess 1;3; cf. Gal 3:26. The relevant bibliography is richer and richer.

15. A variant in Greek here is πάντως/*pantōs*, which would yield the translation: "to save some at all costs." But the reading I have stuck to is attested in a family of Greek manuscripts, in Priscillian, in the Syriac Peshitta, and in the Latin versions (Old Latin and Vulgate): *ut omnes salvos facerem.*

16. Cf. two deutero-Paulines: Eph 1:10: "God has the intention of *recapitulating all beings in Christ, those in heaven and those on earth,*" and Col 1:18–20: Christ in the end will attain "primacy over *all beings,*" and the Father "by means of him will *reconcile all beings to himself.*" The very notion of reconciliation excludes again a forced submission.

always implies a *voluntary* recognition, praise, and thanksgiving. In Philippians 3:21 Paul insists that Christ has the power of submitting "all beings" to himself. This confirms Origen's and Gregory's interpretation of the eventual submission of all in the end announced by Paul as the salvation of all.

In 1 Corinthians 3:14–15 Paul makes it clear that the otherworldly fire does not preclude salvation: "If the work that one built up on the foundation resists, one will receive a reward. If the work is burnt, one will suffer a loss, but *will be saved*, albeit as it were through fire." Either one will be rewarded or one will be saved through fire; no mention of people who will not be saved. On the same line is 1 Corinthians 5:5: a man who has committed a very serious sin must be "handed over to satan for the *ruin/perdition* of his flesh, that his spirit *be saved* in the day of the Lord."

Pseudo-Paulines, Other Letters, and Revelation

1 Timothy, one of the Pastoral Epistles, develops the universalistic thread in Paul's thought. Being handed to satan is presented, as in Paul, as a therapeutic measure (1 Tim 1:20), and we read that Christ entered this world to save sinners (1 Tim 1:15). Most significantly, the author declares:

> God our Savior *wants all human beings to be saved* and to reach
> the knowledge of the truth. For God is one, and one is the me-
> diator between God and humans: the human being Christ Jesus,
> who has given himself in ransom for all. (1 Tim 2:4–6)

(This is conceptually parallel to 2 Peter 3:9: "God wants *nobody to perish*, but all to reach conversion.") Therefore, "We have placed our hope in the living God, who is *the Savior of all humans, especially* [*sc.* but not exclusively] of those who believe" (1 Tim 4:10); "God's Grace has appeared, which brings about *salvation for all humans*" (Titus 2:11).

Similar themes are found in the letter to the Hebrews: in 9:19 Jesus is said to have been sacrificed once and for all to bear the sins of the many; in 9:11–13 he is said to have offered "one sacrifice forever," a voluntary sacrifice, which purifies our conscience (10:5–10). More significantly, in 2:9 Jesus is said to have "tasted death for everyone": 2:14–15 comments that "Since therefore the children share in flesh and blood, he himself likewise partook of the same things, that through death he might destroy the one who has the power of death, that is, the devil, and *deliver all* those who through fear of death were subject to lifelong slavery." Origen and other fathers will strongly rely on 1 Timothy 2:4–6 and on Hebrews for their universalism.

In 1 Peter 3:19–21, Jesus is said to have preached salvation to those who were prisoners in Hades and who once had refused to believe and had therefore perished in the flood. Those who survived the flood in the ark represent those who are now saved through baptism. However, Christ is said to save even the others, those who did not believe and represent those who are not baptized. Henryk Pietras considers this passage to be an expression of universal salvation.[17] Indeed, Christ's descent to hell will play an important role for the supporters of apokatastasis right up to von Balthasar in the twentieth century.

In Revelation 20:10–15 the lake of fire is the second death (cf. 21:8), and those who enter there are death itself and hell, which are no creatures of God. The death of death is clearly the disappearance of death. Sinners too are said to be cast into the lake of fire, but nowhere is it said that they will remain there forever (21:8); the devil will burn there "for ages and ages," which means a *very* long time. According to Origen, it denotes all the future aeons prior to the eventual apokatastasis! In chapter 21, the nations of the earth, who throughout Revelation are Christ's opponents, will in the end bring their wealth into the New Jerusalem, entering as worshipping pilgrims.[18] The doors of the heavenly Jerusalem are said to be permanently open so that those who have completed their purification in that fire can finally enter the holy city. Chapter 22 reveals that inside the city there is a tree of life, an allusion to Genesis and perhaps the symbol of Christ's cross, whose leaves produce "the therapy/healing of the nations" (i.e., those who are still outside Jerusalem). Moreover, the end of every malediction and exclusion and of every pain is proclaimed. The radical destruction that is announced in Revelation does not involve creatures, but evil and death (the same is announced in 1 Cor 15:24–8). The fire that will destroy evil is the same that will purify sinners precisely by eliminating evil.

In this chapter we have seen some of the biblical seeds of hope that were sown into the soil of early Christianity. In the chapters that follow we shall observe how those seeds began to germinate and grow into the plant we know as the doctrine of apokatastasis.

---

17. Pietras, *L'escatologia*, 38, with my review in *Augustinianum* 48 (2008) 247–53.

18. For the motif of the nations bringing their wealth to Jerusalem, see Chan, *The Wealth of Nations*, who shows how Scripture reflects ancient Near Eastern traditions.

2

Universal Restoration before Origen

THE RIDDLE OF IGNATIUS
AND THEOPHILUS OF ANTIOCH

Ignatius, Bishop of Antioch, was born in Syria around 50 AD and was martyred in Rome between 98 and 117 AD. In the corpus of letters of Ignatius, written while he was en route to face his death in Rome, universal salvation is evoked in *Ep. ad Sm.* 2 (belonging to the so-called middle recension[1]): "the Logos, when its flesh was lifted up like the brazen serpent in the desert, dragged *all human beings to itself* for their *eternal salvation,*" with a patent echo of John 12:32. Ignatius' corpus was known to Origen (*Hom. in Luc.* 6:4) and Eusebius (*HE* 3:36) and was preserved in the library of Caesarea. With Christ's crucifixion, Ignatius wrote, "every spell of *evilness has been dissolved*, every chain destroyed; ignorance has been eliminated, the ancient kingdom has fallen into ruin, when the Godhead has manifested itself in human form for the novelty of *absolutely eternal* [ἀΐδιου/*aidiou*] *life*. What has been established by God has begun: from then on, *all beings* have been put in motion for *the providential realization of the destruction of death.*" The death that is destroyed is not only physical, but spiritual: Christ has "performed every justice," that is, the justification of all (*Ep. ad Sm.* 1:1).

While in the work of Justin Martyr (100–165) and Tatian († 185) there is a notion of restoration or apokatastasis, and even the terminology of apokatastasis, it is unclear whether it coincides with universal

---

1. See at least Nautin, "Ignatius." Now Markus Vinzent 2018 for a revisitation of Ignatius' corpus.

salvation. However, in Theophilus of Antioch († 183) it is clearer. He uses the very noun *apokatastasis* in reference to the eschatological restoration, proclaiming that once human beings will have abandoned evil, even animals will be restored to their original meekness. At the same time Theophilus interprets ferocious beasts as a symbol of sinners, as they are interpreted by Origen and in the *Acts of Philip*.[2]

> In the beginning animals were not created evil or venomous, because from the beginning no evil came from God, but all was good and very good, but it was human *sin* that made them evil. When the human being transgressed, they too transgressed. Therefore, when humanity will *return to the state that is in accord with its nature*, and will *no longer do evil*, animals too will be *restored* [ἀποκατασταθήσεται/*apokatastathēsetai*] *into their original meekness*. (*Aut.* 2:17)

Theophilus uses the same key verb in *Aut.* 3:9: Moses gave the Law to the Hebrews, but also to the whole world, and restored the Hebrews into the Land of Canaan, which is also a symbol of paradise. Theophilus thus hints at apokatastasis as universal salvation for humans and animals.

Another second-century Christian apologist, Melito of Sardis († 180), also hints in this direction. In his *Homily on the Passion of Christ*, he states that Christ, "through whom the Father created everything, has the authority to judge and *save all beings*." This is, at least, suggestive, although it falls short of a clear assertion of universal salvation.[3]

BARDAISAN AND CLEMENT

Bardaisan of Edessa

It is rather in Bardaisan of Edessa (154–222), Clement of Alexandria (c.150–c.215), and some so-called apocryphal writings that one can find the clearest antecedents to Origen's full-blown doctrine of apokatastasis as eschatological universal restoration and salvation.

2. See Ramelli, "Mansuetudine," 215–28.

3. An examination of so-called "gnostic" apokatastasis leads to the overall conclusion that this notion does *not* entail universal salvation (although with possible exceptions that deserve further investigation) or the resurrection of the body; therefore, I shall not include a treatment here, not even in abridgement. For a detailed treatment of "gnostic" apokatastasis and all the relevant texts, as well as the problem of the "Gnosticism" category, see my "Apokatastasis in Coptic Gnostic Texts." Further investigation is underway, though.

Bardaisan was a Syriac Christian philosopher and theologian in-
accurately accused of "Gnosticism" by heresiologists.[4] At his school in
Edessa Greek philosophy was studied as well. In the final section of the
Book of the Laws of Countries—basically corresponding to Bardaisan's
Against Fate, in which he defended human free will against determinism, as Origen was later to do—he proclaims the eventual universal
restoration:

> For, just as human freewill is not governed by the necessity of
> the Seven [i.e., the planets], and, if it were governed, it would be
> able to stand against its governors, so this visible human being,
> in turn, is unable to easily get rid of its principalities' govern-
> ment, since he is a slave and a subject. For, if we could do all,
> we would be all; if we couldn't decide anything, we would be the
> instruments of others.
>
> But whenever God likes, everything can be, with no obsta-
> cle at all. Indeed, there is nothing that can impede that great and
> holy will. For, even those who are convinced to resist God, do
> not resist by their force, but they are in evil and error, and this
> can be only for a short time, because God is kind and gentle, and
> allows all natures to remain in the state in which they are, and to
> *govern themselves by their own will*, but at the same time they are
> conditioned by the things that are done and the *plans that have
> been conceived* [*sc.* by God] *to help them*. For this order and this
> government that have been given [*sc.* by God], and the associa-
> tion of one with another, damps the natures' force, so that they
> cannot be either completely harmful or completely harmed, as
> they were harmful and harmed before the creation of the world.
>
> And there will come a time when even *this capacity for
> harm* that remains in them *will be brought to an end* by the *in-
> struction* that will obtain in a different arrangement of things.
> And, once that new world will be constituted, all *evil movements
> will cease*, all *rebellions will come to an end*, and the *fools will be
> persuaded*, and the *lacks will be filled*, and there will be *safety and
> peace*, as a gift of the Lord of all natures.[5]

Bardaisan uses theological passives. It is God who excogitates plans
to help all creatures, i.e., to save them. Like Origen later, Bardaisan too
thinks that God's providence is not incompatible with creatures' free will.
During history, each one is free to adhere to the Good as much or as little

4. See my *Bardaisan of Edessa*.

5. Translation mine from Ramelli, *Bardaisan on Human Nature, Fate, and Free
Will*.

as one wishes, and to experience the consequences of this, but *in the end* Providence guides *all* to salvation. Providence does not allow any creature to be damaged completely and perish, or else to damage completely, doing evil forever. Evil will utterly disappear, as Origen, Gregory of Nyssa, Evagrius, Isaac of Nineveh, Sergey Bulgakov, and other universalists will repeat. To this end, God disposes a work of teaching and persuasion, that those immersed in evil may be purified and healed. Bardaisan again anticipates Origen's theology on this score. Thanks to instruction, "the fools will be persuaded," and not punished eternally. Bardaisan does not even mention retributive punishment anywhere in what survives of his work. He manifestly shares the vision of ethical intellectualism later embraced by Origen; this is why he thinks that instruction will enable the eventual restoration; all will choose the Good when all have achieved a pure, non obfuscated intellectual sight. Knowledge of the Good cannot but produce adhesion to the Good. That the final restoration will be a work of God is another idea that Bardaisan shares with Origen, as well as the description of the final state in apokatastasis as one of peace.[6]

Eusebius (260/65–339/40), who was a fervent admirer of Origen, not by chance appreciated Bardaisan, spoke well of him in his *Church History*, and in his *Preparation to the Gospel* reports long excerpts from his work against Fate (which he clearly had at his disposal in the Caesarea library and was perhaps already in Origen's own library). It is meaningful that Eusebius, in the section of his *Preparation* in which he quotes Bardaisan's arguments against determinism and in defense of free will, cites Origen *together* with Bardaisan (6:10 and 6:11). He clearly noticed that they were arguing on the very same line. It is not accidental either that Didymus (c.313–98), another faithful Origenian and a supporter of universal salvation, appreciated Bardaisan and depicted him in the best light. In general, it is remarkable that the most favorable testimonies on Bardaisan all come from authors who appreciated Origen as well, such as Africanus, Didymus, Eusebius, and the early Jerome.[7]

6. This is attested for Origen, e.g., in *Hom. in Luc.* 36; *Fr. in Matt.* 571 and *Comm. in Io.* 10:39: in the end "peace will be perfect, after the years of the providential economy."

7. See Ramelli, *Bardaisan*.

Clement of Alexandria

Clement of Alexandria (c.150–c.215), an educated convert to Christianity from a pagan background, was a theologian at the famous catechetical school in Alexandria, North Africa. He was a pioneering Christian Platonist and an older contemporary of Origen whose work was certainly known to Origen. Clement entertained a notion of apokatastasis which was open to universal salvation.[8] Like Bardaisan and later Origen, he was a strong defender of human free will and responsibility against determinism.[9] At the same time he emphasized God's mercy, which forgives

8. See Ramelli, "*Stromateis* VII and Clement's Hints of the Theory of Apokatastasis."

9. E.g. *Strom.* 1:1:4:1; 4:24:153:1–2; 2:14–5:60–64. Clement was especially against "gnostic" determinism. Clement explicitly criticized "the followers of Basilides" because they thought that some people would be saved "by nature" and others condemned "by nature" and not on the basis of their free choices (*Strom.* 2:3). The same criticism was addressed by Clement to the Valentinians, who thought that they "will

even voluntary sins: God *"prefers the sinner's repentance to his death . . .
gives* according to one's merits but remits sins" (*Strom.* 2:15:66). In this
context, Clement also uses therapeutic metaphors, which will be dear to
Origen as well: God's aim is to *heal* the sinner.[10] Contrary to the claims of
some,[11] Clement, for instance in *Strom.* 7.16.102, consistently applies the
distinction between *timōria* and *kolasis*, the former indicating retributive
punishment, and the latter therapeutic punishment. He explicitly states
there that God *kolazei*, but never *timōreitai:* God applies therapeutic,
educative punishments, but *not* retributive punishments.

Clement advocated, like Origen, a distinction between sinners and
their sins: the latter must be hated, but not sinners, who are God's creatures (Origen and Gregory of Nyssa will say that they bear the image of
God, which sin can obfuscate and cover, but never cancel).[12] Clement
applies to the devil, too, the criterion of responsibility; according to him,
just as later to Origen, Satan was not compelled *by his nature* to do evil,
but he was free to either choose or reject it (*Strom.* 1:17:83–84). Soon
after, Clement explains the decisional mechanism that gives rise to a
bad choice in terms "ethical intellectualism" (i.e., the view that what you
choose depends on what you know; evil is chosen because it is mistaken
for a good, due to an error of judgment), a line that Origen and Gregory
of Nyssa will keep:

> One never chooses evil qua (as, insofar as) *evil, but because*, at-
> tracted by the pleasure that one finds in it, one *believes that it is
> a good* and deems it enjoyable. . . . We can, nevertheless, detach
> ourselves from the bad choice, however enjoyable it may be, and
> beforehand *we can avoid giving assent to those fallacious images.*

Ethical intellectualism surfaces again in many points of Clement's work.[13]
Gregory of Nyssa will even use this doctrine to explain the so-called

---

be saved by nature" qua gnostics. Salvation must be achieved voluntarily (*Strom.*
6:12:96:1–3; 3:7:58; 1:1:4; 3:9:65; 1:17:83–84; 2:12:54–55; 2:13:69).

10. *Strom.* 2:15:69–71.

11. For instance, the anonymous writing under the pseudonym "koine lingua"
on the blog https://www.reddit.com/r/AcademicBiblical/, under the title "Αἰώνιος
(*aiōnios*) in Jewish and Christian Eschatology: 'Eternal' Life, 'Eternal' Torment, 'Eternal' Destruction?" from 26–27 April 2015.

12. *Strom.* 4:13:93–4; see also 1:1:4:1.

13. E.g. *Strom.* 2:6:26:5; 2:15:62:3; 4:26:168:2; 6:14:113:3; 7:3:16:2, etc. See also my
"Was Patristic Sin Different from Ancient Error? The Role of Ethical Intellectualism
and the Invention of 'Original Sin'", invited lecture, Institute of Advanced Study of the

original sin: Adam and Eve ate the forbidden fruit because, even though this was an evil, they mistakenly believed that it was good. For they had been *deceived* by the serpent.

In *Strom.* 7:2:12 Clement is clear that God's project, aim, and activity is universal salvation:

> The God of the universe has disposed everything for *universal salvation*, in general and singularly. Thus, God did whatever did not prevent the voluntary nature of human choice, and showed this as a help to attain virtue, that in some way even those who are endowed only of weak vision the sole true Omnipotent could be revealed a *good God* who from eternity and *forever saves* through the Son *and is absolutely not responsible for evil.* Thus, it is a work of God's *salvific justice to lead every being to the best* insofar as possible.

God's justice saves.[14] Every punishment decided by God aims at saving the punished, even those who are the most hardened: "And the necessary corrections, inflicted *out of goodness* by the great Judge who chairs—either through the angels who surround him, or by means of preliminary judgments, or with the *complete and final judgment—, force to repentance those who are too hardened.*" Even the punishments inflicted at the Last Judgment, according to Clement—that is, even torments in hell—aim at the conversion of the sinner. Repentance can take place even after the Last Judgment (i.e., in hell), after which the punishments, which aimed at this, will cease. Repentance is therefore not limited to our earthly life, but can take place "both here on earth and *elsewhere*, because there is *no place* where God does not do good" (*Strom.* 4:6:37:7). Thus, punishment in hell will come to an end. God's goodness and its beneficial effects are active even in hell. Christ descended to hell precisely with this goal:

> The Lord brought the good news even to those who were in hell. . . . *God's punishments save and educate!* They *induce sinners to convert* and want them to repent and not to die.[15] . . . It is certainly demonstrated that *God is good* and the Lord is *able to save* with impartial justice those who convert, *here or elsewhere.*

University of Paris, April 2017, forthcoming.

14. See also *Strom.* 1:17:86:1–2, where Clement states that God's Providence directs even human beings' evil deeds to a good end. For God not only does the good, but even turns evil to a good end.

15. Ezek 18:23; 33:11.

> For God's operative power *does not reach only on earth, but it is everywhere, and it operates always.*[16]

Always . . . , even in hell.

Clement deemed the second-century text known as the *Apocalypse of Peter* to be divinely inspired and commented on it in his *Hypotyposeis* (*Outlines*), where he also proclaims that "God saves all, converting some by chastisements, others by their own will, with dignity." This is significant since this *Apocalypse*, as we shall see later, proclaims the eschatological salvation of the damned thanks to the intercession of the just. And this should not surprise us, especially in the light of Clement's conviction that apokatastasis is announced by Paul. In Romans 6:22, Paul declares that the *telos*, the end to which one must tend (identified with the assimilation to God), is life in the world to come. Clement, after referring to this, claims that Paul "teaches that the *telos is the hoped-for apokatastasis*."[17] Universal restoration is the supreme end. Clement is obviously thinking of 1 Corinthians 15:23–28, where the *telos* is described as the eventual destruction of evil and death and the submission of all creatures to God, who will then be "all in all." Clement relies on the authority of Paul to proclaim that the end of all things will be universal restoration and salvation. The very term *apokatastasis* is attested in Clement in other passages in reference to the *telos*. In *Strom.* 7:10:57:1–4 Clement describes the perfection of the soul that has reached knowledge and dwells in the divine as "restoration (ἀποκατάστασις/*apokatastasis*) into the highest place of rest." This restoration will be tantamount to "seeing God face to face." Like Origen later, basing himself on 1 Corinthians 15:25–28, Clement connects this condition to the voluntary submission to the Lord, postulating a salvific passage from incredulity to faith and from faith to knowledge, which, tending to love, leads to the final apokatastasis:

> Love comes after knowledge and fruition after love, and this is when one depends on the Lord through both faith and knowledge. . . . This perfects what is not yet perfect and teaches in advance the *future life* we shall enjoy with the "gods" *in God*, after being *liberated from every punishment and suffering that we sustain because of our sins* with a view to a salvific education. After this payment, *rewards and honors will be bestowed on those who have been made perfect once they have completed their purification.* . . . Then *restoration* [ἀποκατάστασις/*apokatastasis*]

16. *Strom.* 6:6:45–47.

17. *Strom.* 2:22:134:4.

awaits them *in eternal* [ἀΐδιος/*aïdios*] *contemplation*. . . . Thus, *knowledge* rapidly brings to *purification*.

Punishments are again declared to be educative. Clement uses ἀΐδιος/*aïdios* in reference to what is eternal proper, as apokatastasis certainly is. However, it is important to note that only αἰώνιος/*aiōnios* is used in reference to death or punishment in the other world. By refusing to apply ἀΐδιος to these, Clement shows that he does not deem them truly eternal. Only *life* is.

Clement proclaims the final harmony of all beings brought about by Christ (*Protr.* 1:5:2) who "has saved us while we were already close to ruin" (*Protr.* 1:7:4). The *telos* is "deification,"[18] which is grounded in the incarnation. Christ-Logos additionally exerts a therapeutic, purifying, and illuminative function, becoming "a sting for salvation." He waits for unbelievers to believe even after their death, as he is "the Savior of all,"[19] who "almost *compels to salvation* out of a superabundance of goodness" (*Strom.* 7:14:86:6). Christ-Logos, the revelation of God, is the divine Pedagogue who is "God's instrument for the love of humanity: the Lord has compassion, teaches, exhorts, warns, and *saves*."[20]

> This is the highest, most perfect good deed: to be able to convert one from evilness to virtue and righteousness. . . . Providence that governs *is necessarily sovereign and good,* and its power *takes care of salvation* in two ways: either, qua sovereign, *has one repent by means of punishment,* or, qua good, *helps with good deeds*. (*Strom.* 1:17:173:1–6)

No mention of a third way in which divine providence does *not* save. In *Strom.* 2:8:37:5 Clement describes God's Wisdom—who is again Christ—as the cause of all creation and of "the restoration [ἀποκατάστασις/*apokatastasis*] of the elects."[21] Indeed, in 3:9:63:4 he remarks that "It is necessary that generation and corruption take place in the creation until all elects have appeared and there comes *the restoration* [ἀποκατάστασις/*apokatastasis*], so that *even substances will return to their original place*." This testifies to the radical *universality* of the eventual

18. *Protr.* 1:8:4. Clement with this anticipates Origen, Athanasius, Gregory Nyssen, and others.

19. *Strom.* 6:6:46ff.; 7:2:7:6.

20. *Protr.* 1:6:2: Φιλάνθρωπον τὸ ὄργανον τοῦ Θεοῦ· ὁ Κύριος ἐλεεῖ, παιδεύει, προτρέπει, νουθετεῖ, σῴζει.

21. Itter, "The Restoration of the Elect," 169–74.

restoration. Alain Le Boulluec thinks that Clement did not anticipate the doctrine of apokatastasis, later supported by Origen and others, because he understood apokatastasis as the reestablishment of the original plan of God,[22] but this is precisely the way in which Origen himself understood it, and Clement's influence on Origen, in this as in many other respects, can hardly be overestimated.

The αἰώνιον/*aiōnion* fire of which the Gospels speak is not "eternal," but "ultramundane," and its function is to purify and sanctify the sinners' souls (*Strom.* 7:6:34:1–3). Clement does not cease to hope that even heretics can be converted by God, even after death, thanks to God's paternal care:

> May these heretics, too, after learning from these notes, regain wisdom and turn to the Omnipotent God. But if, like deaf snakes, they should not listen to, and understand, the song that has been sung recently but is most ancient, may they be *educated*, at least, *by God*, bearing his *paternal admonitions,* that they may be ashamed and *repent,* and may not happen that, if they behave with obstinate disobedience, they must undergo the *final and general judgment.* Beside this, also *partial educative processes* take place, *which we call chastisements,* which most of us, who belong to the people of the Lord, stumble upon, when we find ourselves in sin: *we are chastised by divine providence just as children are by their teacher or father. God does not punish* [τιμωρεῖται/*timōreitai*]—because punishment is a *retribution of evil with evil*—but *chastises* [κολάζει/*kolazei*] *to help those who are chastised.* (*Strom.* 7:16:102:1–3)

God never exerts retributive punishments, but only educative corrections. Even "heretics" who die without being corrected can still be corrected by God after death. Even the final Judgment delivers sinners to a purifying process. The possibility of purification and salvation after death will be contemplated by a number of later patristic thinkers, from Origen to Gregory of Nyssa, Maximus the Confessor, and Eriugena. The idea that if one does not repent within one's earthly life, there will be no possibility of doing so after death, as though one's free will should be lost, was alien to these thinkers.[23] It was, however, supported by some other patristic thinkers, who did not advocate universal restoration. For example, the

22. Le Boulluec, "Filiación y encarnación según Clemente de Alejandría," n. 107.

23. It is also alien to contemporary theologians such as MacDonald, *The Evangelical Universalist,* 32: "the traditional view that there are no chances to repent after death is also very hard to defend."

late Augustine (treated below), or Aphrahat, the Persian sage, who wrote in Syriac *Demonstrations* between 336 and 345. He seems to be one of the voices that limit the possibility of conversion and improvement to the present life. In *Dem.* 7.27 he states that the present world is the world of grace, but the future one will be the world of justice. "A limit has been imposed to grace: the departure (from this world); after that, there will be no chance of conversion."

SOTERIOLOGICAL UNIVERSALISM
IN SOME "APOCRYPHA"

The Apocalypse of Peter

Not only Bardaisan and Clement, but also some ancient so-called Apocrypha, known at least to Clement and likely (or in some cases certainly) to Origen, form the background of Origen's theorization of universal salvation. The most important of these is the *Apocalypse of Peter*, a Jewish-Christian work of the Petrine tradition.[24] It seems that the *Apocalypse of Peter* is very early—coming from the first half of the second century—and even influenced the biblical book of 2 Peter.[25]

The *Apocalypse of Peter* is preserved in an Ethiopian translation and in Greek fragments, transmitted mainly by Clement himself, who—as previously mentioned—deemed it divinely inspired and commented on it in his *Hypotyposeis*, along with biblical books.[26] In *Ecl. Proph.* 41 Clement speaks of the *Apocalypse of Peter* as "Scripture" (a view shared by Canon Muratori[27]). More than this, he also drew theological ideas from the text, ideas that would find their way in to the Origenian tradition. Clement reports that in this inspired text exposed babies were said to be handed to the care of an angel who will educate and raise them up to full

---

24. Bauckham, "The Apocalypse of Peter" and *The Fate of the Dead*, 160–258.

25. So Grünstäudl, *Petrus Alexandrinus*, received by Frey, *Der Brief des Judas und der zweite Brief des Petrus*, 170–73. Grünstäudl associates 2 Peter with the Petrine literature of the *Apocalypse of Peter*, on which he claims 2 Peter depends, and dates 2 Peter to the second half of the second century, considering it an expression of Alexandrian Christianity.

26. Eusebius *HE* 6:14:1. The *Apocalypse of Peter* is included in the Muratori Canon and in that of Codex Claromontanus among the biblical books.

27. The Muratorian fragment contains a copy of perhaps the oldest known list of the books that compose the New Testament, although its dating is now highly debated.

maturity and wisdom.[28] This idea, that intellectual and spiritual growth will continue in the other world if it was not completed in the present life,[29] will later be shared by Origen and Gregory of Nyssa. Origen will motivate this by observing that "the soul is always endowed with free will, both when it is in this (mortal) body *and when it is out of it*" (*Princ.* 3:2:5). Gregory of Nyssa will take over the idea of the otherworldly growth of dead babies in his *De infantibus praemature abreptis* (*On Babies who Died Prematurely*). In exactly the same work, not by chance, Clement expounds perhaps in the clearest way his theory of apokatastasis, even using the noun *apokatastasis* ("restoration") once and the relevant verb ("to restore") twice:

> According to the Apostle, then, there are firstborns *in the su-preme restoration* [*apokatastasei*]. The firstborns are the Thrones, being powers, because God rested upon them, as upon believers too. For each one, according to one's inclination, has its own degree of knowledge of God, and God rests on this knowledge, when those who have known him have become eternal thanks to knowledge. . . . "[B]eyond every governor, dominion, and power" are those who, among humans, angels, and archangels, have obtained perfection, *returning to the nature of angels at the first moment of the creation*. Indeed, those who, from humans, will have *transformed into angels*, will be instructed by angels for a thousand years and thus *will be restored* [*apokathistamenoi*] *to perfection*. Their instructors, in turn, will pass on to the power of archangels, and those instructed will pass *from the human to the angelic state*, and thus, in given periods, *will be restored* [*apokathistantai*]. (*Ecl. Proph.* 57)

The Ethiopian translation[30] and, more explicitly, the Greek Rainer Fragment (third century)[31] of the *Apocalypse of Peter* include a prediction of the eschatological intercession of the just in favor of the damned and the consequent liberation of the latter from hell. So speaks Christ in the Rainer Fragment:

> I will grant to my called and elect *all those they will ask me to draw out of the punishment*. And I will give them a noble

28. See my "Transformations of the Household and Marriage Theory," 369–96.

29. It is also attested in a quotation from the *Apocalypse of Peter* by Methodius, *Symp.* 2:6, known to Gregory Nyssen.

30. Buchholz, *Your Eyes*; Bauckham and Marassini, "*Apocalypse de Pierre*," 745–74; Bremmer and Czachesz, *The Apocalypse of Peter*.

31. P. Vindob. G. 39756 folii 1r–2v.

baptism *in salvation* in the Acherusian Lake,[32] which is said to be in the Elysian Field, a *share in justice and justification with my saints*. And my elect and I shall go joyously with the patriarchs in my kingdom in the other world, and *for their sake I will keep my promises*, those made to them by me and my Father who is in heaven.

Interestingly enough, the corresponding passage in the Ethiopic translation shows signs of modifications. The reviser clearly tried to eliminate from this passage the patent reference to the salvation of the damned from hell.[33] At any rate, the Ethiopic translation, being complete, helps contextualize the Rainer Fragment. In Chapter 13, the just are said to watch the punishment of the damned. The Ethiopic characterizes it as "eternal," but the underlying Greek is αἰώνιος/*aiōnios*, which indicates a punishment in the world to come.[34] Already at the beginning of Christ's revelation to Peter (Chs. 3–4), when Peter manifests worry for the destiny of sinners, Jesus replies that God, their Creator, has yet much more mercy upon them than Peter himself has. Soon after, he adds: "There is *no being that perishes* for God; there is *nothing that is impossible for God*" (4:5). This is a reminiscence of Matthew 19:26, Mark 10:27, and Luke 18:27, where Jesus responds to his disciples who worry about salvation: "This is impossible for humans, but *everything is possible for God*" (Origen will echo this precisely in support of his doctrine of universal salvation: "*Nothing is impossible* for the Omnipotent; *no being is incurable* for the One who created it").

A close parallel to the *Apocalypse of Peter* is provided by some statements in Rabbinic literature with respect to the idea that the just will intercede for the damned and obtain their liberation from Gehenna-hell: in *Yalkut Chadash*, f. 57.1, we read: "The just (will) bring imperfect souls out of Gehenna," an idea that appears again in *Yalkut Qohelet*: "God created paradise and Gehenna, that those in the former should deliver those in the latter."

The Ethiopic translation of the *Apocalypse of Peter* is part of the Ethiopic version of the "Ps. Clementines." Here, a dialogue between Peter and

32. This is an element of "pagan" mythology. The Elysian fields were the place of the blessed in the other world.

33. Scholars, however, were able to guess the original text even before the discovery of the Rainer Fragment. Cf. Buchholz, *Your Eyes*, 342–62; 425–26.

34. So also in 14:2 behind the Ethiopian "eternal kingdom" there lies "αἰώνιος kingdom," as is proved with certainty by the Rainer Fragment.

Jesus (139rb–144rb) concerns the salvation of sinners. This will come, not thanks to the intercession of the blessed, but thanks to that of Christ before the Father. The Father will have mercy (140rb–140vb); Jesus at his coming will destroy the devil and punish sinners (140vb–141vb). Peter expresses terror regarding these punishments (141vb), but Jesus replies that the Lord will have mercy upon those punished and will give them all "life, glory, and the eternal kingdom," because *he, Jesus, will intercede* for them. This truth, however, must remain a secret, to avoid encouraging sin (141vb–142bv). (As we shall see, Origen will come to share this idea that it is better to mistakenly believe in eternal damnation and abstain from evil and be saved, than know the truth and sin).

In the continuation (146v–157v), entitled "On the Judgment of Sinners," Peter relates to Clement the revelation received from Jesus:

> The Lord did not create Adam for chastisement and correction, but for happiness and joy. After his transgression of the commandment, death follows Adam's life. . . . *After resuscitating him, will God destroy Adam anew with death in hell?* After a *retribution commensurate with his sin*, will God *destroy him again?* Reflect and understand that *God will not have Adam die for a second time.* But let this discourse be a mystery for every human being, just as the preceding one.

Other "Apocrypha"

This conception appears also in Chapter 40 of the second-century *Epistula Apostolorum*, preserved in Coptic and Ethiopic. Here, the disciples are worried about the otherworldly destiny of sinners, and Jesus replies: "You do well to be worried, because the just will be worried about sinners; they pray for them and implore God," asking God to save them. The disciples ask whether that prayer will be fulfilled, and Jesus replies: "*Yes, I will listen to the prayer of the just, which they elevate for sinners.*" Likewise, in the Coptic *Apocalypse of Elijah* (third century) the blessed are said to successfully intercede for the sinners: "The just will contemplate sinners in their punishments, and those who had persecuted, betrayed, or handed them. Then sinners, in turn, will contemplate the place where the just will dwell, and *will participate in Grace.* On that day the just will be *granted that for which they will have often prayed*" (23:11—24:12), i.e. the salvation of sinners.

The same notion appears again toward the end of Book 2 of the *Sibylline Oracles*, which indeed derives from the *Apocalypse of Peter*. It is not accidental that Clement, who deemed the latter inspired, much appreciated the *Oracles*, to the point of stating that St. Paul recommended them, exactly for their eschatological predictions (*Strom.* 6:5). In 2:330–38 the following is declared:

> And to these pious people the immortal and omnipotent God will grant another gift: when they ask him, the immortal God will grant them *to save humans from the violent fire and the eternal gnashing of teeth*. And God will do so after drawing them *out of the unquenchable flame* and removing them from there, *destining them, for the love of his own, to another life in the world to come, for immortals*, in the Elysian Fields, where there are the long waves of the inextinguishable and deep Acherusian Lake.

In the manuscript tradition, at this point, some verses contest the doctrine of universal salvation here expressed (just as it happens in some scholia to Gregory of Nyssa's *De Anima*, where the doctrine of universal salvation is likewise detected and refuted, as I showed in *Gregorio di Nissa*).

The Petrine tradition is rich in statements concerning universal salvation. In the Greek *Martyrdom of the Holy Apostle Peter* 9, stemming roughly from the time of Origen, the language of apokatastasis is prominent. Peter says that the nail that holds together the two poles of the cross is "the turning and repentance [*epistrophē kai metánoia*] of humanity." Even more explicitly, in Pseudo-Linus' *Martyrdom of Blessed Peter the Apostle* 10, likely produced in Rome in the fourth century, Peter declares that Jesus and he himself have cured the bodily infirmities of many people "that the souls of *all* might be saved" (*ut omnium animae salvarentur*). Likewise, dead bodies were resuscitated "that *all* dead souls might be vivified again" (*animae mortuae revivescerent*). In Christ, through the cross, "the mystery of salvation has been accomplished" (*in Christo per crucem factum est salutis mysterium*, 11). "The Lord of the universe," as Origen also called God, suffered "for the salvation of the *whole world*" (*pro salute totius mundi*, 12). The mystery of the cross (*mysterium crucis*) is described as a bond of love (*vinculum caritatis*), because through the cross "God draws *all* beings to himself" (*per crucem ad se trahit omnia Deus*: 12). This is again the same language as Origen's (*tantam est caritatis vim ut ad se omnia trahat*, "so great is the power of love as to draw *all* beings to itself"). The very terminology of restoration comes again to the fore in section 14: "Hanging on a cross, he *restored* [*restituit*] . . . what had been altered by the regrettable error of humans." Thus, in section 15, the Lord is called by Peter "the author and perfecter of salvation" (*auctor et perfector salutis*). Even more explicitly, in section 20, Peter announces that, thanks to the crucifixion of Jesus, "the *whole world* was freed from the chains of eternal death" (*mundus totus aeternae mortis est uinculis absolutus*). Likewise, in the Syriac *History of Shimeon Kepha the Chief of the Apostles* 31, Jesus says to Peter: "I endured death by crucifixion for *the salvation of all*."

The *Life of Adam and Eve*, originally written in Greek, as it seems, was profoundly influential upon Christian authors. In 37:3–6, Adam, after death, repents from his sins, is brought by Michael the archangel to the lake of Hades, and is baptized, even after death. He is forgiven by the Lord and admitted to paradise with Eve. In a Latin manuscript very close to the original Greek,[35] God says to Michael: "Put Adam in paradise, in the third heaven, until the day of the salvific economy, when I *shall have mercy upon all* through my most loved Son."

The *Testaments of the Twelve Patriarchs* (second-third century AD) also offer some interesting soteriologically universalistic hints, for example in the *Testament of Simeon* 7.2: "The Lord will rise someone from Levi as a high priest, and from Judah as a king, God and human. This *will save all nations and the house of Israel*." The same in the *Testament of Joseph* 19.11: "Honor Judah and Levi, because among their offspring there will appear for you *the Lamb of God, who, by grace, will save all the nations and Israel*."[36] The *Testament of Abraham* (late first or early second century AD), which may have influenced the *Apocalypse of Peter*, and the *Testament of Isaac*, which depends on the *Testament of Abraham*, reflect a broadly universalist perspective: God concerned for all humankind, not only for his chosen people.[37] The *Apocalypse of Peter*, in turn, reflects a universalistic trend that goes so far as to suggest universal salvation, as I have shown above. And in a composite work whose final layers stem from the first or second century AD, *1 Enoch* 10:20—11:2, a section that is not entirely consistent with the immediately preceding section, the

---

35. Paris, Bibliothèque Nationale, fonds lat. 3832, ed. Pettorelli, "Vie latine d'Adam et d'Ève," 5–52.

36. See also the *Testament of Dan* 5.10–11: "The salvation of the Lord will rise for you of the tribes of Judah and Levi: He will wage war against Beliar, and take eternal vengeance on your enemies. He will deprive Beliar of his captives, the souls of the saints, and will convert to the Lord the disobeying hearts."

37. See Simkovich, "Echoes of Universalist Testament Literature."

archangel Michael is ordered to cleanse the earth from all injustice, oppression, and sin. All the earth will be cleansed from all sin, punishment,
and suffering, and all human beings will become righteous and will live
in peace and truth.[38]

INFLUENCE OF IRENAEUS' "RECAPITULATION" ON
THE DOCTRINE OF RESTORATION?

Reinhard Hübner has proposed that we can trace Gregory of Nyssa's
Christ-centered doctrine of universal salvation back not only to Origen,

38. *3 Baruch* also suggests a universalistic drift, since it presents God's glory as
related to a concern for all people and control over the cosmos. According to Lloyd,
"Universalism in 3 Baruch," the structure and episodes created by the author of the
text work to downplay Jewish particularism and halakhic commands as a response to
the destruction of the Jerusalem temple by the Romans.

but also to Irenaeus of Lyons in the second century.[39] Irenaeus is thought to have been born into a Christian family in Smyrna, Asia Minor, but is known to us for his ministry as a priest and then bishop in Lyons in Gaul. His celebrated writings were largely directed against the threat that he believed Gnosticism posed to the church.

Irenaeus does not formulate a doctrine of universal salvation, nor a theology of universal apokatastasis. However, he does introduce elements that point toward the doctrine of apokatastasis and very probably inspired those who formulated it after him. The contribution of Irenaeus, whose philosophical competence has been recently re-evaluated by Anthony Briggman,[40] mainly lies in his doctrine of the "recapitulation" (cf. Eph 1:10) of all beings in Christ. Christ "in his work of *recapitulation has united all beings together*, waging war against our enemy, and *entirely defeating the devil*, who at the beginning had imprisoned us" (*AH* 5:21). All humanity will be recapitulated in Christ and reconciled to God in full unity.[41] Christ "*recapitulates in himself all the things that are in heaven and on earth*; heavenly realities are spiritual, earthly ones concern the economy providentially arranged for humans. Consequently, Christ has recapitulated all this in himself, *joining humanity to the Spirit*, and having the Spirit dwell in humanity. Christ himself has become the Head of the Spirit, and gives the Spirit that it may be the Head of humanity" (*AH* 5:20:2). Christ "would not have truly possessed the flesh and blood through which he redeemed us if he had not *recapitulated in himself Adam's ancient molded nature*" (Greek fr. 3 from *AH* 5). Irenaeus even uses the terminology of restoration in connection with that of recapitulation:

> If God had not freely granted salvation, we would never have received it with certainty, and if the human being had not been united to God, it would never have been able to participate in incorruptibility. . . . The Son passes through all the stages of life, *restoring for all the communion with God*. . . . *He really eliminated the kingdom of death*; . . . he had to *destroy sin* and redeem the human being from the power of death . . . *that sin might be destroyed by a human being and the human being might be freed from death*. For, just as because of the disobedience of one

39. Hübner, *Die Einheit des Leibes Christi*, 125–29.

40. Briggman, "Revisiting Irenaeus' Philosophical Acumen" and "Literary and Rhetorical Theory in Irenaeus."

41. See De Andia, "Irénée, théologien de l'unité," 31–48; Steenberg, *Irenaeus*, 44–54.

> human being, molded from virgin earth, all were made sinners
> and had to renounce life, so also was it necessary that, thanks
> to the obedience of one human being, born from a virgin, *all
> be justified and receive grace.* . . . God *recapitulated in himself
> the original whole of humanity,* so to *kill sin, deprive death of its
> power, and vivify humanity.* (*AH* 3:18:1.7)

Again, the vivification of humanity consists not simply in the resurrection of the body, but in the liberation from sin. Christ recapitulates all,
albeit not all at the same time (*AH* 3:16:6.9). Thanks to Christ, no human
being is an enemy of God any longer (frs. 33–34).[42] In 5:23:2, another
Adam–Christ parallel confirms that the recapitulation operated by Christ
is universal: "The Lord suffered death, in obedience to his Father, on the
day on which Adam died due to his disobedience to God. . . . Thus, the
Lord, recapitulating in himself that day, suffered the passion in the day
before the Sabbath, that is, the day on which the human being was created, *thus offering him a second creation* through his Passion, the *new
creation free from death.*" This recreation has an effect on the whole of
humanity. Now, if all humans are recreated and recapitulated in Christ,
the question arises of how people who are eternally damned can be said
to be recreated and recapitulated in Christ.

Irenaeus' concept of recapitulation is similar to that of apokatastasis
as conceived by Origen and Gregory of Nyssa, all the more in that Irenaeus states more than once that in this recapitulation Christ assumes the
whole original human *katastasis* (*formatio*) in order to restore it: exactly
an *apo-katastasis*. In fr. 19 from Book 4, Irenaeus uses the verb "to restore,"
corresponding to the noun *apokatastasis*, to indicate the eschatological
salvific action of Christ: "The Lord, manifesting himself in the extreme
times, has reconstituted/restored [ἀπεκατέστησεν/*apekatestēsen*] himself
for all." Christ subsumed all humanity and brought it back to its state of
original purity. In fr. 5 from Book 5, the verb occurs twice[43] in reference
to God, who will restore humanity in the end thanks to the resurrection:
"dissolved in the earth, it *will be restored* anew. . . . God in his will shall

---

42. "Christ has recapitulated his own creature into himself, thus *saving it.*" Cf. *AH*
5:14:1: the Lord "indicates in this way *the recapitulation, in his own person,* of the
shedding of blood from the very beginning, the blood of all the just and prophets,
and shows that by means of himself their blood will be reclaimed. This would be impossible . . . if the Lord had not *recapitulated all this in himself* and had not become
flesh and blood himself, as in the original constitution of humanity, *saving in his own
person, in the end, what had perished in Adam at the beginning.*"

43. In Greek, ἀποκαταστήσει/*apokatastēsei* and ἀποκαταστήσεται/*apokatastēsetai*.

restore those who once existed, for the life donated by him." Gregory of Nyssa will echo this when he will define the resurrection as the restoration of humanity to its original state before sin (a holistic notion entailing not only the resurrection of the body, but also the restoration of the soul). Indeed, the whole treatment of resurrection in fr. 5 seems to be remembered and echoed by Gregory. Likewise in fr. 10: "life will seize humanity, chase away death, and *restore* humanity alive for God." Also at the end of fr. 15 from Book 5, Irenaeus uses the same verb, "to restore," to indicate the work of Christ who restores humanity to friendship with God.

Humanity is not simply restored to the state preceding the fall, but to a *better* one (this too will be the conviction of Origen and Gregory of Nyssa). Indeed, according to Irenaeus "salvation does not mean a mere return to paradise, but the *growth* from Adam's babyish immaturity to the full maturity of being children of God." This growth is not forced, but comes about through education (this will also be a conviction of Origen). In frs. 23–25 from Book 4, Irenaeus asks why God did not grant humans perfection from the very beginning, and answers, not that only some deserve it, but that humanity, just created, was not yet mature enough to receive it. But it will receive it in the end, thanks to Christ. This is why in Greek fr. 9 from Book 3 Irenaeus calls Christ "the Logos of God and *Savior of all*," and in fr. 16 he declares that God "resuscitated (Jesus) and in him gave salvation to humans." In *AH* 5:20:1, the action of Christ is extended to the church and described in universalistic terms: "She is entrusted with God's Light and God's Wisdom, through which she *saves all human beings*." Irenaeus even anticipates Origen's and Athanasius' idea that Christ's inhumanation enabled the deification of humanity: "God's Logos, Jesus Christ our Savior, *in his unlimited love, became what we are to make us what He is*" (fr. 1 from *AH* 5).

Irenaeus too, like Clement and Origen after him, speaks of painful and even drastic treatment applied by God with a therapeutic and educative aim, e.g., in *AH* 3:20:1, where Irenaeus stresses that God's aim is the salvation of humanity; God "extracts it from the belly of hell." In 20:2 Irenaeus adds that God's plan is the following:

> That humanity, passing through every tribulation and acquiring the knowledge of the moral discipline, and then being granted the resurrection from the dead, and learning by experience what is the source of its liberation, may *eternally live in gratitude toward the Lord, having been granted by him* the gift of incorruptibility, that it might *love God even more*.

Gratitude, liberation, and love clearly do not apply to people eternally damned in hell.

In this chapter, we have laid out some of the important Christian precursors to the full-blown, theologically systematized doctrine of apokatastasis as presented by its most famous exponent, Origen of Alexandria. Origen did not invent the doctrine *ex nihilo*, but instead pulled together and developed threads found in Christian texts dating right back into the early second century and, further still, into the Bible itself. It is to his seminal work that we turn in the next chapter.

3

Origen of Alexandria

Christian Universalism as Biblical and Orthodox

ORIGEN OF ALEXANDRIA

Origen († c.255) was born in Alexandria, Egypt, into a Christian family and he was enrolled in the catechetical school there. He was a very pious believer, devoting himself to prayer, asceticism, and Bible study, and in time became a celebrated teacher and author. Origen was very well educated, both in biblical and Hellenistic wisdom, and unusually gifted as a thinker and teacher. He could rightly be considered both the first systematic theologian of the church and one of its greatest ever biblical exegetes. After a controversy, he was banished from Alexandria in 231/32 by a synod convened by Bishop Demetrius of Alexandria. He made his home in Caesarea, Palestine, after this. Eventually anti-Christian persecution caught up with him and he was imprisoned and tortured under the Emperor Decius, and later died of the injuries received, aged sixty-nine.

Origen is, together with his faithful follower Gregory of Nyssa, the main theorizer of the doctrine of universal salvation—although by no means the only one. He theorized it not simply as a Platonist, but as a *Christian* Platonist, such as he was.[1] His "anti-Platonism," which has been stressed by some scholars,[2] needs to be qualified. Origen did not oppose Platonism tout court (that is, per se, in itself, or in an absolute sense), but rather "*gnostic*" Platonism and "*pagan*" Platonism, in an effort to develop an *orthodox Christian* Platonism.[3] His doctrine of universal restoration and salvation is an excellent example of this nuanced approach to the wisdom of the Greeks.

The principal metaphysical foundation of this doctrine of his consists in the idea that *evil is non-being*; only God—who, qua supreme Good, is the opposite of evil—is Being (*Comm. in Io.* 2:13).[4] This is why

1. Ramelli, "Origen, Patristic Philosophy" and "Origen the Christian Middle-Neoplatonist"; O'Leary, *Christianisme et philosophie*, with my review in GNOMON 84 (2012) 560–63 ; a monograph on Origen's relation to Platonism and imperial philosophy has been for much time and is in the works; it will rest on 25 years on research. A future one on Origen and Plotinus is projected.

2. Emphasized especially by Mark J. Edwards and Panayiotis Tzamalikos with several correct observations.

3. Of course Origen would reject doctrines such as that of metensomatosis (the transmigration of souls), which was incompatible with the Bible and in fact was supported by Plato himself only in a mythical form, while it was "pagan" Platonism that supported it in a theoretical and dogmatic form—and this is what both Origen and Gregory Nyssen countered.

4. "It is the good God who says so ['I am the One who Is'], and it is the same God whom the Savior glorifies when he says: 'No one is good but God the Father.' The one who is *good*, therefore, coincides with the One who *is*. On the contrary, evil and meanness are opposed to the Good as non-being to Being. Therefore, meanness and

to adhere to evil means to become non-being: "As long as we stick to God and adhere to the One who truly Is, we also are. But if we go far from God . . . we fall into the opposite [i.e., non-being]. However, this does not mean the ontological death of the soul" (*Hom. 2 in Ps. 38*, 12). The wicked man's death or reduction to non-being is not a vanishing of the substance of his soul,[5] but his spiritual death (see also *Hom. 2 in Ps. 38*, 1; *Hom. 5 in Ps. 36*, 5). And the destruction of the sinner at the Judgment will be the destruction of his sin, that he may be a sinner no more, but a just man; the otherworldly (αἰώνιον/*aiōnion*) fire will indeed destroy, not sinners, but their evil thoughts (*Comm. in Matt.* 5:10:2).

In fact, an important consequence of the ontological non-subsistence of evil—a Platonic notion—is that it cannot exist forever.[6] In the Bible, this is announced in 1 Corinthians 15:24–26 and Revelation. Origen, followed by Gregory Nyssen,[7] argued that, if God will be "in all" (1 Cor 15:28), then evil, which is the opposite of God, the Good, will necessarily be found in no being any more.[8] Since Origen insists, following this biblical text, that it is "*in all*" that God will be "all," and not only "in few or in many," this means that salvation is definitely universal. But the final vanishing of evil from all humans will be able to take place only thanks to the "inhumanation," death, and resurrection of Christ, as I

---

evil are non-being."

5. This is because the soul was created by God and therefore cannot fall into non-being: "The beings that God created in order for them to exist and endure *cannot undergo a destruction in their very substance*" (*Princ.* 3:6:5). The *logoi* or ontological principles of God's creatures will never pass away (*CC* 5:22).

6. E.g., *Princ.* 2:9:2; 1:7:5; *Comm. in Io.* 2:13; *CC* 4:63; 7:72; *Sel. in Ps.* 56; *Exh. ad mart.* 13; Ramelli, "Christian Soteriology."

7. In *In Illud: Tunc et Ipse Filius* 17 Downing and *De anima et resurrectione* 104–5. See Ramelli, "The Trinitarian Theology of Gregory of Nyssa," 445–78.

8. "When God will be 'all in all' we *cannot admit of evil, lest God be found in evil*. . . . That God is said to be 'all in all' means that God will be all even in the single creatures . . . whatever the rational intelligence, freed from every dirtiness of sin and purified from every obfuscation of evilness, will be able to perceive, grasp, and think, *all of this will be God* . . . , therefore, God will be 'all' for this intelligence . . . because *evil will exist no more*: for this intelligence, everything is God, who is untouched by evil. . . . Therefore, if at the end of the world, which will be similar to the beginning, there will be *restored that condition* which the rational nature had when it had not yet felt the need to eat the fruit of the tree of the knowledge of good and evil, once *every sense of evil is removed*, then for the creature, who has returned pure and unsullied, the One who is the only good God will become all. And *not only in few or in many, but 'in all'* God will be all, when there exists no more death, nor death's sting, nor evil any more, absolutely: then God will truly be 'all in all'" (*Princ.* 3:6:2–3). See also *CC* 6:36.

shall show below: "One human died, and his death not only represented a paradigm of death by devotion, but also produced the *principle and advancement of the destruction of what is evil* and the devil, which ruled upon the whole earth" (*CC* 7:17). Evil has no ontological substance—and thus will have to vanish—because, like death, it was not created by God, the Being.[9] It "did not exist in the beginning and will not exist forever" (*Comm. in Io.* 2:13); "there was a state in which evil did not exist, and there will be one in which evil will not exist any more" (*Exp. in Prov.* 5; *Fr. in Prov.* 5). Origen will inspire Evagrius' famous motto: "There was a time when evil did not exist, and there will come a time when it will no more exist" (*KG* 1:40).

If evil will disappear from all beings, then—as announced in 1 Corinthians 15:28 and Acts 3:20–21—all beings will be restored into the Good, and thus be saved: "A righteous person keeps her hope in the shadow of the wings of God, until *evil will be entirely destroyed. After the abolition of evil and its annihilation into non-being*, this person will no longer place her hope in a shadow, but in the Godhead itself" (*Sel. in Ps.* 56). When every evil is definitely reduced to non-being, all beings will return to the Good, even Satan, who will thus be saved, not qua devil, archenemy, and death, but qua creature of God, after his conversion from evil to the Good.[10] "The devil can return to being an archangel"[11] because he was created an archangel; he became devil due to a wrong choice of his free will, but since his will remains free, he can return to the Good and be saved. Demons do not turn to the Good because they do not want to, and not because they cannot, and they do not want to while they continue to delight in evil, but when they stop doing so, they will return to the Good (*Princ.* 1:8:4). The devil and his angels in the end will not disagree with the final harmonic unity of all—a Platonic ideal that Origen also grounds in John 17: "Once things have begun to rush toward the ideal state in

9. See Ramelli, "1 Cor 15:28."

10. *Princ.* 1:6:3; 3:6:5 "This is why it is also written that 'the last enemy, death, will be destroyed' [1 Cor 15:26], that there may be nothing painful left, when death will exist no more, nor anything opposed, when there will be no enemy left." But the last enemy, who is called "death," i.e., the devil, "will be destroyed, *not in such a way as to exist no more*, but so that he may no longer be an enemy and death. . . . [W]e must understand the destruction of the last enemy as the destruction, *not of the substance* that was created by God, but of the *inclination and the hostile will* that stemmed, not from God, but from the enemy himself. Therefore, he will be destroyed, not in order for him to exist no more, but in *such a way as to be no longer 'enemy' and 'death'*."

11. From Jerome, *Ep.* 124:3.

which all are one just as the Father is one with the Son, as a logical consequence we must believe that, when all are one, there will be no divergence
any more" (*Princ.* 3:6:4). Even demons will no longer be powers of evil,
but will return to their angelic state and ascend the angelic hierarchies,[12]
after a purification and illumination that can take extremely long:

> Every being will be restored to be *one*, and *God will be "all in
> all."* However, this will not happen in a moment, but slowly and
> gradually, through innumerable aeons of indefinite duration,
> because *correction and purification* will take place gradually,
> according to the needs of each individual. Thus, whereas some
> with a faster rhythm will be the first to hasten to the goal, and
> others will follow them closely, yet others on the contrary will
> fall a long distance behind. And in this way, through innumer-
> able orders constituted by those who make progress and, *after
> being enemies, are reconciled with God,* there will come *the last
> enemy,* Death, that this may be destroyed and there may be no
> enemy left. (*Princ.* 3:6:6)

Death—which is no creature of God—will vanish; not even the
devil will be any longer "enemy" and "death." This death is not just the
death of the body, but that of the soul due to sin (so in *Comm. in Rom.*
5:7: "once the death of the soul, which is the very last enemy, has been
destroyed, the kingdom of death, together with death itself, will be wiped
out"). That death will vanish means that all rational creatures will be pure
from sin: "We can say that the death of the world comes to an end when
the sin of the world dies, explaining the words of the Apostle: 'And after
he has put all enemies under his feet, then the last enemy, death, will be
destroyed'" (*CC* 6:36); "*No one will do evil any more,* and evil will govern
no one" (*Hom. in Ies. Nav.* 8:5); "There will be *no one who does evil any
more,* as there will be no evil any more" (*Exp. in Prov.* 5).[13] The liberation

12. "Both in these visible and temporal aeons and in those invisible and otherworldly, God's providence operates in favor of all with measure and discernment, with
regard to order and merit. Therefore, some first and then others, and yet others in the
very last times, by means of heavier and more painful sufferings, long and undergone,
say, for many aeons, in the end *all, renewed by instruction and severe corrections, will be
restored* first among the angels, then in the superior hierarchies; thus all will be gradu-
ally received higher and higher, until they arrive at the invisible and eternal realities,
after running, one by one, the offices of the heavenly hierarchies to be instructed."

13. Thus, in *On the Resurrection* Origen interpreted Ezekiel 37 as both a physical
resurrection and a spiritual restoration from sin, allegorically expressed as a return
of the Hebrews from exile (from Methodius *De res.* from Photius *Bibl.* cod. 234, p.
300a). On Origen's use of allegoresis in his biblical interpretation see, e.g., my "Origen's

of creation from death will be a liberation from the devil (*Exh. ad Mart.* 13); even demons will be freed:

> Let us now see what will be *the liberation of creation and the end of enslavement.* At the end of the world, when souls and rational creatures will be, so to say, pushed by the Lord out of the locks and gates, some will move more slowly due to their laziness, others will fly swiftly with their zeal. . . . But when Christ will have handed the kingdom to God the Father,[14] then these creatures too, which earlier had become a part of the kingdom of Christ, along with the rest of the kingdom will be handed to the Father, that this may rule over them. Thus, when God will be "all in all,"[15] as these also are part of the "all," God will be in them as in all. (*Princ.* 1:7:5)

The importance of free will in Origen does not exclude universal salvation.[16] For in *Princ.* 1:6:3, Origen argues that demons and the devil himself will return to the Good in the end *precisely because* they always keep their free will. The latter does not conflict with God's providential action and universal salvation, as is clear in *Comm. in Rom.* 5:10:212–22: "if all the factors that St. Paul listed cannot separate us from God's love . . . *still less shall our free will be able to separate us from God's love.*" In fact,

> I do not deny in the least that the rational nature will *always keep its free will,* but I declare that the *power and effectiveness of Christ's cross* and of his death, which he took upon himself toward the end of aeons, are so great as to be enough to *set right and save,* not only the present and the future aeon, but also all the past ones, and not only this order of us humans, but also the heavenly orders and powers. (*Comm. in Rom.* 4:10)

Salvation will have to be voluntary, for all, by means of a conversion that will be enabled by the healing action of Christ. For "nothing is impossible for the Omnipotent; *no being is incurable* for the One who created it" (*Princ.* 3:6:5). Christ-God, who created all, including the devil, will be able to heal all, even the devil.[17] "In souls, there is no illness caused

---

Allegoresis of Plato's and Scripture's Myths," received by Marx-Wolf, *Spiritual Taxonomies and Ritual Authority*, 148; by Krulak, "Defining Competition in Neoplatonism," 80–81; by Urbano, "Difficulties in Writing the Life of Origen."

14. 1 Cor 15:28.

15. 1 Cor 15:28.

16. As is claimed, e.g., by Holliday, "Will Satan Be Saved?" 1–23.

17. Origen is using the argument of God's omnipotence, employed by Jesus in

by evilness that is *impossible to cure for God the Logos*, who is superior to all" (*CC* 8:72). It is thanks to Christ-Logos that what Origen foresees in *Princ.* 1:3:6 will be accomplished: "many prophecies mysteriously speak[18] of the *complete elimination of evil* and *rectification of every soul.*" The ultimate end (*telos*) is the restoration even of the devil, who will voluntarily submit to Christ-Logos and be saved.[19] He will be saved only once he has returned to the Good.

Origen's insistence on the importance of free will informed his polemic against "gnostic" (Valentinian) determinism as well as his criticism of the Stoic notion of apokatastasis, which was characterized by an *endless* sequence of aeons/ages in each of which the same people will always behave in the same way. Origen's idea of apokatastasis, on the contrary, entails a *limited number* of aeons, after which the universal restoration will take place (e.g., *Princ.* 2:3:1: "a stage in which there will be no aeon any more"). Moreover, in each aeon, rational creatures' moral choices will not be identical to previous aeons, but different (e.g., *CC* 4:67–8), and the aeons will see the rational creatures' spiritual development. They will offer to all rational creatures the time to get purified, illuminated, and thus voluntarily adhere to God.[20] Soon after accusing the Stoic theory of apo-

---

Matthew 19:25–26 and Mark 10:26–27, in reference to the salvation of sinners.

18. Universal salvation must not be proclaimed to just anyone, because it would be dangerous for the immature who do good out of fear and not out of love (1 John 4:17–9).

19. "'Christ is the firstfruits, then those who belong to Christ, at his coming, and then the ultimate end will come' [1 Cor 15:24]. This ultimate end will indeed take place on Christ's coming, when he will hand the kingdom to God the Father, after annihilating all principalities, authorities, and powers . . . then, *he of whom it is written that 'He exalted himself before the Lord almighty' will be among those who submit*, conquered because he has *yielded to the Logos*, and subjected to God's image, becoming a stool for his feet. Thus, he contemplates the *salvific economy, which leads to the good end.*" In his *Letter to Friends in Alexandria*, Origen stated that not even a fool would maintain that the devil is to be saved, since not even sinners will enter the kingdom of God. As long as they are sinners, and have not repented, they will not enter. Neither will the devil, until he repents and ceases to be "enemy and death."

20. "Likewise, I deem it necessary to investigate whether after this aeon there will be a *correction* and *purification*, even bitter and painful, for those who have not wanted to obey the word of God, and, on the other hand, *teaching and rational education* for others, thanks to which those who already during this life have devoted themselves to this study will be able to *make progress. . . .* And it is necessary to investigate whether after these facts there will be the end of all, or, for the sake of the *correction and purification of those who will still need this*, there will be *another aeon . . .* and whether there will come a stage in which there will be *no longer any aeon*, whether there has already

katastasis of annihilating human free will (*Princ.* 3:3:4), Origen claims that aeons/ages will come to an end; this end will coincide with universal restoration and salvation, "when all will be no more in an aeon, but God will be 'all in all.'"[21] All creatures will pass from being in the aeons to being in God. We ought to stress here that when the Bible mentions aeons, it does not refer to eternity, for only God is truly eternal, while aeons have a limited duration.[22] This implies that all Scriptural expressions such as "αἰώνιος/*aiōnios* death," "αἰώνιον/*aiōnion* fire," or "αἰώνιος/*aiōnios* punishment," which refer to the death, fire, and punishment in the next aeon (αἰών/*aiōn*), cannot be interpreted as "eternal" fire, death, or punishment, because the next aeon, and all aeons, will come to an end, when there will be the passage from the aeons to God.[23] In *Comm. in Io.* 10:39, Origen describes apokatastasis as a passage into the Trinity at the end of time: "the [scriptural] expressions that refer to the preparation of the stones, which are pulled up and prepared for building up the construction, seem to me to certainly indicate the totality of time, that is, the extension that is necessary (for rational creatures) to finally *come to be in the eternal Trinity.*" Origen, indeed, identified the ultimate end with restoration and "deification" (*Sel. in Ps.* 23), "communion with the divine" (*CC* 3:80). It is Christ-Logos who makes the eventual "deification" possible (*Ex. ad Mart.* 25; *De orat.* 27:13). The theology of deification itself, according to Origen, is grounded in Scripture.[24] Origen bases his argument on 1 John 3:2 in *Hom. in Luc.* 29:7: "'We shall be like God, and see God as God is.' You,

---

existed a stage in which there was no aeon, whether there have been and there will be more than one aeon, and whether it will ever happen that there exists *one aeon that is perfectly identical to another*" (*Princ.* 2:3:1). Origen's answer to the last question is clearly negative, in opposition to the Stoics.

21. *Princ.* 3:3:5. Cf. *Comm. in Io.* 13:3: "αἰώνιος/*aiōnios* life" will not be the ultimate stage; it will be the life in the next aeon, in Christ, but that aeon will finish and after "αἰώνιος/*aiōnios* life" the final restoration will come, in which all will be in the Holy Trinity, and God will be "all in all."

22. "Whenever Scripture says, 'from aeon to aeon,' the reference is to an interval of time, and it is clear that *it will have an end*. And if Scripture says, 'in another aeon,' what is indicated is clearly a longer time, and yet *an end is still fixed*. And when the 'aeons of the aeons' are mentioned, a *certain limit is again posited*, perhaps unknown to us, but surely established by God" (*Hom. in Ex.* 6:13).

23. "The *perfection and end of all beings* will be found *in God*, when God will be 'all in all'" (*Comm. in Rom.* 8:13:9); "Those who will have been *reformed and corrected* will remain steadfast in its perfection. . . . The fact of closely adhering to the culmination of its perfection is said to *take place in God*" (*Comm. in Rom.* 3:10:3).

24. Ps 82:6; John 10:34; 1 John 3:2–3; 2 Pet 1:3–4.

too, will have to *become God* in Jesus Christ." And he explicitly relies on Psalm 82:6, as interpreted by Jesus in John 10:34, in *Hom. in Lev.* 9:11:1: "Those who will follow Christ and enter with him the inner parts of the temple and ascend to the heights of heaven will no longer be humans, but, according to Christ's teaching, will be like angels of God [Matt 22:30] It is even possible that there is realized what the Lord said: 'I have said, *You are gods*, you are all children of the Most High." Then, one "must have *become* an angel and *even God*" (*Sel. in Ps.* 23).[25] Thus, there will be a passage from being in time to being in God, i.e., in eternity. For God alone is eternal; none of the creatures is (*Hom. 2 in Ps. 38*, 11).

This is why the life that will be a participation in God's life truly is eternal. Death, on the contrary, which is a consequence of sin and no creature of God, is not eternal:

> *I do not think that this reign of death is eternal as that of life and justice is*, especially in that I hear from the Apostle that *the last enemy, death, must be destroyed.*[26] For should one suppose that the eternity of death is the same as that of life, death will no longer be the contradictory opposite of life, but equal to it. For "eternal" is not the contradictory of "eternal," but the same thing. Now, it is certain that death is the contradictory of life; therefore, it is certain that, if life is eternal, *death cannot possibly be eternal.* . . . When the death of the soul, which is the very last enemy, has been destroyed, also this common death—which, as I said, is a sort of shadow of the death of the soul—will necessarily be abolished, and *the kingdom of death, along with death itself, will be wiped out.* (*Comm. in Rom.* 5:7)

If the death of the soul, due to sin, must be destroyed in the end, then all rational creatures will return to life, free from sin. Origen knew that death is only called αἰώνιος/*aiōnios* ("otherworldly; of the next aeon") in Scripture,[27] and never ἀΐδιος/*aïdios* ("eternal"), which is rather

---

25. Cf. *Princ.* 4:4:8: "The Godhead, who is good by nature, wanting that there might exist beings to benefit, and such as to be able to rejoice in the goods bestowed upon them, created creatures worthy of Itself, that is, capable of understanding It in a worthy way. In reference to these, God declares, 'I have generated *children*'" (Isa 1:2).

26. 1 Cor 15:26.

27. Origen is very much aware that αἰών/*aiōn* and αἰώνιος/*aiōnios* in Scripture almost never imply eternity (in fact, they do so only when they refer to God): "In Scriptures, αἰών/*aiōn* is sometimes found in the sense of something that knows no end; sometimes it designates something that has no end in the present world, but will have in the future one; sometimes it means a certain stretch of time; or again the

reserved to life and beatitude; and indeed the Bible explicitly speaks of
the eventual destruction of death (1 Cor 15:26). Therefore, Origen is certain that life and justice will be eternal, but death will not. For "the whole
aeon [αἰών/aiōn] is long in relation to us, but it is quite short, and is only
tantamount to a few years, in relation to the life of God, of Christ, and of
the Holy Spirit," which is eternal (*Comm. in Matt.* 15:31). Hebrews 1:2,
indeed, declares that the aeon was created by Christ, and on the basis of
this verse Origen claims that the aeons are but a creature of the eternal
God (*Comm. in Io.* 2:10). Eternity characterizes only the Trinity;[28] creatures can become eternal only by grace and as a participation in the life
of the divine Trinity. Thus, Origen *never* describes otherworldly death,
punishment, or fire as ἀΐδια/*aidia*, "eternal." He only calls them αἰώνια/
aiōnia, because they last in the future aeon or aeons, but not after the end
of all aeons, in the eternal restoration.[29] Henri Crouzel, an authoritative
scholar in Origen studies, makes the same point: "The essential reason
why the expression πῦρ αἰώνιον did not seem to Origen to necessarily
imply the eternity of punishment as we understand it, is that the adjective
αἰώνιος retains for him all the ambiguity of the word from which it derives, αἰών. In both Testaments, besides the meaning 'eternity' conceived
as endless duration, there is another, which we translate 'age,' meaning a
long period of time, especially the duration of the present world—hence
the synonymy between 'world' and 'age' (*saeculum*)—or the world to
come."[30]

In *Hom. 4 in Ps. 36*, 8 Origen clearly distinguishes between the future aeon, which will be a temporal interval (*tempus vel saeculum*), and

---

duration of the life of a single person is called αἰών/*aiōn*" (*Comm. in Rom.* 6:5).

28. In Origen, ἀΐδιος/*aidios* is the technical term for the absolutely eternal. It is
only found in reference to God, who alone is eternal and immortal, or to eternal life,
when Origen wants to stress that it will be eternal as a participation in the life of God.

29. This is the argument of my studies on the terminology of eternity and time
in Origen and ancient Christianity, which I set out in detail in *Terms of Eternity* and
The Christian Doctrine of Apokatastasis. Besides many other reviewers of my books
and my relevant articles, Daniel Heide recognized the force of my arguments in his
"Ἀποκατάστασις," 201–20.

30. "La raison essentielle pour laquelle l'expression πῦρ αἰώνιον ne parait pas à
Origène impliquer nécessairement l'éternité du châtiment tel que nous l'entendons,
c'est que l'adjectif αἰώνιος conserve pour lui tout l'ambiguïté du mot dont il dérive
αἰών. Dans le deux Testaments à côté de la signification <éternité> conçue comme une
durée sans fin, on trouve celle, que nous traduisons par <siècle>, de longe période de
temps, spécialement de durée de monde actuel—de là la synonymie entre <monde> et
<siècle> – ou de monde futur" (Henri Crouzel, "L'Hadès et la Géhenne," 320).

the absolute eternity that will come *after* the end of all aeons (*deinceps in aeternitate*). At the end of all aeons, in the eternal restoration, all will come to be, no longer in any aeon, but in God, who will be "all in all" (1 Cor 15:28, commented on in *Princ.* 3:6:2–3).

From that perfect condition, in the eternal restoration, no one will fall again. For the perfection of love, reached in the very end, will admit of no falls, while at the same time rational creatures will keep their free will. Origen argues for all this in *Comm. in Rom.* 5:10:158–240. He begins with a refutation of those who thought that Christ's sacrifice would have to be repeated over and over again, due to the possibility of ever new falls. Origen responds that it needn't be repeated: it occurred *once and for all*, and its effect extends to all rational creatures and all aeons (*Comm. in Rom.* 5:10:235–36; 187–95). Origen then goes on to demonstrate that rational creatures will not continue to fall without end, because there will come an end of all aeons, in the eternal restoration; from that condition no one will fall, since perfect love will prevent this:

> What is that in the future aeons that will *prevent the freedom of will from falling again into sin*? The Apostle tells us this quite pithily, when he states: "*Love never falls.*"[31] This is why love is greater than faith and hope, because it is the only one that *will prevent all sin*. For, if the soul has reached such a degree of perfection as to love God with all its heart, with all its mind, and with all its forces, and its neighbor as much as itself, *what room will be left for sin?* . . . *Love will prevent every creature from falling, when God will be "all in all."*[32] . . . So great is the power of love that it *attracts every being to itself* . . . especially in that God has been the first to give us reasons for love, since he has not spared his only child, but he offered him for all of us. (*Comm. in Rom.* 5:10:195–226)

Love could not impede Satan's or Adam's fall, because their falls occurred *before* the manifestation of Christ's love (*Comm. in Rom.* 5:10:227–30). But the end will be better than the beginning, because in the end rational creatures will adhere to God voluntarily, in so strong a love that they will never fall again as they could fall at the beginning.[33]

31. 1 Cor 13:8.

32. 1 Cor 15:28.

33. The stability of all rational creatures in the Good in the final restoration is indeed attested by *Comm. in Io.* 10:42:26; *Comm. in Matt.* 12:34; *Dial. cum Her.* 26; *Hom. in Reg.* 1:4.

Indeed, "one who is found in the Good eternally and for whom God is 'all things' does *no longer desire to eat* (the fruit) of the tree of the Knowledge of Good and evil" (*Princ.* 3:6:3). And in reference to the Song of Songs:

> If the girls [i.e. rational creatures] will reach Christ's true being, which is incomprehensible and ineffable, they will *no longer walk, nor run*, but they will be, in a way, *tied by the bonds of Christ's love*; they will *adhere to it* and will have *no longer the force to move again*, because they will be one and the same spirit with Christ, and in them the saying will be fulfilled, "Just as you, Father, are in me and I am in you, and we are One, so also may they be one in Us." That this may happen and *all creatures may incessantly and indissolubly adhere to the One who Is*, Wisdom must necessarily *instruct* them on this point and bring them to perfection.

Origen elaborated his doctrine of apokatastasis on the basis of his defense of free will against "gnostics."[34] Thus, Origen's theory of universal salvation, far from eliminating human free will, is in fact grounded in it. Book 3 of his masterpiece *On First Principles* meaningfully begins with a defense of free will against "gnostic" determinism—dictated by his concern for theodicy—and ends with the theory of universal restoration and salvation. Indeed: "God's providence takes care of all, *respecting the choices* of each human being's free will" (*CC* 5:21). The same is argued in *Princ.* 2:9:7[35] and *De orat.* 27:15: "The present aeon is the consummation of many past aeons, as though it were a year of aeons, and after this there will come future aeons, whose beginning is the next one, and in these future aeons God will show *the richness of his grace in goodness*. Even in the case of *the worst sinner*, who has blasphemed against the Holy Spirit, possessed by sin in the whole of the present aeon and in the future from the beginning to the end, after this, I do not know how, God will take *providential care of him*." This providential care mainly takes the form of illumination, instruction, and correction. This is consistent with Origen's ethical intellectualism: one's moral choices depend on one's knowledge; one's will proceeds from one's intellect; it is not independent of it. Evil

34. Ramelli, "La coerenza" and "Origen, Bardaisan, and the Origin of Universal Salvation."

35. "*God takes providential care of all with mercy, and exhorts and pushes all to salvation* by means of remedies from which *each one can profit*. ... God, pre-ordering everything with Wisdom up to the tiniest details, and distinguishing everything with judgment, with a most just retribution has disposed everything so that *every creature may be taken care of and helped in relation to its merit*."

is therefore chosen because it is mistaken for a good, due to insufficient knowledge or a clouding of the intellect (e.g., *Hom.* 1 *in Ps. 37*, 4: "sin here is rightly called *ignorance*"). This is why instruction and illumination are paramount in the process of restoration; these will be imparted by angels and then by Christ.[36]

The whole process will also entail suffering proportional to each one's amount of sins. This means that the otherworldly "punishment" is in fact medical, pedagogical, and purifying.[37] Like the NT, and like Clement, Origen uses *kolasis* in the sense of a punishment that is always corrective. For instance, in the newly discovered Munich homilies, in Homily 2 on Psalm 36.5, fol. 47v, he speaks of the fire that will come after the end of the world (μετὰ τὴν συντέλειαν/*meta tēn sunteleian*) and observes that this fire will punish sinners (κολάζον πῦρ/*kolazon pur*), but in such a way that a sinner will no longer be a sinner: ποιήσει μηκέτι εἶναι ἁμαρτωλόν/ *poiēsei mēketi einai hamartōlon*.

Christ is a physician of souls whose aim is "to heal *all rational souls* with the therapy that comes from the Logos, to make them friends of God" (*CC* 3:54). He can have recourse to drastic remedies, such as cauterization with fire, but he does heal sinners.[38] In *Princ.* 2:10:6–7 Origen interprets many scriptural passages to show that "God deals with sinners in the same way as physicians do with the sick to restore them to health." All will pass through the purifying fire, and the duration of their time in it will be commensurate to each one's sins (*Hom.* 3 *in Ps.* 36, 1). God is said by Scripture to kill and destroy, but only to remake creatures better (*Hom. in Ier.* 1:15–16); his strategy is always "resurrecting."[39]

That all will be saved, and that this will happen because all will come to believe, is particularly clear from Origen's reflection on Romans 11:25–26. In *Comm. in Rom.* 7:13, Paul's prayer for the salvation of Israel will be fulfilled in the end, when the "totality of the nations" will enter and "all Israel will be saved." This prophecy is repeated by Origen over and over again in this commentary, and in other works,[40] and is to be

36. *Princ.* 2:11; 3:6:9.

37. In this perspective, Origen considers even the death decreed by God after the fall as healing and salutary, e.g., in *Comm. in Matt.* 15:15; *Hom. in Lev.* 14:4; a fragment preserved by Methodius from Photius *Bibl.* cod. 234.

38. *Princ.* 2:10:6; cf. 2:7:3; 3:1:15.

39. "He *had me fall* with this purpose: in order for me *to rise again*" (*Hom. in Luc.* 17).

40. E.g. *Comm. in Rom.* 8:1; 8:9; 8:12; 8:9. See also *Fr. in Luc.* 125; *Hom. in Ex.* 6:9;

seen as an expression of universal salvation. The salvation of all Israel and all gentiles will take place through faith: Abraham will inherit "the whole world" because all will be made just by their faith.

One point that must be stressed is that Origen, like Gregory of Nyssa after him, has universal salvation depend on Christ: on his inhumanation, death, and resurrection, besides his healing work as Physician and instructive activity as Logos. Christ's sacrifice, although it took place once, has had the power of healing and rectifying all rational creatures in all aeons (*Comm. in Rom.* 4:10; 2:13:27),[41] and at the same time—thanks to Christ's action of instruction and persuasion—the salvation of all will be voluntary. Christ's sacrifice reconciled all rational creatures with God (*Comm. in Rom.* 10:9:12–4), putting sin to death (4:12:55–78); Jesus, as a high priest, offered himself in sacrifice "for *all rational creatures*" (*Comm. in Io.* 1:35:255). Christ is the savior and propitiatory offering for all, "not only for our sins, but also for the whole world."[42] Christ's sacrifice and resurrection produce the restoration of "every creature" (*Comm. in Rom.* 4:7:41–43), by *making them just* (100–103). Christ's incarnation destroyed sin in flesh (5:1:501–5), and "the whole creation was restored through the Lord's resurrection" (4:7:3). This restoration is "the return of the whole universe to God" (*CC* 4:99). Christ defeats the devil as the holder of the power of death, which is evil (*Comm. in Rom.* 5:3:65–70). Christ destroyed sin,[43] since evil has no power over him, as divine Wisdom (Wis 7:30); his blood shed saves humans more than faith and good deeds (*Comm. in Rom.* 6:11:73–75). And we must never lose sight of the power of Christ's illuminating and healing action (*CC* 8:72).[44] No being is

---

Hom. in Ier. 5:4–5; Hom. in Num. 7:1.

41. "Jesus' blood was so precious . . . that it alone was enough for the redemption *of all.*" In *De orat.* 27:15, too, Origen, reflecting on Heb 9:26 and Eph 2:7, argues that Christ's sacrifice was made once and for all aeons, and in *Fr. in Iob* 387:14 he declares that "the Cross happened once and for all" (*hapax*).

42. *CC* 3:49; cf. 4:28.

43. *Comm. in Rom.* 6:12:64; 67:70–76.

44. "It is not only possible, but also the case that *all rational creatures* will eventually submit to one Law. . . . We profess that at a certain point the Logos will have obtained the hegemony over *all rational creatures* and will have *transformed every soul to the perfection* that is proper to it, when each one, exerting its own free will, will have *made its own choices* and reached the state that it had elected. But we hold that it will not happen as in the case of material bodies, . . . it is not so in the case of illnesses derived from sin. For it is certainly *not the case that the supreme God, who dominates over all rational creatures, cannot cure them.* Indeed, since the Logos is *more powerful than any evil that can exist in the soul,* it applies the *necessary therapy* to every individual,

incurable for Christ: "nothing is impossible for the Omnipotent; no being is incurable for the One who created it" (*Princ.* 3:6:5).

The final restoration itself will be performed by Christ, to whom all rational creatures will submit, and who will hand all of them to God:

> I think that God's Goodness, by means of Christ, *will call back every creature to one and the same end,* after submitting even the enemies. . . . Now, what kind of subjection is that in which all beings must submit to Christ? In my opinion, it is the same subjection in which we too want to be subject to him, the same in which the apostles and all saints are subject to him. . . . For the name of the "subjection" in which we are subject to Christ means *the salvation of those who have submitted,* that *salvation which comes from Christ.* As David too said, "Will not my soul be *subject* to God? For my *salvation* comes from God." (*Princ.* 1:6:1)

Origen bases himself here especially on Psalm 61:1 and 1 Corinthians 15:24–28, and interprets universal submission to Christ as universal salvation also in *Comm. in Matt. Ser.* 8 ("*subjection* means the *salvation* of those who submit"), in *Princ.* 3:5:7,[45] and in *Comm. in Io.* 6:57(37):

> If we grasp *what it means to be subject to Christ,* especially in the light of this passage: "And when all will be submitted to him, he himself, the Son, will submit to him who has subjected everything to him," then we shall understand God's lamb, who takes up the sin of the world, in a way *worthy of the goodness of the God of the universe.*"

The only interpretation of the subjection to Christ *in a way that is worthy of Christ and God* is its identification with salvation. Only purifying suffering and instruction, and not eternal retributive punishment, is *worthy of God.* "Christ reigns in order to *save,*" not to crush (*Hom. in Luc.* 30). He will subject all nations to himself, "that they may devote themselves to *justice, truth, and all the other virtues.* Christ will indeed reign as Justice

according to God's will. And the ultimate end of all things will be *the elimination of evil.*"

45. "Christ's subjection to the Father means the beatitude of our own perfection. . . . If therefore this subjection in which the Son is said to submit to the Father is understood as *good and salvific,* it is perfectly consistent to interpret also the subjection of the enemies to the Son of God, of which Scripture speaks, as *salvific and helpful.* In this way, when the Son is said to submit to the Father, this indicates *the perfect restoration of every creature.* And likewise, when the enemies are said to submit to the Son of God, this means the *salvation,* in Christ, *of those who submit,* and the *restoration of the lost.*"

itself." Likewise, "'He must reign until he has put all enemies under his feet' means 'until all *wicked* have become *righteous*'" (*Sel. in Ps.* 21).

The image of God in every human (Gen 1:26) is blurred by sin, but never cancelled.[46] Its restoration also relies on Christ, the image of God.[47] Each rational creature's voluntary adhesion to God entails the acquisition of the likeness to God—a biblical (Gen 1:26) and Platonic (*Theaetetus* 176B) ideal. The "image" of God is an initial datum that must be recovered; the "likeness" of God is attained thanks to moral improvement in this or the future life; in the end there will be a further passage from likeness to unity, when God will be "all in all" (*Princ.* 3:6:1).[48] The image and likeness of God in each human will be restored thanks to Christ-Logos, as is clear from *Princ.* 4:4:9–10[49] and *Hom. in Gen.* 1:13:

> Let us contemplate unceasingly this image of God [i.e., Christ], so as to be transformed into its likeness. For if the human being, who was created in God's image, has become similar to the devil due to sin, assuming the devil's image, which is against its nature, all the more so *will it receive that form that was given to it according to its nature, through the Logos and its power, assuming God's image.*

The restoration or "palingenesis" will indeed take place at the end of time, "in Christ," who will make all "pure to the highest degree" (*Comm. in Matth.* 5:15:23*). Thanks to Christ's work, "evil will be wiped away from the entire world" and "not even the tiniest sin will remain in the reign of the Father, and the word will be fulfilled that 'God will be all in all'" (*Comm. in Io.* 1:32). The Logos, with its inhumanation, went far from

46. See, e.g., *Hom. in Gen.* 13:4; *CC* 4:83; 2:11.

47. Origen quoted by Athanasius, *Decr.* 27.

48. Cf. *Princ.* 3:6:1: "The fact that Moses said, 'God created it in the image of God,' without mentioning the likeness, indicates that the human being since its first creation was granted the dignity of the image, but *the perfection of the likeness* has been reserved for the end, in that it must attain it by imitating God with its own industriousness. Thus, having been given from the beginning the possibility of the perfection through the dignity of the image, it can achieve the perfect likeness through the works."

49. "Although the intellect, out of laziness, loses its capacity for receiving God in itself in a pure and integral way, however it *retains in itself the possibility* of recovering a better knowledge, when the interior human being, which is also called rational, is *restored to the image and likeness of God* who created it. This is why the Prophet says: 'All the earth will remember and *return to the Lord* and all peoples will knee before him' [Isa 45:22–23]. If one dares affirm the ontological destruction of what has been made in the image and likeness of God, in my view he extends his impiety to the Son of God as well. For this is called in Scripture 'image of God'" (2 Cor 4:4; Col 1:15).

the Godhead out of love for its creatures, who themselves had gone far from the Godhead, that these might "return into its hands." "By following Christ, they will come to find themselves near God" (32:35). This restoration will take place at different times, depending on the different merits of rational creatures, but all will be purified and saved, and evil powers destroyed (37–39). In *Comm. in Rom.* 9: 41:8, 1 Corinthians 15:28 is cited in support of universal salvation, along with Philippians 2:10:

> Once he has 'handed the kingdom to God the Father,' that is, presented to God as an offering all, *converted and reformed*, and has fully performed the mystery of the *reconciliation of the world*, then they will be in God's presence, that God's word may be fulfilled: "Because I live—the Lord says—*every knee* will bend before Me, *every tongue* will glorify God."

The last sentence makes it clear once again that all will voluntarily adhere to God. Of course, the eventual restoration and salvation depends on Christ's sacrifice and divine grace and providence,[50] but this does not contradict human free will. The summit of beatitude is attained by grace (*Princ.* 3:1:12.15). Retribution, or better purification, is commensurate to sins and not eternal,[51] precisely because it has a measure, i.e., it is according to our works, but beatitude after that is a *gift* from God and is commensurate to nothing and can therefore be eternal. After purification, all will reach perfection: "*the end and perfection of all will be realized*. Those who were wicked, after *completely expiating* the punishments inflicted to them *for the purification of their sins*, will *deserve* to inhabit that land" (*Princ.* 2:3:7).[52]

In *Comm. in Io.* 1:16:91 Origen declares that "the end [*telos*] is in *the so-called apokatastasis*" and again quotes 1 Corinthians 15:24–28. As anticipated in the introduction, Origen here refers to an existing tradition concerning restoration, not one that merely possessed the idea of

---

50. Its importance is underlined, e.g., in *Princ.* 2:1:2; 2:9:7; 3:1:17; 3:5:5.

51. "The length of the punishment is *calculated* on the basis of the quality and nature of one's sin. . . . I cannot say with certainty how long we shall remain closed in prison *until we have paid our debt*. If one who owes a small debt is not let out until one has paid the last coin, certainly for one who owes a very large debt *innumerable aeons will be calculated* for the repayment of his debt" (*Hom. in Luc.* 35). If they are calculated, they must have a limit.

52. "'All flesh will see God's salvation' [Luke 3:6]. . . . There is *no one that is excepted so as not to see God's salvation*" (*Hom. in Luc.* 22:5; cf. 32:5).

restoration without the terminology of *apokatastasis*,[53] nor one that had the terminology while meaning something other than universal salvation by it,[54] but a *Christian* tradition that had *both* the *idea and* the *word*. This tradition, in its embryonic form, goes back to the Bible (especially Acts 3:20–21), and then Clement, who, as I have shown, identified the ultimate end with the restoration (*apokatastasis*).[55] Origen interprets the "universal restoration" mentioned in Acts 3:20–21 as the "perfect end" after all aeons.[56] Other biblical passages that—without the terminology of apokatastasis—Origen considered to buttress his theory of universal salvation include 1 Timothy 2:4–6: "God wants all human beings to be saved and to reach the knowledge of the truth," and most especially 1 Corinthians 15:28 ("God will be all in all"), besides Jesus' prayer for unity in John 17. Origen indeed presents the doctrine of universal restoration and salvation as rooted in Scripture.

Origen sets his Christian doctrine of apokatastasis against both the Stoic "pagan" theory of apokatastasis (which denied both human free will and any *final* restoration, with its endless, determined cycles of aeons) and "gnostic" conceptions of apokatastasis (which, unlike Origen's, generally were neither universal—since they mostly excluded some human beings from restoration—nor holistic, because they excluded the resurrection-restoration of the body). Origen, instead, accepted the biblical notion of resurrection and integrated it in his holistic doctrine of restoration.[57]

For those who consider Origen to be a "heretic" (ante litteram, even before the definition of orthodoxy), it is salutary to note that Origen's doctrine of rational creatures and their ultimate restoration and salvation was elaborated in the context of his defense of orthodoxy and divine goodness. It was developed in his case for human free will and his related polemic against "gnostic" predestinationism and the separation between the Old and the New Testament and between justice and goodness in God that both Marcionites and many "gnostics" advocated. This is especially evident in *Princ.* 3,[58] where he starts from this very polemic—

53. See, for instance, the *Apocalypse of Peter*.

54. See the Stoic theory of apokatastasis, overtly criticized by Origen.

55. Origen may have thought of Bardaisan as well, but we cannot be totally sure either that Bardaisan used the word *apokatastasis* or that Origen knew his work.

56. In *Princ.* 2:3:5, as well as in *Comm. in Matt.* 17:19.

57. Thus, for instance, he calls the restoration "the perfection of the resurrection" (*Comm. in Io.* 10:37), when Christ will be with the Father, and thereby God will be "all in all." Gregory Nyssen will emphasize the link between resurrection and restoration.

58. See Ramelli, "La coerenza" and "Origen, Bardaisan, and the Origin of Universal Salvation."

dictated by his concern for theodicy—and ends up with expounding the theory of the restoration and salvation of all rational creatures after their purification and illumination. This saves theodicy by reconciling divine goodness with divine justice. Rufinus understood this and consequently observed that the supporters of universal salvation, i.e., Origen, intended "to defend God's justice and respond to those who claim that all things are moved either by Fate or by chance." Origen, "wanting to defend God's justice, . . . thought that it is worthy of the good, immutable, and simple nature of the Trinity *to restore each one of its creatures*, in the ultimate end, into the state in which it was created from the beginning, and, after long torments that can extend over whole aeons, to *finally put an end to punishments*" (*Apol. c. Hier.* 2:12). Rufinus exactly understood Origen's motivations for the construction of his theory of universal salvation[59] and rightly noticed that theodicy was Origen's main anxiety.

Just as Origen elaborated his doctrine of universal salvation in defense of orthodoxy against the "heretics" of his day—Marcionites and "gnostics"—in the same way Gregory of Nyssa, especially in his commentary on 1 Corinthians 15:28, maintained the very same doctrine against "Arianism." And it is no accident that in this commentary he shows a pervasive influence from Origen.[60] Origen and Gregory indeed put the doctrine of universal salvation in the service of their polemic against "heresy" as well as against "paganism."

ORIGEN'S CRITIQUE OF ANNIHILATIONISM

An alternative to both the eternal damnation of some and the salvation of all, which theoretically could serve theodicy better than the unending physical and mental torment of the lost in hell, was the so-called theory

---

59. See especially *Princ.* 3:5:5: "Nobody but God the Creator of the universe can calculate and *order* each one's merits and at the same time *restore all to one end*, taking into account the various falls and progressions, rewarding virtue and punishing sins, both now and in the future aeon and in all worlds, before and after. God only knows the reason why he allows some to follow their own will and fall . . . whereas he begins to assist others little by little, almost leading them by hand, and restores them to their original condition, placing them on high. Some, having misunderstood this, *unable to grasp that the variety of this disposition has been established by God on the basis of previous causes due to the use of free will, have believed that all that which happens in the world is determined by fortuitous events or fatalistic necessity* and nothing depends on our *free will.*"

60. Demonstration in my "*In Illud*" and "The Trinitarian Theology."

of annihilationism.[61] According to some scholars, this is a view already supported by Paul. Unless one views Paul as a universalist, as Origen and Gregory of Nyssa did, and as has been suggested above in the spirit of their interpretation, one should consider him to be an annihilationist, as Mark Finney does. Paul, argues Finney, distinguished the destiny of believers and non-believers, and he taught that the latter will be "annihilated after judgement."[62] What is common to both universalism and annihilationism is the claim that Paul is not to be regarded as an advocate of an eternal hell.

Annihilationism, which emerged at the very beginning of the patristic age, held that the finally impenitent sinners will cease to exist altogether.[63] This seems to have already been, for instance, the view of Philo of Alexandria, and it is not accidental that Origen, who knew Philo's ideas very well, argued strongly against annihilationism for metaphysical reasons.[64] Origen denied that any soul can ever perish ontologically (*substantialiter*); souls can be morally dead, but they will certainly rise again because their substance never vanishes, since it was created by God and as such it is good. Philo, instead, seems to believe that eternal life is a privilege granted by God only to virtuous souls, whereas the others seem to be doomed to perish altogether. Indeed, in Philo's view, the rational soul alone is immortal and incorruptible, and only those who

61. Pinnock, "Annihilationism," offers a treatment from the systematic point of view, without a focus on patristic eschatology; he takes *aiōnios* in the NT to mean "everlasting," which is not the case unless it refers to God. But he rightly concludes that, as opposed to universalism, annihilationism "maintains the doctrine of hell but without the sadistic aspect. It retains the realism of some finally saying no to God and going to hell but without turning the notion of hell into a monstrosity."

62. Finney, *Resurrection, Hell and the Afterlife*, 161.

63. On patristic annihilationism, see, e.g., Bernstein, *The Formation of Hell*, 205–65. This interpretation of hell has remained an option today, when it is being revived by several theologians. Jonathan L. Kvanvig in a book and in an article for *The Oxford Handbook of Eschatology* presents annihilation of sinners as one possible alternative to eternal hell (viewed either as punishment or as a way to honor individual choices). (Kvanvig, *The Problem of Hell*; Kvanvig, "Hell.") The other alternative is universal salvation, which Kvanvig however, as many others, sees as problematic with respect to individual free will. Against this objection, in the same handbook, Thomas Talbott concentrates specifically on Christian universalism, which has the salvation of all depend on Christ (Talbott, "Universalism"). This, I note, is the doctrine defended by patristic universalists, who were also strenuous defenders of free will, as I have thoroughly demonstrated in *The Christian Doctrine of Apokatastasis*. From their perspective, it would be absurd to reject universalism because it jeopardizes human free will.

64. See my "Philo's Doctrine of Apokatastasis," 29–55.

have exercised it will survive; the others, having renounced their own rational soul, will perish like irrational beings. Origen also claimed that the soul of a person who lives in vice perishes, because in his opinion the soul experiences mortality through "the real death," that is, spiritual death, brought about by sin and vice, as he declares in his *Dialogue with Heraclides* and elsewhere. However, Origen did not regard this perdition and state of "being lost" (*apoleia*) as eternal. For Jesus has come to find and save the lost sheep, and Scripture proclaims everywhere the resurrection of those who have died (*Homilies on Jeremiah* 11.16).

For Philo, and for later patristic annihilationists, the death of the soul is an ontological destruction; for Origen (and his followers, such as Gregory of Nyssa), there can be no ontological or substantial destruction of any soul, since rational creatures were created by God in order for them to exist, and whatever God created is good. This is why they cannot be destroyed ontologically, for such destruction would amount to a defeat for God the Creator. So Origen explicitly rejected Philo's thesis of the substantial annihilation of the soul that chooses evil. On the one hand, he maintains that if one chooses evil, which is non-being, one ends up with non-being, and therefore dies, but this death is *moral*, not ontological. In *Commentary on John*, 2.133 Origen is clear that "the One who is Good, therefore, coincides with the One who Is. On the contrary, evil and meanness are opposed to the Good and non-being to Being. As a consequence, meanness and evil are non-being." If one adheres to God, who Is, one remains in being; if, on the contrary, one rejects God, one falls into non-being (*Homily 2 on Psalm 38*, 12). But Origen, probably polemicizing with Philo, is careful to add that this does not mean that the soul is destroyed or perishes ontologically (*substantialis interitus*). (An alternative to annihilation would have been metensomatosis or reincarnation, but Origen rejected that view outright, denouncing it as impious; Philo might have entertained this view hypothetically or esoterically, as Karjanmaa suggests.)

Origen hammers home in several places that the annihilation of the wicked is not ontological, but spiritual (e.g., *Homily 2 on Psalm 38*, 1). Sinners will actually perish in the other world, but will do so *as sinners* so as to live as saints, once purified from sins. This is a transformation of sinners into saints, not the annihilation of sinners. What will perish ontologically, according to Origen, is rather *evil itself*, sin, which was not created by God. Souls, or better rational creatures, who were created by God, and as such are good, will never cease to exist.[65]

Evil, according to Origen (*CC* 4.63), just as to Plato (*Republic* 445C6), is indefinite, something *aoriston*, like non-being, but virtue is one and simple, and therefore definite, like the Good (i.e., God, the One). What will be burnt away by the "otherworldly fire"[66] will be not sinners, but their "bad beliefs," their "evil thoughts" (*Comm. in Matt.* 5.10.2). Thus, the death and destruction that Philo attached to the soul itself as a consequence of its life of vice, Origen transferred onto the destruction of evil and sin, which results into the purification of the sinner and his ultimate salvation.

The impossibility of an ontological destruction of the soul directly bears on the possibility of universal salvation. In Philo's perspective, only souls—and not bodies—will be saved, and only *some* souls: the souls of those who have led a philosophical and pious life (which from Philo's viewpoint is much the same thing). Origen took over Philo's notion of the restoration of the soul, just as Clement had done, but according to Origen *all* souls, and not only few, will be restored and saved, and they will have back their *bodies* as well, transformed and glorified as souls themselves will be. In this way they will be able to participate in the divine life and to be "deified."

New Testament passages that speak of the destruction of sinners have been taken as references to annihilation, although universalists may note that nowhere is this destruction or death described as eternal (at most, it is said to be *aiōnios*, "otherworldly" or "long-lasting," as in 2 Thessalonians 1:9, "the ruin of the age to come,"[67] but never *aïdios* or strictly eternal). So Origen could note that Scripture announces a resurrection after the destruction or death.[68] The texts variously adduced by the annihilationists are, e.g., Jesus' warning: "Do not fear those who kill the body but cannot kill the soul. Rather fear him who can destroy

65. The same set of ideas underlies another homiletic passage by Origen (*Homily 5 on Psalm 36*, 5). The impious will no longer exist, because he has chosen not to participate in God, who always is, and is Good itself. But, again, the destruction of the sinner in the next world to which Origen refers will be, properly speaking, the destruction of his sin, of evil, so that the sinner will be no longer a sinner, but a righteous person. For evil, when it is no longer chosen by anyone, will vanish according to its ontological non-subsistence (*Commentary on the Song of Songs* 4.1.13).

66. For the translation of αἰώνιον/*aiōnion* as "otherworldly" or "pertaining to the world to come" or "long-lasting," instead of "eternal," see the Appendix.

67. On which see also MacDonald, *The Evangelical Universalist*, 153–54.

68. See my "Origen's Homilies on Jeremiah: Resurrection."

both body and soul in hell" (Matt 10:28), as well as references to sinners thrown into the fire as chaff or weeds (Matt 3:10, 12; 13:30), or to the destruction of sinners in Philippians 3:19 or 2 Peter 3:7; 2:1–3.[69]

Irenaeus might have believed that the wicked will be destroyed, which would fit his doctrine of recapitulation less awkwardly than eternal damnation would (how could the damned be considered "recapitulated" in Christ?).[70] However, his doctrine of recapitulation was a precursor of apokatastasis; he was loved by both Origen and Gregory of Nyssa, who read him through a universalistic lens. Indeed, they tended to see recapitulation and apokatastasis as coincident. A universalistic reading of Irenaeus clearly excluded the alternative, annihiliationistic reading. Perhaps one might dare to argue that even if Irenaeus himself held on to a belief in annihilation, the universalist development of recapitulation theology, which we find in Origen and Gregory, was more true to Irenaeus' own deepest insights and was a legitimate development of his thought.

Arnobius of Sicca is probably the clearest patristic annihilationist. He denied Plato's doctrine of the immortality of the soul, which was instead strongly upheld by patristic universalists such as Origen, Gregory of Nyssa, and Evagrius. Arnobius was clear that "The wicked are cast into hell and, being annihilated, pass away vain in everlasting destruction which is a human's real death" (*Against the Gentiles* 2.14).

Origen, instead, argued from creation: God created all rational beings, including the devil, *in order for them to exist;* nothing and nobody can cause them to cease to exist, not even their own free will. (Of course, the Godhead could cause creatures to cease to exist, but it will never want to do that, since this would be the failure of its creation.) If creatures choose evil, which is non-being, they will end up drifting into non-being, but this is a moral, spiritual condition of death that is distinct from ontological annihilation. From spiritual death it is always possible to be resurrected: therapeutic punishment and instruction will work the required conversion, that the choice of the Good may be voluntary for all. From Origen's and his followers' standpoint, theodicy rules out the eternity of hell, but *also* the annihilation of sinners. What befits God's justice and goodness is only the voluntary conversion of the wicked.

69. For a discussion of biblical support to annihilationism, see Fudge and Peterson, *Two Views of Hell*, and Powys, *Hell*.

70. For instance, Irenaeus thinks that those who do not have the Spirit, but are only "flesh and blood," are dead, because humans are made alive by the Spirit and those who do the works of the flesh will die (*Against Heresies* 5.9–10). This position, even if grounded mostly on Pauline passages, comes close to that of Philo of Alexandria.

4

Universal Salvation in Origen's
First Followers and His Apologists

THE FIRST ALEXANDRIAN ORIGENIANS
AND ST. ANTHONY

Theognostus and Pierius

After Origen's death the catechetical school in Alexandria was directed by Theognostus (in 265–80) and then Pierius. The former wrote *Outlines* (now lost, but summarized by Photius) in which he adhered to Origen's doctrine, including his doctrine of universal salvation, and defended Origen. St. Athanasius, who held Origen and Didymus in high esteem, also praised Theognostus together with Origen. Pierius followed Origen's thought so faithfully as to be called "Origen the Younger."[1] According to Philip of Side, he composed a panegyric[2] on St. Pamphilus, who was a disciple of his and wrote an apology for Origen. Still in the second half of the fourth century, Pierius was admired by the Egyptian Origenian monks dubbed the Tall Brothers, and in particular Ammonius, who read Origen together with Pierius and Didymus, and St. Melania, who read Origen along with Pierius, Basil, and Gregory.[3] All of which is to say that Origen's person and work continued to be esteemed in his native Egypt and wider afield.

---

1. Jerome, *Vir. Ill.* 76; Photius, *Bibl.* Cod. 119.

2. A speech or text in praise of someone.

3. Palladius *HL* 11;4; 55:3.

St. Anthony

The learned monk Hieracas, too, espoused Origen's doctrines, very probably including that of universal restoration. Origen's thought, indeed, spread very early in the Egyptian desert, and St. Anthony (c.251–356) himself—the celebrated father of desert monasticism—is the most prominent example. He wrote many letters to his disciples in which, like Origen, he postulated the original unity of all rational beings (Letter 3:4), who have the same "intellectual essence" (*ousia noera*). Rational creatures fell from that unity into a state of death (Letter 5:16–8).[4] But the

---

4. Spiritual death is a condition of oblivion of one's true nature; the present heavy body and the inclination to evil have clouded the faculties of the mind; this is why rational creatures "have been unable to discover themselves as they were created, that is, as an eternal substance" (Letter 3; cf. 5).

Logos will bring them back to their original state, in a "restoration [*apo-katastasis*] of the spirit" (Letters 2 and 4–6), a restoration to the original "nature of our essence," in virtue and knowledge, without evil any more (Letter 7). Anthony foresees a "resurrection of the heart from the earth" (Letters 4 and 6), which is a spiritual resurrection.[5] The restoration is enabled by the acquisition of knowledge and the awareness of one's spiritual essence. The role of Christ is essential; he came "for *every* rational being" and will free every rational being, once each one has acquired knowledge and discernment (Letter 2). The "resurrection of minds" as well as "the remission of sins" are operated by Christ (Letter 2; see also Letters 3; 5; 6; 7). One might even argue that the spirituality of the early monastics out in the desert was underpinned by the by kinds of theological ideas taught by Origen.

Dionysius of Alexandria

Dionysius († 265), bishop of Alexandria, was a pupil of Origen and wrote a letter on martyrdom to him;[6] as a bishop he also reconciled his teacher with the Alexandrian clergy. The apology for Origen preserved by Photius (*Bibl.* cod. 117) cites Dionysius' works among "the texts in favor of Origen." Indeed, Dionysius composed an Apology for Origen in four books. Athanasius in turn wrote an apology for Dionysius himself. Dionysius wished that all Christians might "entertain sublime and lofty views" about "the divinity, in its glory and its true dignity, about the resurrection of humans from the dead, and about their union with God and their assimilation to God" (*Prom.* 1). He clearly followed Origen with respect to the eventual universal restoration and "deification." This perspective is entirely consistent with his linguistic awareness in regard to the terminology of eternity.[7] He comments on Ecclesiastes 1:4 ("One

---

5. The body, too, will rise as a spiritual body, after the necessary purification taught by the Spirit (Letter 1). Anthony, like Origen, reflects on the meaning of Paul's description of the resurrected body as a "spiritual body" in 1 Corinthians 15:44. Just as Origen maintained that one's risen body will keep the same "form" (in the metaphysical sense of "substance," not in that of "shape") as one's earthly body, and not the material ὑποκείμενον/*hypokeimenon*, which will pass away in that it continually passes away during the present life, so does Anthony state that the risen body will keep one's "invisible essence/substance," which will not pass away with the material flesh (Letter 6).

6. Eusebius *HE* 6:29:4; 6:46:2.

7. See Ramelli and Konstan, *Terms for Eternity*, 116–29.

generation passes away, another comes, but the earth endures *for the aeon* [εἰς τὸν αἰῶνα/*eis ton aiōna*]") remembering well both the scriptural polysemy of αἰών/*aiōn* and αἰώνιος/*aiōnios* and Origen's doctrine of a series of aeons prior to the eventual restoration. Thus, Dionysius remarks that the Bible reads, "for the aeon," and not "for the aeons" (εἰς τοὺς αἰῶνας/ *eis tous aiōnas*); this is why the earth will remain for this aeon, but not for all aeons, and not eternally. Indeed, αἰών/*aiōn* and αἰώνιος/*aiōnios* in Scripture never mean "eternity" and "eternal" unless they refer to God. Commenting on Ecclesiastes 3:11 ("clarify to me the brevity of my days"), Dionysius proves well aware that αἰών/*aiōn* does not indicate eternity, but on the contrary one's life in the present world: "the end of this αἰών/ *aiōn*, that is, of the *present life*."

THE FIRST DEFENDERS OF ORIGEN: GREGORY THE WONDERWORKER AND PAMPHILUS

Gregory the Wonderworker

St. Gregory the Wonderworker (c.213–c.270) was a disciple of Origen and at the end of his studies with him addressed a thanksgiving oration to him.[8] Macrina the Elder († c.340), the grandmother of Basil and Gregory of Nyssa,[9] was a disciple of the Wonderworker, who brought Christianity to Neocaesarea.[10] And the Christianity he brought was *Origen's* Christianity. From Origen Gregory the Wonderworker surely learnt the doctrine of universal restoration; therefore, in *Pan.* 17 he calls Christ "the one who *saves all humans, even those who are half dead and deprived of all*; he is the Protector and *Healer of all*, the Logos, the tireless *Savior of all.*" Rufinus too, toward the end of the first book of his apology against

8. While this has been sometimes questioned, Gregory's paternity of this work is very probable thanks to the attestations of Pamphilus—who in his *Apology* mentioned Gregory as a disciple of Origen and quoted the whole of Gregory's thanksgiving oration (Socrates *HE* 4:27)—Eusebius (*HE* 6:30), Basil, who praises him (*De Spir. S.* 29:74), Gregory of Nyssa—who wrote his biography/panegyric on the basis of the tradition available in his family, including in it a profession of faith whose original was still preserved in the church of Neocaesarea in his day—and Jerome in *Vir. Ill.* 65.

9. Basil traces back the Christian faith of their family to her (*Ep.* 204:6; 210:1; 223:3). Gregory of Nyssa's venerated sister, Macrina the Younger, was named after her.

10. Basil *Ep.* 204:6.

Jerome, attests that Gregory the Wonderworker taught the doctrine of universal salvation. The Wonderworker transmitted this doctrine to Gregory of Nyssa, Macrina the Elder and the Younger, and probably also Gregory Nazianzen, who—as I will show—were all supporters of universal restoration and salvation. So we can trace the line of transmission of Origen's teaching from Origen himself, through his disciple Gregory the Wonderworker, to those we now know as the Cappadocian fathers.

Pamphilus

Origen was a figure of some controversy, even during his lifetime, and this inspired his supporters to write defences or apologies for him.[11] The first to do so was St. Pamphilus Martyr. Pamphilus, a disciple of Pierius in Alexandria (director of the Cathechetical School there), followed in Origen's footsteps by moving from Egypt to Caesarea in Palestine, where he founded a Christian school[12] at which both philology and philosophy were studied and primarily applied to Scripture, and women were received among students just as they were at Origen's school. Pamphilus restored and expanded Origen's Caesarea library with the assistance of Eusebius, his disciple, who wanted to be called "Eusebius (spiritual son) of Pamphilus." During Pamphilus' long detention prior to his death as a martyr (307–10 CE) he wrote an apology for Origen in five books; after his death, Eusebius added a sixth. (Only Rufinus' translation of the first book into Latin is extant.) The seventh accusation from which Pamphilus defends Origen deals with universal salvation. Origen was mistakenly accused of not postulating any punishment in the next world for sinners. On the contrary, as Pamphilus was aware, Origen *did* foresee purifying punishments, even very long ones, for those who most need purification.[13]

11. Origen is the first Christian author for whom ancient scholars composed apologies (Pamphilus and the anonymous cited by Photius *Bibl.* Cod. 117), an anthology, the *Philocalia*, and a commentary, that of Didymus on his *On First Principles*.

12. Eusebius *HE* 7:32:25.

13. An anonymous apology for Origen in five books summarized by Photius (*Bibl.* Cod. 117, 91b–92a) is based on Pamphilus' apology as well as on Dionysius, Clement, Demetrius, and Eusebius. It reports the same eschatological charge against Origen of denying otherworldly punishments. According to Nautin, *Origène*, 100–153 this Apology represents Books 4 and 5 of Pamphilus' Apology.

METHODIUS, A CRITIC OF ORIGEN WHO ESPOUSED UNIVERSAL SALVATION

It would be easy for us, knowing how suspicious the church later became of universalism, to imagine that the controversies surrounding Origen in his day must have been focused around his doctrine of apokatastasis. In fact, in large part this was not the case; indeed, many of his earliest critics were in fact themselves universalists. We can illustrate this by Methodius, Bishop of Olympus in Lycia († 311ca). Methodius is cited by Socrates as an opponent of Origen, but he was also influenced by Origen in many respects, and his few criticisms of Origen's ideas derive from misunderstanding (e.g., of the philosophical terminology of "form" and "substratum" used by Origen in his treatment of the resurrection: Methodius misunderstood the metaphysical form as a sense-perceptible shape). What is more, nowhere does Methodius attack Origen's doctrine of universal salvation. On the contrary, he adhered to it. In the sixth book of Pamphilus' apology for Origen, Eusebius complained against Methodius for writing against Origen even though in fact he embraced many doctrines of Origen's (Jerome *C. Ruf.* 1:11). Methodius in his last work expressed much admiration for Origen, as a withdrawal of previous criticisms.[14]

Methodius starts from the presupposition that God, "according to the Apostle, wants *all human beings to be saved* and attain the knowledge of truth" (*Symp.* 2:7). Like Clement, he considered the *Apocalypse of Peter* to be inspired. Since this text envisages the eventual liberation of the damned from hell ("the river of fire"), it seems that Methodius regarded this doctrine as inspired as well, and therefore supported it. This is confirmed both by several passages from Methodius, which I will quote in a moment, and suggested by his use of terminology: he describes punishment in the next world only as αἰώνιος/*aiōnios* "otherworldly," and never as ἀΐδιος /*aïdios*, "eternal."[15] This is consistent with his adhesion to the doctrine of apokatastasis.

In his dialogue *On the resurrection* and his *Symposium*, Methodius depicts physical death as providential. The death of the body was wanted by God "so that, by means of the dissolution of the body, *sin might be destroyed completely, up to its very roots*" (*De res.* ch. 4). This enables restoration and salvation. Indeed, this is confirmed in the Greek text preserved

14. Socrates *HE* 6:13.

15. See Ramelli and Konstan, *Terms for Eternity*, new ed., 226–27.

by Photius: "Death was given by God as a gift to those who had sinned, for this purpose: that evil might not remain immortal" (*Bibl.* cod. 234). Evil must come to an end. This is the aim of the "skin tunics"—that is, mortality—that God gave to Adam and Eve after the fall: God "prepared the skin tunics, wrapping, so to say, the human being in mortality, with a view to this: that, thanks to the destruction of the body, *all the evil born in it might die*" (ibid.). Indeed, "God excogitated even death *for our sake, in order to eliminate sin: that sin might not perdure in us eternally*" (ibid., p. 296a). God introduced the death of the body for all humans, in order to spare them an eternal spiritual death:

> Our tabernacles will be stably built when the body rises, with bones that are again joined and united to the flesh: then we shall really celebrate a feast for the Lord, when we receive eternal tabernacles, not doomed to perish and dissolve in the ashes of the grave. Now, our tabernacle at the beginning was well solid, but it was shaken by transgression and bent toward the earth, *because God put a limit to sin* by means of death, *to avoid* that the human being, immortal, *living in sin and with sin alive in it, should be liable to an eternal condemnation*. Therefore, he died, and the soul was separated from flesh, so that *sin might die* thanks to (physical) death, given that it cannot survive in a dead person. Therefore, once *sin is dead and destroyed*, I shall rise *immortal*, and I praise God because, through (temporary physical) death, he *has liberated his children from* (spiritual eternal) *death*. (*Symp.* 9:2)

This paves the way to universal restoration and salvation. Physical death limits the duration of evil, and thereby also that of spiritual death. This will not be eternal. Methodius further elaborates on this concept: "God, as Scripture says, *kills and then gives life*, that flesh, after the withering *and the death of sin*, may, like a temple that is rebuilt, be erected again with the same elements, impassible and immortal, while *sin is entirely and definitely destroyed; . . . the very idea of evil will disappear*" (*De res.* 5). "The noble image" of God in humans, mutilated and stained by evil, "will be restored again, intact and perfect, in the same original form . . . because God, in his love for the human being, has not tolerated to leave it in such a condition, that it *might not be culpable forever*, and might not bear the blame indefinitely, but had it resolve again into its original elements, *so that, when God models it again, all defects in it might vanish and disappear*" (*De res.* 6). "In the remodeling, *all defects and flaws will disappear*, and [the human being] will be made again *perfect and pleasant to God"* (*De res.* 7). The resurrection will be a restoration, not only of the body, but also of the soul, liberated from evil:[16] "restoration [*apokatastasis*] into a condition that is free from passions and glorious."

Salvation will be universal: "God's mercy entirely dissolves death, assists humanity, and nourishes the light of the heart. . . . While the first laws, promulgated in the day of Adam, Noah, and Moses, did not succeed in giving salvation to all humanity, *the law of the gospel*, it alone, *has saved all* [*pantas*]" (*Symp.* 10:2).[17] Universal restoration and salvation hinges on Christ:

> The Logos assumed human nature in order to defeat the serpent and *destroy the condemnation* that arose with the fall of human- ity. It is right that the evil one should be defeated by no one else but the one whom he had deceived . . . because the *destruction of sin and of that condemnation* would have been impossible unless the same human being to whom it was said, "dust you are and dust you will be again," *had been created anew and the condemnation had been eliminated* which, because of that hu- man being, had extended to all. For, "As in Adam all die, so *will all be vivified in Christ*," who assumed the nature and stance of Adam. (*Symp.* 3:6)

The choral hymn of the virgins that concludes Methodius' *Sym- posium* can therefore celebrate universal restoration and salvation as follows:

> Corruption has disappeared, and likewise the pains of illnesses that make people shed tears; *death has been eliminated*; *all stu- pidity has perished*; there is no more affliction of the soul which devours, because God's joy has returned to shine over mortals. Paradise is no longer destitute of mortals. By order of God, it is

16. In *De res.* 14, Methodius adduces the same argument for resurrection as Greg- ory Nyssen brings forth in his dialogue *On the Soul and the Resurrection*, and his inter- pretation of the Feast of Tabernacles as a symbol of the resurrection and restoration is very similar to that which Gregory proposes toward the end of the same dialogue: "It means this real tabernacle of ours, which, after *falling into sin* because of the transgres- sion of the law, and after being *broken by sin*, will be assembled again according to his promise, and will be resurrected into incorruptibility, that we may really celebrate, in God's honor, the great and glorious feast of the Tabernacles." This refers not only to the resurrection of the body, but also to the restoration of the whole human nature.

17. Christ has already begun to save all: "*the rule of the evil one*, who once en- slaved the whole of the human race, *was destroyed* . . . when Christ became incarnated" (*Symp.* 10:1).

inhabited again, *as it was in the beginning*, by that humanity who had fallen from it because of the subtle arts of the serpent, and who is now again *incorruptible, fearless, and blessed*. (Strophes 21–22)

Humanity will finally be restored to its original condition, free from sin and evil. Methodius has the fall depend on the devil's deception. Gregory of Nyssa will do the same: Adam and Eve chose evil because it looked good; they were deceived, they produced a false judgment, and this was instilled by the devil. Methodius and Gregory both think that evil is not chosen qua evil, but because it is mistaken for a good. Future purification and instruction will correct that mistake "in the restoration [*apokatastasis*] of the new aeons" (*Symp.* 8:11).

In this chapter we have seen that Origen's influence continued on in his native Egypt—among monks, priests, and others—and further afield, into Palestine and Asia Minor. As a controversial and envied figure he attracted critics, but to start with apokatastasis was not high on the list of issues he was attacked for, and even some of his earliest critics were themselves believers in universal salvation.

5

Fourth-century Origenians I

Eusebius, Marcellus, Athanasius, and Didymus

EUSEBIUS, A CAUTIOUS SUPPORTER
OF UNIVERSAL SALVATION

The refining fire "will come to each soul [*psuchē*] judging each according to its deeds done while alive, and cleansing and refining it by fire, like gold, and purifying the minds [*hēgemonika*] of all." (*Ecl. Proph.* 3.31 [133.20–25])

Eusebius († 339–40), bishop of Caesarea in Palestine, court historian of the Emperor Constantine, and the first source concerning the Ecumenical

Council of Nicaea (325), was a devoted disciple of the Martyr Pamphilus, the apologist of Origen.[1] He cooperated with Pamphilus in composing the apology for Origen and highly praised Origen in *HE* 6. However, he always endeavored to avoid eschatological issues, out of caution, to hide his own penchant for the doctrine of universal salvation. This becomes clear from a very close analysis. One preliminary element comes from his rigorous use of the terminology of eternity.[2] He uses αἰώνιος/*aiōnios* in the sense of "pertaining to the world to come" and as meaning "eternal" *only* if it refers to God, mostly in quotations from Scripture. But he uses ἀΐδιος/*aïdios* in the full sense of "eternal," in reference to God, to the co-eternity of the Son with the Father, and to intelligible entities (i.e., what transcends time or is immutable in time). Eusebius *never* characterizes future punishment or death or fire as ἀΐδιος/*aïdios* or "eternal," but he does describe life and beatitude in the world to come as ἀΐδιος/*aïdios*. For Eusebius regards life and beatitude—but not punishment, fire, and death—as eternal.

In *PE* 7:18:9 Eusebius describes the final restoration as a "rectification," a "setting right" of sin and the return of humanity to its original perfection as its end.[3] Eusebius, like Origen, deems the eventual restoration a work of Christ: "the salvific Logos, who leads to the Father those who walk through It, taking them by hand, and *restoring* [*apokathistas*] them to the kingdom of heavens. . . . *Nobody who walks this Way enters without having been purified*."[4] Like Origen and Gregory of Nyssa, Eusebius depicts the resurrection as a renovation (*anakainizesthai*) and restoration; he employs the very same definition of resurrection as restoration that Gregory will use: "resurrection is a restoration [*apokatastasis*] to our

---

1. On him see now Johnson and Schott, eds, *Eusebius of Caesarea*, and, for a general introduction Johnson, *Eusebius*.

2. See Ramelli and Konstan, *Terms for Eternity*, new edition (2013), 142–57.

3. "*The original sin must be rectified with subsequent remedies*, and it is necessary to rush to the return and *restoration to the condition that is proper and familiar* (to humanity). For the *end of human nature* is not here on earth, and it is not a reduction to corruption and perdition, but it is up *there, from where the first* (human) *fell down*." See also *Eccl. theol.* 2:9:4: "at first she was one thing; then she became something else, and finally is restored again to her original condition;" *Comm. in Ps.* PG 23:92:7: "After their fall God shapes them again, and *restores* them again to their original condition."

4. *Comm. in Is.* 2:9. Cf. *In Luc.* PG 24:580:21–24: "First, he will *restore* them to *safety and good health*, after opening the eyes of the blind and *healing every illness and every weakness of their souls*. Then, he will prepare for them *the spiritual banquet*." Christ, healing souls, liberates them from sin and operates their restoration.

original condition."[5] Eusebius also inherited from Origen the concept of divine punishments as purifying, educative, and healing, which implies their limited duration: "after being instructed by punishment for a short time, they will be restored again to their previous condition" (*DE* 10:6:3).

Eusebius foresees "the gathering and *restoration* of all believers— those who have become worthy of the holy city of God—to one and the same choir."[6] Like Origen,[7] Eusebius often interprets Acts 3:21 ("the times of universal restoration [*apokatastasis*], of which God spoke through his holy prophets from time immemorial") in reference to universal restoration and salvation in the end.[8] In *C. Marc.* 2:4:11 he interprets the words "the times of universal restoration" in Acts 3:21 as referring to the other world, in which *all beings* will have a perfect restoration: "For, what else does 'until the times of universal restoration' signify to us, if not the aeon to come, in which *all beings must receive their perfect restoration*? . . . On the occasion of *the restoration* [*apokatastasis*] *of absolutely all beings*, Paul said that creation itself will be *transformed* from slavery into freedom."[9] Also, commenting on the Transfiguration scene in Luke, Eusebius observes that in the end not only three disciples will fall upon their face, *but all creatures*, since all knees will bend in heaven, on earth, and in the underworld (a reference to Philippians 2:10–11, one of Origen's favorite passages in support of universal salvation).[10]

Eusebius in his exegesis of Isaiah foresees that sinners will be punished; this is symbolized by the destruction of their cities (Isa 25:2), but the inhabitants will be saved and escape from ruin. Sins will be destroyed

5. *Comm. in Ps.* PG 23:1285:56.

6. *Comm. in Ps.* PG 23:1049:22.

7. Especially in *Hom. in Ier.* 14.18 and *Comm. in Matth.* 17:19.

8. E.g. In *Eccl. theol.* 3:14:2 he refers the "times of universal restoration" to the second coming of Christ.

9. In *Eccl. theol.* 3:9:1 (cf. 3:13:1–3) Eusebius interprets again Acts 3:21 in relation to Paul's prediction of the final liberation of all creation from corruption. And in 3:16 he interprets the reference to "breaking in pieces" in Psalm 2:9 as the Son's action of breaking his enemies in pieces, to be understood as aimed at remolding them, restoring them to their original condition. Eusebius deems Psalm 124 entirely devoted to the idea of apokatastasis (*Comm. in Ps.* PG 23:72:26). That this restoration is eschatological is proved by the inscriptions of the immediately following psalms: "Expectation of the future; Edification of the church; The call of the nations; The victory of the army of Christ."

10. *In Luc.* PG 24:549:6–36. This is not one of the fragments on Luke that Alice Whealey, "The Greek Fragments," 18–29, attributes to Eusebius of Emesa.

and sinners will be purified and saved. Christ is "helper and defender," the "Savior of all together," and frees all from error and spiritual death.[11] Eusebius reads Isaiah 25:8 as a prophecy of the final destruction and vanishing of death[12]—not only physical, but also spiritual death. This will be eliminated thanks to Christ and faith. All "will not be subject to death any more, but participate in immortality and in the life of the world to come." Death will return to its original state, which is non-being, because God did not create it.[13] All will first need to be liberated from evil and made worthy of God's promises.[14] The rational creatures who are "worthy of the promises" are those whom Christ will have *made* worthy. They will dwell in Christ, who will be "all things" for all (1 Cor 15:28).

God's Logos revivifies the dead and cures their sins, if these are sins of human scale (*Comm. in Is.* 1:88:53), thus bestowing on them, not only the resurrection, but also "salvation and life in the future world."[15] In *Comm. in Is.* 1.85 Eusebius describes the final restoration, "the culmination of the goods" foreseen by the prophets (Acts 3:20–21), identifying it with God's "original intention" before the creation of the world: the

11. "The Savior of *all together*, who loves humanity, having *liberated the souls of human beings from death* . . . removed *every tear from every face,* . . . *preventing the perdition of so many souls,* out of his love for humanity." In *C. Marc.* 2:4:28 Eusebius likewise calls Christ "the common savior of *absolutely all.*"

12. "He will *destroy* and make *vanish* the face of the one who had power over all: death. . . . The Lord will engulf it in such a way that it will *no longer appear anywhere.* . . . Now, since the last enemy, death, will be annihilated . . . , death, which once swallowed all, will be swallowed in turn."

13. "I shall do so, he says, after I have vanquished the enemy of life, that is, death, regarding which it is said, 'The last enemy will be annihilated, death.' In fact, *it will turn back, that is, to its first constitution, when it did not exist,* because *God did not create death,* but death entered this world because of the devil's envy. When this has happened, all other enemies and adversaries of your Logos will be reduced to impotence and will perish as well" (*In Ps.* 9, PG 23:13).

14. "While the reign of Christ will shine forth in the life of the world to come, humans, from absolutely all peoples, will enjoy it, once *liberated from their ancient sins* and *made worthy of the promises of God.*" Eusebius opposes the punishment of Moab (Isa 16; Jer 31) to beatitude, but Moab represents the powers of evil, and not humans: "Moab means the evil demon and the adverse power. . . . From this single example it leaves to us to understand all the rest that will happen to the powers of evil." Eusebius stresses the final destruction of death and adverse powers; humans will be purified from evil and saved.

15. The impious, that is, those who have not sinned against men but against God, or have sinned in a superhuman degree, will pay the penalty beneath the earth. It is not, however, said that this punishment will be eternal, all the more in that the reference to the existence of the earth itself seems to refer to *intermediate* eschatology.

submission of all enemies and the final annihilation of evil and death: "The facts that were pre-established *before the foundation* of the world, and will be fulfilled *at the end of the aeons;* . . . once *all evilness has been eliminated and the last enemy, death, has been destroyed, God will be 'all in all'*" (1 Cor 15:28). This is simply a representation of Origen's description of the eventual restoration, based on the Pauline passage so dear to Origen.

Eusebius comments on 1 Corinthians 15:24–28, especially in his polemic with Marcellus of Ancyra. In *C. Marc.* 2:4, both of them rely on Origen's exegesis of this passage, in reference to universal salvation. The destruction of all the power of the devil will take place during Christ's eschatological reign: "the end/aim of Christ's reign is . . . that all be submitted to his feet, and when all, in the end, are finally subjected to Christ . . . he will submit to him who has subjected all to him" (*C. Marc.* 2:4:1). When Christ becomes the king of all, "the human being, who once was deceived by the devil, thanks to the power of the Logos will be king and . . . finally defeat the devil" (2:4:9–10). This will happen in "the times of universal restoration [*apokatastasis*]" announced in Acts 3:20–21. These times will come when humanity becomes united with the Logos, and in the future aeon all will receive a full restoration (*apokatastasis*). This will occur when Christ hands his kingdom to the Father, after the submission of all enemies and the annihilation of evil (2:4:12). "All that which concerns humans will receive its ultimate perfection thanks to God's providence and action on the occasion of the Judgement." Indeed, after the Judgement there will come the "rectification of all" and the vanishing of all adverse powers (2:4:13–4). Eusebius agrees with Origen and Marcellus about the universal "rectification" and "restoration" (*apokatastasis*), which he sees in 1 Corinthians 15:24–28.

After the Judgement, there will be the "rectification of absolutely all beings" and "the vanishing of absolutely every adverse power;" then Christ-Logos will submit to the Father and "after the accomplishment of his work," will be one with God, who will be "all in all" (*Eccl. theol.* 2:8). In *Eccl. theol.* 2:14, Eusebius is discussing Psalm 109:1, quoted in 1 Corinthians 15:25 and Acts 3:21, which foretells the "times of universal apokatastasis." Like Origen and then Gregory of Nyssa, who relied on Origen, Eusebius interprets 1 Corinthians 15:25–8 not in the sense of Christ's subordination to the Father, but as the voluntary submission of all, meaning universal salvation:

> The apostle, saying that *all beings* will submit to the Son, in-
> dicated the obedience given *out of a free choice*, and the glory
> . . . that *all beings* will render to him qua *Savior* and king *of
> all together*. In the same way, also his own submission to the
> Father probably does not indicate anything different from . . .
> the *voluntary obedience* which he himself [in his humanity] will
> render to God the Father, once he has *rendered all worthy of the
> divinity of the Father*. . . . In case they are unworthy of it, Christ,
> qua *common Savior of absolutely all*, will take on his reign, a
> *rectifying and therapeutic reign, which will rectify those who will
> be still imperfect and heal those who will still need healing*, and
> will reign, leading under his feet the enemies of his kingdom.
> (*Eccl. theol.* 3:15)

The eschatological reign of Christ will be a healing and purifying reign, which will make worthy of God those who are not yet so, and thus "all, once sanctified, will submit to the Son of God *in a salvific submission*. . . . He will subject *all beings* to himself, and this must be understood as a *salvific submission*. . . . He will bring to God all those who have submitted to him, having put them around himself as a choir" (3:15–6). This will be "the perfect accomplishment of Paul's teaching in the very end: that God may be *all in all*." Indeed, "after the end and perfection of all, at the constitution of the new aeon, God *will no longer inhabit few, but all*, who by then have become worthy of the kingdom of heavens." Then, "God will be 'all *in all*' . . . *filling all*, and the Son will exult and rejoice in the perfect act performed . . . and will continue to reign without end." Eusebius reiterates that Christ will be able to give back "*all*" to the Father only after making them "perfect," "saved," and "completely healed," having sanctified them all as a high priest: "Like a high priest he will *sanctify all* . . . that they may be filled with the unspeakable goods of the Father. For it is in this sense that God will be 'all in all.'" Perfect unity will reign—in Eusebius' view, just as in Origen's view—in the final universal restoration:

> Then God will be *in all*, who will *have been made perfect mean-
> while by the Son* . . . And the Son will hand the kingdom to God,
> presenting him all those with whom he had been entrusted *safe
> and ready for the adoration and the sanctity of the Father*. So God
> will be *all in all* . . . representing all the goods for them.

The final restoration is described by Eusebius again and again, and is identified with "the culmination of the most blessed hope" at the end of this passage and in 3:18: "the most blessed end" is the final condition in which the Godhead "will give itself as a gift to those who constitute the kingdom of Christ, thus coming to be all in all." All will have to be "perfected into unity,"[16] which is a unity of *will*, not of metaphysical substance, for both Eusebius and Origen.[17]

I already noted the epithet that Eusebius attaches to Christ in his works preserved in Greek, such as his exegesis of Isaiah and *Against Marcellus*: "the common Savior of absolutely all" (ὁ κοινὸς ἁπάντων Σωτήρ/ *ho koinos hapantōn Sōtēr*). This is also how Eusebius describes Christ-Logos in *Praise of Constantine* 6.9. The universalistic connotation is also clear, and extraordinarily emphasized, in his *Theophany*, a probably late work preserved in Syriac, where Christ is repeatedly called "the common Savior of all [*d-kl*]" (*Theoph.* 5.1; 5.8; 5.14; 5.16; 5.34; 5.46). He is the Cause of all and "the Savior of all rational creatures," the Universal Savior who bestows logos, wisdom, and all goods upon all creation (1.26–27). This seems not to mean that Jesus merely *offers* salvation to all humans, those of all races and classes, but that he will eventually *achieve* salvation for all, as taught by Origen, Eusebius' hero. In *Theophany* 1.72 and 5.27, Eusebius speaks of the darkness and fire that await those who do not follow the Logos, but not even here, in what may be his last work (at least according to Michael Simmons), does he state that this fire will be eternal. Exactly like Origen, who asserted that Christ with his cross provided the principle and advancement of the destruction of evil and the devil, who ruled over the whole world (*CC* 7.17), so does also Eusebius claim that Christ with his cross inaugurated the definitive liberation of the world from the demons (*Theophany* 3.59).

16. John 17 buttresses the idea of restoration as unity in Origen and Eusebius alike.

17. "Making *us all one thing*, so that we are no longer many, but *all of us are one*, *made one with his divinity* . . . made perfect not in a confusion of substances reduced to one, but in the perfection of virtue brought to its apex, . . . all of us by imitation of God's unity."

HILARY OF POITIERS AND HIS CORPORATE
SOTERIOLOGY

Hilary († 367ca), bishop of Poitiers in Gaul, a devoted anti-Arian,[18] knew and admired Origen, and even translated nearly 40,000 lines from his Greek works into Latin, if we credit Jerome (*Apology against Rufinus* 1). It is therefore not surprising to find that he took over Origen's interpretation of God's actions of destruction as remedial. Commenting on Psalm 2:8–9, he observes that God will bruise and break the nations "in order to reform them." Sinners are slain by God when they die to vices and sins, and are redeemed (*Treatises on Psalms* 139.19). This is typically Origenian exegesis. Moreover, for Hilary, Christ's incarnation is salvific for all humanity, because Christ's body—which is also the church—contains every

---

18. Arius had taught that the divine Son was not of one substance with God, but was rather the most preeminent of all God's creatures. This view was rejected at the Council of Nicea in 325.

human individual ("corporate soteriology" or "physicalist soteriology").[19] This is also what Origen maintained, and this model will be taken over by Gregory of Nyssa. As we shall see later, Eriugena in the ninth century—still a great admirer of Origen—went even further along this line, stating that Christ's incarnation, or better inhumanation, effected the salvation of all creatures: "Thanks to the inhumanation of God's Child, every creature in heaven and on earth has been saved" (*per inhumanationem Filii Dei omnis creatura in caelo et in terra salva facta est*).

Very interestingly, Hilary's interpretation of the Parable of the Lost Sheep—identifying the lost sheep with all of humanity, which is to be restored—coincides exactly with that offered by Adamantius (Origen's byname) in the *Dialogue of Adamantius*. Hilary, referring to Luke 15:4, explains:

> This one sheep is the human being, and by one human being the whole race is to be understood . . . the ninety-nine are the heavenly angels . . . and by us [humans], who are all one [*sc.* because we share the same human nature], the number of the heavenly church is to be filled up. This is why every creature awaits the revelation of the children of God. (*Commentary on Matthew* 18)

Excursus: The Dialogue of Adamantius

Rufinus' version of the *Dialogue of Adamantius* reports exactly the same exegesis. Adamantius' important treatment of apokatastasis in 848e constitutes one of the most outstanding points of contact with Origen's thinking, including his dealing with all rational creatures, his insistence on the negation of an ultimate perdition or ruin (*apóleia*), and his use of the Parable of the Lost Sheep in reference to the apokatastasis. Adamantius, in fact, offers here a real abridgment of Origen's philosophy of history and eschatology.[20]

19. See Scully, *Physicalist Soteriology*. On Hilary's relation to Origen and Augustine: Image, *The Human Condition in Hilary of Poitiers*, and my review in *Reading Religion*: http://readingreligion.org/books/human-condition-hilary-poitiers.

20. Si labitur quis et decidat, *a diuina eius prouidentia nusquam prorsus abscedat, nec omnino aliquid sit quod illi penitus pereat*. Et super omnia adhuc illud uidendum est, quod ad *cunctam rationabilem naturam* quanta et quam minima pars homo est, qui similiter ut ceterae *omnes rationabiles naturae* arbitrii uoluntate donatus est, qui tamen uelut ouis errans per ignorantiae montes et colles *boni pastoris humeris reportatus est et restitutus est* ad illas nonaginta et nouem oues quae non errauerunt. Quid ergo tibi uidetur, qui hoc ita sentis? Ne una erraret ouicula, nonaginta et nouem ouium profectus et gloria debuit impediri? Impeditum namque fuerat, si naturae rationabili

This not only is significant in itself, but it is also all the more revealing in that this discussion is *completely lacking* in the extant Greek. It is only present in Rufinus' version, which is likely to be much closer to the original than the Greek we have today. Whereas it is generally assumed that Rufinus added this passage, I think it is far more probable that the original text did include it, and Rufinus translated it, but it was subsequently expurgated in an act of censorship by the Greek by opponents of the apokatastasis theory. This extensive athetesis[21] probably took place after the official condemnation of Origenism under Justinian in 553. I have argued that the extant Greek is quite late, as is indicated by its linguistic features, all the more in that soon after (849a) Adamantius is declared to have expressed the *orthodox* position. Rufinus, on the contrary, had no problem in leaving the passage in its place, given that, in his view, Origen's position was indeed orthodox (for he identified Adamantius with Origen).[22]

That Rufinus' Latin is a translation from an original Greek text is suggested by the presence of Greek loanwords such as *stadium* and *agon*, which means "battle, fighting," which moreover represent extremely common metaphors in Origen, and by the expression *regressum ad pristinum statum* or "return to the original condition", which is the translation of *hē eis to archaion apokatastasis*. This phrase and conception is typical of Origen, and of Nyssen, who took it over from Origen, in many places and especially in *De anima*, where he defines twice the anastasis as *hē eis to archaion apokatastasis* or "the restoration to the original condition" of our (i.e., human) nature. Origen's use of the phrase *eis to archaion apokathistēmi* or "I restore to the original condition" well attested by Jerome, *Ep. ad Avit.* 3: *per genus hominum reuertantur ad pristinum statum*, which clearly translates the above-mentioned Greek phrase. What is more, in *Princ.* 2.1.1 Rufinus' translation *restituere in statum initii sui* or "to restore into one's original condition" surely renders *apokathistēmi eis to archaion*. The whole sentence is, *praecipue si intueamur illum finem per quem omnia restituenda in statum initii sui* or "especially if we understand that ultimate end through which

libertas arbitrii, per quam illae nonaginta et nouem in summis excelsis profectibus permanserunt, non fuisset indulta, quandoquidem *nec eorum qui quo modo oberrauerant salutem dispensatio diuina despexerit*, sed stadium quoddam praesentem hunc et uisibilem mundum posuerit, in quo, concertantium et aduersantium agone moderato, *certaminis praemia proposuerit regressum ad pristinum statum*, dum *per arbitrii libertatem* quae illuc ducunt eligi et nihilominus et respui quae non sinunt possunt.

21. *Athetēsis* (a setting aside, abolition) is the marking of a passage as spurious.

22. See Ramelli, "The Dialogue of Adamantius." An Oxford critical edition and a monograph are in the works.

all beings are to be restored to their original condition." Soon after, Origen explains how *to archaion* or "the original condition" is to be understood: *illa initii unitate atque concordia in qua a deo primitus procreati sunt . . . illo bonitatis statum*, or: "in that initial state of unity and concord, in wich the were orginally created by God . . . that condition of goodness." The same concept returns in *Princ.* 3.6.6, and there is also an attestation directly in Origen's Greek, in *Co. Io.* 13.3.13: *eis homoion tō archēthen apokatastas*, or "restoring to a state similar to the initial one," which closely corresponds to the aforementioned expression in the *Dialogue*.

Furthermore, Adamantius' phrase *in statum initii sui* or "into one's original condition" suggests that the original condition, exempt from sin, belonged to the human being as its proper state: Origen characterizes the apokatastasis as a return to what is one's own and familiar (*eis ta oikeia*) in *Hom. in Jer.* 14.18. A comparison can be drawn with *Princ.* 1.3.8, where the apokatastasis is described (in Rufinus' translation) as a *redire ad statum suum ac rursum statuere id quod per neglegentiam fuerat elapsum*, or "return to one's own condition and restore what had fallen out of negligence." Now, *rursum statuere* translates a form of *apokathistēmi*, and *ad statum suum* renders *eis to oikeion*, which expresses the same concept as in Origen's *Homilies on Jeremiah*: the apokatastasis will be a return to the state that was proper to the human being at the beginning, a return to one's true nature, as it was in God's plan. Likewise, the original state characterized by beatitude, to which at the apokatastasis all will be brought back, is described by Origen in *Princ.* 1.6.2 as "proper" and "properly belonging to" the human being: *redire et restitui* [sc. *apokathistēmi*] *ad statum suae beatitudinis*, or "to return and be restored to the state of beatitude that belongs to one." Indeed, *suae* very probably renders a form of *oikeios*.

Also, *restitutus est* in the *Dialogue* undoubtedly renders *apokatestathē* or another passive form of *apokathistēmi*, as well as *restitutio* perfectly corresponds to *apokatastasis*. This is the case also with *Princ.* 3.5.7, where Origen is describing the universal apokatastasis as a result of the submission of all to Christ: *inimicorum quae dicitur Filio Dei esse subiectio salutaris quaedam intellegatur et utilis, ut, sicut cum dicitur Filius Patri subiectus*, perfecta uniuersae creaturae restitutio *declaratur, ita cum Filio Dei inimici dicuntur esse subiecti*, subiectorum salus *in eo intellegatur et* reparatio perditorum, or: "the subjection of the enemies to the Son of God, mentioned by Scripture, should be understood as salvific and useful: just as, when the Son is said to be subject to the Father, this announces the perfect restoration of all creatures, so also, when the enemies are said to be subject to the Son of God, the salvation of those subjected should be understood in this, and the restoration of the lost." A parallel instance is also to be found in *Princ.* 3.6.9, where Christ's reign bringing about universal apokatastasis, i.e., the perfecting and restoration of all, is described as a period of illumination and instruction.

Adamantius' statement that the apokatastasis is the reward for the agonistic effort of virtue (*certaminis praemia . . . regressum ad pristinum statum*) perfectly corresponds to Origen's statement in *Comm. in Io.* 13.46.299: "the reward of our Lord should be interpreted as the salvation and restoration of those conquered, since he will rest after restoring them." What is more, the association of the terms *agon* and *certamina* for the description of the present world as a place of exercise and trial in view of the ultimate end in Adamantius' piece on the apokatastasis finds a stunningly precise correspondence in Origen: in *Hom. Gen.* 16.7, where he is allegorizing Jacob's descent into Egypt as the descent of the rational creature into this world, he uses the very same terms in an identical context (of course, here too in Rufinus' translation): *in carne positi agones mundi huius et certamina sustinemus*, or: "once we have been put in the flesh, we have to sustain the struggles and fights of this world." And the homilies, too, like the dialogues, reflect Origen's oral, initially impromptu, performances.

In Adamantius' discussion of the apokatastasis there is also a reference to the Parable of the Lost Sheep (Luke 15:3–7) and to Jesus' action of restoration. This is a parable on which Origen particularly insists, and which he refers precisely to the apokatastasis, which in his thought proves to be grounded primarily in Christ. Only in his extant Greek works, there are many passages in which the soteriological value of this parable is highlighted, for instance, fr. 58b-c on Luke, where he cites John 10:11 joint to Matt 18:12 and Luke 15:3–7. Even more explicit about the connection between the Parable of the Lost Sheep and the doctrine of universal salvation is *Fr. in Ps.* 118.176. In *Fr. in Jer.* fr. 28, too, the parable is related to Jesus' action of saving what is lost or has perished and to his unifying action (unity is one of the essential traits of the apokatastasis according to Origen). In *Fr. in Ps.* 18.6 Origen offers an allegorical exegesis of the parable: Jesus went to rescue the lost sheep when he descended onto the earth and into the underworld. Finally, in *Sel. in Ps.* PG 12.1628, which is very likely to reflect Origen's thought, Origen connects the Parable of the Lost Sheep with the apokatastasis performed by Christ first qua Justice and then qua Wisdom; in this way, he will remove from the soul both evilness and ignorance (the close connection between which will be especially emphasised by Evagrius).

Very interestingly, Macarius of Magnesia (who will be addressed below), who shows many points of contact with both Origen and Nyssen, has exactly the same exegesis in *Apocr* 4.18. Moreover, like Origen, he indicates sloth and negligence as the cause of the primordial fall (ibid.). The presence of exactly the same exegesis, with reference to apokatastasis, in both Hilary and the *Dialogue* and Macarius makes it probable that all depend on Origen's exegesis.

MARCELLUS, AN ORIGENIAN WHO MISUNDERSTOOD ORIGEN?

Marcellus, bishop of Ancyra († 374), was in line with Origen in his anti-Arianism, being one of the anti-Arian bishops at the Council of Nicaea, and indeed was profoundly influenced by him. However, he also misunderstood Origen and fell into the opposite Trinitarian extreme of mono-prosopism or Sabellianism: he posited only one hypostasis or person in the Trinity.

One aspect of Marcellus' dependence on Origen is his adhesion to the doctrine of universal salvation.[23] His exegesis of 1 Corinthians 15:24–28 is the same as Origen's: the eventual submission of Christ to God is the submission of all humanity—Christ's body—to God, and this will be a *salvific* submission: Paul "is speaking of the submission of the cosmos, which will take place in the flesh of Christ, . . . when, he says, all will submit to the Son, we shall find ourselves being his limbs, and thanks to him we shall become children of God. . . . Then he himself will submit to the Father *on our behalf, as the head on behalf of his own limbs.* For, as long as all of his limbs have not yet submitted, he himself, who is their head, has not yet submitted to the Father, because he is *waiting for his own limbs . . . it is we who submit to the Father in Christ*" (*De Incarn.* 20). Christ, "when he remits his spirit into the hands of the Father, hands himself to God qua human being, in order to *hand all humans to God.*"[24]

In Christ, "the human being, who was once deceived (by the devil), is established as king, by means of the Logos" (*C. Aster.* fr. 113). Like Origen, Marcellus—as is evident from the fragments that can be gleaned

23. See Ramelli, "*In Illud: Tunc et Ipse Filius . . .*," 259–74.

24. Ramelli, "*In Illud: Tunc et Ipse Filius . . .*," 13. If this work *On the Incarnation and Against the Arians* is Marcellus' (which is not entirely certain), another close parallel would emerge with Origen's interpretation of the eventual submission of the Son as the submission of humanity and its salvation.

from Eusebius' *Against Marcellus*—regards the submission of all to Christ as a recapitulation, and the restoration (*apokatastasis*) of the Logos as the restoration of humanity. He uses the very words "restoration *of all*" and "rectification *of all*," meaning that all will be made just by Christ, "after the time of the Judgment," at "the complete vanishing of every hostile power," during Christ's reign. Once evil has disappeared and all have been made just, the Son will be able to submit—in his "body"—to God, who will thus be "all in all."[25]

ST. ATHANASIUS THE GREAT,
AN ADMIRER OF ORIGEN

25. See Ramelli, "*In Illud: Tunc et Ipse Filius . . .*"

Athanasius of Alexandria († 373), who represented himself as the great defender of the Nicene faith, was also a great admirer of Origen, who indeed had anticipated the theology of Nicaea. Athanasius' sympathy with Origenian Christians can be seen in numerous ways. He maintained an epistolary correspondence with the Origenian Palladius, the disciple of the Origenian Evagrius, he famously wrote the biography of another Origenian, St. Antony the Great, and he appointed Didymus the Blind as head of the Didaskaleion—Didymus was not only a faithful Origenian, but also (like Evagrius and Palladius, and perhaps Antony), a supporter of the doctrine of universal restoration. Athanasius also composed an apology of the thought of the Origenian Dionysius of Alexandria.

It was not only Origenists that Athanasius supported, but Origen himself. In *The Decrees of the Council of Nicaea*, 27.1 Athanasius quotes Origen as an authority and praises him for his commitment to labor (φιλόπονος/*philoponos*) and for his heuristic work, which Athanasius distinguishes from a dogmatic discourse. Athanasius thereby defends Origen, and quotes his words as authoritative in support of his own Nicene position, viz. the coeternity of the Son with the Father: "Origen the Hardworking wrote some things for the sake of philosophical research and exercise: let nobody consider these to be expressions of his own thought [. . .], for those who seek quarrels he says something in the spirit of investigation. But the Hardworking's own thought is what he states as a definition. Now, after saying a few things as in an exercise, against the heretics, he immediately adds his own thought." Athanasius reports at this point Origen's words on the coeternity of the Son with the Father, on which I have commented elsewhere, demonstrating that what prevailed at Nicaea was in fact Origen's theology.[26] It is ironic, given how many have thought of Origen as a heretic, that Origen's theology prefigured Nicene orthodoxy and that the Nicene-Constantinopolitan Creed shows traces of the influence of Origen and the Cappadocians. (And it should be noted in passing that the Creed comprises among the articles of faith the final judgment, eternal life, and eternal glory—including a profession of faith "in the life of the world to come" (ζωὴ αἰώνιος/*zōē aiōnios*)—but *not* eternal damnation, death, and hell.)

In *The Decrees of the Council of Nicaea*, 25.1, Athanasius also exalts Theognostus, another faithful Origenian, for maintaining that the Son

---

26. See Ramelli, "Origen's Anti-Subordinationism and Its Heritage in the Nicene and Cappadocian Line," and further arguments will eventually appear in a monograph on Origen's philosophical theology.

was born from the Father's essence/substance (*ousia*)—as Origen himself thought. Likewise, in his fourth letter to Serapion, Athanasius praises Origen as "the most learned and active writer among the ancient," and the Byzantine theologian Gobar reports that Athanasius often lauded Origen and Theognostus.[27] Socrates too testifies that Athanasius was a "praiser" of Origen, that he regarded him as "wondrous" and "most hardworking," and that in his *Discourses against the Arians* he adduced Origen's words as authoritative, in defence of the faith in the consubstantiality of the Son with the Father. This may refer to the passage that I have reported above, or to another passage now lost.

Athanasius shared Origen's ideas of evil as non-being and non-existent in the beginning, and sin as moving into non-being (e.g., *On the Inhumanation of the Logos*, 4), as well as the notion that Christ's inhumanation (ἐνανθρώπησις/*enanthrōpēsis*) has a salvific and deifying effect on humanity. Athanasius insists that Christ became human in order for humanity to be deified, for instance in *On the Inhumanation of the Logos*, 54.3: Christ "was made a human being, that we might be deified [θεοποιηθῶμεν/*theopoiēthōmen*]."[28] This idea stems from Origen and Irenaeus, who formulated it as follows in *Refutation of All Heresies*, 3, preface: Christ became what we are to bring us to what he is. The inhumanation has taken place, says Athanasius, "thanks to the love and goodness of God the Father, for the salvation of us humans. [. . .] the salvation of the world has been performed by the same Logos who has created it" (*On the Inhumanation of the Logos*, 1).

Athanasius often displays universalistic overtones: "Flesh was taken up by the Logos to *liberate all humans* and *resurrect all of them* from the dead, *and ransom all of them from sin*" (*Letter to Adelphius*, PG 26.1077). Athanasius declares here that *all* humans will be liberated from sin. He repeats this shortly afterwards: "The Logos became a human being for the sake of *our salvation* [. . .] to *set free all beings in himself*, to lead the world to the Father and to *pacify all beings* in himself, in heaven and on earth" (col. 1081). In 1077A he has recourse to Philippians 2:10, one of Origen's favorite quotations in support of the universal nature of apokatastasis, since he interpreted the submission described there as voluntary and therefore leading to salvation. This is also why in *The Inhumanation of*

---

27. In Photius, *Library*, 232.291b.

28. See also, e.g., *Against the Arians*, PG 26.397.21. Cf. Maftei, *L'incarnation du Verbe* for the salvific value of Christ's inhumanation according to Athanasius.

the Logos, 19.3, Athanasius calls Christ the "Saviour of *all*,"[29] and explains: "That corruption *may disappear from all*, forever, thanks to the resurrection [. . .] *he has paid for all*, in death, all that was owed. [. . .] This glorious deed is truly *worthy of God's goodness to the highest degree*. [. . .] He has set right their neglectfulness by means of his teaching, *having rectified all human things by means of his power*." Remarking about soteriological deeds as worthy of God's goodness is typical of Origen, as is the description of sin as neglectfulness. The argument from what is worthy of God's goodness is adduced by Athanasius also in *On the Inhumanation of the Logos*, 6, in which he remarks that it would be unworthy of the goodness of God that "creatures, which are his work, should be reduced to nothing by the deception of the devil."

Athanasius explicitly speaks of restoration and, like Origen, has it depend on Christ, who, "through his own power, has *restored the whole human nature*" (*On the Inhumanation of the Logos*, 10). The Lord has come "to heal and teach" (43), according to the notion, dear to Clement and Origen, of Christ-Logos as Physician and Teacher. Christ's sacrifice was "offered for *all*," "had death disappear from us, and renovated us" (16.4–5). The effect of Christ's sacrifice is "that death might be destroyed once and for all, and humans might be *renewed* according to the image of God" (13). Thus, Athanasius speaks of a recreation: Christ "has banished death from us and has *created us anew*," bringing the knowledge of God everywhere, even "in the abyss, in Hades" (16; 45). In his festal letter 7.9.31, Athanasius refers to Luke 15:32 on the return to life from spiritual death: "This is the work of the Father's love for humanity and goodness, which not only has people rise again to life from the dead, but makes also grace splendid by means of the Spirit [. . .] by *regenerating the human beings in the image of Christ's glory*." Like Origen, Athanasius too is convinced that all humanity and the angels who have transgressed need the grace of the Logos to be saved (*Ep. ad Afr.* 7), but with that grace they *are* saved—even demons, as Origen also taught.[30]

Like Origen,[31] Athanasius insists on the universal scope of Christ's sacrifice in *The Inhumanation of the Logos*, 8–9, 20, 25, and 32:

---

29. See also *Against the Arians* 1.45, 48, 50; 3.25; 2.59, 69; *Letter to Serapion*, 3.6.

30. As MacDonald, *Evangelical Universalist*, 20, notes, the view that salvation is by grace does not require in the least that anyone be damned.

31. See Ramelli, "The Universal and Eternal Validity," 210–21.

He handed his own body to death *for the sake of all* [. . .] *to drive back to incorruptibility* the human beings who had turned to corruptibility [. . . ,] to stop the corruptibility of *all the other human beings* [. . . ,] *for the life of all.* [. . .] [T]hrough this union of the immortal Son of God with the mortal human nature, *all humans* have been covered with incorruptibility, in the promise of the resurrection. [. . .] He offered the sacrifice *for all* [. . . ,] handing his "temple" to death *for all* [. . .] to *liberate the human being from its first transgression.* [. . .] The body that he first offered *for all* and which he transformed into a way to heaven [. . .] he assumed a body *for the salvation of us all.*

In his festal letters, Athanasius proclaims the defeat of Satan, which clearly also implies liberation from sin: "*The devil*, the tyrant of the world, has been killed" (4.1.3); "Death *and the kingdom of the devil* have been abolished" (4.3.4); "Now that we pass from earth to heaven, *Satan*, like a lightning, falls down from heaven" (24.17, cf. Luke 10:18). Christ "has abolished death and *the one who has the power* of death" (7.26). Christ "overwhelmed the whole army of the devil [. . . ;] neither death nor life [. . . ,] nor any other creature will ever be able to separate us from the love of God" (19.6). "Thanks to the Saviour's death, *hell has been trodden*" (5.3.5). Christ "died *for all* [. . .] to abolish death with his blood [. . . ;] he *has gained the whole humanity*" (6.4.9–10); with a Pauline echo from Romans, "the totality of the peoples has entered, so that *every human* be saved" (27.24). Christ "has redeemed from death and *liberated from hell all humanity*" (10.10.23). Athanasius also quotes Jesus' words, with a strong universalistic thrust, in John 12:31–32: "Now the ruler of this world will be cast out. And I, when I am lifted up from earth, *will drag all humans to myself*" (43.20).

The eschatological universal resurrection will concern not only the body, but also the soul, implying the elimination of evil: "Our Saviour's death has *liberated the world*. By his wounds *all of us have been healed*. [. . .] Which joy will there be for *the total abolition of sin* and the *resurrection of the dead?*" (festal letter 6.9.21–10.23). The resurrection of the dead, for Athanasius, as well as for Origen, goes hand in hand with the eventual abolition of sin. In his festal letter 27.19 Athanasius, commenting on the Parable of Dives and Lazarus (Luke 16:19–31), claims that during the final judgement sinners will repent. For Christ helps sinners to repent (Letter 13.2.6); Christ-Logos kindles faith in people (7.7.26), which is indispensable for salvation. Christ's providential action—for

Athanasius as for Origen—does not contradict human free will, and is infallible: "It does not force one's will beyond what is possible, and love does not address only the perfect, but it descends among those who are in a middle position, and even among those who come third, in sum in such a way as to *redeem all human beings to salvation*. [. . .] *The enemy is cast out*, and all of its army is thrown to the outer side" (festal letter 10.4.8–9).

In Christ's cross there is "the salvation *of all humans in all places*," since Christ "takes away the sins of *the world* and also purifies our souls" (festal letter 14.2.5). Christ, "who is everything for us, also becomes responsible for our salvation in myriads of ways" (14.4.16). Christ "wants the repentance and conversion of the human being, rather than its death. In this way, *evilness, all of it, will be burnt away from all humans*" (festal letter 3.4.8), which will happen, either in this world or in the next, though fire (3.4.9). Now, if *all* humans are purified from evilness (i.e. sin), as Athanasius claims, then all will be eventually saved.

Like Origen, in his oeuvre Athanasius refers the adjective ἀΐδιος/ *aïdios*, "absolutely eternal," to the eternity of God and to intelligible, eternal things, but he never applies this qualifier to punishment of humans, or death, or fire in the future world, thus never stating that these will be truly eternal. He only describes these as αἰώνια/*aiōnia*, in conformity with Scripture and Origen. That he interprets this term as "belonging to the world to come" is patent from his glossing of the biblical statement, "the Lord will reign εἰς τὸν αἰῶνα/*eis ton aiōna*" as "in the future and new world/aeon" (92.28–31). The words of a psalm, "Nations, go away from his land," according to Athanasius mean that "during the [eschatological] reign of Christ they will be cast into the fire of the world to come [αἰώνιον/*aiōnion*]," but its aim is not perdition but conversion: "that these may revive, and those may correct themselves." This fire is corrective, not "eternal," but "otherworldly."

When people dismiss early Christian universalism as an aberration in Christian theology, dreamed up by Origen in the third century under the influence of paganism and later discerned to be heretical, they err on several counts. First they fail to appreciate that Origen's theology of apokatastasis was primarily a synthesis of much earlier Christian ideas, with deep roots in Scripture. Second, they overestimate the shaping influence of pagan wisdom—for while Origen happily adopted and adapted ideas from the philosophies of his day to help explicate his theology, as did all of the church fathers, he sought to evaluate such ideas in the light of the gospel and the Bible. Thus, for instance, he was very critical of the so-called doctrines of apokatastasis found among Stoics and "gnostics" and in no way considered them the inspiration for his own theology. Third, claims that Origen's theology is heretical are usually based on significant and demonstrable misunderstandings of his teaching that became widespread in the church, especially as time went on. However, the fact that such major pillars of early Christian orthodoxy as Athanasius and Gregory of Nyssa stood firmly in his defense ought to give us significant pause before aligning Origen with the heretics. For Athanasius, Origen should instead be seen as one of the theologians upon whose thought Nicene orthodoxy was built. And if Origen is to be dismissed as a heretic for embracing universalism then so should a host of others, including the great St. Athanasius and the Cappadocian St. Gregory of Nyssa.

MACARIUS OF MAGNESIA

Another supporter of apokatastasis along Origen's lines seems to have been Macarius of Magnesia, the author of the *Apocriticus* or *Monogenes*, very probably stemming from the fourth century. He seems to have been a semi-contemporary of Didymus and Gregory Nyssen (on whom see below) and to have followed Origen in his doctrine of rational creatures, originally homogeneous, but then divided into angels, humans, and demons, according to the gravity of their sins and degrees of elongation from God. His very refutation of a Porphyrian polemicist seems to be inspired by Origen's refutation of Celsus.

Hints of the apokatastasis theory are to be found in the sections of his *Apocriticus* or *Monogenes* that are preserved, such as 3.43.2: when Paul says that "God grants mercy to whom he will and hardens the heart of whom he wills" (Rom 9:18), he does not mean "that some are granted mercy by God while others are not granted mercy, but have their hearts hardened, but rather he holds that *all are granted mercy by God and saved*, saying: 'God, who wants all human beings to be saved' [1 Tim 2:4]."[32] But the section in which Macarius was most explicit about apokatastasis is—not accidentally—lost. This is attested by Nicephorus of Constantinople (early ninth century) in his *Epikrisis* against iconoclasm, 12: at the end of the fourth book, now lost (possibly just for this reason), Macarius taught "the crippled doctrines of the impious and apoplectic Origen, and undertook to teach the same things as that wretched man: that the

---

32. Trans. Jeremy Schott and Mark Edwards with slight variations.

chastisement threatened and prepared by God for impious people in the time to come *will come to an end.*"

In *Apocr.* 4.12–18 (186–88 Blondel) Macarius envisages an eschatological renovation, at the end of all aeons, at the second coming of Christ, which is configured as universal restoration. Macarius remarks that every human being at the end of all will receive back the *logos* of a second existence in incorruptibility—which can refer both to the physical resurrection and to the restoration of each one to virtue. He adds that in the same way the whole world, after perishing (at the "end of the world"), will be renewed in a greater beauty and in impassivity (*apatheia*). As a silver vase that has become tarnished over time is molted and shaped again, more beautiful and without rust, keeping its *logos*, likewise this world will be purified from the rust of sin coming from disobedience, but it will retain and improve "the *logos* of its essence" (*ousia*), an expression that was already used by Origen. Just as Origen said about the resurrection of the body of each human, as well as about the end of the world, so does Macarius claim that the visible shape of the world will pass away, but the Logos of the Creator, which remains in the creation, will never pass away, but will rather renovate the universe (*epanakainisei to pan*).[33] The Logos Creator (ὁ δημιουργὸς λόγος/*ho dēmiourgos logos*) will create again the whole nature of creatures (πᾶσαν τῶν γενητῶν φύσιν/*pasan tōn genētōn physin*) in a second and better creation (δευτέραν ἀναλαβεῖν καὶ βελτίω γένεσιν/*deuteran analabein kai beltiō genesin*). Macarius employs the same metaphor used by Gregory of Nyssa at the end of his dialogue *On the Soul and the Resurrection* for God's action of restoration of all rational creatures. It is also significant that the notion of the deception of the devil by the incarnate Christ is shared by Origen, his faithful followers Gregory Nyssen and Rufinus, and Macarius himself.

DIDYMUS THE BLIND OF ALEXANDRIA, A FAITHFUL FOLLOWER OF ORIGEN

Didymus († 395/98) was another of the celebrated leaders of the catechetical school in Alexandria. Like Origen before him, he was an

---

33. Even though he does not expand on apokatastasis in Macarius, Volp, "The Fashion of this World," too thinks that Macarius was a supporter of this doctrine and that in general he had an Origenian eschatology: Even if without any reference to Macarius' texts, Volp states that for him "there only ever will be one ἀποκατάστασις at the end of all times" (889), as Origen already postulated.

exceptionally learned teacher with an ascetic spirituality; he was also "an extremely explicit defender of Origen."[34] As we have already seen, it is reported that it was Bishop Athanasius of Alexandria who—fully aware of Didymus' adhesion to Origen's thought, including the doctrine of universal salvation—is reported to have appointed him the head of the catechetical school, where he served for almost half a century. Didymus wrote a commentary, now lost, devoted to the defense and clarification of Origen's treatise *On First Principles* because it was widely misunderstood (Socrates *HE* 4:25). This commentary, also cited by Jerome at the beginning of his work against Rufinus, was the first Christian commentary on a work of a Christian author outside the Bible.[35]

Didymus foresees a final state in which all will be free from sin. Christ, he avers, cannot reign where sin reigns; when sin will be found in no one, *then* the Lord will reign eternally (*Fr. in Ps.* 69:23). The biblical "αἰώνιος/*aiōnios* punishment" is not "eternal," but cathartic and therapeutic, "in the world to come."[36] Didymus, like Origen, is well aware of the many meanings of αἰώνιος/*aiōnios* (*Comm. in Iob* 76:11ff.).[37] He thus

---

34. Jerome *C. Ruf.* 1:6. According to Jerome (in his preface to his translation of Origen's *Homilies on Ezekiel*), Didymus defined Origen "the second teacher of the churches after the Apostle(s)." According to Rufinus, in his preface to his translation of Origen's *On First Principles*, Jerome himself described Origen "the second teacher of the churches after the apostles." Jerome, indeed, in his preface to the treatise on the Hebrew names, calls Origen "teacher of the churches after the apostles." The Origenian Palladius visited Didymus four times. St. Anthony praised Didymus as endowed with spiritual sight (Socr. *HE* 4:25). Three of Didymus' disciples were Origenians: Rufinus, the early Jerome, and Gregory Nazianzen.

35. See my "Commentaries" in *The Cambridge History of Later Latin Literature*, ed. Gavin Kelly and Aaron Pelttari, forthcoming; *Origen of Alexandria's Philosophical Theology*, in preparation.

36. Cf. Ramelli and Konstan, *Terms for Eternity*, new ed., 135–42; "Time and Eternity," in *Routledge Companion to Early Christian Philosophy*, ed. Mark Edwards, forthcoming.

37. He writes: "It must be noted that αἰώνιος is said in several ways: in the expression, 'αἰώνιος God,' it means beginningless and endless; for the divinity is called αἰώνιος by virtue of having neither a beginning nor an end of its existence. But αἰώνιος is something different when used in the expression, 'things unseen are αἰώνια': for these things are not αἰώνια in the way God is, but rather because they do not perish but remain forever in the same condition. And αἰώνιος is meant differently again when it is measured against the present time, as when it is said: 'the sons of this αἰών are wiser in their generation'; for the time that extends over the life of a human being is also called an αἰών. Indeed, it is laid down concerning the Hebrew who did not wish to be freed in the seventh year, that 'he will be your slave unto the αἰών': for no slave of a human being remains one forever, even after his death. It is in this sense that Paul too

calls the eternal life, which lasts not only throughout the future aeon (αἰώνιος/*aiōnios*), but beyond all aeons in eternity (ἀΐδιος/*aïdios*), "salvation beyond the aeons [ὑπεραιώνιος/*hyperaiōnios*]" (*Comm. in Zach.* 2:370).

Like Origen and Gregory Nyssen, Didymus also drew a close connection between resurrection and restoration. He considered the eventual restoration to be the spiritual aspect of the resurrection. Not only will the body be resurrected as a spiritual body and no longer as a psychic body, but there will be a spiritual restoration of all humans to their original and perfect condition, characterized by virtue and freedom from evil. The final universal restoration will be universal salvation, understood by Didymus as the return of all souls to God, in a perfect unity that will subsume all multiplicity. The theme of unity in apokatastasis is an Origenian heritage.[38] In *Comm. in Io.*, fr. 2, on John 3:35–36, Didymus describes the purification and subsequent restoration of fallen rational creatures:

> This is said about rational creatures. Since, among all of them, there are also some who have become wicked, know how these *will have a restoration [katastasis] once they have arrived in the hands of the Son*, obviously after *rejecting the evilness* that they had, and *assuming virtue*. For one should not pay attention to those who propound sophisms, claiming that only those rational beings who have sanctity are called.

For Didymus, just as for Origen and Nyssen, the eventual apokatastasis will clearly depend on *Christ*. The use of *katastasis* in reference to the final restoration is common in Didymus, who indeed prefers *katastasis* to *apokatastasis* and prevalently refers it to the initial condition that will be eventually restored.[39] *Katastasis* in his works also indicates

---

writes [1 Cor 8:13]: 'if flesh causes my brother to stumble, I will not eat flesh through the αἰών,' using this term in place of 'throughout my life.'"

38. See my volume of Novum Testamentum Patristicum devoted to *John 13–17*, and my "Harmony."

39. In *Comm. in Iob* col. 2:14 *katastasis* indicates the original condition of rectitude from which a rational creature has fallen; in *Comm. in Eccl.* col. 232:22 the noun indicates the original unity of all rational creatures; this unity is conceived by Didymus as *a unity of concord and will*, as it is in Origen. In *Comm. in Eccl.* col. 15:11 *katastasis* refers again to the original condition, the dwelling place of all rational creatures, which is also the place of virtue; this is also the condition to which they have to return. The original condition of the human being coincides with being in the image and likeness of God; when it goes far from this condition (*katastasis*), it loses its own identity (*Comm. in Ps. 29–34* col. 221:6).

beatitude in the next world, which awaits the virtuous (*Comm. in Eccl.* col. 213:12), and even refers to the final "deification" (*theia katastasis*, "divine state"). After leaving all that is of this aeon, the rational creature, once purified from evil and vices, attains its home, which is the divine condition (358:20). A process of rectification will bring about the blessed, final *katastasis* of imperturbability and peace thanks to the grace of God; this condition will be Christ himself (*Comm. in Zach.* 1:65). Didymus describes the eventual deification, especially in *Comm. in Ps. 35–39* col. 234:22, in *Fr. in Ps.* fr. 845 and in *In Gen.* col. 222:3, in which he characterizes it as perfect beatitude. Deification is "to become God," to reach a divine condition: *Comm. in Eccl. (3–4:12)* col. 101:26. It is union with God and adhesion to the Good; it is described again as a *katastasis* in *Fr. in Ps.* fr. 641a:9. The final apokatastasis is depicted also in *Comm. in Zach.* 1:265 as a state of peace after the war against the powers of evil, after which there will be no fighting left.

Like Clement, Origen, and Gregory of Nyssa, Didymus too maintains that the otherworldly fire will be purifying and will consume, not creatures, but evil:

> It is impossible that wood, grass, and straw disappear *in such a way as not to exist any more*, but they [i.e., sinners] will disappear *insofar as they are grass* and so on. Indeed, *this fire of the corrective punishment is not active against the substance, but against [bad] habits and qualities.* For this fire consumes, *not creatures*, but certain conditions and certain habits" (*Comm. in Ps. 20–21* col. 21:15).

Like Clement, Origen, and Nyssen, Didymus insists on the therapeutic nature of suffering and sees the Lord as a physician who employs drastic remedies, but for no other end than salvation (*Comm. in Iob* 50). No creature is evil by nature,[40] but due to a free choice; this is why, through purification, all will be able to convert to the Good and be restored and saved: "He calls us *to salvation*. The verb 'they will return/convert' indicates that *nobody is evil by essence*, by nature, but rather by

---

40. Didymus, like Origen, supports the notion of the ontological non-subsistence of evil. Evil emerges from a wrong choice of rational creatures' free will (*Comm. in Iob* 114–5); "when the agent ceases to want evil, the latter has *no more ontological subsistence*, . . . for evil is not a *substance* [*ousia*], but it arises and receives its existence in the moral choice: when the deception ceases, evil too disappears." In Didymus' ethical intellectualism, evil is the consequence of a bad choice, which results from a deception, of a lack of clear knowledge.

free choice. If evil had the power to push free choice toward something else, something alien, *the Good will have the power to call it back to its original condition*" (*Comm. in Ps. 20–21* col. 54:20). God-the-Good is the agent of restoration and salvation, through Christ's work and the works of angels and holy humans:

> The Savior in fact came to *look for what was lost and save it*. He looks for the soul, *in order to lead it to salvation, to bring it back to its original condition*. Now, just as the Savior does this *by means of instruction* and perfecting into what is good, likewise the disciples of the Savior, angels and human beings, do so. (*Comm. in Ps. 35–39* col. 267:20)

> The Father has given to Christ the power and dominion *over all beings*, that *no being* that has been handed to him should *perish*: for this glory, too, passes through us, because it was necessary that *the totality of* those who will have submitted to him and have arrived in the hands of the *omnipotent* Logos of God *be saved* and remain among the goods that have no end, so that it need no longer suffer the tyranny of death, *nor be liable to corruption and sins, nor have to undergo punishment for ancient evils*. (On John 17:1)

The insistence on "instruction" as a means of liberation from sin is consistent with Didymus' ethical intellectualism, which he shared with Origen, Gregory of Nyssa, and other Origenians. In this perspective, the original sin is considered by Didymus, just as by Gregory, to be essentially due to a deception, that of the devil, which made the soul see things opposite to the truth (*Comm. in Eccl.* 82–83). Original sin was thus due to a deception, a lack of knowledge. Sin depends on an obfuscated intellectual sight. This is why Christ's illumination and instruction will liberate all souls from sin.

Didymus (*Comm. in I Cor.* 7–8) observes that believers will be saved first, then all the others will. This will be a return to the original condition:

> Then it will be the end [*telos*], *ordered and established as corresponding to the beginning*. . . . Therefore, it is necessary that Christ reign over the beings, as they progressively add themselves, *up to the totality*, until *all* [*pantes*] *those who are enemies because of sin have submitted to him*, and Christ has *destroyed every tyrannical power*, after which the first evil itself, death, is destroyed, in that *every* [*pasa*] *soul*, now subject to death, which is joined with evil, *will be joined to Christ*.

Like Origen, Didymus thinks that the death that will be destroyed as the last enemy is *spiritual* death, not only physical death. The dominion of death will have an end because it had a beginning and thus is not eternal (*Comm. in Rom. Fr.* 3–4). Evagrius, Didymus' disciple, will use this same argument in reference to evil: since there was a time when evil did not exist, there will be a time when it will no more exist (*KG* 1:40).[41] Evil's destruction amounts to universal restoration and salvation. Consistently with this, Didymus explains that punishment will be commensurate to sin.[42] Sufferings will continue until the Lord, as a judge, "has made the sinner just" (*In ep. can. br. enarr.* p. 34). Christ transforms sinners into the just, through instruction and purifying suffering. (Origen similarly observed that Christ's work will be accomplished only when he has made the very last sinner just.) According to Didymus, Christ takes away the sin of the world to restore humans into their original image and likeness of God their creator; they will thus be again "worthy of being loved" (68).

God liberates people even from spiritual death, the "second death," in the world to come:

> God not only keeps creatures in life, but also brings back to life those who have lost it, by resurrecting them from the dead. This is why we rise again, not by confidence in our own power, lest we should fall off life, but in God, who *will vivify us even in case we should end up in death*. . . . Now, this *is not written concerning ordinary life and death*, because he says: "God, who has liberated, and liberates, and will *liberate again, from such a serious death*; God in whom we have put our hope." For he is speaking of *the death that seizes the soul away from life in the world to come*. . . . Whoever is in evil lives according to evil, and whoever errs because of it *loses the life one had according to evil*, in order to proceed, by *doing good, toward the blessed life*. (*Comm. in II Cor.* 16 and 22)

Didymus insists that nobody can be pulled away from the hands of the Father; even when Job is persecuted by the devil, not even the devil could separate him from God's love (*Comm. in Iob* 23). This is why in *Comm. in Eccl.* 156 Didymus identifies the death of the soul with the "last/extreme death" (probably a reminiscence of 1 Corinthians 15:26,

---

41. See below in the section on Evagrius.

42. This principle of commensurability is still emphasized by some contemporary theologians, such as Gregory MacDonald. MacDonald, *The Evangelical Universalist*, 11.

death as "the last enemy"), but he opposes to it the redemption and resurrection operated by Christ, who can rise from death not only the body, but also the soul, having it live "for eternity" (whereas death is never declared to last "for eternity"): "A dead has been *risen*, even after *losing the soul*, since that impious soul had *descended to the last death*. Therefore, the Savior, when he *detaches someone from sin and impiety*, behold, has *operated a resurrection;* . . . the daughter of the head of the synagogue did not die, because she had been *made just*. . . . . Those who *have risen in the soul* then possess it *for eternity*." Indeed, Didymus is certain that each and every action of divine providence is aimed at the salvation of rational creatures (*Comm. in Eccl.* 116).

6

Fourth Century Origenians II

The Cappadocians and Evagrius

BASIL OF CAESAREA

As we have already seen, Gregory Thaumaturgus (Wonderworker) brought not only Christianity but specifically *Origen's* thought to Cappadocia. This, by means of Macrina the Elder, and her granddaughter Macrina the Younger, entered the family of the latter's brothers, Basil of Caesarea and Gregory of Nyssa. Basil thus inherited Origenist sympathies from his godly sister and grandmother. He ordained Evagrius—an Origenian—a lector; a letter of Evagrius was even ascribed to him in which the final chapter expounds the doctrine of apokatastasis as a return to the initial unity (Evagrius, *Ep. fidei* = [Bas.] *Ep.* 8; cf. Evagrius, *Ep. ad Mel.* 5). Also, Chapter 6 of Book 2 of Origen's *On First Principles* was even ascribed to Basil under the name *Sermo de incarnatione Domini*, *Homily on the Incarnation of the Lord*! And so it happened that Origen's chapter, under the name of Basil, was used by Leo the Great to confirm the dogmas of Chalcedon.

Basil also collected many passages from Origen's works in his *Philocalia* together with Gregory Nazianzen—the attribution is traditional and probable—and he highly praised Gregory the Wonderworker, a direct disciple of Origen (Letter 28), as well as other disciples or estimators of Origen, such as Dionysius of Alexandria, Eusebius, Firmilian of Caesarea, and Africanus, all of whom he includes among the champions of orthodoxy. Basil exalts Gregory the Wonderworker elsewhere also (e.g., Letter 204; *De Spir. S.* 29:74). Even Basil's criticism of extreme allegoresis in his *Hexaëmeron* must not be understood as directed against Origen, but against "gnostics" or Manichaeans, all the more so in that Basil is deeply influenced by Origen. Toward the end of his life, Basil in his tract *On the Holy Spirit*, which is full of Origenian themes, at § 73 shows high respect of Origen. And Basil in turn was highly esteemed by Gregory Nyssen, his brother, a strong supporter of the doctrine of universal salvation, who speaks of him in sublime terms at the beginning of *The Creation of the Human Being*, and at the beginning of his *On the Soul and the Resurrection*. Indeed, Gregory devotes this important dialogue, which very clearly supports the doctrine of apokatastasis, to the memory of his venerated brother Basil.

Basil shared with Origen the conviction that otherworldly sufferings will not be physical, and that this world is a school for acquiring the knowledge of God. What is more, Basil's Commentary on Isaiah[1] is full of Origenian themes relevant to the doctrine of universal salvation. In

---

1. The authenticity of this commentary has been questioned by some, but on weak grounds.

Comm. in Is. 2:85, Basil, like Origen in his *Homilies on Jeremiah*, interprets God's declarations that he will not forgive his people as pedagogical threats. Commenting on Chapter 9 of Isaiah, Basil claims that if one recognizes one's sins then the punishment for it becomes temporal, and not eternal, and the fire is purifying. Basil reads Isaiah 9:1–6 as an expression of "the dogma of *salvation.*" The Logos-Angel (i.e., Announcer) knows the great plan of God, that is, God's *salvific* plan, which had remained hidden for centuries, but now is clear. The power which is on the Logos' shoulders is referred by Basil to the cross: "since when he was lifted up on the cross he has *drawn all people to himself.*" This reference to John 12:31–32 is overtly universalistic and is connected by Basil with the equally universalistic 1 Corinthians 15:24–28:

> The peace given by the Lord extends for all eternity; it knows neither boundaries nor limits. Indeed, *all beings will submit* to him, and all will recognize his authority. And when *God will be all in all,* once those who created confusion with apostasies will be *restored to peace,* they will *sing praises to God in a symphony of peace.*

Rebels are not destroyed or excluded or forcibly submitted, but they are reintegrated in the universal peace. The Logos descended "out of mercy, especially for the weakest." And again, Basil insists on the preventive, therapeutic, and educative value of the punishments decided by God for those who abstain from evil out of fear and not yet out of love.[2] Basil reflects that, until one finally converts, one sin generates another, like darnel, but this will be burnt in the otherworldly purifying fire:

> God's threat manifests God's beneficial action: *Iniquity will be burnt away as by fire.* Indeed, our good Master, as a benefit to human beings, *providentially established that the matter provided by iniquity should be consigned to annihilation.* It will be *devoured by fire* like dry darnel and *burnt away....* If we unmask sin by means of its admission, we shall reduce it to dry darnel, deserving of being devoured by the *purifying fire.*

Therefore, soon after, again in his commentary on Isaiah 9, commenting on the verse "The whole earth has been burnt by the impetus of the Lord," Basil interprets this fire, which is punitive, as purifying: "He shows that earthly things are handed to the *punishing fire for the sake of the soul. . . . He does not threaten destruction, but shows the purification,*

---

2. "Beating is necessary with people of this kind: . . . we do not convert unless we are struck."

according to what the Apostle says: 'If one's work is burnt, one will suffer loss, but will be saved; only, as through fire' [1 Cor 3:14–15]." Basil, like Paul, does not contemplate the case of people who pass through fire and are *never* purified.

According to Basil, sins "unto death" can be cured (*Comm. in Is.* 4.4). Referring to 1 Corinthians 15:28, Origen's *locus classicus* in support of apokatastasis, Basil offers an exegesis that is in full continuity with that of Origen: "All beings will be subject to Christ . . . when God is 'all in all', even those who now excite discord by revolt, having been pacified, will praise God in peaceful concord" (*Comm. in Is.* 9.6). Likewise, "All beings will be made subject to Christ's rule . . . ; those made subject to his rule will obtain restoration" (*Comm. in Is.* 16.4–5). The same equation between submission and restoration-salvation that is clear in the last two passages, was posited by Origen, whom Basil is patently following.

The interpretation of the destruction brought about by God as beneficial to sinners is also entirely Origenian: "I shall burn . . . that I may purify. . . . This is how God is angry: that he may bestow benefits on sinners" (*Comm. in Is.* 1.24); sinners will be destroyed *qua sinners*, that they may cease to be disobedient and become holy. This is what Origen said about Paul: God destroyed Paul the traitor and persecutor, to make him Paul the apostle of Jesus Christ.

Moreover, Basil admits of the intercession of the saints for the sinners, which liberates the latter from their suffering (*Or.* 10, PG 31,624).[3] And his linguistic use is consistent with that of Origen and Gregory of Nyssa: he calls "eternal" (ἀΐδιος/*aïdios*) only life in the other world; punishment, fire, death, etc., are *never* called so by him, but are only styled αἰώνια/*aiōnia*.[4]

Further evidence that points to Basil's penchant for the theory of universal restoration is found in a text by a friend of Augustine, who had no sympathy at all for that theory.[5] It is Paulus Orosius' *Warning about the Error of the Priscillianists and the Origenists* (*Commonitorium de errore Priscillianistarum et Origenistarum*), which was prepared for

3. The only passage in which it is said that αἰώνιοι/*aiōnioi* sufferings will be eternal, on the grounds that otherwise αἰώνιος/*aiōnios* life could not be eternal (short *Rules* for the monks 267, PG 31:1264:30–1265:47), is very probably spurious, or else inspired by a pastoral concern similar to that of Origen. See full discussion in my *Apokatastasis*.

4. See Ramelli and Konstan, *Terms for Eternity*, new ed., 182–209, and here below.

5. See my "Basil and Apokatastasis: New Findings"; on Orosius' role in the Origenistic controversy see also Heil, "Orosius, Augustine, and the Origenist Controversy in the West."

Augustine around the year 414. In section 3, pp. 160–62, Orosius reports that two men, both named Avitus, travelled one to Jerusalem and the other to Rome, and brought back from there "one Origen, and the other Marius Victorinus." Both, however, concentrated more on Origen and "began to propose many ideas from Origen as wonderful." At this point Orosius expounds these Origenian doctrines, first those which he deems orthodox, and then those which he regards critically. The good Origenian doctrines spread by the two Aviti, according to Orosius, concern the Trinity, the creation of everything by God *de nihilo*, the goodness of all creatures, and the exegesis of Scriptures.

Next comes the most interesting part of Orosius' exposition, and the most relevant to Basil's theology and its relation to Origen's doctrine of universal restoration. For Orosius states that not only the two aforementioned Aviti, but *also Basil* taught some Origenian doctrines that Orosius deems debatable, among which is universal restoration (pp. 161–62). Orosius probably means Basil of Caesarea, the Cappadocian, since he describes him as "St. Basil the Greek," and since Basil's good knowledge of Origen's ideas is beyond doubt. Basil taught such doctrines "in the most holy way," but Orosius later realized that they were in fact problematic.

The first of the doctrines that Orosius deems incorrect, but that Basil taught on the basis of Origen, is the eternal preexistence of creatures in God's Wisdom, which would make them coeternal with God. Basil said that "God never began to create all that he has created." Of course, this is a misunderstanding of Origen's doctrine of the eternal preexistence of the ideas or *logoi* or paradigmatic models of all creatures in God, before their creation as substances (*Princ.* 1.4.4–5). Orosius passed on this misunderstanding to Augustine (*Against the Priscillianists and the Origenists*, 8.9).

The second Origenian doctrine taught by Basil is that all rational creatures had one and the same origin and nature or substance/essence, and became differentiated at a certain point into human souls, demons, and various angelic ranks, according to their different moral choices. This division is on the basis of the principle that "a slightest sin deserved a higher rank." This doctrine is correctly ascribed to both Origen and his followers, including the Cappadocians.[6]

---

6. The initial and final union is indeed one of essential nature, as all rational intelligences (*logokoi*) have the same nature, even if some are now human while others are angelic or demonic. This union is not to be confused, however, with the idea that all *logikoi* are *one and the same being* as each other or as God. Rather, the eschatological union will be a union of wills, since all the wills of rational creatures will be oriented towards the Good, i.e. God, instead of being dispersed in a multiplicity of lesser good

Another Origenian doctrine attributed to Basil by Orosius is the creation of the world (without further specification whether the sense-perceptible world or the intelligible world or the intellectual creation, but the reference seems to be to the sense-perceptible world) only after the fall of the souls, for their purification. This is not entirely correct from Origen's point of view, but is the way Origen's doctrine was often represented.

But the Origenian doctrine of Basil on which Orosius concentrates most of all is precisely that of universal restoration, because it is also the one that worries him the most:

> They taught that the "eternal fire" [*ignem aeternum*], in which sinners will be punished, is neither true fire nor eternal. For they maintained that the above-mentioned fire is in fact the punishment of one's own conscience. Indeed, according to its Greek etymology [αἰώνιος / *aiōnios*], *aeternum* does not mean "perpetual, eternal, unending, everlasting" [*perpetuum*]. They [i.e. the Aviti] also adduced a Latin testimony: it is written in Scripture, *in aeternum*, and after *aeternum* it is added as an explanation: *in saeculum saeculi,* "in the aeon of the aeon" [i.e. not "eternally"]. Therefore, all the souls of the sinners, after the purification of their conscience, will return to the unity of the body of Christ.
>
> They wanted also to make the following assertions about the devil, but they did not prevail: given that the devil's substance, which was created good, cannot perish/be annihilated [*perire*], at a certain point the devil's evilness will be entirely consumed, and his substance will be saved.

This point, too, will appear again in Augustine, *Against the Priscillianists and the Origenists,* 5.5 and 8.10, and will return also in Eriugena (below) concerning all sinners (*malitia eorum . . . in aeternum peritura,* "their evilness will perish in eternity"). Jerome's Letter 124 to Avitus is likely to have inspired Orosius' Origenistic dossier, but interestingly enough there is no trace of Basil whatsoever in Jerome's letter; therefore, the reference to Basil as a supporter of universal restoration and salvation must have come to Orosius through another source.

Basil's teachings concerning universal restoration, as reported by Orosius in the above block quotation, are the following four:

1) The fire of hell is not true fire, i.e., not a sense-perceptible or material fire, but rather the punishment of one's own conscience. This is

---

or even evil objects of will.

indeed a doctrine that Origen and his followers, down to John the Scot Eriugena, did express; being a fire that "cannot be extinguished," it cannot be the material fire we experience in this world, which can be quenched by means of water and such like.

2) The fire of hell is not eternal, because it is called in Greek, in the New Testament, αἰώνιον/*aiōnion* (and not ἀΐδιον/*aidion*), and αἰώνιος/ *aiōnios* does not mean "eternal" outside of technical Platonic vocabulary (see Appendix). For αἰώνιος/*aiōnios* in Scripture means "remote," "ancient," "mundane," "long-lasting," and "otherworldly," or "pertaining to the future aeon." (In the Bible, αἰώνιος/*aiōnios* conveys the meaning of eternity only when it refers to God, and this because of God and not due to its intrinsic semantic value.) That πῦρ αἰώνιον/*pur aiōnion* means "fire in the next world" or "long-lasting fire," not "eternal fire," was indeed clear to Origen and to most Greek patristic authors, including Basil himself.

A special investigation into Basil's terminology of eternity exactly confirms this awareness of his. As I mentioned above very briefly, Basil uses ἀΐδιος/*aïdios*, meaning "absolutely eternal," in reference to the absolute eternity of God, of the Son, who is eternally generated (especially in his polemic against the "neo-Arian" Eunomius), of the Spirit, of divine attributes, or in reference to eternal and intelligible realities, and to the future life, which is described in this case as eternal proper. The same is the case with "eternal victory" (ἀΐδιος νίκη/*aïdios nikē*). In the case of angels, the state that existed before the creation of this world, and is apt to the powers that are beyond the world, not only is beyond time in the present world (ὑπέρχρονος/*hyperchronos*), but it even lasts through the aeons (αἰωνία/*aiōnia*), and is absolutely eternal (ἀΐδιος/*aïdios*), that is, beyond all aeons. Here Basil clearly distinguishes the meanings of ἀΐδιος/ *aïdios* and αἰώνιος/*aiōnios*, reserving the sense of absolute eternity for the former. He observes that "some people attach to the aeons [αἰῶνες/ *aiōnes*], too, the name of 'eternal' [τοῦ ἀϊδίου/*tou aidiou*]," but he keeps the two distinct, thus showing that he was well aware of the semantic difference between αἰώνιος/*aiōnios* and ἀΐδιος/*aïdios*, and knew that only the latter means "eternal."

Basil uses αἰώνιος/*aiōnios* in scriptural citations, for instance in the sense, frequent in the Septuagint, of "remote, ancient" (so, for example, he glosses the biblical ὅρια αἰώνια/*oria aiōnia*, "ancient boundaries," with ὅρια πατέρων/*oria paterōn*, "the boundaries of the ancestors," and definitely not "eternal boundaries"), or also in the sense, "enduring through generations," in the contrasting couple πρόσκαιρα/*proskaira* and αἰώνια/

aiōnia, "ephemeral" and "long lasting." But he does not use αἰώνιος/ *aiōnios* in the sense of "eternal," apart from scriptural quotations concerning God. Most often, Basil uses the Gospel phrase ζωὴ αἰώνιος/*zōē aiōnios*, "life in the world to come." He paraphrases Jesus' words that one who hates one's own life/soul in this world will preserve it for life in the other world (εἰς ζωὴν αἰώνιον/*eis zōēn aiōnion*). Drawing on John, Basil describes ζωὴ αἰώνιος/*zōē aiōnios* as life tout court, in that it is the true life, and is Christ.

Opposed to this and similar positive ideas—such as αἰώνιος/*aiōnios* glory, etc., which are also widely attested in Basil—is, among Basil's expressions, αἰσχύνη αἰώνιος/*aischunē aiōnios*, "shame in the other world," this too a quotation from the Bible, and αἰώνιος καταφθορά/*aiōnios kataphthora*, "ruin/perdition in the next world," and, above all, πῦρ αἰώνιον/ *pyr aiōnion*, "otherworldly fire," another biblical expression, e.g., in *Prol.* 7 PG 31.673. Here Basil cites Jesus' words about people who have not done works of mercy and are sent to fire in the other world. In *Prol.* 8 PG 31.685, Basil paraphrases Scripture when he says that the just will go to life αἰώνιος/*aiōnios* and the kingdom of heavens, while sinners will be sent to punishment/correction αἰώνιος/*aiōnios*, where, as Scripture has it, the worm does not die and the fire cannot be put out as they do and can in this world. The same opposition, life αἰώνιος/*aiōnios* vs. punishment/correction αἰώνιος/*aiōnios*, is found again in *Prol.* 31.892, in which punishment in the other world is exemplified by the αἰώνιον/*aiōnion* darkness, "otherworldly darkness."

A parallel negative phrase in Basil's work is "αἰώνιος/*aiōnios* death," i.e., death in the world to come. In *Homilies on Psalms* 61.4 this expression does not indicate an eternal damnation, but death in the sense of separation from God in the next world for those who have chosen delights in this world, instead of electing virtue and the suffering that virtue always brings about in this world: "to choose a temporary pleasure and because of it to receive death in the other world/long-lasting death [θάνατος αἰώνιος/*thanatos aiōnios*], or to choose suffering in the exercise of virtue and use it to receive delight in the other world/enduring delight." Indeed, Basil's thought here is perfectly parallel to that of his brother Gregory of Nyssa in his reflections on the Parable of Dives and Lazarus in *The Soul and the Resurrection*: Lazarus chose the true good, and therefore suffering, in this world, and has rest and comfort in "Abraham's bosom" in the other world, while Dives chose delight and vice in this world (apparent goods), and thus suffering in the next. But this does not mean in the least that for Gregory the otherworldly suffering of the wicked will be eternal (indeed, Gregory thought that even the devil will be healed and saved). Neither does it need to mean so for Basil.

That αἰώνιος/*aiōnios* in all of these cases refers to the world to come, in accord with the biblical use, is clear from *Consolation to a Sick Person*, PG 31.1720, where it is stated that a rich man, if rich in virtue, will be rich also in the next world, but if deprived of virtue, he will be "poor in the world to come," αἰώνιος/*aiōnios*. The same is also clear from Basil's glossing αἰωνία ζημία/*aiōnia zēmia* ("loss in the world to come"), as opposed to αἰωνία ἐλπίς/*aiōnia elpis* ("hope for the world to come," and not "eternal hope") with τὴν ἐπερχομένην ζημίαν/*tēn eperchomenēn zēmian* ("the penalty to come"), thus equating αἰώνιος/*aiōnios* punishment with punishment "to come." Therefore, penalty αἰωνία/*aiōnia* means punishment "in the future world," and not "eternal" punishment.

Again, Basil contrasts the present moment (πρόσκαιρον/*proskairon*) with the future time (αἰών/*aiōn*), and the use of ὕστερον/*hysteron*, "later," confirms that αἰώνιος/*aiōnios* means "pertaining to the future aeon," the "later world," and not "eternal," Thus, the worm αἰώνιος/*aiōnios* is that which is in the future aeon. Basil has martyr Gordius say: Should I reject Christ, "so that I may gain the reward of a few days? But I shall pay the penalty for this for the entire aeon to come" (αἰῶνα ὅλον ζημιωθήσομαι/*aiōna holon zēmiōthēsomai*). The martyr adds: "It is obvious madness to die with art, and with evil and treachery to prepare for oneself punishment/correction in the world to come (αἰωνίαν κόλασιν/*aiōnian kolasin*)." The "entire aeon to come" refers to the next aeon, which will last until the end of the aeon itself, or of all aeons.

It is remarkable that Basil uses ἀΐδιος/*aïdios*, "eternal," only in phrases that denote the future life and beatitude, and *never* in phrases that signify damnation. Like Origen, Gregory of Nyssa, and other patristic thinkers, and like the Bible itself, he never speaks of ἀΐδιον /*aidion* fire or ἀΐδιος/*aïdios* punishment. This choice, at least linguistically, rules out an otherworldly fire or punishment conceived as absolutely eternal, all the more so in that Basil clearly endows αἰώνιος/*aiōnios* with the sense of "pertaining to the world to come." This strict linguistic consistency is well understandable in an author who was very familiar with Origen's writings, as well as with the Greek Bible.

3) Basil's third doctrine related to universal restoration, according to Orosius as reported in the block quotation above, is that all the souls of sinners, after due purification, will be restored to the unity of Christ. This is exactly the doctrine of universal restoration and unification (ἕνωσις/

henōsis) that Origen taught, followed in this closely by Gregory of Nyssa. Now it is most interesting that, according to Orosius, this doctrine was also shared by Basil. While this may seem to be a gross mistake at first sight, the preceding notes on Basil's terminology of eternity and the analysis that I have conducted, especially with regard to his *Commentary on Isaiah*, reveal that Orosius' claim is certainly plausible.

4) Basil's fourth doctrine related to apokatastasis, according to Orosius, is that the devil, being a creature of God, is good in his substance, and his substance cannot be destroyed; therefore, after a full purification, with the total destruction of his evilness, he too will be saved in his substance. This is exactly Origen's argument in *Princ.* 3.6.5, followed by Gregory Nyssen and later on by John Eriugena. Basil too, even though with many doubts, left the door open to this possibility.

GREGORY NYSSEN

A Case for Gregory's Universalism

Basil's brother Gregory, bishop of Nyssa (c.335–c.395), absorbed the Origenian form of Christianity—including the doctrine of universal restoration—from his older sister and venerated professor St. Macrina the Younger († 379), a Christian philosopher[7] and ascetic. In his dialogue *On the Soul and the Resurrection,* Macrina is presented as arguing for universal resurrection and salvation. But the doctrine of universal salvation can be found in practically all of Gregory's works, from all periods of his life.

Besides the dialogue *On the Soul,* the work of Gregory in which the doctrine of universal salvation is treated most extensively is a short commentary on 1 Corinthians 15:28,[8] where Gregory overtly states even the salvation of the devil.[9] Gregory here describes universal salvation as the highest fulfillment of hope.[10] In this work, as in many others, he was closely inspired by Origen.[11] The very passage he is commenting on (1 Cor 15:28) was Origen's favorite in support of universal salvation. Like Origen, Gregory interprets the final submission of all to Christ announced in this biblical verse as the salvation of all. Christ's submission to God is understood by Gregory, just as by Origen,[12] as the submission, and consequent salvation, of all rational creatures, who are "the body of Christ."

From the metaphysical point of view, Gregory's argument is based on the final annihilation of evil.[13] But this is enabled by Christ, in whom humanity is made connatural with the Good (i.e., God), and all evil disappears from humanity. The Good, in the end, will reach even "the extreme limit of evil," and "nothing will remain opposed to the Good." All will be united to God. All humanity, all rational creatures, and the whole of creation will become "one body."[14] That salvation will be universal is clearly affirmed by Gregory: "*No being* will remain outside the number

7. See Silvas, *Macrina the Younger,* who regards Macrina as the mother of Greek monasticism and perhaps of cenobitic monasticism, and rightly emphasizes the philosophical character of her Christianity, which she transmitted to Gregory.

8. The Latin title is *In Illud: Tunc et Ipse Filius.*

9. See my *"In Illud,"* 259–74.

10. See also *De beat.* PG XLIV 1196:11. This phrase had already been used by Origen in *Fr. in Matth. 78.*

11. I have demonstrated this in detail in *"In Illud"* and, with further arguments, "The Trinitarian Theology," 445–78.

12. See my "Origen's Anti-Subordinationism," and "The Father in the Son, the Son in the Father."

13. See my "Christian Soteriology and Christian Platonism."

14. See my "Harmony between *Arkhē* and *Telos.*"

of the saved" (*In Illud* 21 Downing); "*no creature* of God will fall out of the Kingdom of God" (*In Illud* 14 D.). This will be a consequence of the purification of all beings from evil and their restoration to a state free from evil: "*Every being* that had its origin from God will return such as it was from the beginning, when it had *not yet received evil*" (*In Illud* 14 D.). Like Origen, from 1 Corinthians 15:28 Gregory deduces that if God must eventually be "all *in all*" then evil will no longer exist in *any* being, because God, the Good, could never be found in evil. Gregory is directly drawing on Origen, *Princ.* 3:6:2–3.

The dialogue *On the Soul and the Resurrection* between Gregory and Macrina is a Christian version of Plato's *Phaedo*. Here, Macrina plays the role of Socrates, leading the discussion, and argues for the resurrection of all the dead in such a form as to include the restoration and salvation of all, because the resurrection is not only of the body but also of the soul, which is freed from sin through purification. Macrina envisages "the *universal harmony of all rational nature* that one day will obtain in the Good. . . . When finally, after long cycles of aeons, *evilness has disappeared*, only the Good will remain, and even those creatures [i.e., demons] will concordantly and unanimously admit the sovereignty of Christ." (*De an.* col. 72B).[15] Even demons will submit to Christ and be saved!

Macrina, like Origen, insists that otherworldly sufferings are healing, and not retributive (e.g., cols. 88A–89B). Souls who have not yet liberated themselves from sins and passions on earth must do so in the other world. The primary cause of this purification is God, who attracts the soul to himself, not to punish it, but to have it back; if a soul is covered with evil, that attraction will cause suffering as a side effect (cols. 97B–100C):

> It is not the case that God's judgment has as its main purpose that of bringing about punishment to those who have sinned. On the contrary, as the argument has demonstrated, the divinity on its part does exclusively what is good, separating it from evil, and attracting [the soul] to itself, *with a view to its participation in beatitude*, but the violent separation of what was united and attached to the soul [i.e., evil] is painful for the soul that is attracted and pulled [by the divinity to itself]. . . . It seems to me

15. I use my edition, *Gregorio di Nissa sull'anima*, which is also based on the collation of the Coptic translation (much more ancient than the extant Greek manuscripts; it has allowed me to restore several readings). Ekkehard Mühlenberg's critical edition in GNO has received some of my readings. Further my "Gregory of Nyssa on the Soul (and the Restoration)."

that the soul too must suffer whenever the divine power, *out of love for human beings, extracts for itself what belongs to it* from the ruins of irrationality and materiality. For it is neither out of hatred nor for punishment of an evil life, in my view, that those who have sinned are inflicted suffering by the One who *claims for itself and drags to itself all that which has come to being thanks to it and for it*, but the Godhead, for its part, as its principal and better purpose *attracts the soul to itself*, i.e., the Source of every beatitude; however, as a side effect, there occurs necessarily the aforementioned suffering for the one who is pulled [out of evil] in that way.

The amount of sin that is found in each one determines the duration of the purifying suffering; the flame of the "otherworldly fire" (αἰώνιον/ *aiōnion* fire) will be applied for a shorter or longer time, depending on the amount of sin that must be purified.[16] The aim of the purification is the complete annihilation of evil (*De an.* 100–105A). The Gospels emphasize the necessity of purification, which must be commensurate with the amount of evil/impurity accumulated by each one (Matt 18:23–25; Luke 7:41); and the idea of measure excludes that of an eternal duration:

> *Evil must necessarily be eliminated, absolutely and in every respect, once and for all, from all that is,* and, since in fact it is not . . . , neither will it have to exist, at all. For, as evil does not exist in its nature outside will, once each will has come to be in God, *evil will be reduced to complete disappearance,* because no receptacle will be left for it. . . . God's right judgment is applied to all, and *extends the time of the restitution of the debt according to its amount;* . . . the complete eradication of debts does not take place through any monetary payment, but the debtor is handed to the torturers, *until he has paid his whole debt.* . . . [T]hrough the necessary suffering, he will eliminate the debt accumulated by means of participation in miserable things, which he had taken upon himself during his earthly life. . . . [A]fter taking off all that which is alien to himself, i.e., sin, and getting rid of the shame deriving from debts, he can achieve a condition of freedom and confidence. Now, freedom is assimilation to what has no master and is endowed with absolute power, and at the beginning it was given us by God, but then it was covered and hidden by the shame of debts. Thus, as a consequence, everything that is free will adapt to what is similar to it; but virtue

---

16. *De an.* 100 CD–101A = 448 Ramelli. On Origen's theology of freedom here, see my *Social Justice*.

admits of no masters: therefore, everything that is free will turn out to be in virtue, since what is free has no master. Now, God's nature is the source of all virtue; so, in it there will be *those who have attained freedom from evil*, that, as the Apostle says, "*God may be all in all.*" (*De an.* 101–4)

The goal of every soul is its increasing participation in the divine goods forever (*De an.* 105AD), an ideal that derives from Origen.[17] In her concern—shared already by Origen—that the awareness of universal salvation may bring about moral relaxation, Macrina warns that the purifying process will be hard (*De an.* 157BD); however, it will achieve its aim, that is, universal salvation. In her exegesis of the Parable of Dives and Lazarus, Macrina (*De an.* 81A–84D) interprets Luke 16:19–31 as a warning that the soul must be freed from the "fleshly glue"—passions that keep it stuck to sins—to "rush toward the Good"; each soul, sooner or later, will do so (*De an.* 85B–88C).

The Feast of Tabernacles is interpreted as a symbol of the eventual universal salvation: all rational creatures will be happy, in harmony and unity, after the vanishing of evil (*De an.* 132C–136A). Philippians 2:10 is also read—as it was by Origen—in support of universal salvation (*De an.* 136A), since it foresees the "universal harmony with the Good" in the end. The interconnection between resurrection and restoration, and thereby salvation (*De an.* 145C–149B), is clear from the very description of the resurrection as the restoration (*apokatastasis*) of human nature to its original condition, free from evil. This does not mean that Gregory intended to "reduce" the restoration to the mere resurrection of the body, as has been suggested,[18] but that he wanted to put forward—in the footsteps of Origen—a "holistic" and much richer concept of the resurrection. This will be, not simply the resurrection of the body and its transformation to an immortal body, but the restoration of the soul and all the intellectual and spiritual faculties of the human being to their prelapsarian state, through a purification from evil. The resurrection of the body is but the beginning of the full resurrection-restoration. Those who are still covered with sin will undergo a process of purification for their resurrection-restoration to be complete, as Macrina explains. But all will eventually achieve the state that was planned by God for humanity from the beginning: free from evil, suffering, decay, and death. For

17. See my *Gregorio di Nissa sull'anima*, introductory essay with argument and documentation.

18. Especially by Maspero and Taranto; see below.

"human nature was something divine, before the human being acquired the impulse toward evil" (*De an.* 148A). God's intention is the restoration of all humans to their original perfection with a view to their endless spiritual development. God will liberate all from evil, which is alien to human nature, so that in all the image of God will return to shine forth (*De an.* 157C–160C).

Gregory supports the doctrine of universal salvation in all kinds of his works, from all periods of his production and all literary genres, e.g., in a "catechetical handbook" such as his *Catechetical Oration*, in a consolatory work such as *On Prematurely Dead Babies* or *On the Dead*, in a dialogue such as that *On the Soul*, and in an exegetical short work such as that on 1 Corinthians 15:28, as well as in other works. As for the *Catechetical Oration*, it is significant that Gregory decided to support the theory of universal salvation, in its most radical form—including the salvation of the devil—in a handbook for *all catechists*, among the *basic* Christian teachings:

> It is proper to the just to distribute things to each one in accord with his or her merits, and it is proper to the wise neither to subvert justice nor to separate the good purpose inspired by love for the human beings from the Judgement according to justice, but to join both these elements together in a fitting way, rendering to justice what it deserves, without parting from the goodness of the purpose inspired by love for the human beings. Let us now consider whether these two elements can be detected in what has happened [in Christ's deception of the devil].[19] The rendering of what one has deserved, through which the deceiver [i.e., the devil] is deceived in turn, shows God's *justice*; the purpose of the fact is a proof of the *goodness* of its agent. For it is typical of justice to render to each one those things whose principles and causes one has initially provided as a foundation . . . and it is typical of wisdom not to fall down from the Good in the modality of rendering similar things for similar things. . . . From the point of view of justice, the deceiver [i.e., the devil] receives in exchange those things whose seeds he has sown by means of his own free choice. . . . Christ, who is just, good, and wise at the

19. Gregory insists that Jesus Christ deceived the devil just as the devil had deceived the human being at the beginning. The devil deceived Adam and Eve by having them deem the eating of the forbidden fruit something good, while this was something evil. Jesus deceived the devil by having him deem Jesus a common human, while he was God. This is also why Gregory can state that, being God, Christ will eventually convert the devil to the Good.

same time, used the intention of deception aiming at the *salvation* of the destroyed. In this way, *he benefited not only the one who had perished* [i.e., the human being], *but also the one who had perpetrated that ruin against us* [i.e., the devil]. For, when death is approached by life, darkness by light, and corruption by incorruptibility, there occurs the *disappearance of the worse element and its passage into non-being*. This is *beneficial to the one who is purified* from those worse elements. . . . [T]he approach of the *divine power, like fire*, to death, corruption, darkness, and whatever product of evilness had grown upon the inventor of evil [i.e., the devil], produced the *disappearance of what is against nature* and therefore benefited the nature [i.e., of the devil] with the purification, even though the above-mentioned separation is painful. Indeed, *not even the adversary himself would doubt that what has happened is just and salvific at the same time*, in consideration of the benefit produced. . . . Once, after the revolving of long ages, *evil has been wiped out from nature*, while now it is completely mixed and confused with it, when there will be *the restoration of those who now lie in evilness into their original state, a unanimous thanksgiving will be elevated by the whole creation*, both those who have been punished in purification and those who did not need even a beginning of purification. *These and such things are allowed by the great Mystery of the inhumanation of God*. For, thanks to all the respects in which Christ has mixed with humanity, having passed through all that is proper to the human nature, birth, nourishment, growth, and having even gone as far as the trial of death, he has accomplished all the tasks I have mentioned, *both liberating the human being from evil* and *healing even the inventor of evilness* [i.e., the devil]. (*Or. cat.* 26)

The restoration and salvation enabled by Christ is so universal, says Gregory, that it will even incorporate Satan, the deceiver, whose purification is "both just and salvific." Sin is presented as the result of deception and ignorance. Gregory in *De hom. op.* 20 says about the forbidden fruit: "it *seems* to be good, but, in that it causes the ruin of those who taste it, it turns out to be the culmination of all evil." Adam and Eve ate it because it seemed to be good, and it seemed so to them because they were deceived by the devil.[20] But Christ saved both humanity and the devil, by liberating them from evil, which is alien to their nature. Manifestly Gregory, like

20. *Or. cat.* GNO III/4, 26,3–5: "the adversary, having mingled evilness to the human faculty of choice, produced an obfuscation and darkening of the capacity for reasoning well." Sin comes from an obfuscation of the intellect.

Origen, has universal salvation depend on Christ—his inhumanation, sacrifice, and resurrection—and on divine grace.

What Christ performs is essentially the radical eviction of evil. That evil must eventually disappear absolutely is repeatedly asserted by Gregory in the dialogue *On the Soul and the Resurrection*, in the commentary on 1 Corinthians 15:28, in the *Catechetical Oration*, and in a number of other works, including the treatise *On the Titles of the Psalms*, GNO V 100:25 and 101:3. Here Gregory proclaims that "evil does not exist from eternity [ἐξ ἀϊδίου/*ex aidiou*], and therefore it will not subsist eternally. For what does not exist always will not exist forever either." This is why there will come a "complete elimination of evil." "Being in evil properly means *non-being*, since evil itself has *no ontological subsistence* of its own; what originates evil, indeed, is rather a lack of Good" (*In inscr. Ps.* GNO III/2, 62–63). That the final eviction of evil depends on Christ is repeated by Gregory in *De trid. sp.* GNO IX 285:7–286:12 and even more clearly in *De v. Mos.* 2:175: "Out of love for us . . . Christ has accepted to be created just as we are, to *bring back to being* what had ended up out of being," that is, "out of the Good, far from God."[21] Restoration to being means that evil, qua non-being as no creature of God the Being, will have to vanish (*In Inscr. Ps.* GNO III/2, 101:18–21 and 155[22]). Evil is also *limited*, while God is unlimited; therefore, to remain in evil indefinitely is impossible—something on which Bardaisan, well known to Gregory, had already insisted. "The mutability of human nature does not remain stable,

21. The same idea of universal salvation as "restoration among the existing beings" performed by Christ appears in *Hom. in Eccl.* 2.305.10–13. It is a restoration to what does not perish or is not lost (*apollymi*); thanks to Christ humanity no longer passes on to non-being, i.e., evil. *Apollymi* (to become lost/destroyed) is the keyword of the Lukan Parables of the Lost Sheep, the Lost Drachma, and the Prodigal Son, all of which are found again (Luke 15); in Matthew 10:6, Jesus sends his disciples to find again the lost sheep of the house of Israel; in Luke 19:10 the Son of Man is said to have come to seek and save the lost. Thus Gregory, like Origen, does not interpret *apollymi* in the sense of a definitive perdition: what was lost and had perished is found by Christ and restored to being. Thus, in *De virg.* 13 Gregory interprets the Parable of the Lost Drachma in reference to the restoration.

22. "The nature of evil is unstable and *passes away*. It did *not come into existence in the beginning with the creation* . . . and it will *not continue to exist eternally* along with the beings that have ontological consistence. For the beings that derive their existence from *the One who is the Being* continue to be eternally [*dia pantos*]; but if anything is *out of the One who is*, its essence is not in Being. This thing, therefore, *will pass away and disappear in due course, in the universal restoration* [*apokatastasis*] *of all into the Good.* Consequently, in that life which lies before us in hope *there will remain no trace of evil.*"

not even in evil. . . . As a consequence, after the extreme limit of evil, there comes again the Good. . . . Even if we should have crossed the boundary of evilness and reached the culmination of the shadow of evilness, we *shall return to living again in the Light"* (*De hom. op.* 21).[23]

Universal restoration and salvation is the end of all (*telos*), as is clear from *De mort.* 60:26–27 Lozza and *On the Titles of the Psalms*, since the whole Psalter is a progression toward the *telos*, which is beatitude (*In Inscr. Ps.* GNO V 25–26). This is why the last psalm in the Psalter describes, according to Gregory, the glorification of God by all creatures, finally liberated from evil and death (GNO V 66:7–9; 16–22; 67:3–6; see also *In Inscr. Ps.* 57 and 87 GNO V 86:4–5; 13–14). All rational creatures, humans and angels, will join in this final thanksgiving that will mark universal salvation (*In Inscr. Ps.* 1:9).[24]

The eighth beatitude describes the eventual restoration and salvation of all sinners, "the restoration into heavens of those who had fallen into captivity," that of sin (*De beat.* PG 44:1292B; cf. *De or. dom.* PG 44:1148C). In *De vit. Mos.* GNO VII/1, 57:8–58:3, Gregory interprets Moses' outstretched hands—which saved not only the Hebrews, but the Egyptians too, i.e. sinners—as a type of the salvific effect of Christ's cross, which saves sinners. The plague of darkness indicates that Christ's cross can dissipate even the "outer darkness" of hell (Matt 8:12). Since "after three days of suffering in darkness, even the Egyptians participated in light," this passage (Exod 10:21) announces "the restoration [*apokatastasis*] that we expect will come to pass in the end, in the kingdom of heavens: *the restoration of those who had been condemned to Gehenna, . . .* the 'outer darkness.' Now, *both this and the 'outer darkness' are dispelled* when Moses outstretched his arms *for the salvation of those who lay in darkness."* The "outer darkness" image of hell appears again in Gregory's exegesis of Psalm 59. Sinners will be pushed into the external darkness, but he does not say that this confinement will be eternal. For sinners will eventually be purified from sin: "Instead of human creatures, *what will be destroyed and reduced to non-being will be sin. . . .* When all that is *evil has disappeared,* 'they will know'—says Scripture—'that God is the Lord of Jacob and of the ends of the earth.' . . . There will be *no evilness left anywhere; . . .* evil, which now reigns over most people, *will have been*

23. Likewise in *De mort.* 19 Lozza Gregory proclaims the infinite permanence of human beings in the Good, that is, God, who is infinite, and not in evil.

24. The same idea is found at the end of the dialogue *On the Soul and the Resurrection* and *In d. nat. Salv.* GNO X/2, 237–38.

wiped out." In his (probably) last work, the *Homilies on the Song of Songs,*
4, Gregory continues to proclaim universal salvation: the end (*telos*) of
all is:

> that love may always increase and develop, *until the One who*
> *"wants all to be saved and to reach the knowledge of truth"* [1 Tim
> 2:4] *has realized his will,* . . . until the good will of the Bride-
> groom *is accomplished.* And this good will is that *all human be-*
> *ings be saved and reach the knowledge of truth.*

God wants universal salvation and God's will shall come true in the end.

The last of these homilies is replete with references to the final
restoration and its conclusion describes the restoration of all, after the
purification of all from evil, which confirms that Gregory continued to
support the doctrine of universal salvation until the end of his life.[25] All
will come to be in communion with God:

> . . . *all will be unified* with one another, in connaturality with the
> only Good, thanks to perfection. . . . The run for this beatitude is
> *common to all the souls of every order;* . . . it is a natural impulse
> *common to all* that of tending to what is blessed and praised
> . . . until *all* look at the same object of their desire and *become*
> *one and the same thing* and *no evilness will any longer remain in*
> *anyone.* Then God will really be 'all *in all*.' For all, thanks to the
> *union* with one another, will be joined in *communion* with the
> Good, in Jesus Christ Our Lord." (GNO VI 466–7)

Universal salvation will pass through the restoration of the image
of God in all humans (e.g., *De virg.* 12 GNO VIII/1, 302), which can be
blurred by sin but never cancelled.[26] For humanity was created precisely
in the image of God, and will be restored to that state (*De hom. op.* PG
44:188CD: "*the restoration of those who have fallen to their original condi-*
tion. Indeed, the grace that we expect is a sort of *re-ascent to the first*
kind of life, given that it lifts up again into paradise the being who had
been chased from it"). In *De perf.* GNO VIII/1, 194–95 Gregory makes it
clear that this restoration of the image of God depends on Christ and on

25. This also disproves claims, such as Salvatore Taranto's (and partially Giulio
Maspero's), that Gregory upheld this doctrine only initially, but then dropped it. See
below.

26. "God's goodness can never be found separate from our nature, . . . but it is
always present in every person; it may become obfuscated by the concerns or pleasures
of life, and then it is unknown and hidden, but it is *immediately found again,* as soon
as we reorient our thought to God" (*De virg.* GNO VIII 300).

divine grace (e.g., *Or. cat.* 16; *De hom. op.* 17; *De mort.* 20–21). And "the grace we expect is the restoration to the original life that brings back to paradise those who had been chased out of it. . . . [O]ur restoration into the original condition makes us *similar to angels*" (*De hom. op.* 17). This angelic life is similar to that of Gregory's sister St. Macrina as described by him in her biography. Likewise, Lazarus "kept himself free from sin for the whole duration of his life, and, when the scenery of this world disappeared for him, because the enemy had been defeated already during his earthly life, he was *immediately found among angels*. . . . This is *the dance and roaming with the angels*, the bosom of the patriarch who receives Lazarus in himself, and the inclusion in the *joyful symphony of the choir*" (*In Inscr. Ps.* 2:6).

Once again, a close lexical analysis is paramount to evaluate Gregory's eschatological thought and avoid falling into mistakes and misunderstandings. He speaks without problem of an αἰωνία/*aiōnia* suffering for those who are purified in the other world (*C. usur.* PG 46:436), because with this he—like the Bible, Origen, and other church fathers—does not mean an "eternal" suffering, but a suffering of a certain duration, albeit long, in the next world.[27] He also speaks of a διαιωνίζουσα/*diaiōnizousa* suffering in fire (*De benef.* GNO IX 100:5): this will extend through the aeon to come, but *not* in the final restoration, as is clear from the dialogue *On the Soul and the Resurrection*. Also, the "incessant lamentation" in *Adv. eos qui cast. aegre fer.* GNO X/2, 328:16 means that those who are suffering purifying punishments are continually lamenting, but it does not specify that this suffering will go on eternally. The "αἰώνιον/*aiōnion* fire" is the purifying fire in the other world, and it is not an "eternal fire." It enables the final universal restoration and salvation by burning away sin from all rational creatures.[28] I have already warned that the same care

27. Due to his misunderstanding of αἰώνιος/*aiōnios* as "eternal," Germanus of Constantinople (eighth century, preserved by Photius *Bibl.* Cod. 233), since he found in Gregory expressions such as "αἰώνιος/*aiōnios* punishment" but also the doctrine of universal restoration and salvation, thought that Gregory's manuscripts had been interpolated by Origenists who added the parts on universal salvation. But another opponent of universal salvation, Severus, simply recognized that Gregory supported the doctrine of universal restoration and did not find a problem in his use of "αἰώνιος/*aiōnios* punishment," clearly because he was aware of the meaning that Gregory attached to it (in Photius *Bibl.* Cod. 232).

28. "The nature of evil, at last, will be reduced to non-being, completely disappearing from being, and God's purest goodness will embrace in itself *every* rational creature, and *none* of the beings that have come to existence thanks to God will fall out of the kingdom of God, when every evilness that has mixed with beings, as a kind of

must be used in the study of the the terminology of "perdition" (*apollymi* and related terms) in Gregory, which for him never indicates a definitive damnation or death.

Gregory focuses his soteriology on Christ's inhumanation and sacrifice. First, Christ assumed human nature entirely, thus sanctifying its whole "lump" (*De perf.* GNO VIII/1, 203–7). Then he performed his sacrifice of sanctification and redemption, as great High Priest and propitiatory victim at the same time (175–76; 186–87).[29] Stretching his arms on the cross, Christ embraced and unified all, and attracted all to himself (*Or. cat.* 32); the cross is a recapitulation of all.[30] Gregory relies on Ephesians 1:10, about Christ's recapitulation of all, and Acts 3:21, on the second coming of Christ, which will bring about "universal restoration [*apokatastasis*]."[31] Christ's risen body transmits the resurrection to all of humanity, his "body."[32] This is especially emphasized in *Or. cat.* 16: "Just as the principle of death, becoming operative in the case of one human being [i.e., Adam], from it passed on to the whole human nature, likewise the principle of the resurrection, from one human being, and through it, extends to the whole of humanity."[33] With his resurrection Christ has all

---

spurious matter, will have been *consumed by the fusion of the purifying fire*, and thus every being that has come to existence thanks to God will *return to being such as it was at the beginning*, when it had *not yet received evil*" (*In Illud*, 13–14 D.).

29. See also *CE* 3 GNO II 140; *De tr. sp.* GNO IX 286–88.

30. *De tr. sp.* GNO IX/1, 298–303; *CE* 3, GNO II, 121–22. The four dimensions of the cross, indicated by its four arms, make it clear that "all heavenly and infernal realities and the extremes of all that exists are governed and kept together by the One who in the figure of the cross has manifested this great and ineffable power" (*CE* GNO II 121–2). Christ's sacrifice took place on the cross and not in another way (*De tr. sp.* GNO IX,1 298–9) because "this figure of the cross, divided into four arms that stretch out from the central crossing, indicates the omnipresent power and providence of the One who was manifested upon it . . . there is *no being that is not found under the providence of divine nature*, most absolutely, above heaven, under the earth, and up to the extreme limits of all that exists . . . You are the one who permeates all, becoming the link of all, uniting in yourself all the extreme limits: You are above and are present below, Your hand rests on one extreme and Your right hand governs on the other." (*ibid.* 300–301). "By means of the figure of the cross the Godhead indicates its power, which keeps all beings in its custody. This is why Scripture says that it was necessary that the Son of the Human Being not simply 'should die,' but 'should be *crucified*,' that, for those who are more insightful, the cross could become the proclaimer of the Logos of God, because in its form it proclaims the omnipotent lordship of the One who has offered himself on it, and who is 'all in all'" (*De tr. sp.* GNO IX 303:2–12).

31. *Contr. c. Apoll.* 55, GNO III/2, 224–26.

32. *In S. Pascha* GNO IX 245–53; *Or. cat.* 37, GNO III/4 93–95.

33. The same motif of the unity of all humans in Christ, by whom the whole "lump"

of humanity raise with him and cancels death, the consequence of Adam's sin (*Contr. c. Apoll.* 21, GNO III/1, 160–61). In *Or. cat.* 32, too, Gregory insists that the resurrection of all humanity is enabled by the resurrection of Christ, who has the same nature as humanity. This universal resurrection in Gregory's view is a restoration of body, soul, and intellect. "The totality of human nature" will thereby achieve perfection and even "deification," according to God's intention (*De hom. op.* 22; *De an.* 129BC; 152A).[34] God's intention will definitely be realized, even if some will need a long purification to this end. Gregory does not admit of cases in which some people will *never* get purified. Indeed, the aim of Christ's resurrection was "to restore the original grace that belongs to human nature, and thus allow us to return to the absolutely eternal [*aïdios*] life" (*Or. Cat.* 16). Only life is eternal in the strict sense of the term (*aïdios*). Gregory never describes as *aïdios* death, punishment, or fire in the world to come.[35] In Christ humans become God, in a "deification" that will be full and eternal (again *aïdios*):

> The human being surpasses its nature by becoming, from mortal, immortal, from corruptible, incorruptible, from ephemeral,

---

of humanity is sanctified and joined to the Father, is also exploited in *De perf.* GNO VIII/1, 197 and 206: "by assuming in body and soul the first fruits of the common nature, he *has sanctified it*, preserving it in himself *pure from every evil and uncontaminated*, to consecrate it in incorruptibility to the Father of incorruptibility, and to attract to himself, through it, *all that belongs to the same species by nature* and is of the same family, in order to readmit those disinherited to the *inheritance of filial adoption*, the enemies of God to *the participation in his divinity*." See also *Hom. in Cant.* GNO VI 467:2–17. Gregory insists on the notion of kinship (*syngeneia*) of all humankind and between humankind and Christ in *De perf.* GNO VIII/1, 197–9. With the *syngeneia* between Christ and all humans Gregory motivates "the common salvation of human nature" (*Contr. c. Apoll.* GNO III/1, 154).

34. "God's *intention is one and only one*: after the realization, through each single human, of the *full totality*—when some will be found to have been already purified from evil during the present life, while others will have been *healed by means of fire* for given periods, and yet others will have not even tasted, in this life, either good or evil to the same extent—to *bestow on all the participation in the goods that are in the Godhead*, of which Scripture says that no eye has ever seen, no ear has heard, nor are they graspable through reasoning. Now, this, I think, is nothing but *coming to be in the Godhead* itself." Cf. *Or. cat.* 32: "Because the totality of the whole human nature forms, so to say, *one living being*, the resurrection of one part of it [i.e. Christ] *extends to the whole*, and, in conformity with the continuity and unity of the (human) nature, *passes on from the part to the whole*."

35. See Ramelli and Konstan, *Terms for Eternity*, 2nd ed., chapter on Gregory; "Time and Eternity," in *The Routledge Handbook of Early Christian Philosophy*, ed. Mark J. Edwards, forthcoming.

absolutely eternal [*aïdios*]; in a word, from human being *becoming God*. For one who has received the honor of becoming Son of God will surely possess the dignity of the Father, and inherits all the goods of the Father. (*De beat.* GNO VII/2, 151).

Only Christ allows the deification of humanity, because in him human nature is joined to the divinity: "by participating in the purest being, human weakness is *transformed into what is better and more powerful*; . . . human smallness is united to divine greatness" (*CE* 3:4). In this union, God's nature is affected by the weaknesses of human nature, but human nature receives divine perfections. "The two (natures) must become one, and the conjunction will consist in a transformation into the better nature" (*De beat.* 7). Not only humanity, but even all of creation will become "one body" in the final restoration (*In Illud* 20 D.); salvation is as universal as possible: "*no being* will remain outside the number of the saved" (21).

Both Gregory and Origen deemed the doctrine of universal salvation not only compatible with, but even grounded in, each rational creature's free will and responsibility. For each will have to adhere to the Good *voluntarily*, if necessary after a process of purification and education. God alone is pure Good and always remains in the Good.[36] Rational creatures are free and must choose the Good freely: "'virtue has no master' and is voluntary: what is forced by compulsion and violence cannot be virtue" (*De hom. op.* 16; cf. 4). This is why in *De an.* 101C–104A otherworldly purification is presented as a restoration of freedom in virtue after enslavement to sin. Human nature is free because it is in the image of God.[37] (This is also why the social institution and practice of slavery is illegitimate in Gregory's view.[38]) Free will is a gift from God, "the noblest and most precious of blessings" (*Or. cat.* 5). And true freedom will be achieved once all have been purified and illuminated, thus reaching "the knowledge of the truth" (1 Tim 2:4). Reaching this knowledge means "the salvation of the whole human nature" (*In Illud* 23:15–18 D.). The original sin was due to deception (*De hom. op.* 20), but in the end the illumination and knowledge reached by every human being will make it impossible to choose evil in the false conviction that it is good. No one will choose

36. *De an.* 120C; *Or. cat.* 7; *Hom. in Eccl.* 8; *Hom. in Cant.* 2.

37. Homily 4 on Ecclesiastes; *De mort.* 15. God could have spared evil to humans by turning them toward the Good, even against their will, but this would have deprived them of their dignity of "image of God." Because the Godhead possesses freedom of will, its image too must possess it. See my *Social Justice*, Chs 4–5.

38. See Ramelli, *Social Justice*.

evil; therefore, evil will vanish. The mind's clouding over, resulting from passions, will have to be purified:

> Therefore, that *free mastery over ourselves could remain* in our nature, but *evil be removed* from it, divine Wisdom excogitated the following plan: allow the human being to do whatever it wanted and taste all the evils it wished, and thus *learn from experience* what it has preferred to the Good, and *then come back*, with its desire, to its original beatitude, *voluntarily, banishing from its own nature all that which is subject to passions* and irrationality, by purifying itself in the present life by means of meditation and philosophy, or by plunging, after death, into the purifying fire. (*De mort.* 15, p. 64 Lozza)[39]

Restoration, with the consequent salvation, must be voluntary; apokatastasis does not cancel each human's free will, but it rather depends on it, as Origen had also thought (*Comm. in Rom.* 4:10). For Gregory, the full manifestation of Christ-Logos will eliminate irrational passions and ignorance and will "persuade every soul who does not believe," so that "all nations and peoples" will submit and be saved (*In S. Pascha* GNO IX 246). Salvation will be the result of freedom because Gregory, like Plato and Origen, is convinced that one is free—as God is, who is pure Good— only when one chooses the Good, being free from passions and deceptions; if one chooses evil one is enslaved to evil,[40] produced by clouding of the intellect, error, and ignorance.

This is why purification must entail instruction in the next life, if one has not achieved it in the present one: "the medication of virtue has

---

39. A very similar rationale underlies the concept of hell as educative put forward by a contemporary theologian, MacDonald, *The Evangelical Universalist*, 136: "If we think of hell as the state in which God allows the painful reality of sin to hit home . . . God simply withdraws his protection that allows people to live under the illusion that sin is not necessarily harmful to a truly human life. The natural consequences of sin take their course, and it becomes harder and harder to fool oneself into believing the seductive lies of sin anymore. In this way hell is educative and points us towards our need for divine mercy."

40. "If, thanks to our solicitude in the present life or purification by fire in the future one, our soul will be able to *liberate itself from those which, among the emotions, are irrational* [i.e., passions], nothing will be left to prevent it from contemplating the Good. For *the Good is such as to attract, so to say, by its own nature, every being* that looks at it. Thus, if the soul can be purified from every sin, it will certainly stay in the Good. Now, the Good is by nature identical to the Divinity, with whom the soul will be united thanks to its pureness, in that it will be found joined to what is proper and familiar to itself" (*De an.* 89CD).

been applied to the soul in the present life, in order to cure its wounds. But if the soul does not heal, a therapy has been predisposed for it in the life that follows the present one."[41] Purifying instruction is a therapy for the soul, as Clement and Origen also put it.[42] The soul's maladies and cancers "on the occasion of the judgment will be cut away and cauterized by that ineffable Wisdom and Power of the One who, as the Gospel says, heals those who are unwell/evil [kakoi]" (Or. cat. GNO III/4, 33:6–9). The judgment is in fact a healing action of God, just as physical death, decreed by God after the fall, is in fact beneficial. Gregory, like Methodius and Origen, deems death a way of saving all humanity. God withdrew immortality and freedom from passions (apatheia) from the human being and threw death onto it, but "not in such a way that it should persist eternally" (13): "the mortality of the nature of irrational animals was put around the human nature, created for immortality, for a providential purpose:" to save it (16–18). Indeed, "the human being is dissolved again into earth, like a clay vase, so that, after being purified from the dirtiness that has been received by it, it could be fashioned anew into its original form through the resurrection. . . . [A]fter the destruction of the matter that had received evil, God through the resurrection will fashion again our 'vase,' recreating it from its elements into its original beauty."[43] Death destroys what is unsuitable for the next, blessed life: "What happens to iron in fire, when the fusion destroys what is useless, will also happen when all that which is superfluous will be destroyed through dissolution in death, and our body will be set right through death." Physical death frees humans from passions and directs their desires to God.[44]

41. Or. cat. 8. Those who have been purified in this life will enjoy beatitude immediately at the resurrection, but the others will have to be purified by fire in the other world over "long aeons" (Or. cat. 8 GNO III/4, 191). Salvation will come "thanks either to solicitude in this life or to purification afterwards" (De an. 89). For "some have already been purified from evil during the present life, while others are healed by fire in the future, for the necessary time."

42. Cauterizations and amputations are drastic but successful therapies (Or. cat. 26). God will heal all humans from sin—the illness and death of the soul—with two medicines: virtue in this life or a "therapy" (therapeia) in the next, which can be more or less drastic depending on the seriousness of a soul's illness. This therapy will be administered at the judgment (Or. cat. 8 GNO III/4, 31–34).

43. GNO III/4, 29:17–22; 31:19–21. Cf. De mort. GNO IX 55–62.

44. "Scoriae will disappear, those things to which the impulses of our desires are now directed: pleasures, richness, love for glory, power, anger, haughtiness, and the like. Thus, our impulse, once liberated and purified from all this, will turn in its activity only to what is worth desiring and loving: it will not altogether extinguish our natural

A Reply to Scholars Who Deny that Gregory Was a Universalist

Gregory's support of the doctrine of universal salvation is manifest throughout his works and acknowledged by many scholars.[45] However, some have demurred. According to Salvatore Taranto—who cannot demonstrate his claim—Gregory rejected universal salvation; he knew this doctrine "in Origen's 'version,' which he probably did not deem acceptable."[46] According to Taranto, Gregory "affirms the existence of an eternal state of damnation" and "over time, Gregory will detach himself more and more from the Alexandrian's eschatological positions."[47] But none of the few texts he adduces claims that sinners' sufferings will be eternal: a basic misunderstanding of the meaning of αἰώνιος/$aiōnios$ is at work here.[48] No passage from the dialogue *On the Soul and the Resur-*

---

impulses toward those objects, but will transform them in view of the immaterial participation in the true goods."

45. E.g., Ludlow, *Universal Salvation*, and *Gregory of Nyssa*, of which see my review in *Review of Biblical Literature* 04/2008 [http://www.bookreviews.org/BookDetail .asp?TitleId=6173]; Tsirpanlis, "The Concept of Universal Salvation in Saint Gregory of Nyssa," 42–43; Daley, *The Hope of the Early Church*, 85–88; Harrison, *Grace and Freedom according to St. Gregory*; Pietras, *L'escatologia nei Padri della Chiesa*, 104; McGuckin, "Eschatological Horizons"; Harmon, "The Work of Jesus Christ and the Universal Apokatastasis," 225–43 and "The Subjection of All Things in Christ," 47–64. See also Harmon, *Every Knee Should Bow*.

46. Taranto, *Gregorio di Nissa*, 615–55. Quotation from 618, my translation.

47. Taranto, *Gregorio di Nissa*, 615–16.

48. E.g., Taranto cites *De an.* 101:17 to claim that Gregory affirmed an eternal punishment in the next world (632). But here that punishment is called αἰώνιον/$aiōnion$, not "eternal," and in the immediate context Macrina argues for universal salvation through purification: evil must disappear in the end; thus, those who have sinned more will be purified longer; the duration will be proportional to one's sins, not infinite (which would exclude proportionality). Gregory then asks: "But what would be the benefit of this good hope for one who considers what great an evil is to suffer pains even just for one year, and if that unbearable pain should endure for a *long* [αἰώνιον/ $aiōnion$] *interval*, which consolation remains from the hope for a remote future to one whose punishment extends to *the measure of a whole aeon* [αἰῶνα/$aiōnia$]?" Macrina replies that this is exactly why it is necessary to keep one's sins as limited as possible, "and *easy to heal* [εὐθεράπευτοι/$eutherapeutoi$]." Taranto renders αἰώνιον/$aiōnion$ as "eternal" instead of "long" (but "eternal interval" is a contradiction in terms), αἰών/ $aiōn$ as "eternity" instead of "aeon" (but "eternity" is incompatible with "measure"), and εὐθεράπευτοι/$eutherapeutoi$ as "curable" instead of "easy to heal," thus implying that there are also sins that are "incurable" even for God, rather than "difficult to heal." But, like Origen, Gregory thought that *nothing* is incurable for the Creator, and indeed Macrina goes on to argue that sins are like debts that must be extinguished by torments, whose duration will be proportional to the sins' amount. This rules out

rection or from other works corroborates the claim that Gregory "affirms the existence of a destiny of eternal suffering for those who do not allow grace to transform them and do not open themselves to virtue."[49] And to claim that "[t]his position is affirmed above all in *On the Soul and the Resurrection*"[50] is simply incorrect. Gregory's texts in fact show that he followed Origen's doctrine of universal salvation up to the minutest exegetical and doctrinal points.[51] Gregory even proves to be more radical than Origen in openly proclaiming universal salvation, including that of the devil (*Or. cat.* 26 *et al.*), while Origen was much more worried about divulging this idea. Taranto cites as an example of Gregory's alleged distancing himself from Origen over time the fact that in Gregory "the persuasion that the final state is a return to the initial one will always remain, although, with the deepening of his reflection, Nyssen will see the former as exceeding the latter" (618). But Origen already deemed the end not *identical* to, but *better* than, the beginning, and insisted even more than Gregory on the difference between being in the image of God (from the beginning) and attaining likeness or assimilation to God through voluntary efforts, perfect assimilation being reserved for the end.

Gregory states, to be sure—as Taranto notes[52]—that only those who will be worthy of blessedness will inherit it (*De beat.* 1209), but this does not contradict universal salvation. For Gregory does not declare that, if one is still unworthy at his death, one will never become worthy of beatitude through postmortem purification and instruction. Likewise, Gregory admits the final judgment (*In sex. Ps.* 188–91 McDonough), but he does not state that the punishments it may decide must be eternal. Taranto quotes several passages concerning the last judgment, such as *Hom. in Eccl.* 4, where Gregory distinguishes two immediate outcomes of it, the kingdom of heavens and Gehenna; *Hom. in Cant.* 15, with the mention of "crying and gnashing of teeth" (Matt 8:12); *In S. Pascha* 680, with the scriptural images of punishment by fire, darkness, and worm, and the distinction between those who will have "a resurrection of life" and those who will have "a resurrection of judgment" (John 5:28–29);

---

unlimited torments and is the reason why Macrina concludes that once all have been liberated from their sins, all will come to be in God (104A).

49. Taranto, *Gregorio di Nissa*, 617.

50. Taranto, *Gregorio di Nissa*, 617.

51. See my "The Trinitarian Theology" and *Apokatastasis*, section on Gregory Nyssen.

52. Taranto, *Gregorio di Nissa*, 618.

and *In S. Pascha* 653, on the judgment and the otherworldly punishment of those who have followed Satan. But in none of these passages, or anywhere else, does Gregory assert the *eternity* of punishments in the world to come. Taranto maintains that Gregory at a certain point realized that "the creature's freedom demands the possibility of an uncertain future, a possibility that does not conflict with the necessity of the complete vanishing of non-being [i.e., evil]."[53] This, however, does not rule out universal salvation. For this "uncertain future"—of beatitude or of purifying suffering, depending on one's deeds—in Gregory's view is located after one's death and *before* the final restoration; at the restoration, once all have been purified, evil will be no longer chosen by anyone and will thus vanish. Indeed, when "the enemy will have definitely disappeared and passed to non-being . . . there will be *no sinner* when there will be no sin left." This ultimate state, and not the intermediate state of painful purification, will endure "eternally" (*In Ps.* 1:9).[54] Taranto misunderstands Gregory's eschatology mainly because of an incorrect rendering of crucial Greek terms such as αἰώνιος/*aiōnios*, and because he deems free will incompatible with universal salvation, overlooking Gregory's ethical intellectualism, according to which all minds, once purified and healed, will *voluntary* adhere to God.

Giulio Maspero, who has contributed much valuable scholarship on Gregory Nyssen's theology, also tends to deny that Gregory supported universal salvation.[55] He does well to emphasize that it is necessary to study Gregory's works diachronically, but as we have seen such a study does not reveal a growing detachment from Origen's eschatology, but a constant presence of the doctrine of universal salvation throughout

53. Ibid., 620.

54. Taranto claims that Gregory regarded the doctrine of universal salvation as a product of reasoning, but not revealed by the Bible. He cites *De mort.* 20–21, where Gregory, after describing the eventual restoration as one and the same light and grace shining in all humans after the destruction of evil and death, observes that "the *logos*" provides an important teaching concerning the salvific destiny of the dead. Here *logos* means, not "rational argument," as Taranto surmises, but, "Scripture" (a meaning that it often bears in Gregory): for Gregory has just adduced 1 Corinthians 15:26, 1 Thessalonians 4:13, and John 17: these provide the teaching to which Gregory refers. That universal salvation is based on the Bible for Gregory is indeed manifest from his commentary on 1 Corinthians 15:28, the main passage in which he grounds this doctrine together with John 17.

55. *La Trinità e l'uomo*, 176ff.; with the observations by Ramelli, *Gregorio di Nissa sull'anima*, first Integrative Essay and nn. 76–80; Maspero, *Trinity and Man*, 76–94, reviewed by Ilaria Ramelli in *RBL* 2009.

Gregory's literary career, from start to finish. Maspero says that this doctrine is reflected solely in *De vit. Mos.* 2:82 and *Or. cat.* GNO III/4, 91,[56] but in fact it also appears in the dialogue *On the Soul and the Resurrection*, the commentary on 1 Corinthians 15:28, the *Catechetical Oration*, the works *On the Infants* and *On the Dead*, the *Life of Moses*, and so on until the late Homilies on the Song of Songs, where Gregory still insists that God's will is for universal salvation and that this will shall be fulfilled. The very salvation of the devil is maintained not only in the dialogue *On the Soul*, as Maspero states,[57] but at least also in *Or. cat.* 26, as I showed earlier. Another flaw of Maspero's, as well as others', argument lies in terminological misunderstandings. In *De benef.* GNO IX 100:5 Gregory describes suffering in the other world as διαιωνίζουσα/*diaiōnizousa*, which means "lasting for the whole aeon to come," and not "eternally," which would mean beyond all aeons (for Gregory, in the absolute eternity of *apokatastasis*). This is confirmed by *De an.* 101, where otherworldly punishment is described in the same way, but where it is also presented as limited and commensurate with one's sins, and universal salvation is endorsed.[58] In *Ad eos qui cast.* GNO X/2 328:16, "ἄληκτον/*alēkton* lament" (3 Mac 4:2) means a lamentation that is unbroken *while it lasts*, not a lamentation that lasts eternally. I already pointed out that *apollymi*—in *De beat.* GNO VII/2 135–36, another passage adduced by Maspero against universal salvation in Gregory, and elsewhere—does not imply an eternal perdition. The "worm that does not die" and the "unquenchable fire" are Gospel expressions—also used without any qualms by Origen and other supporters of universal salvation—which do not mean eternal punishment, but a fire and a worm unlike those of this world, which die and can be extinguished. By contrast, the otherworldly fire and worm cannot be stopped from their work until it is completed.

A deeper misunderstanding concerns the interpretation of universal restoration (*apokatastasis*) in Gregory as "only a synonym of resurrection" that does not imply universal salvation.[59] But Gregory's description of resurrection as the restoration of human nature to its original state does not entail the reduction of the restoration to the resurrection of the body, but rather a much richer and holistic notion of resurrection: not just the rising of the body, but the restoration of all humanity in body,

---

56. *La Trinità*, 183–84 = *Trinity and Man*, 81–82.

57. *Trinity and Man*, 91.

58. See my "Αἰώνιος and αἰών"; "time and Eternity."

59. *Trinity and Man*, 91–2.

soul, and intellect to its original condition of freedom from evil (*De an.* 156C; *In Eccl.* GNO V 296:16–18). On the other hand, Maspero stresses the value of personal freedom in Gregory. As we have seen, this is indeed true of Gregory, and of Origen as well, but in their view this is not an impediment to universal salvation. For the final submission of all rational creatures to Christ and God will be *voluntary* and will come after the necessary purification and illumination. There will definitely be a reward or punishment for each one's deeds, but punishment, being purifying, will not last forever. After the resurrection one can be condemned (*De perf.* GNO VIII/1 204:9–205:14), because sinners must first be purified from what is unworthy of God, but let me repeat, Gregory does *not* state, here or elsewhere, that this condemnation will be eternal. Gregory pastorally warns that otherworldly punishments may last long and be harsh (*De beat.* 5, etc.), but he never ever avers that they will be eternal. He expressly states that they will finish for all; after which, "no being will remain outside the number of the saved" (*In Illud* 21 D.).[60] This is one of Gregory's clearest assertions of universal salvation, along with *In Illud* 14: "No creature of God will fall out of the kingdom of God." Indeed, if Satan will convert and be saved (*Or. Cat.* 26), it is difficult to think that some humans will not.

GREGORY NAZIANZEN

Gregory of Nazianzus († 390ca), who was educated together with Basil and was friends with him and his brother Gregory of Nyssa, was also the teacher and mentor of Evagrius, whom we shall consider soon. All these men, along with Basil's and Nyssen's sister Macrina, were supporters of apokatastasis (Nyssen and Evagrius being the strongest, with Origen).

---

60. Maspero adduces *In inscr. Ps.* GNO V 174:22–175:25, mentioned above, concerning people who will be chased out of the holy city and punished with the deprivation of ("hunger for") goods. This deprivation, however, is not said to be eternal. Indeed, first Gregory comments on Psalm 59:13–14, speaking of the very end, when evil is destroyed. Then he comments on v. 15, which repeats v. 7: "then the psalm takes up again the same discourse concerning those who return in the evening and are hungry." This is why Gregory here goes back from the ultimate end (universal salvation) to punishment for sinners "after the present life" and before the end of aeons. I already pointed out that Gregory in this whole passage states that all sinners will be purified from evil, which therefore will vanish. Maspero thinks that for Gregory those who remained fixed in evil in this life will enter eternity statically, but this overlooks God's attraction on all souls, which has the collateral effect of pains for those who are immersed in evil, but God's aim is to extract them from evil, and this aim will be fulfilled.

Gregory Nazianzen defended Origen, declaring the most controversial aspects of his thought, including that of the eternal destiny of rational creatures, to be still open to rational research and not dogmatically defined (*C. Eun. Or. Prod.* 27:10). Not accidentally, this passage, analysed in my *Apokatastasis* and further in the Origen monograph, inspired Origenistic monks. Indeed, the so-called condemnation of Origen came about when in Christianity the commitment to research faded away in favor of dogmatization and institutionalization.

The sixth-century theologian Stephan Gobar attests that Nazianzen admired Origen and called him "lover of the Good."[61] He defined Origen "the pumice stone of all of us" (*Suidas*, s.v. *Origen*), i.e. a thinker who refines other people's thought. Nazianzen, together with Basil, is probably the author of the *Philocalia*, an anthology of Origen's works from which hints of the doctrine of restoration are not absent. Gregory highly praises Origen in *Or.* II 107, saying that he took from him his interpretation of Genesis 1:3 and calling him a "wise man, capable of grasping the depth of a prophet."

Many have suggested that Gregory's criticism of the preexistence of souls in *Or.* 2:48–9 and 4:114–19 is directed against Origen. (The same claim is also made of Gregory Nyssen in his repudiation of the preexistence of souls.) However, this is unlikely to be the case. Origen is not even mentioned in this context and, contrary to popular belief, he did not support such a doctrine.[62]

Like Gregory Nyssen and Methodius, Nazianzen too thinks that physical death is providential because it cuts short sins, thereby also limiting punishment in the other world. Humanity "even in this has a benefit: death, and the fact that its sin is cut away, that *evil may not be immortal. Thus, punishment turns out to be an act of love for humanity. For I am convinced that this is how God punishes.*"[63] Nazianzen, like Clement, Origen, and Nyssen, believes that all punishments inflicted by God are remedial and beneficial to the punished.[64]

---

61. In Photius *Bibl.* cod. 232, p. 291b.

62. See my *Preexistence of Souls?*; further in "Origen" and "Gregory of Nyssa," both in *A History of Mind and Body in Late Antiquity*, ed. Anna Marmodoro.

63. *In S. Pascha*, Or. 45; PG 36:633:14–17 = *In Theoph.* Or. 38; PG 36:324:49–53.

64. In the same *Or.* 38 (PG 36:324:45–47) Gregory embraces the same interpretation of the Genesis "skin tunics" as Origen's and Gregory Nyssen's: not the body per se, which the human being possessed already before the fall, but the *mortality* of the body and its being *liable to passions*.

Gregory's oration *In Sancta Lumina* (*Or. 39 On the Holy Lights*), which deals with the baptism of Christ and not accidentally begins with a reminiscence of Origen,[65] in Chapter 15 puts forward the notion of an extreme baptism that purifies: "What is fire? *The consummation of what has no value* and the fervor of the Spirit. What is the axe? The *cutting away of what is incurable in the soul,* even after death. What is the sword? It is *the Logos' cutting action, which divides the Good from evil.*" Postmortem punishments are not retributive, but *healing.* The "extreme baptism" in fire removes evil from the soul: in the other world, sinners "will be *baptized in fire, in an extreme baptism,* more painful and longer, which devours matter as chaff *and consumes the lightness of every sin*" (PG 36: 356BC). This suffering will be long, but not eternal; it purifies the soul and once achieved this task it will come to an end. Gregory is reminiscent of 1 Corinthians 3:14–15, with the mention of chaff and straw and the declaration that people will be saved either at once or *through fire.* Neither Paul nor Gregory contemplate the case of people who will *not* be saved.

Jesus "did not come for the just, but for sinners, for their conversion. . . . And Paul, in turn, gave preeminence to love because he looked at justification, rectification, and correction. . . . *God rejoices in nothing else but the correction and salvation of a human being.* This is *the end to which every discourse and mystery tends*: that you may become the lights of the world, *vivifying power for the other humans.*" In *Or.* 41:12 Gregory foresees the overcoming of the "great chasm" between the damned and the blessed. This can take place thanks to Christ, the same who has overcome the chasm between the Creator and the creatures with his inhumanation.

What is more, Gregory appropriates the doctrine of his friend Gregory of Nyssa in *Or.* 40:36 PG 35:409D3–5, supporting it as the only one that—as Origen maintained—is "worthy of God":

> I know of a *purifying fire,* which Christ came to kindle on earth. Christ is called "fire" himself with metaphorical and mystical words. This fire *consumes matter and the evil disposition,* and Christ wants that it is kindled as soon as possible. For he ardently wants the Good to be made immediately, since *even the inflamed coals he gives us in order to help us.* I also know a fire that is *not only purifying,* but *also punishing*: it is the fire of Sodom, which pours down like rain on all sinners, mingled with divine storm and sulphur; it is that which is prepared for the devil and his angels; it is that which goes forward before the face

of the Lord and burns his enemies all around, and the one that
is even more fearful than these are: the one that is mentioned
along with the worm that does not die, a fire that, for sinners,
cannot be quenched, but endures during the future aeon. For
all these aspects pertain to the destructive power, unless it is
not dear to someone to think, even in this case, that *this fire is
applied for the love of human beings*, and in a way that is *worthy
of the One who punishes.*

The other way—i.e., the idea of a fire that is only retributive and not
also purifying—is considered unworthy of God. Even the example of the
inflamed coals, from the Old Testament, comes from Origen. Gregory
often insists on the therapeutic aim of God's punishments (*Or.* 16:6):
"*educating us* both with strokes and with threats, *using his wrath to open
up a way for us, out of a superabundance of goodness*, God begins with
the lighter remedies, to avoid needing the most radical, but, if necessary,
has recourse even to the most drastic, in order to *educate*." Even the most
drastic punishments are a form of "education" (*paideusis*). In *Or.* 3:7, PG
35:524B, Gregory refers to 1 Corinthians 3:12–15, in which the divine
fire is described as purifying: it will consume in everyone whatever is
unworthy of eternal life.[66] In *Carm.* 2:1:1:545ff., PG 37:1010, Gregory depicts again the otherworldly fire as "purifying" in that it will devour evil.
Of course Gregory speaks, with the Gospel, of "external darkness," but he
does not say that it will be eternal. Gregory uses αἰώνιος/*aiōnios* ("otherworldly") in reference to these, and not ἀΐδιος/*aïdios* ("eternal"), which
he reserves for life and beatitude.[67] Gregory too, like Origen, interprets
the otherworldly suffering of sinners in a spiritual way, as the torment of
being far from God and remorse (*Or.* 16:8–9). Again, he does not say that
this torment is eternal. The final judgment will consist in the awareness of
one's sins and the "worm that does not die" is continuous remorse (*Carm.*
1:2:15:100 = PG 37:773).

One of the most important testimonies comes from the fourth theological oration *On the Son* (30:6). Like Gregory of Nyssa, Nazianzen first
observes that the Son appropriated humanity with all its sins "in order
to *consume in himself the worst part*, as fire consumes wax." Then he proclaims that the darkness of evil will be completely dispelled and expressly
speaks of apokatastasis as the union of all rational creatures to God:

66. Cf. *Carm.* I 2,15,99 = PG 37,773.

67. See Ramelli–Konstan, *Terms for Eternity*, 185–89 on Gregory Nazianzen.

"God will be *all in all*" [1 Cor 15:28] *in the time of the restoration* [*apokatastasis*], when we will be no longer many, like now, with various movements of the will and passions, and it will not be the case that we carry in ourselves only little or nothing of God, but we shall be *all entirely conformed to God*, able to receive God wholly, and *God alone*. This is the perfection *we aspire to*, and it is especially Paul himself who guarantees this.

The final unity of all in the restoration is not a confusion of substances, as if we all merge into one undifferentiated entity, but a uniformity of *wills*, as it is in Origen and in Gregory of Nyssa. Even the vocabulary, "movement (of wills)," is Origenian. All wills shall be oriented toward God, the Good.

Gregory is also clear that restoration depends on Christ and is universal: "Christ's suffering, through which *all of us—not just some and not the others—have been restored*" (*Or.* 33:9, PG 36:225B). The Greek verb is the correspondent of *apokatastasis*. Christ "came in human form in order to *restore humanity*, . . . collected the mortals and *formed them into unity and placed them into the arms of the great Divinity*, after *washing away every stain* with the blood of the Lamb, and, as the head of mortal humanity, lifted it up on the path to heaven."[68] Likewise Gregory insists on the universal purification performed by Christ, who "offered his blood to God and *purified the whole cosmos*; he underwent the torment of the cross and *nailed sins onto it*."[69]

Since apokatastasis is the work of Christ, for Gregory, it is not surprising that he uses the very term ἀποκατάστασις/*apokatastasis* in reference to Christ's ascension in *Or.* 41:11: in the ascension Gregory saw all humanity ascend with and in Christ. And in *Or.* 39.16 Nazianzen remarks that Christ's baptism symbolized his ascension, when he "carries up the *whole world* with him, and sees the heavens open which Adam had closed to himself and to his posterity." Nazianzen overtly speaks of universal restoration again in *Or.* 44.5. He uses numbers, like Origen and Maximus the Confessor, to describe the present life followed by the ultimate end. The seven represents this life, the eight the life to come, which will depend "on our good works in this life and *universal restoration* [ἀποκατάστασις πάντων/*apokatastasis pantōn*] in the next."

In *Carm.* 1.5.548 Gregory announces that humans will experience either fire or illuminating light in the afterlife, "but whether *all will later*

68. *Carm.* 1:2:1:161–67, PG 37:535.
69. *Carm. dogm.* 2:76–77.

partake of God, let it be discussed elsewhere." He does not avoid putting forward Origen's and Gregory Nyssen's view, but simply defers consideration of it. In *Or.* 36 Gregory meditates on the salvific value of Christ's inhumanation: he became a human being "so as to work as leaven for the entire lump of humanity: having taken up that which was condemned, he liberates *all* from condemnation." In *Carm.* 35.9 Gregory avers that Christ by his sacrifice "loosed *all* those who groaned under the chains of Tartarus [hell]." In *Or.* 42 Christ's descent to hell is said to have liberated, and have brought salvation to, *all* visible and invisible creatures. The theme of the harrowing of hell is enhanced by the poem entitled *Chistus patiens*, which is traditionally attributed to Gregory Nazianzen, and which may, or may not, be by him. Verses 1934–35 of the poem proclaim the belief that Christ "will liberate from Hades as many mortals as it has imprisoned." That this Hades is to be understood as hell is suggested by its being called by Nazianzen "Tartarus" (i.e., the place of torment in the other world) in the passage I just quoted from *Carm.* 35.9.

Pulling together the threads of the above discussion, we can say that Gregory Nazianzen seems to interpret Christ's inhumanation, death, descent to Hades, resurrection, and ascension, as well as otherworldly divine punishments and the final consummation, in universalist ways. While he does not proclaim the universality of salvation with the same clarity as Origen of Gregory of Nyssa, he certainly appears to have a penchant for it.

EVAGRIUS PONTICUS

Evagrius of Pontus († 399)[70] served as a lector under Basil in Neocaesarea and then a deacon under Gregory of Nazianzus in Constantinople (380 AD), rising to the level of archdeacon. He then moved to Jerusalem, where he became a monk, before finally moving to Egypt, where he lived out a monastic life. Evagrius was profoundly influenced by Origen, Neoplatonism, and the Cappadocians, of whom he was a disciple. He wrote to Rufinus, Gregory Nazianzen, Melania the Elder, and John of Jerusalem, all admirers of Origen. He supported a universal restoration of all rational creatures to their initial unity with God, after a sequence of aeons. This is especially clear in his *Chapters on Knowledge* (*Kephalaia Gnostica*: KG) and *Letter to Melania* (both lost in Greek, not accidentally, but thankfully preserved in Syriac). Evagrius too, like Origen and Gregory Nyssen, sees

---

70. Casiday, *Evagrius*; Sinkewicz, *The Greek Ascetic Corpus*; Ramelli, *Evagrius'* *Kephalaia Gnostika* and "Evagrius' and Gregory's Relations."

this restoration as the result of the work of Christ, who intercedes "for the whole rational nature, and separates some from evilness, and others from ignorance" (*KG* 5:46). The soul fell down from the superior rank of intellect, but in the restoration it will return to being an intellect (*KG* 2:29): a unified intellect, subsuming body and soul into itself; the true being of rational creatures is that which they were in the beginning and which they will recover in the end (*Sent.* 58). All will be restored to unity: "*all* will become coheirs of Christ, *all* will know the holy Unity" (*KG* 3:72). For Evagrius, just as for Origen, rational creatures share the same nature, but they became divided into angels, humans, and demons according to their free choices (not even demons are evil by nature, but only by misuse of the will),[71] but all of them will return to unity in the eventual restoration, when evil and ignorance will be wiped out (*KG* 4:29: "when *evil will be eliminated, ignorance will no longer exist among rational creatures*, because ignorance is the shadow of evil").[72]

For it is an extremely strong tenet of Evagrius' thought—as of Origen's and Gregory Nyssen's, but possibly still more hammered home in Evagrius—that evil will eventually disappear, according to its ontological non-consistency, just as it did not exist at the beginning, for it is not a creature of God. The ontological and even chronological priority belongs to the Good, i.e., God:

> If death comes after life, and illness after health, clearly vice, too, is secondary vis-à-vis virtue; for vice is the death and illness of the soul, but *virtue is anterior to it.* (KG 1:41)

> *Evil is not a substance that actually exists*: it is the absence of Good, just as darkness is a lack of light. . . . *There was a time when evil did not exist, and there will come a time when evil will no longer exist.* But *there never has been a time when the Good did not exist, and there will be no time when it will no longer exist.* (*Ep. ad Anat.* 23 and 65)[73]

Just as evil is secondary vis-à-vis the Good, so too is divine judgment—which deals with the effects of the choice of evil instead of the Good—secondary vis-à-vis providence (*KG* 5:23–24). Providence leads every creature to salvation by destroying sin (*KG* 1:28), but at the same time respecting all rational creatures' free will (*KG* 6:43). Providence

---

71. *KG* 4:59; 3:34; 1:63.

72. Suffering in hell will consist in ignorance, while beatitude consists in knowledge (*Gnostikos* 36; *KG* 6:8).

73. Cf. *KG* 1:40; *Praktikos* 1:65.

"pushes rational creatures *from evilness and ignorance to virtue and sci-ence* . . . and never abandons them . . . until they reach the Holy Trinity" (*KG* 6:59; 6:75). Providence will lead rational creatures through purifica-tion, which will be painful, but limited and commensurate to one's sins (*KG* 4:34). The *telos* is when all intelligences are in the Unity, where "inef-fable peace" obtains, and where the intelligences—with a reminiscence of Gregory of Nyssa—are in eternal tension, because they can never get sated of God.[74]

It is no surprise that Evagrius, like Origen and Gregory of Nyssa, interprets 1 Corinthians 15:24–28 as a proof of the eventual universal submission to Christ and God, which is salvific and means perfection and knowledge:

> Christ's feet are ascesis[75] and contemplation, and if he will put all his enemies under his feet, then *all will know ascesis and con-templation*. If all nations will come and worship the Lord, then clearly also those who wage war will, and if this is the case, *the whole nature of rational creatures will submit to the Name of the Lord*. When Christ will no longer be impressed in various aeons and in names of every kind, then he himself will be *submitted to God the Father*, and will delight in the knowledge of God alone, which is not divided over the aeons and the spiritual growing of rational creatures. (*KG* 6:15; 6:27; 6:33)

Evagrius' notion of the aeons is similar to that of Origen: the series of aeons, in which rational creatures are purified and grow, is limited; it began with the creation and will end with the eternal apokatastasis.[76] Every aeon begins after the end of the preceding one and the relevant judgment, in which the place that rational creatures will occupy in the new aeon is determined on the basis of each one's merits or demerits (*KG* 3:38; 3:47). During the aeons, angels and divine providence help rational creatures to liberate themselves from passions and instruct them,[77] a pro-cess that also entails suffering (*KG* 3:18). For Evagrius, just as for Origen and Gregory of Nyssa, what will be burnt like chaff (Matt 3:12) will be sins, not sinners (*KG* 2:26).

Resurrection will not be merely a restoration of the body, which will transition from mortality to immortality, but also one of the soul, which

74. Ibid. 4:51; 1: 7; 1:65.

75. Ascesis is the practice of spiritual discipline.

76. *KG* 5:89; see also 4:38.

77. *KG* 6:35; cf. 3:5; 6:76.

will become free from passions, and of the intellect, which will acquire true knowledge.[78] Thus, resurrection is the restoration of the *whole* human being, just as it is for Gregory Nyssen. All rational creatures have been created by the Godhead for itself (*KG* 4:1) and Christ helps them to turn to God:

> All nations have been called by our Savior to eternal life.[79] Who will be able to express God's grace? Who will observe the criteria of providence, and how Christ leads the rational nature through the various aeons toward the union of the Holy Unity?[80]

In his *Letter to Melania* Evagrius expounds his ideas on the history of salvation. In the beginning, the Godhead, the Unity, created pure intellects from itself ("first creation"), but out of neglectfulness almost all of these fell from "essential knowledge" and became souls,[81] which God endowed with bodies suited to their state ("second creation"). This was the result of the "first judgment" performed by Christ, who divided rational creatures into angels, humans, and demons in accord with the depth of their fall. The second creation is not a punishment, but God's providential way to allow rational creatures to return to their intellectual state and attain salvation in contemplation. This process is enabled by Christ. The Logos is the only intellectual being that did not decay from "the knowledge of the Unity" (*KG* 1:77), and voluntarily adopted the body of the fallen rational creatures to help them reach essential knowledge. All will do so, including demons, because this is the end of all rational creatures (see also *KG* 5:61). Evagrius thought of God's creation as divided into eight days, which reflects the seven days of God's creation of the world (Gen 1) plus the eighth day of eschatological rest "beyond" creation, bringing creation to its final goal. On the seventh day Christ will reign over all rational creatures, and on the eighth all will return to Unity. When God, who is One, is in all, plurality as a mark of discord will disappear.[82] The material creation was made by the Godhead "through its Power and Wisdom, i.e., the Son and the Spirit, that human beings might know, and get close to, God's love for them. . . . The whole ministry of the

78. *KG* 5:19; 5:22; 5:25; 2:15.

79. *KG* 4:26; cf. 1:90; 2:59.

80. *KG* 4:89; cf. 1:72–73. Indeed, the miracles worked by Christ are the symbol of the purification of rational creatures in the world to come (*KG* 3:9).

81. See also *KG* 4:28.

82. Cf. *Letter on Faith* 7; *KG* 1:7–8; 4:19; 4:81.

Son and the Spirit takes place through creation, *for the love of those who are far from God*" (Ch. 2). Only the rational creatures who are already very close to God are helped directly by the Logos and the Spirit (Chs. 3–4). The initial fall—Evagrius claims, as Gregory of Nyssa does—transformed the human being from the "image of God" to an image of animals liable to passions (Ch. 9). But there will come the restoration in the end:

> And there will be a time when the body, the soul, and the intellect will cease to be separate, with their names and plurality, because the body and the soul will be elevated to the rank of intellect. This conclusion can be drawn from the words, "that they may be one in us, as You and I are One."[83] And thus there will come a time when *the Father, the Son, and the Spirit, and their rational creation, which makes up their body, will cease to be separate,* with their names and plurality. This conclusion can be drawn from the words, "God will be *all in all*" [1 Cor 15:28]. (*Ep. ad Mel.* 5)

In Chapter 6 Evagrius, after noting that the intellect, because of the wrong use of its free will, fell to the state of soul and further to that of body, proclaims that the body, the soul, and the intellect, "thanks to a transformation of their wills, will become one." And all intellects in turn will become one with God:

> *They will no longer be many, but one, in God's infinite and inseparable Unity,* in that they are *united and joined to God.* . . . Before sin operated a separation between the intellects and God, like the earth that separated the sea and the rivers, they were *one with God,* without distinction, but when their sin was manifested, they were separated from God. . . . The rivers were eternally in the sea, just as rational creatures were eternally in God. In fact, even though they were entirely united to the Godhead in its wisdom and creative power, their creation proper had a beginning; however, one should not think that it will have an end, because they are united with God, who has no beginning and no end.

83. John 17:22.

7

Apokatastasis in Antioch

DIODORE OF TARSUS AND
THEODORE OF MOPSUESTIA

The doctrine of universal restoration and salvation was also upheld at Antioch in the second half of the fourth century by Diodore of Tarsus († 390ca), founder of the catechetical school near Antioch, and in the early fifth century by his disciple Theodore of Mopsuestia († 428). The Syriac mystic St. Isaac of Nineveh, who also supported apokatastasis (see below), attests that both Diodore and Theodore professed this doctrine and taught that the duration of otherworldly punishments will be commensurate to the gravity of sins and not infinite (*Second Part*, 39:8–11). Isaac goes on to report Diodore's idea that otherworldly suffering will last for a temporary period, whereas blessedness will last for all eternity, and "not even the immense evilness of demons can overcome the measure of God's goodness" (39:11–3). He quotes from Diodore's *On Providence*, where Diodore very probably made the connection between divine providence and apokatastasis as its main goal.

Another witness here is Solomon of Basra, a thirteen-century supporter of the doctrine of universal restoration and salvation, who in the last chapter of his *Book of the Bee* agrees with Origen's view that the doctrine of universal salvation must be preached only to those who are spiritually advanced. He then exemplifies the theory of universal restoration by excerpts from Isaac of Nineveh, Theodore of Mopsuestia, and from Diodore of Tarsus' book on the salvific economy known as *On Providence*:

139

Saint Theodore the Exegete says: "Those who have here chosen fair things will receive in the world to come the pleasure
of good things with praises; but the wicked who have turned
aside to evil things all their life, when they have *become ordered
in their minds by penalties* and the *fear* that springs from them,
and *choose good things*, and *learn how much they have sinned*
by having persevered in evil things and not in good things, and
by means of these things receive the knowledge of the highest
doctrine of the fear of God, and become instructed to lay hold of
it with a good will, will be deemed *worthy of the happiness of the
Divine liberality*. For he [i.e., Jesus] would never have said, '*Until*
you pay the uttermost farthing' [Matt 5:26], unless it had been
possible for us to *be freed from our sins through having atoned
for them by paying the penalty*; neither would he have said, 'he
shall be beaten with *many* stripes,' or 'he shall be beaten with
few stripes' [Luke 12:47], unless it were that the penalties, being
meted out according to the sins, should *finally come to an end*."
These things the Exegete has handed down in his books clearly
and distinctly.

So also the blessed Diodore, who says in the *Book of the Salvific Economy*: "A lasting reward, which is worthy of the justice
of the Giver, is laid up for the good, in return for their labors;
and *torment for sinners, but not everlasting*, that the immortality
which is prepared for them may not be worthless. They must
however be *tormented for a limited time, as they deserve, in proportion to the measure of their iniquity* and wickedness, according to the amount of the wickedness of their deeds. This they
will have to bear, that they *suffer for a limited time*; but immortal
and *unending happiness* is prepared for them. If it be then that
the rewards of good deeds are as great (in proportion to them)
as the times of the immortality which are prepared for them are
longer than the times of the limited contests which take place
in this world, the torments for many and great sins must be
very much *less than the greatness of mercy*. So then it is not for
the good only that the *grace of the resurrection* from the dead is
intended, but also for the wicked; for the grace of God greatly
honors the good, but *chastises the wicked sparingly*."

Again he says: "God pours out the wages of reward beyond
the measure of the labors (wrought), and in the abundance of
his goodness he lessens and *diminishes the penalty* of those who
are to be tormented, and in his mercy he shortens and *reduces
the length* of the time. But even so, he does not punish the whole
time according to (the length of) the time of folly, seeing that *he
requites them far less than they deserve, just as he does the good*

beyond the measure and period (of their deserts); for the reward is everlasting. It has not been revealed whether the goodness of God wishes to punish without ceasing the blameworthy who have been found guilty of evil deeds (or not), as we have already said before. . . . But *if punishment is to be weighed out according to sin, not even so would punishment be endless.* For as regards that which is said in the Gospel, 'These shall go away into αἰώνιος/ *aiōnios* punishment, but the righteous into αἰώνιος/*aiōnios* life' [Matt 25:46], this word αἰώνιος/*aiōnios* [Syr. *l-'olam*] is *not definite*: for if it be not so, how did Peter say to our Lord, 'You will not wash my feet *l-'olam*' [John 13:8] and yet he washed him? And of Babylon he said, 'No man will dwell therein *l-'olam*' [Isa 13:20], and behold many generations dwell therein. In the *Book of Memorials* he says: 'I hold what the most celebrated of the holy fathers say, that he cuts off a little from much. The penalty of Gehenna is a human's mind; for the punishment there is of two kinds, that of the body and that of the mind. That of the body is perhaps *in proportion to the degree of sin*, and he lessens and diminishes its duration; but that of the mind is *l-'olam*, and the judgement is *l-'olam*.' But in the New Testament *l-'olam* [αἰώνιος/*aiōnios*] is *not without end.*"[1]

Diodore conveys the notion that the eventual restoration will reveal that the resurrection is a grace for all humans, including the wicked. For, if the latter were resurrected only to be punished, the resurrection would no longer be a good, because for them it would be better not to rise again. This is the same idea as expressed in a fragment of Theodore, Diodore's disciple, which I shall discuss in a moment. The second passage from Diodore shows his awareness of the meaning that αἰών/*aiōn* and αἰώνιος/*aiōnios* (Syriac *'olam* and *l-'olam*) have in the Bible: he is very clear that they do *not* indicate eternity. This insight emerges not only in the fragment from Solomon, but also in some of Diodore's preserved Greek works.[2]

Shortly after Isaac, in the eighth century, John of Dara confirms that "Diodore of Tarsus, in the book that he wrote on the salvific economy, and Theodore, a disciple of his and the teacher of Nestorius, in many passages claim that *damnation will come to an end*" (*On the Resurrection of Human Bodies* 4:21). Diodore's lost work on the salvific economy is

1. I quote, with small changes, the translation of *The Book of the Bee* by E. A. Wallis Budge, Oxford: Clarendon, 1886, 139–41.

2. Esp. his commentary on Psalm 48:8.

the same as quoted by Solomon of Basra. It may well have disappeared precisely on account of the doctrine of universal salvation it defended, which came to be regarded by the church with great suspicion.

Theodore Bar Konai, while discussing the question whether those who are in Gehenna can be made worthy of the kingdom, says:

> Some among the wise and learned, such as Saint Diodore and the blessed Exegete [Theodore of Mopsuestia], have alluded to this *in an enigmatic way*, by adducing that God is not only just, but also *merciful*, and that *it becomes the One* who judges with justice to have sinners suffer in a measure that is *proportional to their sins* and then make them *worthy of blessedness*.[3]

This fragment shows that one of the arguments that Diodore and Theodore used in support of universal salvation is the theological argument already used by Origen and his followers: the universalist eschatological outcome is the only one that *becomes God*. The allusive way in which Diodore and Theodore spoke of universal salvation, together with the loss of most of the works in which they did so, explain the reason why their doctrine of universal salvation is generally not realized, or sometimes is questioned, by scholars.

Further confirmation of the testimonies I have adduced so far can be found in a Syriac fragment from Diodore, cited by 'Abdisho: "Punishment . . . for the unjust, yet *not eternal*, . . . but such as they will be tormented *for a given limited time, commensurate with their sins*."[4] Indeed, Diodore, like Clement, Origen, and Gregory Nyssen, regarded the punishments established by God as therapies:

> As an expert surgeon, God applies to us, or allows others to apply to us, heavy and difficult conditions, as though they were a *cauterization or a surgical incision*. . . . God does everything *for the sake of our good*. (Commentary on Psalm 4)

Diodore insists on the same concept in his commentary on Psalm 39; all sufferings inflicted by God are healing and educative: "I realize that all of your scourging is aimed at *correcting and improving* a person . . . in order to *improve their soul*. . . . I must accept a punishment that is *commensurate with the limits of my life*." Moreover, Diodore understands

---

3. *Liber Scholiorum*, 2:63.

4. Assemani, *Bibliotheca Orientalis*, 3:1:324.

the universal submission to Christ as a joyous submission (*Comm. in Ps.* 2). In this way, it will coincide with universal salvation.[5]

In his preface to his own commentary on the Psalms, Diodore heavily criticizes those who believe in the Creator but not in divine providence.[6] He cannot have had Epicureans in mind, since they believed in gods that were not the Christian God. Those he spoke of must have been Christians who did not believe in the power of the providence of God. For Diodore, God's providence is that which in all ways and by all means provides for the salvation of all. In *On Providence* he argued that providence leads to universal restoration. Thus, those who believe in God but not in providence are those Christians *who believe in God, but not in the eventual universal salvation*, which is the triumph of divine providence. Generally no satisfactory identification is proposed of those who allegedly believe in God but not in providence. But this is because these statements of Diodore's, preserved in Greek, are not read in the light of the Syriac fragments and testimonies on universal restoration. When the Greek and Syriac sources of evidence are put together, the identity of those he criticizes becomes clearer.

A Greek testimony on Diodore's disciple, Theodore, comes from Photius, who in *Bibl.* cod. 177 is giving a summary of his *Against Those Who Claim That Humans Sin by Nature and Not by Intention*. Photius says that in this treatise Theodore appears to "suffer from the heresy of Origen, at least in that *he suggests the end of punishment*." He adds that Theodore indeed proclaimed that the resurrection will be followed by the restoration, for Theodore writes, "in that restoration [*apokatastasis*] *that comes after the resurrection*."

A Latin fragment from Theodore argues: "How can the resurrection be considered a grace, if those who are resurrected will be inflicted a *punishment that does not result in a correction?* . . . Who is so foolish as to believe that so great a good will become the occasion for *an infinite torment* for those who rise?"[7] The resurrection cannot result in an eternal and merely retributive punishment, if it has to be a glorious gift and

---

5. This universal submission is the object of Diodore's reflection also in *Comm. in Ps.* 45 and 8, where he also develops the so-called theology of the image, one of the pillars with which Origen and Gregory Nyssen buttressed their theory of apokatastasis.

6. On the importance of providence in Diodore's Commentary on the Psalms see Wayman, *Diodore the Theologian.* Its close link to apokatastasis is pointed out in my *Apokatastasis,* section on Diodore.

7. PL 48:232.

good, and not a damage. The resurrection will be, not only physical—in which case it can actually become the occasion for an infinite torment—but also spiritual, so as to bring about reformation and purification. Photius indeed observes that Theodore "maintained an odd doctrine concerning the resurrection of sinners" (*Bibl.* cod. 81). For Theodore is confident that in the future aeon humans will be "immortal, impassible, and free from sin" and insists on his holistic notion of the resurrection in *Comm. in Gal.* 3:26: "Once they have received immortality, they *will sin no more.*"

A Syriac fragment preserved in Isaac of Nineveh's *Second Part*, 3:3:94 likewise supports the idea that otherworldly punishments will be limited in time and will not endure forever. It comes from a lost work of Theodore's, *On Priesthood*. And another Greek testimony confirms these fragments: Leontius of Byzantium (who in turn was a crypto-Origenist)[8] accused Theodore of supporting universal restoration, deeming eternal damnation a mere threat, and thinking that Christ will give mercy to everybody.[9] Here Leontius seems to have misunderstood the teaching in question, for neither Diodore nor Theodore thought that sinners will *not* be punished. They rather thought that punishments will not be eternal, in that they will be therapeutic and commensurate with sins.

Theodore, like Diodore, knew the exact meaning of αἰώνιος/*aiōnios* in the Bible; this is why in the prologue to his commentary on Psalm 2 he correctly interprets "αἰώνιος/*aiōnios* condemnation" as "condemnation in the world to come." And this is also why he defines αἰών/*aiōn* not as "eternity," but as "an interval of time" (*Comm. in Gal.* 1:4). Theodore likewise glosses "αἰώνιος/*aiōnios* life" with "life in the world to come." The same is the case with "αἰώνιος/*aiōnios* death," "αἰώνιον/*aiōnion* fire," and the like. Theodore describes otherworldly torments only as αἰώνιοι/*aiōnioi*, "future," and *never* as ἀΐδιοι/*aidioi*, "eternal" (see *Fr. in Matth.* fr. 28:8). Thus, he applies ἀΐδιος/*aidios* to the future life when he wants to emphasize its eternity and αἰώνιος/*aiōnios* when he wants to indicate that it pertains to the world to come, or in Scriptural quotations. But ἀΐδιος/*aidios* is *never* used by him of future punishment, fire, or death. For these Theodore *only* uses αἰώνιος/*aiōnios*. (He uses the latter also in

---

8. See, e.g., Perczel, "Maximus on the Lord's Prayer," 229, based on the studies of David Evans, *Leontius* and "Leontius."

9. *Contra Nestorianos et Eutychianos* 3; on Leontius see now the important work by Brian Daley, *Leontius of Byzantium: Complete Works.*

various OT quotations, where it bears its typical significance of "remote," "ancient," "long-lasting," or refers to a succession of generations.)

Theodore uses the very terminology of apokatastasis: "not to have them fall into perdition, but to fashion them anew; . . . to fashion them anew after they had fallen *and to restore them again into their original condition*" (*Comm. in Ps.* 8). The very expression "to restore to one's original condition" (with the verbal correspondent of *apokatastasis*) is the designation of the eventual restoration in Origen and Gregory Nyssen. Theodore, like Origen,[10] thinks that God destroys or kills only to rebuild in a better state. Physical death is a gift of God which puts a limit to sin and thus to otherworldly punishment; it destroys the human being to remake it anew free from evil.

Also like Origen, Gregory Nyssen, and his own teacher Diodore, Theodore interprets the eventual universal submission to Christ as universal salvation: "the submission of a soul that is not sad, but joyous, is a *submission* [*subiectio*] that produces, *not suffering, but salvation* [*salvatio*]" (*Comm. in Ps.* 3:11).

Theodore proclaims the universal redemption operated by Christ: "In his own body Christ has realized the salvific economy for us. With the suffering of his own body he has provided the *universal remission of sin and elimination of evils*" (*Comm. in Ps.* 40). Thus, Theodore can describe the eventual universal restoration (*apokatastasis*) as a recapitulation operated by Christ:

> God has recapitulated all beings in Christ . . . as though he made a renewal that epitomizes all, *a restoration of the whole creation,* through him. . . . This will come to pass in a future aeon, when *all humanity and all powers endowed with reason will adhere to him,* as is right, and will obtain mutual concord and *stable peace.* (*Comm. in Eph.* 1:10)[11]

The first catechetical school in the early church was that in Alexandria, and we have seen how several influential universalists came out of that. What is much less well known is that the other early Christian "catechetical" school, that in Antioch, was founded by a Christian believer in universal salvation, Diodore of Tarsus, and had another high-profile

10. See my "Origen's Exegesis of Jeremiah," 59–78.

11. Likewise, commenting on Ephesians 1:10, Theodoret, who followed supporters of apokatastasis such as Diodore of Tarsus and Theodore of Mopsuestia, attributes to Christ "the restoration of the whole creation," when "all rational creatures" will be in concord and peace.

universalist as one of its first teachers, Theodore of Mopsuestia. In other words, both of the two main centers of exegesis and theology in the Christian world of this period were at least open to the notion of apokatastasis.

TITUS OF BASRA

It is fitting at this point to briefly mention Titus of Basra, or Bostra. Titus, a follower of Diodore of Tarsus active under the reigns of Julian and Valens (361–78) and the author of a treatise *Against the Manichaeans* in four books, was, according to the Byzantine theologian Stephen Gobar, among the closest followers of Origen together with Gregory of Nyssa, Gregory of Nazianzus, Alexander of Jerusalem, St. Athanasius of Alexandria, and others (quoted by Photius, *Library* 232). Concerned as he was with theodicy, like Origen, Titus claimed that punishments in the next world will not be eternal. In *Against the Manichaeans* 1.32, he teaches that hell itself, "the abyss, is a place of torment and chastisement, but *not eternal*. It was created for it to be a medicine and help for sinners. Sacred are the stripes that are remedial to those who have sinned. Thus, we do not lament the abysses of hell, knowing rather that these are places of torment and chastisement aimed at the correction of sinners." This aligns well with Titus' anti-Manichaean interpretation of Genesis 3: the fall of the protoplasts[12] testifies to God's providence: it allowed the human being to exert its free will; the death that came about as a result of this is beneficial (as Origen, Methodius, and Gregory of Nyssa underscored), in that it offers rest to the just and prevents sinners from sinning further. It is not surprising that Titus in *Against the Manichaeans* 4.12.20 cited Origen with admiration, stating that he had denounced and fought all the heresies of his time.

---

12. The protoplasts here are Adam and Eve, created by God at the beginning (from *prōtos*, "first," and *plasma*, "created by molding"). See also my section on the Antiochenes in *Apokatastasis*; "The Doctrine of Apokatastasis in the Antiochene Theologians," Invited Patristics Seminar, Oxford University, April 2012, and "Isacco di Ninive teologo della carità divina e fonte della perduta escatologia antiochena" in *La teologia dal V all'VIII secolo tra sviluppo e crisi*, 749–68. On Titus see my review of Paul-Hubert Poirier, Agathe Roman, Thomas Schmidt, Eric Crégheur, José H. Declerck, eds., *Contra Manichaeos Libri IV: Graece et Syriace; cum excerptis e Sacris Parallelis Iohanni Damasceno attributis Titus Bostrensis*, Hugoye 18.2 (2015) 446–52.

8

The Latin Origenians

The influence of Origenian theology spread from the eastern church to the western church. In part, the school in Egypt played a role in this dissemination, as we will see in this chapter, for two influential scholars active also in the West, Jerome of Stridon and Rufinus of Aquileia, both studied there and both acquired a deep admiration of Origen there. Both played a part in making his works available in Latin to churches in the West.

JEROME AND RUFINUS SUPPORTERS OF UNIVERSAL SALVATION. JEROME'S U-TURN & RUFINUS' PROGRAM

Jerome

Jerome (c.347–420) at various times worked in Rome, where he also worked for Pope Damasus, Gaul, and Alexandria (where he studied with Didymus the Blind), ending his days in a cave near Bethlehem. He was one of the great scholars of the early church, best known for the Vulgate, his translation of the Bible into Latin.[1] Between the end of the fourth and the beginning of the fifth century, Jerome embraced the doctrine of universal salvation as well as the rest of Origen's thought and exegesis, being a fervent admirer of Origen, whom he deemed "the greatest teacher of the ancient church." In his *Commentary on Nahum* he took over Origen's therapeutic notion of otherworldly punishments, and on this basis argued that in the end all the world, and even the devil, will be cured and thus saved. Indeed, in this commentary and in that on Habakkuk, Jerome criticized heretics of the past, but never Origen. In *Comm. in Eph.* 4:16 (PL 26:503) Jerome speaks overtly of "universal restoration" (*restitutio omnium*), as the reconstitution of all into their original state, in which even "the fallen angel will begin to be what it was created to be." He adds: "In the universal restoration [*in restitutione omnium*], when Jesus Christ, the true Physician, will come to heal the body of the whole church, now dispersed and lacerated, each creature will recover its place or condition according to the measure of its faith and knowledge of the Son of God; . . . [each] will recover its original condition and will begin to be again what it had originally been." In *Comm. in Eph.* 1 he had no problem in admitting the eventual salvation of all rational beings, including the devil.[2] In these commentaries, indeed, Jerome almost translated Origen literally or paraphrased his commentaries.

Again following Origen, Jerome in his *Commentary on Hosea* 11.8 remarks that God does not "strike to destroy forever, but to correct" sinners, the same that he observes commenting on Zechariah 12:9. Jerome clearly follows Origen's line when in his *Commentary on Galatians* 5.22 he insists that "no creature perishes eternally." Likewise in *Commentary on Micah* 5.8, Jerome, as Origen did, claims that death—meaning the death of the soul—will visit the impious, but only for a limited time, "until their impiety will be consumed." In the same *Commentary on Micah* 7.8, he uses Origen's, Nyssen's, and Evagrius' argument that after the payment of

1. Although the Vulgate was probably only partially his own; its significance is pointed out in my "The Bible," in *Wiley-Blackwell Companion to Word Literature*, I, forthcoming.

2. See Rufinus *Apol. c. Hier.* 1:34–37; 43–45.

the "very last coin" otherworldly punishment will come to an end. And in his *Commentary on Jonah* 2.6, Jerome declares that thanks to his death and descent to hell, Christ set free all those who had been shut up there (likewise in *Comm. in Is.* 45.7).

In Letter 33:5 to Paula (385) Jerome strongly defends Origen against his critics, calling "rabid dogs" those who maintained that at the Roman synod presided over by Pontianus Origen was condemned for dogmatic reasons. Jerome correctly observes that Origen was in fact only criticized for disciplinary reasons, and this out of sheer envy, because his accusers "could not bear the glory of his eloquence and learning, and because when Origen spoke all the others seemed to be mute." In Letter 42:1 to Marcella, likewise, Jerome praises Origen as a teacher of spiritual life, calling him "really a man of steel [*vere Adamantius*]." In *Vir. Ill.* 54, his portrait of Origen is not less celebratory than Eusebius' portrait of Origen in *HE* 6 is. All documents are examined in my future Origen monograph.

By 390 or 391, commenting on the Psalms, Jerome still upheld the eventual elimination of sin in the final restoration. In particular, commenting on Psalm 145(146):9, he stated—like Origen and Gregory of Nyssa—that no creature will ultimately remain outside the number of the saved. At this point Jerome still maintained that demons, who are now opposite powers, will in the end submit to Christ and conform to Christ's will; indeed Jerome, following Origen, taught that humans will be able to improve themselves or fall not only in the present world, but also in the future.[3] Jerome also taught that "at the end of the aeon(s) all beings *will be restored into their original condition*, and all of us will be made one and the same body and will be reformed into the perfect human being, and thus the Savior's prayer will be fulfilled in us: 'Father, grant that, as You and I are One, so too may they be one in Us' [John 17:22]."

Rufinus, about whom we shall say more soon, asserts that neither Jerome nor he himself supported an impious doctrine by maintaining universal salvation. In particular, he reports that Jerome said that

> it befits the character of the Trinity, who is good, simple, and immutable, to hypothesize that *every creature*, at the end of all, will be *restored* into the state in which it had been created at the beginning, and this will take place after a *long punishment*,

---

3. Reported by Rufinus *Apol. c. Hier.* 1:26–35. We must stress, however, that Origen thought that future falls would only be possible in the ages prior to the apokatastasis, *not once the apokatastasis was realized.*

even coextensive with the duration of all the aeons, inflicted by
God to every creature, not because God is angry, but in order
to correct, because God is not excessive in punishing iniquity,
and since the intention of God, as Physician, is that of healing
humans, he will *put an end to their punishment*.[4]

Here we see again that recurring Origenian theme: that the eventual universal salvation "befits God." This is the theodicy that—to Jerome's mind,
at least at that time—is "worthy of God."

It is highly significant that Jerome, at the end of the fourth century,
in his commentary on Jonah 3 attests, like (Ps.?)Basil and Augustine, that
still in his day most people believed in the apokatastasis of all rational
creatures, including even Satan: "I know that most people interpret the
story of Nineveh and its king as a reference to the eventual forgiveness of
the devil and of all *logika*." Jerome is most probably speaking here not of
the views of ordinary Christians in churches, whose beliefs we know very
little about, but of the claims of exegetes. Most of the biblical scholars, he
says, believed in the eventual salvation of even the devil. Of course, we
need to exercise some caution in how much weight to give this claim, but
it remains interesting.

But then Jerome, at a certain point, for political convenience during
the "Origenistic controversy," changed his mind and his (at least official)
evaluation of Origen.[5] But even after his U-turn, Jerome did not criticize
the eventual salvation of all human beings, but only that of the devil.[6]
And still in *Ep.* 85 (400), written long after his volte-face against Origen,
he privately recommended to Paulinus of Nola, as the best treatment of
the question of free will, the third Book of Origen's *On First Principles*,
in which universal salvation is most clearly expounded. So, Jerome's turn
against Origen was more pragmatic than principled and was never a
complete turn.

4. Quoted by Rufinus *Apol. c. Hier.* 2:1–11.

5. On Jerome switching ideas for political convenience, see my *Christian Doctrine
of Apokatastasis*, 627–41 (esp. 636–41).

6. *Comm. in Matt.* 14:10; *Ep.* 124:3; *Comm. in Io.* 7.

Rufinus

While Jerome had made at least a half-turn away from Origen, his fellow Western and former friend Rufinus (340/45–410), who had also been a disciple of the Origenian Didymus the Blind for eight years,[7] never abandoned his admiration of the Alexandrian master. After breaking with Jerome, Rufinus returned to Italy and began a program of systematic translation of Origen's works into Latin, to help all Latin readers see that Origen was no heretic. He began with Pamphilus' apology for Origen (397) and Origen's *On First Principles* for his friend Macarius, who requested this translation in order for him to be able to counter astral determinism, the view that our actions are controlled by the stars. Rufinus was well aware that Origen's doctrine of rational creatures and their universal salvation had been elaborated and used *against* astral and "gnostic" determinism. In *Apol. c. Hier.* 2:12 he observes that the supporters of universal salvation—and of course he was thinking of Origen first of all—wanted

> to defend God's justice [i.e., theodicy] and thus refute those who claimed that everything is determined by Fate or by accident. . . . [E]ager as they were to defend God's justice . . . [they maintained that] it *becomes that good and immutable and simple nature of the Trinity to restore all of its creatures*, in the end, into that condition in which they were created at the beginning, and, after long sufferings over whole aeons, to finally *put an end to punishments*.

Again, for Rufinus, just as for Origen and the former Jerome, universal salvation *befits God*.

---

7. Rufinus *Apol. c. Hier.* 2:15.

AMBROSE AND AMBROSIASTER: SOME REMARKS

Saint Ambrose (c.340–97), a Roman Senator who in the fourth century became the most famous bishop of Milan, exerted a remarkable influence on the early Augustine and can be regarded as the main agent of his conversion. Ambrose, who—unlike Augustine—had a perfect mastery of Greek, having received an education commensurate with his status, knew Origen's works very well and was profoundly influenced by them. Ambrose was following in Origen's footsteps (like Eriugena later on: see below) when in *On Faith* 5.8.106 he declared that "the mystery of God's inhumanation is *the salvation of all creation*, according to what is written: 'That, apart from God, he might taste death *for the benefit of all*' ... as can be read also elsewhere: '*Every creature* will be liberated from enslavement to corruption.'" Even his exegesis of Hebrews 2:9 and Romans 8:21 is the same as Origen's, who remarked: "The whole creation brings in itself the hope for the liberation from enslavement to corruption, when the children of God, who have fallen and are now dispersed, will be brought back to unity" (*Princ.* 3.5.4).

Ambrose's remarks also resonate with Origen's and Gregory of Nyssa's claims, when in *On Sacraments* 2.6 Ambrose notes that death puts an end to sins and the resurrection remolds human nature into a better state. This is exactly what Gregory of Nyssa argued. Likewise, in *Death Is a Good Thing*, 4, Ambrose, like Methodius and Gregory, insists that "death is the end of sin." Commenting on Psalm 44, Ambrose takes up Origen's line in his *Homilies on Jeremiah*: Christ first destroys sin, that what is better may be planted afterwards instead of sin.[8] The same Ambrose, while commenting on Psalm 1, with specific reference to Psalm 18:42 ("I will destroy them"), notes that what is destroyed by God "is not annihilated, but *changed for the better.*" This is precisely Origen's often-repeated point.

Drawing on St. Paul, in his *Exposition of Luke* 15.3, Ambrose observes that when the Gospels says that the Son of Man came to save that which was lost (Luke 19:10), this means all human beings, since, just as all humans die in Adam, all will receive life in Christ. Anticipating what Eriugena will articulate, Ambrose in *On Faith* 5.7–8 not only identifies "the mystery of the inhumanation" of Christ with "the salvation of the whole creation," as I mentioned, but also offers an exegesis of 1 Corinthians 15:28 that is the very same as Origen's and Nyssen's: the eschatological submission of Christ to the Father will be achieved when all become obedient and believe and do God's will; then, and only then, will God be "all in all." This being "in all" is explained by Ambrose, when commenting on Psalm 62:1, in the sense that God will be in all not simply by his power, as now, but "by their free will." For all will voluntarily adhere to God. This is universalism.

Commenting on Philippians 2:10, Ambrosiaster, an anonymous imitator of Ambrose, interprets Paul's words in the sense that "the Father has granted to the Son that, after the crucifixion, all beings should be saved in the Son's name." And commenting on Ephesians 1:9–10, he foretells that "every being, in heaven and on earth, will attain the knowledge of Christ and be restored to the state in which it was created."

8. See Ramelli, "Origen's Exegesis of Jeremiah"; referred to in Arnold, *Der Wahre Logos des Kelsos*, 593.

AUGUSTINE: FROM SUPPORTER TO OPPOSER OF
UNIVERSAL SALVATION

Augustine (354–430) was a native of North Africa, a teacher in Carthage, then Rome, and finally Milan. It was here that, after a long spiritual search, he converted to Christianity, very much under the influence of

Ambrose, of whom we have just spoken. He moved back to Africa and was ordained a priest in 391 then Bishop of Hippo in 395. Without question, Augustine is among the most important theologians in the history of the Christian church, exerting a *massive* theological influence on the western church. Origen's influence on Augustine will make the object of a specific research.

In the 420s Augustine was engaged in a polemic against Pelagianism,[9] which he and others mistakenly believed to have been inspired by Origen's thought. In this context, he felt the need to oppose Origen's ideas and in particular rebuked "those merciful Christians who refuse to believe that torments in hell will be eternal."[10] Among these, Origen was "the most merciful of all" in that he even hypothesized the eschatological salvation of the devil.[11] Augustine had been misinformed (also by Orosius' *Commonitorium*) about Origen's exact doctrine of restoration; he was convinced that Origen had taught "unending shifts between misery and beatitude, and the infinite fluctuation between these states" (*CD* 21:17).[12] On the contrary, Origen thought that these vicissitudes will definitely come to an end with the end of all aeons, in the eventual universal restoration.

Here Augustine insisted that suffering in hell will be eternal and that it is a Platonic and Origenian mistake to understand it as limited.[13] Augustine was only seeking to be true to Scripture, but he knew little or no Greek and was unaware that "*aeternus* (eternal) fire" in his Latin Bible translated the Greek "αἰώνιον/*aiōnion* fire," which, as we have seen, does not necessarily mean "eternal fire," but "otherworldly fire" or "long-lasting fire." Unfortunately, in Latin, both ἀΐδιος/*aïdios* and αἰώνιος/*aiōnios* were rendered with *aeternus* (eternal), which generated a terrible

9. Pelagianism essentially rejected the notion of divine grace and the necessity of grace for the salvation of a human being, while both Origen and Augustine thought that divine grace is indispensable to human salvation.

10. *De gest. Pel.* 1:3:9.

11. See also *C. Iul.* 5:47 and 6:10, in which Augustine refutes the thesis of the eventual conversion and salvation of the devil, ascribing this idea to Origen. He does not even take into consideration that it was rather Gregory of Nyssa who supported it more decisively and overtly than Origen.

12. In *De haer.* 43 Augustine—equally unfoundedly—accuses Origen of teaching an infinite sequence of aeons in which the devil will be purified and rational creatures will fall again and again, with no end.

13. PL 31:1211–6 = CSEL 18:151–57. See also *De haer.* 43, in which Augustine insists that Origen learnt the doctrine of universal salvation from the Platonists. It must be noted, however, that Plato himself did *not* believe in universal salvation.

confusion that surely facilitated the birth of the idea of "eternal" punishments in hell.[14] Because of his lack of awareness, Augustine in his *To Orosius* (5:5; 8:10) argued that the fire of hell must be "eternal," otherwise the eternal beatitude of the just could not be eternal.[15] Again, falling into the same linguistic misunderstanding, in *De gest. Pel.* 1:3:10 Augustine declares that the church does well to criticize Origen and his followers who think that "the torment of the damned will end at a certain point, while the Lord called it 'eternal' [*aeternum*]." But, of course, the Lord only called these torments "eternal" in the *Latin translation* of the Bible, which unfortunately was all Augustine was able to fully understand. And this Latin translation, alongside Augustine's *huge* influence on the western church, played a significant role in marginalizing Christian universalism for many hundreds of years to come.

But Augustine had not always been a defender of eternal torment. Many years earlier, when the target of Augustine's polemic was not yet Pelagianism, but rather Manichaeism, Augustine used against the latter the same metaphysical arguments that Origen used against "gnostics."[16] This, especially in his double treatise *On the Customs of the Catholic Church and on the Customs of the Manichaeans*.[17] It is not accidental that in this same work Augustine also embraced the doctrine of universal restoration, whether he knew that it was Origen's or not. For in *De mor.* 2:7:9 he declared: "God's goodness [*Dei bonitas*] . . . *orders all creatures* [*omnia*] *that have fallen* . . . *until they* return to the original state from which they fell." This is the very same notion that Origen had expressed in *Princ.* 1:6:1, which may have reached Augustine in a compilation or partial translation anterior to Rufinus': "God's goodness [*bonitas Dei*], by means of his Christ, *calls back all creatures* [*universam creaturam*] to one and the same end."[18] God's goodness, for both Origen and the young Augustine, is not simply God's kindness or generosity or mercy, but first

14. See Ramelli and Konstan, *Terms for Eternity*, new edition, 47–80.

15. This is the same argument as presented in the passage included in Basil's monastic rules in the form of questions and answers, which is probably interpolated. Origen had already refuted it in his *Commentary on Romans*, where he demonstrated that, if life is eternal, death cannot possibly be eternal.

16. See my "Origen in Augustine: A Paradoxical Reception," endorsed and confirmed by Perczel, "St. Maximus on the Lord's Prayer," 229; by Pollmann, "The Broken Perfume-Flask"; and by Cameron, "Origen and Augustine."

17. PL 32:1309–78; ed. J. B. Bauer CSEL 90, 1992.

18. God's goodness is also at the center of *Comm. in Io.* 6:57: the eventual universal submission to Christ must be understood as universal salvation because only this will be "worthy of the goodness of the God of the universe."

and foremost, on the ontological plane, it is God's being the absolute Good, and since God is the true Being, evil, which is opposite to God the Good, is non-being. As Augustine explains in the rest of the passage in question (*De mor.* 2:7), the creatures that have fallen are precisely rational creatures, who, with their free choices, acquire merits or demerits. On the basis of these, God assigns them to different orders—in Origen's view, the orders of angels, humans, and demons—all the while never abandoning them and never allowing them to end up by disappearing into evil-non-being. God's providence guides these creatures until they return to the original condition from which they have fallen.

This whole passage is so replete with Origen's ideas that Augustine felt the need to disavow it in his later *Retractations*: "That all beings will return to the condition from which they fell should not be understood in the sense of Origen's theory . . . for those who will be punished in the eternal fire do not return to God, from whom they detached themselves" (1:7:6). Given the closeness of Augustine's thought to Origen, at least in his anti-Manichaean phase, it is not surprising that a collection of texts from Origen's *On First Principles* has been ascribed to Augustine under the title *On the Incarnation of the Logos to Ianuarius*. Besides Karla Pollmann, István Perczel, and Michael Cameron, Daniel Heide, too, explicitly accepts my reconstruction of Augustine as a supporter of apokatastasis in his anti-Manichaean phase.[19]

It is also of interest that a prominent fourth-century Christian Neoplatonist such as Marius Victorinus exerted some influence on Augustine. For Victorinus is likely to have had a penchant for the apokatastasis theory. Marius Victorinus—a Platonist born a pagan who converted to Christianity rather late in his life, becoming a Christian Platonist—composed a treatise against Arianism. Here in 3.8 he states that Jesus Christ "will save all beings into life" and in 1.57 he details that Christ fulfilled the mystery so that all life in flesh, filled with eternal light, should return to heaven, free from all corruption." Universal salvation performed by Christ is but a consequence of the creation performed by Christ-Logos: "The Logos was made 'all in all,' generated all beings, and saved them" (1.26). Victorinus seems to have had some sympathy for apokatastasis, which is not surprising in a Christian Platonist who knew and esteemed Origen. This, and possibly also the influence of Ambrose, and the transmission of Origen's texts, anthologies, quotations, and translations, as well as the metaphysical monistic needs of Augustine's anti-Manichaean

19. Daniel Heide, "Ἀποκατάστασις," 206; Heidl, *Augustine*, whom I receive and discuss in *Apokatastasis* and in "Origen in Augustine."

polemic, may go a little way to explaining Augustine's early openness to apokatastasis.

Before leaving Augustine, it is worth mentioning a tantalizing glimpse he offers into the faith of ordinary believers on the issue of hell. Augustine comments that there are "very many" Christians who, on the basis of their beliefs about divine goodness and mercy, react with horror at the thought of eternal torment (*Ench.* 112). While not wanting to build too much on this brief aside, it at least suggests that in Augustine's day universalist belief was not some obscure idea hidden away in a few dark corners of the church. Augustine, however, did his part in ensuring that it would become such.

JOHN CASSIAN

John Cassian (c.360–435), who became a monk in Palestine and eventually brought eastern monasticism to the West, founding an Egyptian-style monastery in Gaul, is an important although possibly problematic figure to discuss.[20] Here I am concerned with the *Conferences* that have been handed down under his name and were attacked by Prosperus of Aquitania, who tended to present them as close to Pelagianism—which they are not. Cassian's *Conferences* are a series of questions and long answers by Egyptian hermits. *Conference* 13 in particular diverges from Augustine's mature doctrine of grace,[21] which in more Origenian circles was perceived as a new form of predestinationism, similar to that which Origen had opposed in some "gnostics" all his life long. (Cassian was not alone in opposing Augustine's theology of human freedom and divine grace, a theology that represented a significant innovation within the Christian tradition to that point—Vincent of Lérin similarly opposed Augustinian predestinationism.) According to Cassian's *Conference* 13, God does not predestine some people to salvation from the beginning and in a gratuitous way. Human free will, instead, must choose the Good, and God's grace will assist it. Even if free will orients itself toward evil, grace will intervene to reorient it toward the Good. Indeed, salvation necessarily requires God's grace (Ch. 6).

> [God]wants *all human beings to be saved* and to reach the knowledge of truth [1 Tim 2:4]. Indeed, Scripture says: "Your Father who is in heaven does not want any of these little ones to be lost/to perish" [Matt 18:14]. And again: "God does not want to have a soul perish, but he calls it back" [Ezek 33:11; 2 Pet 3:9], thus demonstrating that even those who have gone far from God *will not perish completely.* . . . "Because I live—says the Lord—*I do not want the sinner to die, but to convert and live*" [Ezek 18:23]. . . . If God does not want any of these little ones to perish, how could we imagine without serious blasphemy that God does not want *all humans to be saved, but only some instead of all?* Should

20. Panayiotis Tzamalikos maintains that most of the works ascribed to John Cassian (late fourth to early fifth cent.) were originally composed in Greek by a Palestinian monk, Cassian the Sabaite, who lived in the time of Justinian and was well steeped in the Origenian tradition. We will not address this hypothesis here.

21. In his mature doctrine of grace, Augustine posited that after the original sin, all humanity cannot avoid sinning (*non posse non peccare*). This is why humanity is a "lump of condemnation" or "damned mass" (*massa damnationis, massa damnata*). God inscrutably chooses some people and predestines them to salvation, while the others are doomed to damnation. This solution was often perceived as a double predestination, which still Eriugena in the ninth century rejected in his *De praedestinatione*.

some ever perish, these would perish *against God's will.*[22] . . . Just as a physician who is benevolent to the utmost degree, for the sake of our salvation God will bring us what is opposite to our will, and sometimes he delays and prevents our bad intentions and mortal attempts, that they may not have their horrible effect. And while we rush toward death, God *pulls us back toward salvation* and, while we are even unaware of death, *saves us from the jaws of hell.* (Ch. 7)

God's benevolence for the creatures is so immense that God's providence not only accompanies our will, but it also precedes it, and "shows the way of salvation to those who are in error" (Ch. 8). Indeed, in Chapter 9 God is said to be found by those who were not looking for him, and to always extend his arms toward those who do not believe and refuse him; God "*calls those who resist and drags humans to salvation against their own will.* To those who want to sin he steals away the faculty of realizing their plans and in his goodness he prevents those who are falling into evilness." With Origen, the author insists (Ch. 11) that divine grace or providence and human free will are not opposed to each other. If one turns to the Good, divine providence helps him or her; if one is "lazy or cold" (both adjectives reflect Origen's moral terminology), divine providence exhorts one's heart, so as to form good will in it. Many a time God snatches people from the danger of spiritual death even without them being aware of this (Ch. 14). Nobody knows all the ways in which God "drags humanity to salvation" (Ch. 15). Cassian criticizes the doctrine of justification by faith, insofar as he thinks that not even that may be necessary, let alone human works of righteousness; with this he does not deny the value of faith or works, but he puts *divine grace* before anything else.[23] And grace, in his view, does not operate only in some, as Augustine thought, but in *all*:

God *brings salvation* to humanity in various and infinite ways, . . . *compelling some to salvation even against their will.* . . . God is the first who calls us to himself; while we are still ignorant and reluctant, *God brings us to salvation.* . . . God, the Father of all, works *all in all*, as the Apostle says,[24] like an extremely good father or an extremely kind physician. And now he puts in us

22. This is hypothetical; Cassian is not stating that some *will* perish.

23. "God's Grace is superabundant and many a time overcomes the restricted limits of a person's lack of faith" (Ch. 16).

24. Paul in 1 Cor 15:28.

the germs of salvation and offers to each of us zeal in each one's free will. . . . [N]ow God *saves people, even against their will and without their awareness, from an imminent ruin and a precipitous fall.* . . . God drags those who do not want and resist him, and *compels them to want the Good.* . . . "You will know that I am the Lord when I have benefited you for the sake of my Name, *not according to your bad behavior, not according to your evil works,* o house of Israel. . . . The God of all operates *in all* in such a way as to exhort, protect, and fortify, but without taking away from us *that free will which God has given us.* . . . Human intellect and reason cannot entirely grasp how God operates everything in us and yet, at the same time, everything can be ascribed to our free will." (Chs. 17–18)

The Last Exponents of Patristic Thought

VARIOUS AUTHORS WITH HINTS OF UNIVERSALISM

Sinesius of Cyrene

Synesius of Cyrene (373–414) was a Neoplatonist and a disciple of the Neoplatonist philosopher and scientist Hypatia of Alexandria, whom he venerated and to whom he wrote letters. He interpreted the Trinity in the light of Neoplatonic triads of principles. When he was made a bishop, he wrote to his brother (Letter 105) saying that he was unwilling to give up his philosophical convictions:

> Philosophy is opposite to the beliefs of the masses: I shall certainly not admit that the soul is posterior to the body, . . . [nor] that the world is doomed to perish with all of its components. . . . I regard the resurrection as *something mystical and ineffable.* I am far from sharing the ideas of the multitude.

That the soul is created either with the body or prior to the body, that the intelligible world is eternal (in God), and that the resurrection is not only of the body but also of the soul and intellect are all aspects of the Origenian tradition that Synesius seemingly takes up, along with the allegorical and spiritual exegesis of Scripture. This allowed him to interpret the resurrection as both physical and spiritual, as a restoration not only of the body, but also of the soul to the Good. And since the resurrection is universal, as Scripture announces, the restoration too will be so.

Indeed in his ninth *Anacreontic Ode* Synesius highlights the salvific consequences of Christ's descent to hell: "He liberated the souls from their sufferings," and in his *Ode to the Savior* he sang: in the tomb, Christ as God has purified the earth, the air, the demons, and hell itself, becoming "the Help for the dead."

Isodore of Pelusium and John Chrysostom

Isidore of Pelusium was an Egyptian monk in the first half of the fifth century who tried in vain to defend John Chrysostom (c.349–407), Archbishop of Constantinople, before Theophilus of Alexandria, who was angry with John because he, together with his deacon Olympia, had received and protected some Origenian monks—supporters of the doctrine of universal salvation—in Constantinople. After John's death in exile in 407, Isidore exhorted Cyril of Alexandria to rehabilitate John's memory. Like Origen, he privileged the spiritual sense of Scripture and upheld the Nicene Trinitarian theology. The sixth-century Byzantine theologian Gobar attests that Isidore was accused of "Origenism," but the accusation, according to Gobar, was groundless.[1] John Chrysostom himself, in *Hom. Phlm.* 3, insisted that Gehenna has an educative function: "But why do I speak of slaves, who easily fall into these sins? But let a man have sons, and let him allow them to do everything they want, and let him not punish them; will they not be worse than anything? Tell me, in the case of men then, it is a sign of goodness to punish, and of cruelty not to punish, and is it not so in the case of God? Since he is good, he has therefore prepared Gehenna." Chrysostom, although he was not a consistent or explicit supporter of soteriological universalism, was viewed by Jerome as an Origenist sympathizer.[2]

Philoxenus and Barsanuphius

Philoxenus of Mabbug († 523), a Syrian Christian writer, basing himself on Romans 8:22, seems to have attributed to Christ the restoration of the whole creation: "through his renewing activity, which changes death into life and the corruptible into incorruptibility, all creatures obtain an

1. Reported by Photius *Bibl.* cod. 232, p. 291b.
2. Bady, "Les Traductions latines anciennes de Jean Chysostome," 310.

amazing restoration and transformation" (*Commentary on Matthew-Luke*, fr. 12). But it is especially meaningful that even Barsanuphius of Gaza, who is regarded as an anti-Origenist, in his Letter 569 recommended that Christians should pray for the salvation of the whole world, including "heretics" and "pagans." He declared that three saints pray for this—one of these being himself—and "*they will indeed achieve God's great mercy.*" Therefore, he seems to have embraced universal salvation, although in a somewhat cautious and indirect way.

SYRIAC MONASTICISM: BAR SUDHAILI AND PSEUDO-DIONYSIUS

Bar Sudhaili's Pantheism

Especially through Evagrius and his disciples, Origen's thought exercised a heavy influence on Egyptian and Palestinian monasticism. Stephen Bar Sudhaili (c.480–c.543) was a monk from Edessa who absorbed an advanced form of Evagrian Origenism in Egypt. He is very probably the author of the *Book of the Holy Hierotheus*,[3] in which he supported a doctrine of universal salvation that came dangerously close to pantheism, in that he claimed that all creatures in the end will join the very *substance* of God. This goes far beyond the eschatological unity of *wills* taught in the earlier Origenian tradition. It is arguably the extreme form of Origenism represented among various Palestinian monks in the early sixth century, including Bar Sudhaili, that provoked the reaction against Origen that followed. Unfortunately, their critics made no distinction between the Origenist teaching of the monks and Origen's own teaching. In their minds, because Origen was the source of inspiration for the monks he obviously taught the heresies that they affirmed. Thus it was that Origen became a "heretic."

---

3. Hierotheus is the name, or probably byname, of the venerated teacher of Ps. Dionysius. While some have proposed to identify Hierotheus with Proclus, the "pagan" Neoplatonist, I rather suspect that he was a Christian theologian. There are reasons to suppose that he might have been Origen—or else Ps. Dionysius, following the double reference scheme (Christian + 'pagan' Platonism) that is proper to his whole work, might even have referred at the same time to both.

Pseudo-Dionysius:
Apokatastasis as Universal Return to the One

The texts known as the *Corpus Dionysianum* were destined to become some of the great works of Christian theology, exerting a large influence in both the eastern and the western churches, right up to this day. The author, probably a Syrian Christian working in the sixth century, presented himself as Dionysius the Areopagite[4]—the first-century Athenian philosopher who converted to Christianity as a result of Paul's Areopagus speech (Acts 17:34). Pseudo-Dionysius, or simply Dionysius, was an

4. Louth, *The Origins of the Christian Mystical Tradition* and *Denys the Areopagite*; de Andia, *Denys l'Aréopagite et sa postérité*; Schaefer, *The Philosophy of Dionysius*, on *DN*; Dillon and Wear, *Dionysius the Areopagite*; Coakley and Stang, *Rethinking Dionysius*, with my review in *RBL* 2010. His audience genuinely believed the work to come from Dionysius (or Denys) himself. It is only since the fifteenth century that scholars started to question that attribution. I argue for Origen's influence in "Origen, Evagrius, and Dionysius," in *The Oxford Handbook to Dionysius the Areopagite*, Oxford, forthcoming.

Origenian and Evagrian, as especially Perczel and I have shown, with different arguments. It is arguably to Origen and his tradition that Pseudo-Dionysius refers when he speaks of "theology" and "theologians,"[5] and when he describes God as "Monad and Henad"[6] (*DN* 1:4) he is not quoting Proclus (the pagan Neoplatonist), who never refers to God using this couple of terms, but Origen (*Princ.* 1:1:6).[7] Furthermore, the concept of divine love—not only as charitable love (ἀγάπη/*agapē*), but also as passionate love (ἔρως/*erōs*), which is so much developed in Dionysius—is a clear example of the influence of Origen (who probably drew not only on the Platonic tradition, but even more on his exegesis of the Song of Songs). Gregory of Nyssa and Methodius had already been influenced by Origen in this understanding of divine love. Pseudo-Dionysius in turn was also influenced by Gregory, another supporter of the doctrine of universal salvation.[8]

Now, one passage in which Pseudo-Dionysius develops the doctrine of apokatastasis as the restoration of unity and of the image and likeness of God, in the same way as Origen conceived it, is *DN* 1:4. (The use of the present tense instead of the future or the past is typical of Pseudo-Dionysius, and motivated by the fact that God transcends temporality):

> You will find, so to say, that the whole hymnology of the theologians disposes the divine names in a revealing and hymnic way according to the beneficial procession of the principle of the divinity. Therefore, in practically all the theological teaching, we see that the principle of the divinity is celebrated as "Monad and Henad" because of the simplicity and unity of its supernatural indivisibility. By it we are unified as by a unifying power, and by a supramundane act of reunion of our divisible alterity we are assembled into a monad that is the image of God and a union that is in God's likeness.

In *Princ.* 2:1:1 Origen calls the original unity of creation "Henad" (according to a Greek fragment); Rufinus glosses "unity and concord" (*unitas et concordia*, which emphasizes the concord of wills and rules out the direct identification of this creatural Henad with God, whom Origen defined as "Monad and Henad"). Pseudo-Dionysius also called God

5. Perczel, "Théologiens et magiciens," 54–75.

6. Both Monad and Henad mean "unity, one" and they were used by Origen to describe God: God is "Monad and Henad."

7. Perczel, "God as Monad and Henad," 1193–1209.

8. See Ramelli, "Apokatastasis and Epektasis."

Monad and Henad, since he was inspired by Origen. Ps. Dionysius seems to be clearer, in the above-quoted passage, that the unity of the Henad is the original divine unity that is recovered in the final apokatastasis. In that unity, human beings also recover the image and likeness of God (Gen 1:26). They will become a creaturely Monad and Henad, analogous to God's Monad-Henad. The "unifying power" of which Pseudo-Dionysius speaks is probably the Intellect or *nous*; in *DN* 7:2 the "intellectual power" is in the image of God and tends to achieve unity. In particular, it realizes unity in the soul by bringing it to its state of image and likeness of God—as it was in God's original plan—by means of a "contraction of the divisible alterities." This is Platonic language meaning both the qualities of the body and the relevant movements of the soul (a similar idea occurs in Gregory of Nyssa's dialogue *On the Soul and the Resurrection*). This intellectual unifying power, for the Christian Pseudo-Dionysius, is Christ. Christ's prayer for unity in the Last Supper discourse (John 13–17) and sacrifice for unity (John 11:51–52) was applied already by Origen to unity in the eventual restoration (e.g., *Princ.* 3:5:4). Dionysius, in turn, commenting on Christ's title "Peace," declares that Christ is "the only and universal Principle and Cause that, superior to all beings in indivisibility, as with chains that embrace together the various separated beings, determines and limits all things." In *EH* 1:1 Jesus is said to be the Intellect that "unifies again the many alterities and makes us perfect in the divine life that is an image of the Henad." This perfectly corresponds to the initial passage of *DN* 1:4.[9]

Pseudo-Dionysius constructs apokatastasis as the third Neoplatonic movement, that of "return" (after "immanence" of the first Principle, the Godhead, in itself, and the "procession" of all beings from that Principle in creation):

> The Cause of all is "all in all" according to Scripture [1 Cor 15:28], and must certainly be praised for being the Giver of existence to all, the originator of all beings, which *brings all of them to perfection*. It holds them together and protects them. It is their seat, and *has all of them come back to itself*, and this in a *unified, irresistible, absolute*, and transcendent manner. (*DN* 1:7)

9. This seems to be a description of apokatastasis in the form condemned in the Fifth Ecumenical Council 553, anathema 14 (which is considered to echo Evagrius *KG* 2:17) against those who say "that all rational beings will form one Henad . . . and in the restoration that is the object of their myths there will be only pure intellects, just as it was in the preexistence they babble about."

Indeed, God is "the cause of the perfecting of all beings." This is consistent with a universalistic perspective, and there seems to be more to this. Pseudo-Dionysius informs readers that he has written extensively, also on the basis of biblical quotations, on the universal peace and restoration that have been planned from eternity and will be realized when, thanks to Christ, God will be "all in all." He says that he expounded all this in his *Outlines of Theology*, which came before his treatise *On Divine Names* (*DN* 1:1), but is now lost.[10] The reference to 1 Corinthians 15:28 makes it even clearer that in his *Outlines* Pseudo-Dionysius tackled apokatastasis and buttressed this theory with Scripture and perhaps the authority of former theologians. Among these, Origen was almost certainly prominent.

Pseudo-Dioysius offers the following table of contents of his *Outlines*:[11] affirmative theology, that is, divine nature one and triune, the Father, the Son, and the Spirit; the Father is the supreme and undivided Good, and from the heart of this Goodness lights have sprung forth, meaning the Son; the Son became human, and the rest that has been revealed by Scripture or the sages. The *Outlines of Theology*, Pseudo-Dionysius explains, were much shorter than his *Symbolic Theology*, because they proceeded from God, the first Principle, to the creatures and "the last things." Thus, like Origen in his *First Principles*, Pseudo-Dionysius in his *Outlines* began with the Trinity as first Principle and proceeded to the creatures, arriving at eschatology, which depends on Christ's "admirable gifts." It is no accident that it seems to have been an eschatology close to that of Origen, who also thought that universal salvation depends on Christ's gifts. Nicephorus Callistus (1256–1335) mentions the *Outlines* among Pseudo-Dionysius' lost works.[12] In the first Syriac tradition, on

10. "What could one say of Christ's love for humanity, a love which pours out peace? Jesus operates all in all and performs an *ineffable peace*, established *from eternity*; he *reconciles people to himself in the Spirit*, and, *through himself and in himself, to the Father*. I have *abundantly spoken of these admirable gifts in my Outlines of Theology*, where my own testimony is joined to that of the holy inspiration of Scripture / of the wise" (*DN* 11:5; 221 Ritter).

11. *TM* 3:1, p. 146:1–9.

12. *HE* 2:20. In Psellus, *Or.* 1,784, the expression *Outlines of Theology* may, or may not, refer specifically to the title of Pseudo-Dionysius' work. This possibility is all the more interesting in that the passage at stake refers to the evaluation of Origen's thought: "In their writings [of Origenian authors] there are also some expressions that are full of piety, and *Outlines of Theology*. . . . [T]he famous Origen, a contemporary of the philosopher Porphyry, was very well steeped in Christian theology, and embraced the Christian life as well, but originated all heresies." If *Outlines of Theology*

the contrary, this work is not declared to have been lost, and some references may even give the impression that it was read, as I shall show in a moment. At any rate, if Pseudo-Dionysius composed his *Outlines* and these dealt with universal salvation, it is easy to guess how it is that this work was (intentionally) lost.

Pseudo-Dionysius displays the ontological premises underpinning the restoration of all creatures, including even demons (*DN* 4:23–26). Here he draws on the metaphysical tenet of the ontological non-substantiality of evil, which "does not exist per se," but is a "kind of lack," and, with Origen, Gregory of Nyssa, and Evagrius, argues that no creature is evil by nature: neither souls, nor demons, nor irrational animals. "In the whole of nature" evil does not exist. If demons were evil by nature, they would not come from the Good and would not even *be*. But at the beginning they were good, their very essence (*ousia*) is good, and insofar as they exist they *are* good. They have become evil in that they have ceased to possess and exert the divine goods; even in their case, evil is a perversion of their own nature. However, as Dionysius goes on to argue, with Origen and Gregory Nyssen, evil is "unstable"—for stability belongs to the Good only—and cannot possibly endure forever. Not even demons will be evil eternally. Nor will they cease to exist, because in that they are, and live, and think, they are good (qua creatures of God the Good).

Emiliano Fiori notes that in his extremely few explicitly eschatological passages Dionysius speaks of punishments (*Ecclesiastical Hierarchy* 7.3.6–7; *Divine Names* 4.35).[13] These, however, are not said by him to be eternal. Also, Fiori remarks that when Dionysius speaks of apokatastasis and salvations he is not referring to eschatology, since the verb tense is the present. However, Dionysius uses the present tense on account of the atemporal eternity of God (emphasized by his philosophical model, Proclus), and not because he is not referring to eschatology.

It is remarkable that the Origenian thinker who wrote the *Corpus Dionysianum* chose to ascribe his teaching to Dionysius, the Athenian philosopher who converted to Christianity. In this way, Pseudo-Dionysius wanted to present the Origenian theological tradition, including the doctrine of restoration, as the true *Christian philosophy*.[14]

---

refers to Pseudo-Dionysius' work, clearly this work is here embedded in the Origenian tradition.

13. Fiori, "The Impossibility of Apokatastasis in Dionysius," 831–43.

14. See my review of *Re-Thinking Dionysius*: in *RBL* March 2010: http://www.bookreviews.org/pdf/7361_8021.pdf.

Pseudo-Dionysius' works enjoyed wide diffusion and success among West Syriac authors and were immediately translated into Syriac by Sergius of Resh'aina, himself an Origenian and Evagrian, who also wrote an important introduction to his own translation. The manuscript containing his translation is the most ancient manuscript in the world that includes the *Corpus Dionysianum* and is anterior to all Greek manuscripts that include it.[15] While often scholars deem the *Outlines of Theology* a fiction—i.e., Pseudo-Dionysius never wrote this work, but he wanted his readers to believe that he had written it—Sergius in his introduction (117) cites this work together with the *Divine Names* as the most important Dionysian work, in that it deals with the loftiest science. Sergius gives the impression that he has read the *Outlines*, in which Pseudo-Dionysius treated universal restoration.[16]

In summary, while Pseudo-Dionysius does not proclaim universal salvation from the roof tops, the influence of the Origenian tradition on his work seems clear once one is open to look for it and that influence included the theology of apokatastasis: nothing is evil by nature, for evil is non-being; rather, all things came from the Good God, and are ontologically good by virtue of that reality, and through Christ all things will return to unity in God.

THE CONDEMNATION OF ORIGEN
IN THE SIXTH CENTURY

The radicalization of Origenism among monks in Palestine in the first half of the sixth century, also favored by the circulation of Evagrian works and expressed in the *Book of the Holy Hierotheus* (in which apokatastasis espoused forms of Christian pantheism), precipitated the so-called condemnation of Origenism wanted by Emperor Justinian in 543 and 553. This condemnation was not directed against Origen's own thought (though Justinian was oblivious to this), but rather at a misconstruction of his ideas and a number of distortions and radicalizations of Origen's doctrines. This is the way in which Justinian received an account of

15. Cf. Perczel, "The Earliest Syriac Reception of Dionysius," 29–30.

16. John of Scythopolis, after Sergius' translation, prepared the Greek edition of the *Corpus Dionysianum*, on which all the subsequent editions were based. John's comments on the corpus often reveal that he is aware of the Origenian interpretation of which many passages in the *Corpus* were susceptible. He sought to defuse such interpretations in such a way as to determine later "orthodox" interpretations of it.

Origen's ideas from his theological counsellors, who were hostile to the radical Origenism of their own day.[17] A contemporary source, Cyril of Scythopolis, traces sixth-century Origenism back to "Pythagoras, Plato, Origen, Evagrius, and Didymus" (*Vita Cyriaci* 12). The same was done by Justinian and his counsellors; thus doctrines of sixth-century Origenism were misattributed to Origen himself.

The above-mentioned association of Origen with Plato and Pythagoras is telling: it points to a *believed* link between Origen's ideas—and specifically that of apokatastasis—and the idea of the transmigration of souls (i.e., reincarnation). However, while the notion of transmigration of souls (*metensomatosis*) was supported by both Pythagoras and Plato, it was *not* defended by Origen, who explicitly rejected it as being opposed to the "end of the world" foretold by Scripture. So against *metensomatosis* Origen set forth the Christian doctrine of *ensomatosis* (which did not imply the transmigration of a soul from one body to another).[18] It is a doctrine of apokatastasis *embedded within that of the transmigration of souls* that was condemned by Justinian's Fifth Ecumenical Council (553), *not* Origen's own doctrine of apokatastasis. In the earlier Provincial Council of Constantinople in 543, after Justinian's exhortation, it was declared that, "If anyone claims or maintains that the punishment of demons and of impious men is of limited duration and will come to an end sooner or later, or that there will be the complete restoration [*apokatastasis*] of demons and impious men, let this be anathema." In the Second Council of Constantinople (553), one of the fifteen anathemas—which were, however, formulated by Justinian *before* the opening of the council and appended to its proceedings—sounds: "If anyone supports the monstrous doctrine of apokatastasis, let this be anathema." The reference, as mentioned, was to a doctrine of restoration inscribed within that of the preexistence of souls. This is suggested by looking at the anathemas as a whole, and by the fact that the doctrine of apokatastasis was also held by Gregory Nyssen, yet no mention is made of him in either 543 or 553. Certainly, Gregory did not embrace a doctrine of apokatastasis embedded within that of the transmigration of souls—but neither did Origen.

Moreover, the aforementioned association between Origen and the Greek philosophers corresponds to an old heresiological cliché (that is, a commonplace used by heresiologists, those who collected and denounced

17. See Ramelli, *The Christian Doctrine of Apokatastasis*, 724–38. New work is underway by both István Perczel and myself.

18. See Ramelli, "Origen."

"heresies" or deviant doctrines, mostly asserting that these derived from philosophy), which both Cyril of Scythopolis and Justinian in his Letter to Patriarch Mennas of Constantinople used against Origen. This also fits very well with Justinian's hostility to both Origenism and the "pagan" Neoplatonic School of Athens, which he shut down. Justinian's Letter to Mennas attacks a number of doctrines that he attributed to Origen himself, but were certainly not Origen's, such as the coeternity of creatures with God, the preexistence of disembodied souls, the sphericity of the risen body (but also the denial of the risen body and the eschatological destruction of the body, ascribing two inconsistent theses to Origen!), besides the transmigration of souls mentioned above. In particular, Justinian linked the preexistence of disembodied souls to *metensomatosis* in Origen, while Origen himself rejected both doctrines.[19] In his letter, Justinian also criticized apokatastasis for making people lazy in obeying God's commandments, but this was already Origen's own pastoral concern. This is why, as we have seen, Origen reserved the doctrine of apokatastasis only for those who were advanced, and did good not out of fear but out of love for the Good—God.

The so-called "condemnation of Origen"—three centuries after his death!—was in fact a maneuver by Justinian and his counsellors, which was ratified by ecclesiastical representatives only partially, which is not to say not at all.[20] The 553 Council of Constantinople was wanted by Emperor Justinian, and not by Vigilius (537–55), the bishop of Rome, or by other bishops. Vigilius was forced to travel to Constantinople by the emperor's order, and would not agree to declare that the council was open; therefore, Justinian had to do so himself, and Eutychius, the patriarch of Constantinople, presided. Vigilius' documents, finally emanated by a council that was not even wanted by him, remarkably do not even contain Origen's name. On May 5, the council began its works against the "Three Chapters,"[21] with about 150 bishops, in the Basilica of Haghia Sophia. Pope Vigilius was absent, like the other Italian bishops. On May 14, he published the *Constitutum*, which condemned sixty passages from Theodore of Mopsuestia, but he refused to anathematize the dead theologian, or Theodoret and Ibas. (This must also have been his position with regard to Origen, who died long before Theodore and in good standing

19. See my "Origen."

20. See my "Constantinople II 553." Also, Richardson, "The Condemnation of Origen."

21. The "Three Chapters" in question were the writings of Theodore of Mopsuestia, certain writings of Theodoret of Cyrus, and the letter of Ibas of Edessa to Maris.

with the church.) Vigilius also forbade the conciliar bishops from going on without his approval. The council, however, cancelled the name of the pope from the diptychs in the seventh session, and Vigilius was imprisoned in Constantinople by Justinian, while his counsellors were exiled. In the eighth and last session, on June 2, the conciliar bishops published fourteen anathemas against the Three Chapters. They also proclaimed the perpetual virginity of Mary (eighth session, canon 2, DS 422: *aeiparthenos*, "perpetually virgin"). Pope Vigilius, on December 8, finally approved the condemnation of the "Three Chapters" (the aforementioned Theodore of Mopsuestia, Theodoret of Cyrrhus, and Ibas of Edessa, now considered "heretics" qua their relation to so-called Nestorianism), and in 554 Vigilius published a second *Constitutum*, which, however, did not even mention the Constantinople Council. The churches of Milan, Aquileia, and Spain did not recognize this council (this was the so-called Three-Chapter Schism), and Isidore of Seville did not hide his hostility to Emperor Justinian, who in fact was its sole promoter.

The anathemas that concern us, fifteen in number, appear in an appendix to the council's Acts and were already prepared by Justinian before the opening of the council; he simply wanted the bishops to ratify them. So, it is uncertain that these anathemas should be considered *conciliar* (i.e., proceeding from a council). In them Origen is considered to be the inspirer of the *"Isochristoi."* This was the position of the Sabaite opponents of Origen, summarized by Cyril of Scythopolis, who maintained that the council issued a definitive anathema against Origen, Theodore, Evagrius, and Didymus concerning the preexistence of souls and apokatastasis, thus ratifying Sabas' position (*Life of Sabas* 90).

Justinian was more of an administrator than of a theologian and cared more for the unity of the church and the empire than for theological doctrines, as Volker Menze also emphasized.[22] The main concern of the 553 Constantinople Council was the Christological doctrines of the "Three Chapters," *not* Origen. Ancient Popes Vigilius, Pelagius I (556–61), Pelagius II (579–90), and Gregory the Great (590–604) deemed the Second Council of Constantinople as exclusively concerned with "the Three Chapters"; they never mentioned it in connection with Origenism or with apokatastasis. They never speak as though they were aware of a "condemnation of Origen" stemming from that council. If, as it seems, Origen himself is never named in the authentic acts of the

22. Menze, *Justinian and the Making of the Syrian Orthodox Church*, Oxford: OUP, 2008.

council,[23] then Origen was never formally "condemned" by the church.[24] However, the condemnations of later Origenistic doctrines were *felt* to be directed against Origen, as well as against Didymus and Evagrius. This had a significant impact on the future of apokatastasis within Christian theology.

In passing over Gregory of Nyssa for condemnation, the church, which was fast becoming anti-Origenian, had to bring his work into line, for having such a high profile theologian "off message" was not good. Gregory's ideas concerning the purifying nature of otherworldly suffering were applied to purgatory, rather than Gehenna, to allow for the erroneous conclusion that Gregory admitted of the eternity of hell. Furthermore, the manuscripts that transmitted his works had interpolations and glosses intended to show that Gregory in fact did not support the doctrine of universal salvation,[25] clearly because it was highly embarrassing to have a saint in the church who proclaimed such a "heretical" theory. This embarrassment about having a universalist saint is the reason why Germanus of Constantinople in the eighth century expressed the widespread assumption that Gregory's works were interpolated by heretics who "dared instill in the pure and most holy source of his writings the black and dangerous venom of Origen's error, surreptitiously ascribing this foolish heresy to a man who is famous for his virtue and

---

23. Anathema 11 mentions Origen, but his name appears in the last position in a list of heretics, and it is the only name of the list that is out of chronological order: "Arius, Eunomius, Macedonius, Apollinaris, Nestorius, Eutyches, *and Origen*." The draft of this anathema, prepared in Justinian's *Homonoia*, had this list, but it did not include the name of Origen, which most probably was inserted into the proceedings of the council later. Several anathemas of the council as handed down, including those that mention Origen, did *not* belong to the original Acts, but appear to be later interpolations. The original Greek text of the acts of this council is lost, and suspicions had already been raised in 680 CE (at the Third Ecumenical Council of Constantinople) that the original Greek acts of the 553 council were interpolated. For this reason, Norman Tanner SJ (*Decrees of the Ecumenical Councils*, 106) excludes the anathemas from his edition of the Acts of the Councils, noting that they "cannot be attributed to this council". This is also one of the reasons why Henri Crouzel SJ ("Les condamnations subies par Origène et sa doctrine") argued that Origen was never officially condemned by the church and wished that the church could rehabilitate Origen—who spent all of his life in its defense and even, like Maximus, died as a Confessor.

24. This is the reason that some Catholic and Orthodox theologians have been able to reappropriate Origen's teachings for the twentieth- and twenty-first-century church.

25. See my edition in *Gregorio Sull'anima*, which also presents and comments on the glosses and interpolations.

learning."[26] In this way Gregory was remolded into a saint more acceptable to changing standards of orthodoxy.

What is clear is that from the mid-sixth century onwards it became
widely believed that apokatastasis was off limits (and an investigation into
the causes of the rejection of apokatastasis in late antiquity is underway),
even though only a specific version of it had been condemned, and this
had a significant impact on the tradition. From now on theologians with
such leanings had to find subtle and indirect ways of expressing them for
fear of being branded as heretics.

26. Quoted by Photius *Bibl.* Cod. 223. However, we have an important confirmation from the time of Justinian of the presence of this doctrine of apokatastasis in
Gregory's and the other Cappadocians' writings. It is offered by an ascetic from the
desert of Gaza, Barsanuphius' Letter 604. A monk has asked him why Origen's doctrines, especially apokatastasis, were supported by orthodox authors, and even saints,
such as the Cappadocians. Barsanuphius did not at all deny that the Cappadocians
supported the doctrine of apokatastasis, but simply observes that even saints can have
a limited understanding of the mysteries of God.

MAXIMUS THE CONFESSOR: CRITICIZING ORIGENISTIC VIEWS AND EMBRACING ORIGEN'S TRUE THOUGHT

Maximus the Confessor (580–662), after being an assistant of the Byzantine Emperor Heraclius, was abbot of the monastery of Philippicus in Chrysopolis, across the water from Constantinople, before moving to Carthage in Egypt. He is best known for his defense of the Chalcedonian idea that Christ had both a divine and a human will, a belief for which he was exiled, tortured, imprisoned, and eventually died. But while he was convicted as a "heretic," his reputation was quickly revitalized after his death and he was sainted; indeed, the controversial view that he suffered for the faith became accepted by the whole church at the Sixth Ecumenical Council in 680–81. Today Maximus is highly esteemed as a theologian in both East and West, and is the object of increasing scholarship.

Maximus had read Origen, Didymus, and Evagrius, all supporters of universal restoration. However, he lived after Justinian's anathemas, which created a new and hostile context for those engaging Origen's thought. Maximus himself was charged with Origenism and in a trial in 665 he had to respond to such accusations (*Life of Maximus*, BHG 1234.23A;93A). Mor Michael Rabo, or Michael the Syrian, based on a polemical treatise by a priest, Simon of Qeneshre, in his *Chronicle*, 423–25, depicts Maximus as an Origenian, committed to the doctrine of apokatastasis. The same is repeated in the anonymous *Chronicle to the year 1234*, 130.

That Maximus supported the doctrine of restoration in the form of universal salvation is debated in modern scholarship. E. Michaud in 1902,[27] V. Grumel in 1928,[28] and then Hans Urs von Balthasar[29] thought that Maximus did adhere to the doctrine of universal salvation, albeit prudently and without professing it overtly. This idea has been rejected by Brian Daley, but picked up again by Torstein Tollefsen.[30] What are we to make of this?

It is certainly true that Maximus criticized Origenism, but Maximus' criticism of Origenism does not involve Origen's own doctrines,[31] and even less that of apokatastasis. The latter is notable for its absence from Maximus' criticisms of some Origenistic tenets. According to Michaud, Maximus embraced the doctrine of universal salvation with no hesitations; if in some passages he seems less willing to admit of it, it is because the tone of those passages is moral and not theological. What is clear is that Maximus never states the eternity of hell. Grumel thought that Maximus was inspired by Gregory of Nyssa on this score, albeit expressing himself with caution after the Justinian business.

27. Michaud, "S. Maxime le Confesseur et l'apocatastase"

28. Grumel, "Maxime le Confesseur," 457.

29. Balthasar, *Kosmische Liturgie*, 355–58.

30. Daley, "Apokatastasis and 'Honorable Silence,'" 309–39; Tollefsen, *The Christocentric Cosmology*, 103: "universal salvation, that is to say, a salvation of all created beings." See also Ayroulet, *De l'image à l'image*; Blowers, *Maximus the Confessor*.

31. The doctrine of the body that Maximus criticizes in *Amb.* 42 is *not Origen's own*. For he did not maintain the preexistence of disembodies souls (see my "Preexistence of Souls?") nor that "bodies were invented as a punishment for souls due to the anterior evilness of incorporeal beings" (*Amb.* 42:1328A) nor that bodies will disappear completely after the resurrection (1333A). Origen was clear that only the Trinity can subsist incorporeally (see my "Origen"). Likewise, it is not Origen's, but a post-Evagrian doctrine, that the initial henad (i.e., substantial unity) of rational creatures fell and acquired bodies as a punishment (1069A).

Hans Urs von Balthasar,[32] followed by Polycarp Sherwood,[33] observed that in Q. ad Thal. prologue and 43, Maximus interprets the two trees of the garden of Eden—that of life and that of the knowledge of Good and evil—in a moral and anthropological sense, but he states that the spiritual exegesis of that passage is better. However, he does not expound it, in order to "honor with silence" the "depth" of this meaning. Maximus uses the same reticence in reference to Christ's victory over evil. The mystical doctrine to be covered in silence is Origen's doctrine of universal salvation. Maximus did not profess it overtly not only due to the Justinian incident, but also because of his pastoral concerns—which Origen himself shared—that the preaching of this doctrine before spiritually immature people might lead to moral relaxation. I remark that at the end of Q. 43 Maximus observes that those who are endowed with wisdom, which is a gift of grace, know that what is bad can be so in one respect and not in another, and likewise what is good and noble can be so in one respect and not in another. In the prologue, Maximus exalts again the "most blessed silence, superior to human thought." He connects this with the telos, the eschatological discourse, and the ultimate participation in the divine, ineffable goods, and it may well be related again to the doctrine of apokatastasis. I would also add Amb. 45:1356C, where Maximus decides to keep his silence on the "more sublime" interpretation of the beginning, namely the creation of the first human being free from any passion or sin. The beginning is reflected in the end, with the restoration of humanity to a condition without passions or sin. The similarity between the beginning and the end is indeed declared by Maximus, e.g., in Amb. 71:1412D: "The first and the last things are similar to one another and are truly, while . . . all that comes between them passes away," according to the principle of similarity between beginning and end that was defended by Origen (and by Plotinus, as will be shown in a future, systematic comparison between the two), and was already suggested in the Letter of Barnabas 6:13: "Behold, I make the last things [ta eskhata] the first." Now, according to Maximus, at the beginning, "sin did not belong to human nature" (Amb. 5:1048B), therefore it will not in the end. In Amb. 48:1361D Maximus applies again silence to the ultimate end, beyond both the present and the future aeon, the supreme culmination of all goods.

---

32. Balthasar, Kosmische Liturgie, 355–58.

33. Sherwood, The Earlier Ambigua of Saint Maximus.

In *Q. et dub.* 19, Maximus takes over the notion of apokatastasis of Gregory of Nyssa and comments that the church knows three kinds of apokatastasis:

1) the restoration of an individual to its original condition thanks to virtue;

2) the restoration of human nature thanks to the resurrection, which makes it incorruptible and immortal;

3) the eschatological restoration of the faculties of the soul, "decayed due to sin," to their pre-lapsarian state, for which Maximus expressly refers to Gregory of Nyssa.

The equation between resurrection and restoration also derives from Gregory. The restoration of the faculties of the soul will be an ontological restoration that will annul the effects of sin and therefore evil. This restoration too will be universal: "For as the whole of human nature in the resurrection must recover the incorruptibility of the flesh in the time we hope for, so also the subverted faculties of the soul, in the long sequence of aeons, will have to lose the memories of evilness that are still found in itself. Then the soul, after crossing all the aeons without finding rest, will arrive at God, who has no limit." The souls will eventually know God. Maximus is reminiscent of 1 Timothy 2:4: "God wants all human beings to be saved and to reach the knowledge of the truth." All will attain the knowledge of God, albeit not all will immediately attain participation in them (*Q. et dub.* 99). This participation, however, can well come later.

This proposal is strongly suggested by a parallel passage in which Maximus treats again the eventual restoration. He states that the transformation of humans will shall take place "thanks to the change and general renovation that will come to pass in the future, *at the end of all aeons*, by the work of God our Savior: *a universal renovation of the whole human nature*, natural and yet by grace."[34] If human will is transformed in this way, no one will be able to obstinately remain in evil forever. Indeed, the purified and renewed souls will reorient themselves toward God. In *Q. ad Thal.* 59 Maximus similarly states that due to sin human noetic faculties had shrunk, but they will be restored (the verb is precisely the corradical of *apokatastasis*). In this same passage, Maximus also develops the Origenian and Gregorian theme of *anastasis* (resurrection) as *apokatastasis* (restoration) and of the latter as the restoration to virtue, thus

---

34. *In Ps. 59*, PG 90:857A.

displaying the three meanings of apokatastasis that he delineates in *Q. et dub.* 19.

In *Q. ad Thal.* 60 the aim of God from before the foundation of the world is individuated in Christ's inhumanation (i.e., the union of divinity with humanity) and in the "recapitulation of all creatures into God." This is the goal of God's providence and "the mystery that manifests God's great intention" which existed before all the aeons. Christ-Logos announces and manifests this intention (in Isa 9:5 he is called "the announcer of the great intention"), showing "the abysmal depth of the Father's goodness." This converges with *Amb.* 41. The end (*telos*) will take place when every movement of creatures will cease and they will know the One in whom they will have been made worthy of dwelling, in the "fruition offered to them—inalterable and always the same—of the One who will be known by them." In this way, "we shall receive the deification unceasingly operated beyond nature" thanks to the Son, who, "by means of his inhumanation, personally accomplishes the mystery of our salvation. . . . For the Creator of the substance of beings according to nature had also to be the author of the deification, according to grace, of the creatures brought to existence, that the Giver of being might also appear as Giver, by grace, of 'always being well.'"[35]

Maximus seems to have inherited from Clement his discourse about living, living well, and living always: the Logos Creator, in the beginning, has given us "living" (τὸ ζῆν/*to zēn*), then, as teacher, he has taught us "living well" (τὸ εὖ ζῆν/*to eu zēn*), so as to offer us, in the end, "living always" (τὸ ἀεὶ ζῆν/*to aei zēn*, *Protrepticus* 7.3). The distinction between living and living well was already established by Aristotle (*Pol.* 1252b29: frs 5 and 9 Walzer), but Clement added the third element, "living always," or "eternally" (τὸ ἀίδιον ζῆν/*to aidion zēn*, *Protr.* 7.1).

In *Car.* 1:71, Maximus states that God will unite to all humans, those who are worthy of this and those who are unworthy. This would not seem to imply for Maximus the deification of all humans.[36] Nevertheless, this is God's aim, from before creation to now. In *Amb.* 42:1329B (cf. 65:1392B) Maximus remarks that those who cannot participate in the Good who is God will suffer, but he does not state that this exclusion will be eternal. In *Q. ad Thal.* 59, it is said that those who are worthy of God will enjoy being united to God, while the unworthy will suffer in that

---

35. Some centuries later Jesus will proclaim to Julian of Norwich: "all shall be well" and "I shall make all things well." See below the section devoted to Julian.

36. Larchet, *La divinisation de l'homme*, 652ff.

union. Again, it is not stated that this suffering will be eternal; only for beatitude does Maximus state that it is eternal and beyond all aeons. In *Amb.* 21:1252B, Maximus observes that those who have sinned following their passions, in the future world will remain far from the relation with God; this will be their punishment even for many aeons, but Maximus does not say that this state will endure after the end of all aeons. Passages that some scholars have interpreted as references to eternal damnation[37] in fact cannot support this hypothesis, because Maximus here uses the adjective αἰώνιος/*aiōnios* in reference to the future judgment or punishment, and we have already shown that this does not mean eternal, except when applied to God.

The hypothesis of an eternal permanence of evil, which the existence of everlasting hell requires, contradicts Maximus' theory of the ontological non-subsistence of evil, which he shares with Origen, Gregory of Nyssa, and Evagrius, and which he expresses in many places.[38] In *Q. et dub.* 10, Maximus interprets the eschatological Sabbath in a mystical way, as a renunciation of evil and the disappearance of evil. Maximus can thus conceive of an αἰώνιος/*aiōnios* ("otherworldly") permanence in evil, but *not* of an ἀΐδιος/*aidios* ("eternal") permanence in evil. The mystical "eighth day," the day after the Sabbath rest, corresponds to this absolute eternity. Maximus, indeed, admits of spiritual progress also in the world to come, after the resurrection (*Amb.* 63). For the latter coincides with the first mystical Sunday, but after this there comes the New Sunday and many other feasts, which bring about a progressive participation in the

37. E.g., Moreschini, *Storia*, 733–37. The following are the passages adduced: *Carit.* 1:55: whoever is outside love is passible of "αἰώνιος/*aiōnios* judgment" (which is not an "eternal judgment," but the judgment that will take place in the other world); 1:56: whoever hates his neighbor deserves "αἰώνιος/*aiōnios* punishment"; 1:57: whoever speaks against his neighbor falls out of Christ's love and deserves "αἰώνιος/*aiōnios* punishment"; 2:34: passions and ignorance deserve "αἰώνιος/*aiōnios* punishment" (these refer not to eternal punishment, but punishment in the world to come). *Lib. Ascet.* 27 mentions Isaiah's prophecy on the "αἰώνιος/*aiōnios* place" or otherworldly place of punishment for sinners, where their fire will not be quenched and their worm will not die. These biblical expressions indicate a qualitative difference between the fire and worm of the other world and those of this world, which can be quenched and killed; they do not imply absolute eternity. In *Q. et Dub.* 173 all beings are said to have a place in God's *logoi*: if some go away from them, renouncing their own *logos* in order to follow other things that have no ontological consistence (i.e., evil), they will incur the "αἰώνιος/*aiōnios* judgment" (i.e. judgment in the other world); there is *no* mention of eternal condemnation.

38. E.g., *Amb.* 42:1332A; *Amb.* 20:1237C; *Amb.* 7:1085A, and *Quaest. ad Thal.* prologue.

divine goods and are called "mysteries." The same succession of present aeon > death > future aeon (with the resurrection) > further feasts and purifications is found in *Amb.* 50:1368D. In *Amb.* 59, in the framework of Christ's descent to hell, Maximus is clear that one can come to adhere to God even after death, by means of conversion and faith.

The second coming of Christ at the end of the world will determine "the *transformation* of the universe and the *salvation* of our souls and bodies" (*Amb.* 42:1332D), because Christ "leads and invites all to his glory, insofar as possible, with the power of his inhumanation, being the initiator of *the salvation of all*, and *purifies the stains of sin in all*" (1333A).[39] In *Amb.* 7:1097AD Maximus, after introducing the Adam–Christ parallel, highlights the recapitulation of all in Christ, realized through "the mystery of God's most holy coming into the human being, made necessary by transgression." In *Amb. ad Thom.* 5:1049A, Maximus describes Christ's inhumanation in the following terms: "when he became a human being he lifted up human nature together with himself, making it into a mystery." In 4:1044AD and 1045B, he articulates this concept:

> Christ destroyed our worse element, that is, the law of sin that comes from transgression. . . . He saved the human beings who were kept prisoners by sin, paying in himself the price of our ransom, and even had them participate in divine power. . . . He realized the *complete salvation of all humanity*, making his own all that our humanity is. . . . He wanted to make me the lord of the devil, who, by means of deception, lorded it over all like a tyrant. . . . [T]hrough passible flesh he *deifies the whole humanity*, which had become earth by effect of corruption, . . . with a view to the perfect submission by which he will bring us to the Father after saving us and making us like himself by grace. . . . This is the mystery of our salvation.

Maximus too, like Origen and Gregory of Nyssa, seems to envisage the ultimate salvation and deification of all humanity. Due to circumspection, Maximus strategically ascribes these clearly universalistic

---

39. By "insofar as possible" I do not think that Maximus is expressing hesitancy about the final outcome. Rather, I think it qualifies the degree to which it is possible to share Christ's glory. He says, with Origen, that each one will need his time and his providential care, and that no one will reach the same glory as Christ, since Christ is God and no human is.

statements to "a man, holy in thought and life," whom he asked for illumination. In this way he presents the idea of universal salvation as a "holy thought."

In *Amb.* 42 Maximus himself is adamant that the aim of divine providence is the restoration of humanity: "Look for the main reason [*logos*] of the birth of the human being, a reason that keeps its stability and never abandons it. Also, consider what is the way of its education due to sin, in accord with God's educative economy, whose end is the correction of those who are educated and the perfect return to the *logos* of their birth, that is, their restoration [*apokatastasis*]." Christ is the main agent of divine providence, and in *Amb.* 31:1280A Maximus consistently declares that "Christ-God has filled the supernal world, *divinely realizing in himself the salvation of all*" (1280D). In Christ, human nature is restored to its perfection, freedom from passions, and incorruptibility. Christ thus performs the restoration (*apokatastasis*) of human nature (*Q. ad Thal.* 42), on which Maximus insists also in *Q. ad Thal.* 61. In *Amb.* 3:1276AB, too, Maximus comments that Jesus' birth from a virgin was necessary to the restoration of human nature, which also entails its deification.[40]

In *Q. ad Thal.* 65 the mystical Sabbath that is to come must be honored with silence, which reinforces the impression that Maximus is referring to universal restoration. It will subsume all mystical feasts and will see the cessation of all movements and the passage of all into God. After that there will be no dimension or extension any more. In *Amb.* 10, likewise, the eighth day of apokatastasis is indicated as truly eternal (ἀΐδιος/*aïdios*), as "a day without sunset and with no end."

Maximus insists on the universal and meticulous action of divine providence, which he, like Origen, does not consider to be in conflict with our freedom of will.[41] Maximus, like Origen, makes much of free will[42]

---

40. Maximus drew from Origen and Gregory of Nyssa the idea that the distinction of humanity into genders and procreation is secondary; the human being that is in the image of God is neither endowed with a heavy, mortal body nor male or female. See my "Origen" and "Christian Platonists in Support of Gender Equality", in *Otherwise than the Binary*, eds. Danielle Layne and Jessica Elbert Decker, forthcoming. Maximus' concept of the prelapsarian human body (*Amb.* 45:1353A) is similar to that of Origen and Gregory of Nyssa: a less thick body, harmonious, not liable to passions, and immortal. So will it be also after the resurrection. Maximus highlights the idea of the restoration of the original integrity of the human being thanks to the Logos' inhumanation (*Q. ad Thal.* 21).

41. E.g., *Amb.* 10:1108C: "it is present to all in all" to help all attain virtue.

42. E.g., *Myst.* 24; *Amb.* 65:1392D; *Opusc.* 1, PG 91:25B; *Q. ad Thal.* 6:280D.

and excludes any automatic salvation: "The mystery of salvation belongs to people who want it, and not to people who are forced to submit to it."[43] In Q. ad Thal. 61 Maximus remarks that God gave to humanity an absolutely eternal (ἀΐδιος/aïdios) life and will *restore* it again (the verb is again the corradical of *apokatastasis*). In *In Or. Dom.* 82, Maximus describes absolutely eternal (ἀΐδιος/aïdios) life as the restoration (*apokatastasis*) of humanity liberated from sin and the law of sin.

Like Origen, Maximus also describes the *telos* using 1 Corinthians 15:28:

> The Godhead will really be *all in all*, embracing all and giving substance to all in itself, in that no being will have any movement separate from it and nobody will be deprived of its presence. Thanks to this presence we will be, and will be called, gods and children, body and limbs, because we will be *restored to the perfection of God's project.*" (*Amb.* 7:1092Cff.)

Humanity alienated itself from this project with the fall; this is why God introduced physical death, but—as Origen, Gregory of Nyssa, and Methodius also thought—in this God was at work "administering our salvation, that, by loving non-being [i.e., evil], instructed then by suffering, we might learn to reorient our intellective faculty toward the Being." It is not accidental that, in this connection, Maximus describes Jesus Christ as "the restorer" (ἀποκαθιστάμενος/*apokathistamenos*) of all (PG 91.1400BC). The action of restoration will be performed through the reorienting of the free wills of rational creatures towards the Good: "God, as he alone knew, completed the primary principles [λόγοι/*logoi*] of creatures and the universal essences of beings once for all. Yet he is still at work, not only preserving these creatures in their very existence, *but effecting the formation, progress, and sustenance of the individual parts that are potential within them.* Even now in his providence he is bringing about the assimilation of particulars to universals, *until he might unite creatures' own voluntary inclination to the more universal natural principle of rational being through the movement of these particular creatures toward well-being, and make them harmonious and self-moving in relation to one another and to the whole universe*" (Q. ad Thal. 2).[44]

---

43. Q. 1309C4–11; *In Or. Dom.* CCG 23:154ff. Maximus emphasizes the voluntary nature of the submission of all to God in the end also in 1076Aff. and the retention of free will even in the final deification. He agrees again with Origen.

44. Trans. Blowers and Wilken.

Now in this restorative reorienting of wills, Christ's role is paramount, in particular through his cross. For the crucifixion "effects the utter abolition of all unnatural qualities and movements that have added themselves to our natures owing to the disobedience, and restores all the original natural qualities and movements. In this apokatastasis, not even one of the *logoi* of creatures will be found falsified" (*Q. ad Thal.* 445–51). Not . . . even . . . one. István Perczel agrees with me that this claim "has a strong universalist taint, as normally all of Maximus' statements about the complete restoration of the human nature in Christ do have."[45] Indeed, writes Maximus, Christ, "having reconciled humans in himself, leads them through the Spirit to the Father" (*The Lord's Prayer* 73–74). What he has effected is "the apokatastasis of the impassible nature oriented towards itself" and not towards evil, "the abolition of the law of sin," and "the destruction of the evil tyranny that had imprisoned us through deceit," i.e., the devil's deception of humans by making them believe that evil and sin are good (77–85). Maximus clearly interprets sin according to the doctrines of ethical intellectualism, just as Origen and Gregory of Nyssa had done.

Not only Christ's cross, but also his inhumanation is pivotal to the restoration. Indeed, Maximus takes over Origen's motif of the generation of the Son in the heart and will of the believers, who are thus saved. The Son "becomes incarnate through those saved," in whom the likeness to God is attained, through a voluntary effort, in the reshaping of the will according to the divine likeness. The *logos* of such a person becomes a dwelling place of the Holy Spirit, as well as of the Father, and gives birth to the Son from its will; this makes the soul of this *logikon* a virgin mother, having no male-female dualism in itself, and therefore no decay (352–402). The ideal of the unified *nous* is clearly an Evagrian legacy. As Maximus puts it in *Questions to Thalassius* 60, the ultimate *telos*, for which all things exist and in view of which all things are ordained is "the recapitulation of all the beings that God has created." For Christ "has established himself as the innermost depth of the Father's Goodness." Due to the mystery of Christ, all beings in all aeons have received their beginning/principle and end/fulfilment in Christ.

István Perczel also agrees with me that Maximus' thought has much in common with that of Origen and Evagrius and, explicitly referring to my treatment of apokatastasis in Maximus in my 2013 monograph, he

---

45. Perczel, "St. Maximus on the Lord's Prayer," 239.

concurs that "Maximus partly allowed for apokatastasis and partly even explicitly exposed this doctrine."[46] In many ways, despite his understandable caution, it seems fair to think of Maximus as a true heir of Origen.

SEVENTH–EIGHTH CENTURY SYRIAC ASCETICS: ISAAC AND JOHN

Isaac of Nineveh

A near contemporary of Maximus, the seventh-century Syriac ascetic St. Isaac of Nineveh († c.700), knew Evagrius' work very well, including his *Chapters on Knowledge* in their non-expurgated Syriac version, which bristle with passages relevant to the doctrine of apokatastasis. Like Evagrius, Isaac also composed *Chapters on Knowledge*: these coincide with the third chapter of his Second Part, discovered by Sebastian Brock in 1983 (ms. syr. e. 7, Bodleian Library, Oxford). Moreover, he knew Ephrem, John the Solitary, Macarius, Abba Isaiah, and probably Bar Sudhaili. He retired from his bishopric in Nineveh after just five months and became a hermit in the mountains.[47] Like Clement, Origen, and Gregory of Nyssa, Isaac is profoundly convinced that sufferings inflicted by God can only have a therapeutic and pedagogical aim, not a retributive one:

46. Perczel, "St. Maximus on the Lord's Prayer," 226–27. According to Perczel, five anecdotes in John Moschus' *Spiritual Meadow*, 4, 8, 19, 96, and 104, indicate that Maximus and his circle harbored sympathy for the Origenists of their day ("St. Maximus on the Lord's Prayer," 255–71). Indeed, Moschus' stance appears to be the opposite of that of the anti-Origenist Cyril of Scythopolis and his Sabaite circle.

47. His works, which address monks, are divided into a First, a Second, and a Third Part. The First is comprised of eighty-two homilies, soon translated into Greek; the Second Part, in forty-three texts, has never been translated into Greek; the Third Part has become available to scholars only recently, thanks to Sabino Chialà's 2011 edition, *Isacco di Ninive: Terza Collezione*, in CSCO Syri 246 (Corpus Scriptorium Christianorum Orientalium). Brock, "Four Excerpts," offers the edition and translation of four new excerpts never edited so far; Hansbury, *Isaac's Spiritual Works*, offers a text and translation from which Isaac's doctrine of apokatastasis emerges. Nestor Kavvadas, *Isaak von Ninive*, points out the frictions between East Syrian episcopacy and the anchorite mystical movement as represented by Isaac, and draws out of Isaac's writings, and especially the *Kephalaia Gnostika* (the same title as Evagrius' masterpiece), the underlying structure of Isaac's thought on the working of the Holy Spirit, with the tension between the here and now and the "new world" that can be momentarily anticipated in the present world. Recently Scully, *Isaac of Nineveh's Ascetical Eschatology*, is in full continuity with my treatment of Isaac's eschatology and soteriology in *The Christian Doctrine of Apokatastasis*.

"God corrects with love, never inflicts evil in return for evil, but he only wants his image [i.e., the human soul] to recover its good health."[48] In this way, every soul will return pure from passions and evil, as it was in the beginning.[49] For God "loves the whole human nature, not the single person" (*Third Part* 6:31), which means that God loves the creature itself—which is good qua created by God—independently of the sins that the single persons may commit. The love of God surpasses sins and evil.

Even the death decreed by God after Adam's sin was only apparently a punishment, but in fact it was a benefit (as Methodius, Gregory of Nyssa, and Maximus also maintained): God "established death as though it had been a punishment for Adam, because of his sin, . . . but under the appearance of something fearful, he concealed his eternal intention concerning death and the aim that his Wisdom wanted to reach: . . . death would be the way to transport us *to that splendid and glorious aeon*" (*Second Part* 39:4).

Indeed, that God does not reason or act in terms of retribution is demonstrated by the incarnation and the passion of Christ: "Is the coming of Christ in any way commensurate with the works of the generations prior to it? Does this infinite compassion seem to you a retribution for those evil deeds? *If God is one who punishes, and does so by retribution, what adequate retribution can you possibly see here?*"[50] So, hell (Gehenna) cannot be an eternal punitive retribution: "Even regarding the affliction and condemnation of Gehenna, there is some hidden *mystery*, with which the wise Creator has taken as a point of departure for his future success the evilness of our actions and will. He uses this as a means to bring his salvific plan to perfection. This plan remains hidden to both angels and human beings, and it also remains hidden to those—demons or humans—who are undergoing suffering, for the whole duration of the suffering itself."[51] This clearly implies an end for this duration. Thus, in his definition of a merciful, compassionate heart in Homily 74, Isaac declares that this "burns for the whole creation: for the human beings, the animals, demons, every creature. . . . It cannot stand listening or seeing

48. *Spiritual Teachings*, Slavonic *Philocalia* 260.

49. "The soul, according to its nature, is untouched by passions. These are something that added itself later [this is also Gregory of Nyssa's and Evagrius' conviction], due to the sin committed by the soul. But before that, the soul was luminous and pure, thanks to the divine illumination, and *so will it be again*, when it returns to its origin" (*Spiritual Teachings*, Slavonic *Philocalia* 25).

50. *Second Part* 39:16.

51. *Second Part*, 39.

the slightest evil or sadness in the entire creation. Therefore, this person prays among tears, every moment, for the irrational animals, for the enemies of truth, and for all those who harm her, that they may be saved and forgiven. In the immense compassion that arises in her heart, which is in the image of God, beyond measure, she even prays for snakes," which are associated with the fallen angels. Indeed,

> If we said or thought that what concerns Gehenna is not in fact *full of love and mixed with compassion*, it would be an opinion tainted with blasphemy and abuse at our Lord God. If we even say that he will hand us to fire in order to have us suffer, to torment us, and for every sort of evil, we ascribe to the divine nature hostility toward the rational creatures that God has created through grace. The same is the case if we state that God acts or thinks out of retribution, as though the Godhead wanted to avenge itself. Among all of God's actions there is none that is not *entirely dictated by mercy, love, and compassion*: This is the beginning and the end of God's attitude toward us. (*Second Part,* 39:22)

This is among the clearest statements in the Origenian tradition on the nature of torment in Gehenna, all the more striking given that it was written in the seventh century, after Justinian's anathemas.

John of Dalyatha

Another Syriac monk and abbot with universalist sympathies was John of Dalyatha (c.690–780).[52] John was influenced by a number of patristic authors who had been supporters of apokatastasis: Diodore of Tarsus, Theodore of Mopsuestia, Evagrius, Gregory of Nyssa, Pseudo-Dionysius, and Isaac of Nineveh, as well as Babai's commentary on Evagrius' *Chapters on Knowledge* and St. Anthony, who in turn was influenced by Origen. So his theological inclinations are not hard to imagine.

Referring to God's clothing Adam and Eve in Genesis 3, John wrote that the "garment of light," which after the original sin was lost to humanity and replaced by the "skin tunics" (which for Origen, symbolized mortality and heavy corporeality), will be recovered, thanks to Christ and the help of angels (*Disc.* 7). Christ is, for John, just as for Origen, the

52. An English translation of his letters is Hansbury, *The Letters of John of Dalyatha*. See also Brock, "Some Prominent Themes," 49–59; Seppälä, "Angelic Mysticism," 425–33.

"physician of souls" (Letter 5:18; cf. 11:1). Christ is God's purifying fire itself, "in which the Creator has *purified* the creation" (Letter 4:6). Christ is "the fire that cannot be quenched," precisely that of hell, which kills to give better life (Letter 15:2). This notion was hammered home by Origen especially in his *Homilies on Jeremiah*.

In his prayer in Letter 42:1, John calls Christ "the ocean of our forgiveness." Evildoers "in the world to come" (αἰωνίως/*aiōniōs*) will experience God as a dark and mortal ocean (Letter 50:12–4), but not "forever." Indeed, the Godhead will "regenerate rational creatures in the likeness of its glory" and in *Ep.* 43:22, John renders well the Gospel expression "αἰώνιον/*aiōnion* fire" with "heavenly/divine [*shmynyt'*] fire," not "eternal fire." In Letter 47:2 John clearly describes only otherworldly beatitude, and not otherworldly torments, as eternal.

Christ's blood is that which purifies, shed as it was for the sake of forgiveness (Letter 14:3). It has "entirely paid the debt contracted by our evil will" (Letter 5:3). John often insists on God's love, which "liberates us from the prison where we have imprisoned ourselves, *even when we would not like*: may Your power prevail over us!" (Letter 5:4). (The idea that God even goes against our will to save us is typical of the *Conferences* ascribed to John Cassian.) In Letter 40:7, John of Dalyatha envisages the end as "the reconciliation and unity of all those separated," since these were "created for that unity." Those who are too little or lacking forces will be helped (Letter 40:11), because that will be "the unified place, which unifies those who are divided" and which is separated from this world by a boundary of silence (Letter 40:6). In Letter 31:2, Christ's great prayer for unity (John 17:21) is cited. (I will examine its enormous impact on patristic philosophical theology in Novum Testamentum Patristicum John 13–17.)

In Letter 49:9, John, like Evagrius, places the contemplation of God's providence *after* that of the final judgment, and observes that in the contemplation of the "totality of humanity as the image of God in which it was created" there is no longer "either righteous or sinner . . . either man or woman, but Christ fully appears in everyone."[53]

53. This letter may be by Joseph Hazzaya, another Syriac mystic who was deeply influenced by Origen and Evagrius. In this case it would testify to the presence of the doctrine of apokatastasis in Joseph too.
It is no wonder that, under the influence of John, Dionysius Bar Tsalibi in the twelfth century commented on Evagrius' *Chapters on Knowledge*, where Evagrius supported apokatastasis, including by showing that the contemplation of divine providence comes after that of divine judgment. My supposition is confirmed by Nestor Kavvadas,

With John of Dalyatha we will take our leave of the eastern church in the patristic period and move across to the Latin West. There the outstanding universalist at the end of the patristic period was John Scotus Eriugena.

ERIUGENA, THE LATIN HEIR OF GREEK PATRISTICS

John the Scot "Eriugena," meaning "the Irishman" († 877ca.), headed up the Palatine Academy under Charles the Bald, in Gaul, which prospered under his leadership. He was a gifted scholar, fluent in Greek, which was unusual in the Latin West at this time, and a definitive supporter of the doctrine of universal restoration and salvation. This comes as no surprise if one considers that his main sources were Origen, Gregory of Nyssa, Pseudo-Dionysius, and Maximus the Confessor. Of Gregory he even translated into Latin the treatise *On the Creation of the Human Being*, and of Origen he definitely knew and cited the treatise *On First Principles*. The very structure of his masterpiece, *Periphyseon* (*On Natures*), corresponds to that of Origen's *On First Principles,* the only anterior synthesis of Christian philosophy that can be compared to it. Both works, not accidentally, begin with the treatment of God as Universal Principle or Cause. Moreover, in both works the argumentative structure is the same: philosophical demonstrations are always joined to biblical support (and patristic support, in case of Eriugena). It is telling that Eriugena's homily on the

Joseph Hazzaya on Providence, who argues that his aim was to derive apokatastasis from Theodore of Mopsuestia.

Prologue to the Gospel of John was long believed by many—including Thomas Aquinas—to be a work of *Origen*'s! It is equally telling that Prudentius of Troyes accused Eriugena of embracing "*Origen*'s foolishness."[54] In addition, Eriugena also translated the works of Pseudo-Dionysius into Latin, adding his own commentary on them.

Let us consider some of the evidence regarding his universalism. In his work *On Predestination*, John the Scot insists on the ontological non-substantiality of evil (3:2–3; 7 and 10), an idea that by now we are well acquainted with as one of the main metaphysical pillars of the doctrine of universal restoration. For, if evil is basically not, it cannot possibly endure forever.

Eriugena is adamant that the root of all sins is not free will per se, which is a gift from God, but "the perverse movement of the rational substance that makes a bad use of the freedom of its own will" (*De praed.* 5:5–6). This movement tends to nothingness, which is "the bottom of evil" (*De praed.* 18:9). But the Godhead does not abandon its creatures; this is why it establishes a limit to the evildoing of sinners—with their death—lest it tend to the infinite (*De praed.* 18:7). And the very torment of evil wills in the other world (i.e., the torment of hell) is described by Eriugena as "a most secret operation" (*De praed.* 2:5), which enables the final return (*reditus*) of all sinners to the Good (i.e. God), the First Cause from which they had their very existence. Even the demons' evilness will be reintegrated into the final unity.

While the substance of sinners, which was created by God, will live forever (*semper permansura*) and enjoy beatitude in the end, "the evilness that is found in their perverse will is doomed to perish in eternity."[55] Their evilness, not the will itself, will thus disappear, and what will remain of them will ultimately be their good substance, restored to union with God. Indeed, in his *Periphyseon* Eriugena envisages a universal restoration as the conclusive cosmic movement: the initial movement was the passage from the unity of God to the division and multiplicity of creation, and the final movement will be (Platonically) the return of multiplicity to unity. According to Eriugena, the movement of reunification of all in God begins with the human being itself: the first distinction that will be eliminated is that between man and woman, which was first introduced because of sin and reduced humanity to a "bestial and corruptible kind

54. *De praed. adv. Joh. Erig.* 1011A.

55. "Their own malice/evilness is doomed to perish in eternity/ forever" (*Malitia vero, in perversa illorum voluntate reperta, in aeternum peritura*) (*Periph.* 5:931A).

of multiplication." This will be abolished thanks to Christ, in whom there is neither man nor woman (Gal 3:28), and this will happen "when human nature will be restored to its original condition,"[56] which is "in the image of God." After the unification and restoration of human nature, the earth and paradise will also be joined together (*Periph.* 2:8), and this again thanks to Christ, who in his resurrection united not only man and woman, but also earth and heaven (*Periph.* 2:10). Eriugena foresees the final restoration of all humanity to its original integrity,[57] in which it "will very clearly see the greatness and beauty of the image [of God] created in itself." In his view—as in Origen's and Gregory of Nyssa's—the restoration of humanity is made possible by Christ's inhumanation: for it is in Christ that human nature has been restored (*restaurata est*).

The human being was made for life in paradise and not for death on earth (*Periph.* 5:2), and it will return to life. The death of the body is the death of death (*Periph.* 5:7) and the beginning of restoration:

> The first *return to the origin* of human nature takes place when the body is dissolved and returns to the four elements of the sense-perceptible world of which it is composed.
>
> The second will take place at the resurrection, when each one will receive his or her own body back, after it has been reconstituted by the concourse of the four elements.
>
> The third will take place when the body becomes spiritual.
>
> The fourth will take place when the spirit—and, to speak more clearly, the whole human nature—will return to the primordial causes that are always and immutably in God.
>
> The fifth will be when nature itself, along with its causes, will proceed toward God, just as the air proceeds toward light. For *God will be all in all* [*omnia in omnibus*] when there will be nothing but God alone. (*Periph.* 5:8)

In *Periph.* 5:20 Eriugena explains that it is always inferior levels of reality that are subsumed and transformed into the superior ones: "the two genders are transformed into the human being, because the differentiation into sexes is inferior to the human being; the earth, which is inferior, is transformed into paradise; the earthly bodies, because they are inferior, will be transformed into heavenly bodies. Then there will follow the reduction of every sense-perceptible creature to unity and its transformation into intellectual, so that the whole of creation will

---

56. *Quando humana natura in pristinum restaurabitur statum* (*Periph.* 2:6).

57. *Ad pristinam integritatem restituatur* (*Periph.* 4:7).

become intellectual. In the end, the whole of creation will be reunited to its Creator, and will be one in God and with God. And this is the end and perfection of all visible and invisible things, *as all visible realities will be transformed into intellectual ones, and all the intellectual ones into God*, with an admirable *unification [adunatio].*" Apokatastasis will be the universal return of all beings to unity in God. All creatures of God will experience it:

> The *whole universe* has been *restored [restitutus est]*, for now in a special sense, in God's only-begotten Logos, who got incarnated and became a human being, but at the end of the world it will be restored [*restaurabitur*] in the same Christ in a general and universal way. Indeed, what he accomplished in himself in a special way, will he perform *in all* in a general way. And I mean, not only in all humans, but in every sense-perceptible creature. For the Logos of God, when he received human nature, *omitted no created substance*, which he did not receive in human nature. Thus, by receiving human nature, he received every creature in himself. Christ has saved and restored [*salvavit et restauravit*] *human nature*, which he received; therefore, Christ has undoubtedly *restored* [*restauravit*] *every creature*, visible and invisible. (*Periph.* 5:25)

When Christ took on humanity, he took on the entire creation, and this is why he can restore it. For Eriugena, too, it is clear that universal restoration and salvation depends on Christ. Likewise, he states that it is a matter of both faith and intelligence that "thanks to the inhumanation of the Child of God [i.e., Christ] *every creature*, in heaven and on earth, *has been saved.*"[58] In *Periph.* 5:27 Eriugena articulates this more:

> If God's Logos has assumed humanity, it has not assumed only one part of it, but *all of it, in its wholeness.* Now, if it has assumed all of it, it certainly *has restored [restituit] all of it* in itself, because in it *all beings have been restored [restaurata sunt omnia]*. He has left *no member of humanity*—entirely adopted by it—*prey to the eternal punishments* and the chains of evilness that cannot be broken, as evilness is followed by the misery of torments.[59]

---

58. *Omnis creatura, in caelo et in terra, salva facta est* (*Periph.* 5:24).

59. *Nihil humanitatis, quam totam accepit, perpetuis poenis insolubilibusque malitiae, quam tormentorum calamitas sequitur, nexibus obnoxium reliquit.* For Eriugena's remarkable assimilation of Stoic ἐκπυρώσεις to the Christian conflagration, see Jeauneau, "La Métaphysique du Feu," 299–318.

No human creature will be punished in hell eternally. In this respect, Eriugena definitely follows Origen and Gregory of Nyssa. Likewise, he is persuaded that all rational creatures will return to the enjoyment of their natural goods and will be restored into an angelic state (*Periph.* 5:32). The eventual restoration will indeed be universal, and will take place in three phases or modalities:

1) the material world will return to its causes or principles, (Medioplatonically) conceived as Ideas in the mind of God (*Periph.* 5:21 and 5:39).

2) There will be "the general return of the *whole human nature, saved* in Christ, to the original condition of its creation and to the dignity of the image of God" (5:39).

3) The blessed "will overcome, in a superessential manner, all the limits of nature up to the Godhead itself, and will be one and the same thing in God and with God" (5:39).

It is no surprise that Eriugena contests Augustine's interpretation of 1 Timothy 2:4, which in his view is distorted and misleading. While that passage reads, "God wants all human beings to be saved," Augustine claimed that "all human beings" there means "all those predestined."[60] This interpretation is unacceptable, according to Eriugena, who in *De praed.* 19 opens up the possibility of the eventual restoration.

However, Eriugena does make a distinction between all humans, who will be restored and saved, and the more restricted group (which may be distinguished from the rest either forever or in an initial phase), of those who will eat the fruit of the tree of life and be deified:

> This return [*reditus*] is considered in two ways, one of which teaches the *restoration* [*restaurationem*] *of the whole human nature* in Christ, whereas the other does not limit itself to contemplating the restoration *per se,* in a general sense, but also the *beatitude and deification* [*deificationem*] of those who will ascend to the Godhead itself. For one thing is to return to paradise, and another to eat the fruit of the tree of life; . . . its fruit is the blessed life, eternal peace in the contemplation of the truth, which is properly called de*ification* [*deificatio*]. (*Periph.* 5:36)

Like Pseudo-Dionysius, thus, Eriugena too draws an equation between the "return" or *reditus* (the third metaphysical moment in

60. *De corr. et gr.* 14:44.

Neoplatonism) and the restoration or *restauratio/restitutio*. This return and restoration (*apokatastasis*) is universal. All beings will be restored to God. However, only some beings—at least at an initial stage—enjoy deification by grace.

Daniel Heide, in an otherwise valid study of apokatastasis,[61] supports the widespread view that Eriugena distinguishes apokatastasis and theosis (deification), on the grounds that, unlike Origen, Eriugena distinguishes nature and will. However, I would note that the latter distinction was precisely emphasized by Origen, who availed himself of it in his argument for the salvation of the devil. I suspect Eriugena ultimately overcomes the apokatastasis-theosis divide in the supreme epistrophe or reversal/return, as the resolution of all beings in their principles and of these principles in God. According to Heide, for Eriugena, "the perverse wills of sinners shall be subject to everlasting punishment,"[62] but this is not exactly what Eriugena says; he rather states: *malitia eorum in aeternum peritura*. If evil perishes forever from the will, the will becomes good. It is not the will that is tormented forever, but evil that will be destroyed forever, just as had Origen maintained.

In *Periph.* 5:929A–30D Eriugena quotes, in Rufinus' translation, a very long passage from Book 3 of Origen's *First Principles*, which comments on 1 Corinthians 15:26. Origen here is speaking of the end/perfection/consummation of the world, which is the supreme good to which every rational nature tends, when God will be "all in all." This means that God will be all goods for every single creature, once they are purified from their vices. Given this purification, Origen can say that evil will remain nowhere. This will be the restoration of the original state of humanity. Origen, and Eriugena with him, underline that God will be not only in few or in many, but in *all*, absolutely, once both evil and death have vanished altogether. In such a condition, harmony and unity will reign, and there cannot be disagreement (930C).

And what of the devil? Eriugena notes that death, "the last enemy" (1 Cor 15:28)—an appellative of the devil, i.e. spiritual death—must disappear. But the devil is not destroyed in his substance, which is good in that it is a creature of God; rather, Eriugena explains, using Origen's very words, that the devil's perverse will shall be abolished: so he will be destroyed as "enemy and death," but not as a creature of God. For "nothing

---

61. Heide, "Ἀποκατάστασις," 195–213.
62. Heide, "Ἀποκατάστασις," 209.

is impossible to the Omnipotent, no being is incurable for the one who created it." The last sentence is that in which, as I have argued, Origen corrected Plato with respect to those who are "incurable."

Eriugena, who is quoting Origen extensively, remarks that Origen is clearer than Ambrose—his follower—on this score (930D): Ambrose stated that the demons will not remain forever, that their evilness may not be absolutely eternal, but this can mean either that the demons will be eliminated together with their evilness (annihilationism) or that their evilness will perish, while their substance will remain. Origen clearly embraced the latter option, and Eriugena overtly followed him.[63]

It must be noted that it is Alumnus,[64] the disciple, who objects to the doctrine of apokatastasis on the grounds that it conflicts with the (supposedly) "eternal" punishments mentioned in Scripture. Alumnus, as many commentators maintain, represents Eriugena before his encounter with the Greeks, while Nutritor, the master, represents Eriugena illuminated by his Greek theological education.[65] So it is clear that finally Eriugena, as Nutritor, sides with Origen, not with Augustine. And indeed he quotes Origen as authoritative on universal apokatastasis.

It is not accidental that it is especially for its universalism, clearly and avowedly influenced by Origen, that Eriugena's *Periphyseon* was criticized and even condemned some centuries later, in the thirteenth century. Eriugena, however, like Origen, died in peace with the church and during his life, again like Origen, was even a defender of "orthodoxy" against "heresies" concerning God's predestination.

---

63. In his (otherwise very positive) review of my *Apokatastasis* monograph, Mark Edwards states that I omitted Eriugena's quotation of Origen *Princ*. 3.6.5 on the devil *nouissimus inimicus* ("she omits to cite his alleged quotation of *De Principiis* 3.6.5, which concurs with the received text of Rufinus in all respects except that it introduces the noun *diabolus*"; Edwards, Review, 724), but in fact I cited and discussed it thoroughly on pp. 797–98, since this is one of the crucial points that Eriugena makes in support of universal restoration, and one in which he deliberately intends to make clear his dependence on Origen—his greatest inspirer after more than six centuries.

64. Alumnus (or the disciple) and Nutritor (or the master) are the two main characters of the *Periphyseon*.

65. Moran, *The Philosophy of John Scottus Eriugena*, 201.

The Middle Ages and the Early Renaissance

FRAGMENTS OF EVIDENCE FOR CONTINUING HOPE

The Middle Ages were not a hospitable time for Christian universalists, and lacking any official permission from the church to entertain a larger hope, we tend to find such notions appearing among people at the fringes, and sometimes developed in theologically heterodox forms. In this final chapter, we shall consider scattered fragments of evidence for continuing hope in its various forms, both orthodox and heterodox, among ordinary believers, theologians, heretics, poets, and mystics.

Aelfric's Testimony about Tenth-Century Anglo-Saxon Universalistic Trends

We have a tantalizing fragment of evidence from England just over a century after Eriugena's death concerning the hope that some at least may be rescued from hell. The Anglo-Saxon bishop Aelfric of Eynsham, at the very end of the tenth century, in his eschatological homily *On the Feast Day of the Virgins*, testifies to the theology of some unnamed opponents, whom he calls "heretics." These Christians, apparently at that time, believed that "the holy Mary, the Mother of Christ, and some other saints, after the Judgment will harrow the sinners from the devil."[1] This may or

---

1. *Aelfric's Catholic Homilies, Second Series*, vol. 2, nr. 39, 373. See Cubitt, "Apocalyptic and Eschatological Thought," esp. 45–46.

may not be witness to a continuing stream of Origenian thought at the grassroots—its focus on Mary and the saints seems to place the emphasis in a different place from the tradition we have been considering—but it certainly indicates that the idea of one's fate being sealed at death continued to be a cause of concern to Christians, who sought resources from their tradition to open up a wider hope.

Theophylact

In the eleventh century, Theophylact, the archbishop of Akhrida in Bulgaria († 1107), commenting on our core text 1 Corinthians 15:28, observed that "By these words some understand the elimination of evilness, because God will be 'all in all' clearly once sin has ceased to exist." He is probably speaking of contemporary theologians, although this might also refer to earlier church fathers. Certainty eludes us.

Amaury de Bène

Amaury de Bène († c.1207), a teacher of logic and theology at the University of Paris, and his followers are reported to have embraced universalistic doctrines. In 1206, the church forced him to revise his positions, which are basically unknown to us, but were obviously felt to be dangerous. This feeling of genuine concern is indicated by the fact that Eriugena's *Periphyseon* was only condemned at that time (1225), centuries after it was written, because of its influence on Amaury.[2] The latter was condemned by the 1215 Lateran Council.[3] That his followers proclaimed universal salvation is not totally certain, though they promised that they would bring all humanity to perfection. Some of Amaury's ideas passed on to the so-called Brothers and Sisters of the Free Spirit (thirteenth-fifteenth centuries).[4] In their view, God is "all in all," not only in the end—as is proclaimed in 1 Corinthians 15:28—but already now; as a consequence, sin and its punishment are not really existent. In their

---

2. See Cohn, *The Pursuit of the Millennium*, 152–56.

3. Cf. Cross and Linvingstone, *The Oxford Dictionary of the Christian Church*, 48. Amaury was accused of pantheism, of teaching that God permeates the whole universe, and of asserting the impeccability of his followers. This is why they were condemned in 1209 or 1210.

4. Cohn, *The Pursuit*, 156–86.

view, it is not exactly the case that all *will be* saved, because all are *already* saved. Some fringes of this movement seem to have believed in a universal absorption in God in the end, in a kind of pantheism. Hell and purgatory were regarded by these people as mere psychic states.[5] They rejected the mediation of the church and even of Christ, given that they deemed themselves in communion with God.

William Hilderniss

In the early fifteenth century, a Carmelite named William Hilderniss attached much more importance to Christ's mediating role than Amaury's followers: all creatures will be saved by Christ's suffering. However, the consequence he drew from this was very far removed from the positions of the patristic supporters of universal salvation: he seems to have thought that one's personal merits or demerits are completely irrelevant, and that hell does not exist, not even in a temporary an purgative form.

Cathars

Universalistic aspects can also be found among the Cathars, a sort of Manichaean dualistic revival movement that flourished between the twelfth and fourteenth centuries in northern Italy and southern France. They regarded death as a liberation from the body, which enabled communion with God. Some of them thought that in the end evil will definitely be removed (a tenet of Origen's, Gregory of Nyssa's, and Evagrius' eschatology). One branch of the Cathars even thought that the judgment has already taken place and that hell consists in suffering in this world. Christ's work is thus deprived of significance; indeed, the Cathars, in their matter-spirit dualism, even denied Christ's incarnation.

The forms of universalism we find in mediaeval heresies, such as Catharism, differ from that of the church fathers we have examined, who remained inside the church and, as I have shown, even elaborated their theodicy in defense of Christian orthodoxy and *against* the heresies of their day. Unlike these fathers, the mediaeval heretical groups that supported universalism often were against the church and did not recognize

5. Cf. Cohn, *The Pursuit*, 172–73.

it.[6] In many cases they had a poor exegetical and theological formation and made very little, or nothing, of Christ's mediative work.

Among the Poets

Several fourteenth-century English and French vernacular poets show universalistic drifts, even though in general their universalism is restricted to the baptized. William Langland (c.1332–c.1386) composed an allegorical poem that, in its last part, narrates the history of Christianity in an allegorical fashion.[7] This poem exists in at least three recensions; Recension B stems from the seventies of the fourteenth century and expounds eight visions of a dreamer, Will. In the last four visions (*passus* 15–20) the Soul, as a prosopopoeia, criticizes the church qua institution and emphasizes the importance of charity. The guardian of the Tree of Charity is Piers Plowman, who highlights the value of Christ's Passion and struggle against death and hell (*passus* 18). A debate between Christ and Lucifer is also staged. In the whole poem, there are many references to Christ's passion and its salvific effect. Langland especially underscores God's love and mercy and explicitly excludes an eternal condemnation, at least for Christians:

> Fiends and fiendkins · before me shall stand,
> And be at my bidding · wheresoere me liketh.
> And to be merciful to man · then my nature asketh;
> For we be bretheren of blood · but not in baptism all.
> But all that be my whole bretheren · in blood and in baptism,
> Shall not be damned to the death · that is without end; . . .

> And I, that am king of kings · shall come in such a time,
> Where judgement to the death · damneth all wicked;
> And if law wills I look on them · it lieth in my grace,
> Whether they die or die not · for what they did ill.
> Be it anything bought · the boldness of their sins,

> I may do mercy through righteousness · and all my words true.
> And though holy writ wills that I be avenged · on them that did
> ill, . . .

6. Ludlow, "Universalism in the History of Christianity," 198–99.

7. See at least Mairey, "Pratiques de l'allégorie dans la poésie anglaise du XIVème siècle," 266–88.

They shall be cleansed clearly · and washed of their sins
In my prison purgatory · till *parce* is called,
And my mercy shall be showed · to many of my bretheren.
For blood may suffer blood · both hungry and a'cold,
But blood may not see blood · bleed, without pity.[8]

(*Piers Plowman* B 18:374–96A)

The salvation of all Christians seems to have been supported by various English and French vernacular authors, especially Jean de Mandeville, Margery Kempe, and Langland himself.[9]

K. Tamburr has shown the importance of the motif of Jesus' descent to hell from the Anglo-Saxon age to the Reformation, in liturgical, homiletic, and devotional works, as well as dramatizations of the Passion, iconographical stories, and apocryphal works (especially the *Gospel of Nicodemus*, which exerted a profound influence on this literature).[10] In English liturgical texts Christ's descent to hell is often deemed a sign of the liberation of the whole church from the power of evil. Its connection with universal salvation is especially evident in the above-mentioned *Piers Plowman*.

8. Fendes and fendekynes bifore me shul stande/And be at my biddyng wheresoevere be me liketh./Ac to be merciable to man thanne, my kynde it asketh,/For we beth bretheren of blood, but noght in baptisme alle./Ac alle that beth myne hole bretheren, in blood and in baptisme,/Shul noght be dampned to the deeth that is wihouten ende . . . And that I am kyng of kynges shal come swich a tyme/There doom to the deeth dampneth alle wikked;/And if lawe wole I loke on hem it lith in my grace/Wheither thei deye or deye noght for that thei diden ille./Be it any thyng abought, the boldnesse of hir synnes,/I may do mercy thorugh rightwisnesse, and alle my wordes trewe/And though Holy Writ wole that I be wroke of hem that diden ille –/Nullum malum impunitum –/Thei shul be clensed clerliche and clenewasshen of hir synnes/In my prisone Purgatorie, til Parce it hote./And my mercy shal be shewed to manye of my bretheren;/For blood may suffre blood bothe hungry and acale. / Ac blood may noght se blood blede, but hym rewe.

9. Cf. Watson, "Visions of Inclusion," 145–87; Hill, "Universal Salvation in Piers Plowman B, XVIII 390," 323–25.

10. Tamburr, *The Harrowing of Hell in Medieval England*.

MYSTICS

Marguerite Porete

Marguerite Porete († 1310) was a learned French-Flemish mystic, perhaps a beguine, who was burnt at the stake after a trial because her ideas were deemed "heretical."[11] She wrote the *Mirouer des simples ames* (*Mirror of Simple Souls*), where elements of the Origenian tradition show up, as well as traces of Pseudo-Dionysius' apophaticism and Eriugena. Like Origen, Marguerite bases the impeccability of souls on love. Just as Maximus the Confessor, Marguerite honors with silence the mystery of universal salvation: "Paradise? Would you not assign something else to them? For in this way even murderers will attain paradise, if they will ask for mercy! . . . But about this, since you so wish, I will keep my silence" (Ch. 121).

Meister Eckhart

The great Christian Platonist Meister Eckhart (Hochheim, Thuringia, 1260–Avignon 1328) was a German Dominican theologian and

11. See Field, *The Beguine, the Angel, and the Inquisitor.*

philosopher with mystical instincts.[12] Kurt Flasch has recently argued that Eckhart should be thought of as a philosopher more than a mystic;[13] I agree that Eckhart was indeed an important philosopher, but would add that these two aspects are not incompatible with one another, as is proved, for instance, by Plotinus, Origen, and Gregory of Nyssa. Ekhardt was *both* a philosopher *and* a mystic.

With Eckhart we can trace an influence from the Origenian tradition. Eckhart knew and cited Origen, from whom, more or less directly, he derived a number of ideas, including that of the birth of Christ in one's soul. Eckhart frequently quotes Origen, fifty-one times in his oeuvre, even though many of these quotations seem to be indirect, mediated through Thomas Aquinas' *Catena aurea* or the *Glossa ordinaria*.[14] Eckhart, however, read directly at the very least Origen's *Homilies on Genesis*, in Rufinus' Latin translation.[15] He also cites Eriugena's homily on the Prologue of John, *Vox spiritualis aquilae* (*The Voice of the Spiritual Eagle*), as a homily of Origen (a misattribution shared also by Aquinas and highly indicative of Eriugena's indebtedness to Origen). Others in Europe in the Middle Ages know Origen's works and ideas: Peter Lombard (1100–1160) appreciated Origen both as an exegete and as a theologian, Albert the Great (c.1200–1280) valued him as a biblical allegorist, but rejected some of his doctrines, and Thomas Aquinas (1225–74), who cited Origen 168 times, often refuted what he deemed Origen's doctrinal errors. But Eckhart, unlike his Scholastic colleagues, never criticized Origen in any way; rather, he treated him as an authority and derived from him important doctrines.

Eckhart's very method, studying texts from the Holy Scriptures, whose philosophical content he set out through philosophical arguments, is the same as Origen's and Eriugena's. Like Origen, he regarded

12. On whom see, e.g., McGinn, *The Mystical Thought of Meister Eckhart*; Woods, *Meister Eckhart*; Hackett, *A Companion to Meister Eckhart*.

13. Flasch, *Meister Eckhart*. On Plotinus, Origen, and Nyssen mystics and philospohers see my "The Divine as Inaccessible Object."

14. Thomas Aquinas' *Catena aurea* is Thomas' extensive commentary on the Gospel of Luke. The *Glossa ordinaria* was a collection of glosses on the Bible, taken from patristic authors and thereafter, printed in the margins of the Vulgate. These glosses were widely used in cathedral schools from the Carolingian period (Eriugena's times) onward; their use declined in the fourteenth century.

15. Rubino, "*Ein grôz meister*: Eckhart e Origene," usefully collects all of Eckhart's quotations of Origen (153–65); a comprehensive study now in Elisabeth Boncour, "Eckhart lecteur d'Origène," PhD dissertation Paris 2014.

Scripture as a work of philosophy. In his definition of the subject matter of the gospel message—"the gospel contemplates being insofar as it
is being [*ens in quantum ens*]" (*Commentary on John*, 444)—Eckhart is
repeating Aristotle's very definition of metaphysics or "first philosophy."

The central theme of Eckhart's German homilies—the presence of
God in the individual soul, and the birth of Christ in the soul of the just—
stems from Origen. Also in a Latin work, his *Commentary on Exodus*,
207, Eckhart speaks of a spiritual conception that is immediately a giving
birth (*parturitio sive partus*). God the Father bears his Son in the ground
of the soul (the seat of the divine presence in the human being). This
motif, as Duane Williams has pointed out, amounts to applying to God
a female act and characteristic.[16] The male Father-God turns out to be
a female Mother-God, against the backdrop of a strong apophatic drift,
deeply aware of the impenetrable mystery of God. Origen had obviously
in mind the Septuagint version of Psalm 110:3, in which God says to the
Son, "before the morning star, I brought you forth from my womb"—
where God the Father is clearly represented as a Mother. Meister Eckhart
surely had Origen in mind, and also knew the Psalm. But it is in his vernacular homily *On the Noble Person* that Eckhart explicitly cites Origen
as "the great master" (*der grôze meister*) who described God's image, i.e.
the Son, as being "in the ground of the soul" as a seed and a spring of living water. He is echoing Origen's homilies, on Exodus, on Psalm 36, and
especially on Genesis (13.4, also cited in Eckhart's second Latin Commentary on Genesis, 193). Two whole homilies of Origen on Genesis, 12
and 13, are explicitly quoted by Eckhart in his second Latin *Commentary
on Genesis*, 189–203, about five kinds of inner, divine seed.

In his German Homily 41, Eckhart explicitly cites Origen (*Homilies
on Jeremiah* 9.4) to the effect that whenever one has good thoughts or
deeds one is born anew in the Son, to support his own view that when
we are "without why"[17] we are reborn in the Son and the Son is born
in us. And, even without citing him, Eckhart is echoing Origen's *Homilies
on Luke* 22.3 in his Latin *Commentary on John*, 117, when he says that
it is useless that Christ-Logos became flesh if he is not also born in the
individual. Eckhart also drew on Origen's *Homilies on Numbers* 23 for
the motif of God's joy at the birth of the Logos in one's soul, in his second

16. Williams, "Feminist Theology and Meister Eckhart" 275–290.

17. This odd expression is a typical notion of Marguerite Porete. Being "without
a why" means to give up reason altogether and surrender to this free state of "living
without a why"—which is not irrational, but supernatural.

Latin *Commentary on Genesis*, 180, and elsewhere.[18] God accomplishes in the soul the birth of the Son during the life of the soul in time, continuously and repeatedly. The soul thus becomes by grace what the Son of God is by nature and can thus share in the attributes and works of God, including the creation.

Like Origen, Eckhart insists that creatures are "nothingness" (*nihileitas, nulleitas*) in comparison with God. According to the papal bull of 1329, *In agro dominico* ("In the Lord's Field"), which posthumously condemned some propositions of Eckhart as "heretical," the latter asserted that "it may be conceded that the world was from eternity." This is a charge that was also leveled against Origen, although Origen was clear that what existed from eternity in the mind of God were the ideal paradigms and *logoi* of all creatures, and *not their substances*, which were created in time.

Origen had maintained that Christ is Justice itself—he does not participate in Justice, does not possess justice as a quality, but rather *is* Justice—and all the just participate in Christ, in a way becoming Christ. Eckhart elaborated on this and went further, basing himself on the notion of "becoming Christ." He claimed that the just person is Justice itself (like Christ). This is also why in his Latin *Commentary on Wisdom*, 44, he can aver that "all the just, qua just, are one," because they are Justice itself. Therefore, it is not righteous deeds that make a person just, but the just will do righteous deeds. Like Origen, Eckhart regards highly the works of charity, especially service to the poor.[19]

Like Eriugena, Eckhart maintained that the human being, as the mediator of the world, leads all creatures back to God, and Christ, who stands at the center of humanity, is the key to redemption. He is the sinless human being who restores the universal harmony. His temporal birth is included in his eternal birth, which also continually happens in the ground of the soul of the just. In his passion and death there is an overwhelming power that draws humans to God. Origen had similarly maintained that the cross of Christ was so powerful as to be enough to set right and save all rational creatures.

While he does not develop a consistent doctrine of universal restoration or salvation, Eckhart insists on the remedial nature of punishment.

18. See McGinn, "The Spiritual Heritage of Origen," who, however, does not discuss Origen's and Eckhart's eschatologies.

19. On Origen's attitude toward the poor, and his position that wealth is tantamount to theft, see my *Social Justice and the Legitimacy of Slavery*.

In his second *Commentary on Genesis*, probably stemming from his time in Strasbourg after 1313, Eckhart notes that the Genesis story of the fall teaches mythically/allegorically (*parabolice*) that any human being can fall into sin, and that "the punishments of the sinners bring them back to virtue and to the Lord of virtues" (*de poenis peccatorum reducentibus ad virtutem et Dominum virtutum*, 3.135). Indeed, like Origen (and Plato), Eckhart sees in suffering the most effective and most valuable means of purification. For suffering is a participation in the cross.

Eckhart mentions hell in various places—as virtually all the supporters of apokatastasis did—but he says that what burns there is "nothing" (*das Nicht*, German Sermon 5b). This is punished forever (Latin Sermon 43.1.427), but this is a limit concept, to contemplate and expect as a mental exercise (45.467) and in prayer (47.2.489). As Bardo Weiss notes, hell for Eckhart is "only the greatest suffering imaginable, . . . only an example of a huge suffering, which can befall also a righteous person, but without depriving her of her salvation."[20] In this sense, hell is not an eschatological condition to be feared. In Latin Sermon 41.1.414 hell is punishment for sins, but not eschatological—let alone that Eckhart speaks dramatically much less of hell than of salvation and bliss. Eckhart never uses fear of hell as a motivation for good behavior. Suffering the pains of hell according to God's will even signifies salvation for a person (*Pf.* 1.10). Whoever has been touched by truth, goodness, and righteousness, or has seen an angel, even just once, could even wish to stay one whole millennium in hell for that (*Pf.* 1.11; German Sermon 15). The righteous are so steadfast in their righteousness that they would not even notice the torments of hell (German Sermon 6). The humble person could force God even into hell (15). Eckhart paradoxically associates virtuous people with hell.

Thus, there is no unambiguous evidence that Eckhart rejected the doctrine of universal restoration; rather, his great admiration for Origen, his healing and purifying notion of punishment, his concept of the restoration brought about by Christ, and his concept of hell, all suggest that he may have had a penchant for this perspective.

---

20. *Die Heilsgeschichte bei Meister Eckhart*, Mainz: Grünewald, 1965, 177. He studies the original sin and the role of Christ, Mary, and the church in the salvific economy in Eckhart, as well as his eschatology (166–80).

Catherine of Siena

St. Catherine of Siena (1347–80) was an Italian mystic, a Dominican ter-
tiary, who was later canonized and proclaimed a Doctor of the Church. In
her biography, written by her spiritual director Raymond of Capua, she
voices the same desire as the just in the *Apocalypse of Peter* treated above:
"Lord, how can I be happy as long as one of those who were created like
me in your image and likeness, be lost or be taken from your hands? I do
not want any of my siblings, who are united with me in nature and grace,
to be lost . . . should your truth and your justice permit, I would want
hell to be destroyed, or at least no soul, from now onwards, to descend
there."[21] This is not a dogmatic declaration of apokatastasis, but the out-
pouring of a heart that yearns for such an outcome. Origen himself had
previously noted that the presence of any in hell forever would diminish
the heavenly joy of the saints, but also the body of Christ himself: "if the
delight does not seem to be complete for you who are a member, if another member is missing, how much more does our Lord and Savior, who
is the 'head' and the originator of the whole body, consider his delight to

---

21. *Vita di Santa Caterina scritta dal Beato Raimundo di Capua* (Siena: Cantagalli,
1982), 27.

be incomplete as long as he sees one of the members to be missing from his body" (Origen, *Hom. in Lev.* 7.2.10).

Julian of Norwich

Julian of Norwich (1342–1416/7),[22] an English anchoress faithful to the church, whose formation probably took place in the local Benedictine community in Norwich, during a severe illness in 1373 received many visions.[23] These were divided into "imaginative" and "intellectual" visions, and were published in the *Revelations of Divine Love in Sixteen Shewings*,

22. Critical edition Colledge and Walsh, *A Book of Showings*; Windeatt, *Revelations*, with a critical edition of the shorter and longer versions, based on all available manuscripts. See Baker, *Julian of Norwich*; Dutton, *Julian of Norwich*; Sweetman, "Sin Has Its Place, But All Shall Be Well"; Hill, *Women and Religion*; Whitehead, "Late Fourteenth-Century English Mystics," 367–70; Delrosso, etc., *Nuns*, on Julian of Norwich onwards; Rolf, *Guide to Julian*.

23. The name Julian is probably not that of this woman, who is anonymous, but that of the church of St. Julian close to which she was an anchoress.

in a shorter and older form and in a later and longer one (1393). Here the conviction of universal salvation is grounded in the mystery of the love of God. In her Revelation 13 Christ overtly declares:

> By the same Might, Wisdom, and Goodness that I have done all this, by the same Might, Wisdom, and Goodness *I shall make well all that is not well*. . . . It behoved that there should be sin; but *all shall be well, and all shall be well, and all manner of thing shall be well.*

Julian takes over Origen's, Gregory Nyssen's, Evagrius', and Pseudo-Dionysius' doctrine of the ontological non-subsistence of evil: "I saw not sin: for I believe *it hath no manner of substance nor no part of being*, nor could it be known but by the pain it is cause of." There is no evil that will not be turned into Good. As Christ explains, his work is much more powerful than sin:

> Since I have *made well the most harm*, then it is my will that thou know thereby that *I shall make well all that is less*. . . . I can *make all thing well, I will make all thing well, and I shall make all thing well*; and thou shalt see thyself that *all manner of thing shall be well.*

This also shows that according to Julian, just as according to Origen and Gregory of Nyssa, restoration is entirely grounded in Christ.

Julian, like Origen and Gregory, understands the ultimate outcome of all in the light of 1 Corinthians 15:28 ("God will be all in all"): "The oneing [= making one] of *all mankind* that shall be *saved unto the blessed Trinity*." This is why Julian can see Christ regarding all humanity as though it had no sin in it: it is humanity as it will be in the end, restored to its purity and freed from all evil, that Christ sees.

Just as Peter in Acts 3:21 announced the universal restoration that God planned from eternity, so too Julian announces this "great work" of God: "This is that Great Deed ordained of our Lord God from without beginning, treasured and hid in His blessed breast, only known to Himself: by which *He shall make all things well*. . . . For like as the blissful Trinity made all things of nought, right so the same blessed Trinity *shall make well all that is not well*." As for the impious, wicked Christians, demons, and Satan, Julian objects that all these will be unable to be included in the universal "being well," but Christ replies to her by means of the argument of God's omnipotence that was used both by Jesus in the Gospel and by Origen in support of universal salvation: "That which is impossible to thee is *not impossible to me*: I shall save my word in all things and I *shall make all things well.*"

In Revelation 16 Julian, like Origen, emphasizes that God does not want humans to do the good out of fear, but out of love. In the end "We shall see verily the cause of all things that He hath done; and evermore we shall see *the cause of all things that He hath suffered.* And the bliss and the fulfilling shall be so deep and so high that, for wonder and marvel, all creatures shall have to God so great reverent dread, . . . *marveling at the greatness of God the Maker.*" Julian notes the disproportion between "the endlessness and the unchangeability of His love" and the finitude of sins and evil. Gregory Nyssen too was well aware of this disproportion and from it he concluded the eventual victory of God—the Good over evil.

Julian's concept of universal salvation is based on the very nature of God, who is Love: "And I saw full surely that ere God made us He loved us; which *love was never slacked* nor ever shall be. And in this love He hath done all His works, and in this love He hath made all things profitable to us, and *in this love our life is everlasting.*" It is Gregory of Nyssa's argument in his homilies on the Song of Songs ("call God 'Mother' and you will not be mistaken, because God is Love, as John stated [1 John 4:8, 16]").[24]

Lady Julian offers a good note on which to close. While expressing the larger hope in very evocative and moving language, language that in some ways can mask the sophisticated theological notions undergirding it, she was careful not to do so in a way that could be seen as undermining the church, to which she was always unwaveringly committed. Hers was an orthodox Christian universalism, cautiously expressed, and committed to existing within the boundaries of the *ekklēsia*.

24. Julian assigns maternity to God, and likewise to Christ in his divine nature, as many other mystics have done. Jesus himself compares himself to a hen with her chicks, and in the Old Testament God compares himself to a mother. What is more, as seen, in Psalm 110 (Septuagint) God says to the Son that Godself brought him forth "from his/her womb" before all times ("before the morning star," before Lucifer and the creation of all the angels). This characterization of God as a Mother, as well as of the Son/Wisdom as a Woman, was well remembered by Bardaisan, Clement, Origen, Gregory of Nyssa, and Eriugena.

Conclusion

A Christian Hope over 2000 Years, Grounded in Christ and God as the Absolute Good and Supported in Defense of Orthodoxy

From the very first Christian centuries—as is clear from what I have pointed out so far—a number of Christian thinkers supported the doctrine of universal salvation. Some Platonic church fathers—among whom we find Origen, Gregory of Nyssa, and Evagrius—were convinced that God alone is the Good and the Being; creatures can only participate in the Good and in Being. However, due to their free will, creatures are also capable of falling into evil (i.e., non-being). Evil has no positive existence, being no creature of God, but is a *lack* of Good and thus a *lack* of Being. Rational creatures who choose evil face spiritual death, but there is a resurrection from it thanks to Christ, the only human being without evil. By assuming all humanity in himself, Christ abolishes evil from it. At the same time, every rational creature will have to adhere to the Good *freely*. Furthermore, these fathers were certain that, sooner or later, all will voluntarily adhere to the Good, because all rational creatures, whose *logos* is in the image of Christ-Logos, after knowing the Good with a pure and not obfuscated intellectual sight, will love it. No rational creature will be saved *against* its will! Instead, what these fathers were certain of is that in the end all will *want* to be saved and will voluntarily adhere to the Good and be brought to God, the Good, by Christ. They based their conviction, among else, on creation, ethical intellectualism, and the work of Christ (incarnation, crucifixion, resurrection).

For these authors, such as Origen and Gregory of Nyssa, the resurrection of Christ, which took place historically, is also the anticipated realization of the glorious eschatological resurrection of the "body of Christ," which is all humanity (and, since Christ is the Logos, all rational creatures). This resurrection is all humanity's liberation, not only from physical death, but also from spiritual death. These fathers entertained a *holistic* view of the resurrection, not only of the body, but also of the soul, which is purified from evil and restored to the integrity of its faculties, currently corrupted by sin. This idea is developed by Maximus the Confessor, too. Purification will go on for as long as is necessary, as a part of this process of resurrection-restoration. *God himself* is the "purifying fire" that performs this, according to St. John of Dalyatha.

Origen in *Comm. in Io.* VI 295–96 declares that the eventual submission of all creatures to God must be understood "in a way that is worthy of the goodness of the God of the universe." Therefore, it cannot be a *forced* submission, but it must be a spontaneous submission, which implies a conversion and coincides with salvation. "The name of the submission with which we submit to Christ indicates the salvation [*salus*] of those who submit, a salvation that comes from Christ" (*Princ.* I 6,1). According to Origen, and to the fathers who supported universal salvation, this doctrine is preferable, and in fact offers the only acceptable account of eschatology, not because it is better from the anthropological or psychological point of view, or else because it depends on a metaphysical or cosmological necessity, but first and foremost because it is better from the *theological* standpoint. And it is better theologically because it is the only one that is *worthy of God*. Likewise, in *CC* IV 13 Origen declares that the only way to conceive the purifying fire in a manner that is worthy of God is to understand that God, like fire, burns evil in sinners, thus purifying them: "God is said to be a fire that consumes. But let us investigate *what becomes God to consume*. And let us establish that *God, like fire, consumes evil* and its works." This is the idea of God as a purifying fire that will reach John of Dalyatha. God does not destroy sinners, but their sins, thus purifying sinners, and resurrecting them from the death of the soul—the death that comes from sin. This death is not eternal: it will be destroyed as "the last enemy" (1 Cor 15:26). As Origen argues in *Comm. in Rom.* V 7, since St. Paul reveals that death will disappear, it is impossible to believe that the kingdom of death will be eternal as that of life and justice is. Eternal life and eternal death are a contradiction in terms: if life is eternal, death cannot be eternal, as Origen puts it in his syllogism.

In the history of Christian thought, universal salvation is not the isolated fruit of one mind, Origen's, who is supposed to have been excessively influenced by Greek philosophy and to be a "heretic" (but in fact whose purported "condemnation" is the product of misunderstandings, hostility, prejudice, and even envy). Universal salvation has a much wider tradition, rooted in the Bible itself. Before Christianity, no philosophy or religion—not even mystery religions—had supported universal salvation proper (and Zoroastrianism, as I argued in an essay in 2017, began to teach universal restoration only *after* the spead of patristic apokatastasis). In Stoicism, restoration was an infinitely recurrent cosmological necessity, not final salvation, and Origen explicitly criticized it. As for Plato, whose ideas Origen was accused of following in the elaboration of his own doctrine of universal salvation, in fact he did *not* believe in universal salvation. On the contrary, he repeatedly affirmed that some sinners will never be purified and will suffer forever in hell (Tartarus), although the doctrine of infinite cyclicity, fully elaborated later, will relativize this theory. And the so-called "gnostics" mainly thought that *the elite* would participate in the apokatastasis, and that without their bodies. So, in fact, it was *Christian theologians who first proclaimed the message of universal restoration.* (The restoration of all souls was admitted by some late Neoplatonists—albeit without the resurrection of the body—but this was most probably under the influence of the already well-established Christian doctrine of universal restoration and salvation.[1])

The doctrine of universal restoration and salvation is eminently Christian and is rooted in the Bible, where many passages, especially from St. Paul and the Acts of the Apostles, inspired it. Other texts that were long deemed part of Scripture before the canon was finally settled, such as the *Apocalypse of Peter*, also suggested universal salvation. Precisely because they regarded it as grounded in Scripture, most supporters of universal salvation, from the church fathers to Julian of Norwich to our day, did not intend to oppose the church. Many of these, indeed, are saints, and some are martyrs, such as Pamphilus. Origen and St. Gregory of Nyssa, the main patristic supporters of universal salvation, even elaborated this doctrine in defense of Christian orthodoxy and

1. This will be the subject of my second scientific monograph on apokatastasis. After the study on apokatastasis from the New Testament to Eriugena (2013), the next will focus (*Caelo volente et adiuvante*) on "pagan" philosophical notions of apokatastasis, from ancient to late-antique philosophy, and the third on its rejection. See the Introduction.

theodicy against the "heretics" of their day (Origen against "Gnosticism" and Marcionism, and Gregory against "Arianism"); both related the argument for universal salvation to that of the non-subordination of the Son to the Father in the interpretation of 1 Corinthians 15:28. Both Origen and Gregory, and many other Christian supporters of universal salvation during the centuries, are clear that the salvation of all depends on Christ, and not on any metaphysical or cosmological necessity, or a necessity of any other kind. Universal salvation as a *Christian* hope and a *Christian* doctrine consistently continued over the two millennia of Christianity.

This is not a doctrine that arises from moral relaxation—as it was depicted during the Origenistic controversy—but the expectation of the total victory of God over evil, which is grounded in the inhumanation, death, and resurrection of Christ, his work as Logos-teacher and physician, and in God's "goodness." This goodness is not simply God's kindness or mercy, but it is God's being the absolute Good—with the relevant corollary of the ontological non-substantiality of evil, which is doomed to disappearing. Evil will not exist any longer when in the end no one will choose it any more, once all have been illuminated, purified, and healed. Purification, according to all the supporters of universal salvation,[2] will be commensurate to each one's sins and therefore finite. Death itself in any case puts a providential limit to everyone's sins—as Origen, Methodius, Gregory of Nyssa, and others later reflected, up to our day—so that their purification will not have to go on forever. As Gregory Nyssen most forcefully argued, God alone is infinite, while evil is finite. Universal restoration and salvation depends on the grace of God, who "wants all humans to be saved." Gregory of Nyssa was clear, right until the end of his life, in his homilies on the Song of Songs, that this divine will *shall* be fulfilled ("until the One who wants all humans to be saved has reached his aim"). The Christian hope, which is given voice by St. Paul in 1 Corinthians 15:24-28, is that in the end, when all have been purified and illuminated by Christ-Logos and all evil has been eliminated, all those who were enemies will submit in what Origen and many theologians over the centuries regarded as a salvific submission, whereas "the last enemy," death, which is no creature of God, will be destroyed. Then will St. Paul's prophecy come true that "God will be all in all" (1 Cor 15:28).

2. With the sole exception of the very few who thought that there will be no otherworldly punishment/purification at all for anyone.

APPENDIX I

The Meaning of *Aiōnios*

I briefly summarize here the results of Ilaria Ramelli and David Konstan, *Terms for Eternity*, which are highly relevant to the present discussion.[1] For all the original texts, *loci*, and further bibliography, I refer to the most recent editions of that monograph, as well as to further research that has eventually appeared in my *Tempo ed eternità in età antica e patristica*. Further new research will appear in "Time and Eternity," in the forthcoming *Routledge Companion to Early Christian Philosophy*. Specifically for ancient philosophy, I also refer to Wilberding, "Eternity in Ancient Philosophy."

    Terms for Eternity surveys the uses of two ancient Greek adjectives—*aiōnios* and *aïdios*, commonly translated as "eternal"—from their earliest occurrences in poetry and pre-Socratic philosophy down

---

1. The book has received very positive reviews, e.g., by Carl O'Brien in *The Classical Review* 60.2 (2010) 390–91 [journals.cambridge.org/article_S0009840X10000272]; in *International Review of Biblical Studies / Internationale Zeitschriftenschau für Bibelwissenschaft und Grenzgebiete*, ed. Bernhard Lang, 54 (2007/2008), (Leiden: Brill, 2009), 444, 1901; by Danilo Ghira in *Maia* 61 (2009) 732–34; by Shawn Keough in *Ephemerides Theologicae Lovanienses* 84.4 (2008) 601; by Joel Kalvesmaki, *Guide to Evagrius Ponticus*, summer 2014 edition (Washington, DC, 2014), evagriusponticus. net. Referred to by Réka Valentin, "Immortality in the Book of Wisdom in the Context of the Overlapping Worlds," *Studia Universitatis Babes-Bolyai, Theologia Catholica Latina* 55.2 (2010) 85–99, esp. 86; in *The Cambridge Companion to Socrates*, ed. D.R. Morrison (Cambridge: Cambridge University Press, 2011), x; by Gregory MacDonald, *The Evangelical Universalist* (2nd ed., Eugene, OR: Cascade, 2012), xv; by James Gould, *Practicing Prayer for the Dead* (Eugene, OR: Cascade, 2016), 107, 269; repeatedly by Steven Nemes, "Christian Apokatastasis: Two Paradigmatic Objections." *Journal of Analytic Theology* 4 (2016) 67–86: philpapers.org/rec/NEMCA;10.12978/jat.2016-4.181913130418a; etc.

through the Septuagint (and a thorough comparison with the Hebrew Bible), the New Testament, and the Christian theologians, from the earliest to Maximus the Confessor. The monograph examines the rise of the idea of infinitely extended time (generally denoted by *aïdios*), and Plato's innovative introduction of a concept of a timeless eternity, which in Platonic technical vocabulary—and *only* there—was denoted by *aiōn*, with *aiōnios* meaning "eternal" in the sense of "transcending time." In all the rest of Greek literature, however, and—what is most relevant to us here— in the Greek Bible, *aiōnios* has a wide range of meanings, but does *not* denote absolute eternity.[2] Since only *aiōnios*, and never *aïdios*, is applied to the punishment of humans in the afterlife, Origen could find support in the biblical usage for his doctrine of universal salvation and the finite duration of hell.

At the beginning of Greek philosophy, with the Presocratics, the term *aïdios* seems to be well attested in the sense of "eternal," although without any connotation of metaphysical transcendence. For instance, Heraclitus referred *aïdios* to the perpetual movement of things that are eternal and to the cyclical fire, which is god. Among the Eleatics, Parmenides is said to have described the "all" as *aïdios*, in that it is ungenerated and imperishable. Democritus too argued that time was *aïdios*, on the grounds that it was ungenerated, and that the whole of things too was eternal (*aïdion to pan*). It would appear, in sum, that the term of art for eternal things—all that is ungenerated and imperishable—among cosmological thinkers in the period prior to Plato was *aïdios*, never *aiōnios*. In addition, *aïdios* is the standard adjective meaning "eternal" in non-philosophical discourse of the fifth century as well.

Plato introduced the concept of metaphysical, timeless eternity, in reference to the model that the demiurge followed in creating the sensible universe by looking "to the eternal" (*to aïdion*). In a crucial passage in his *Timaeus*, Plato remarks that the created universe was seen to be moving and living, an image of the eternal gods (*tōn aïdiōn theōn*, 37C6), and adds that it was itself an "eternal living being" (*aïdion*). Plato goes on to say that it was the nature of the living being to be *aiōnios*, but that this quality could not be attached to something that was begotten (*gennēton*). The creator therefore decided to make "a kind of moving image of eternity" (*aiōnos*), and so as he arranged the universe he made "an eternal image [*aiōnion eikona*] moving according to number of the

---

2. Allin, *Christ Triumphant*, 93–98 agrees that *aiōnios* in Scripture and in most church fathers does not mean "eternal."

eternity [aiōnos] which remains in one," and this he called "time." Plato
seems to have found in the term aiōn a special designation for his notion
of eternity as timeless; and with this new sense of aiōn, aiōnios too seems
to have come into its own as a signifier for what is beyond time. However,
Plato's conception of a timeless eternity remained specific to Platonism
in antiquity.

In Aristotle's oeuvre there are nearly three hundred instances of
aïdios, which is Aristotle's preferred word to designate things eternal. It
is clear that Aristotle was not moved to adopt Plato's novel terminology,
whether because he perceived some difference between his own concept
of eternity and that of his teacher, or because he felt that aiōnios was an
unnecessary addition to the philosophical vocabulary, given the respect-
ability of aïdios as the appropriate technical term for eternity.

In the Stoics, aïdios occurs over thirty times in the sense of that
which endures forever. It is applied to bodies and matter, the realities that
truly exist according to Stoic materialism, and above all to god or Zeus.
To the extent that the Stoics employed aiōnios and aiōn, however, there is
either a connection with their specific view of cosmic cycles, as opposed
to strictly infinite duration, or else the noun occurs in phrases indicating
a long period of time. Thus, in Stoic terminology—as generally in all of
Greek literature, apart from technical Platonic language—aiōnios does
not mean "absolutely eternal," a meaning that is reserved for aïdios.

The Epicureans, too, regularly employed aïdios to designate the eternity of such imperishable constituents of the universe as atoms and void.
Epicurus uses aiōnios in reference to the future life that non-Epicureans
expect, with its dreadful punishments: that is, to an afterlife in which Epicureans do not believe, and which does not deserve the name "eternal"
(aïdios), properly reserved for truly perpetual elements.

Coming to the Bible, in the Septuagint, aïdios occurs only twice,
both times in late books written originally in Greek: 4 Maccabees and
Wisdom. In addition, there is one instance of the abstract noun, aïdiotēs,
again in Wisdom. On the other hand, aiōnios occurs with impressive fre-
quency, along with aiōn; behind both is the Hebrew 'olām, which has a
wide range of meanings, but per se does not mean "eternal." Only when it
refers to God can it acquire this meaning. For example, aiōnios can refer
to a time in the remote past or future, or to something lasting over generations or centuries, or can even mean "mundane," with a negative connotation. Of particular interest is the mention in Tobit 3:6 of the place of
the afterlife as a topos aiōnios, the first place in the Bible in which aiōnios

unequivocally refers to the world to come. In 2 Maccabees, the doctrine of resurrection is affirmed and *aiōnios* is used with reference to life in the future world. This meaning will become prevalent in the New Testament.

The adjective *aïdios*, as mentioned, occurs in the Septuagint only in 4 Maccabees and Wisdom. In Wisdom, which is saturated with the Greek philosophical lexicon, Wisdom is defined as "a reflection of the eternal [*aïdion*] light" that is God. In 4 Maccabees, an impious tyrant is threatened with "fire *aiōnion*" for the entire age or world to come (*eis holon ton aiōna*). But here we find the expression *bios aïdios* or "eternal life" as well, in reference to the afterlife of the martyrs; this blessed state, moreover, is opposed to the lasting destruction of their persecutor in the world to come. This contrast between the parallel but antithetical expressions *olethros aiōnios* ("otherworldly ruin") and *bios aïdios* ("eternal life") is notable: whereas retribution is described with the polysemous term *aiōnios*, to life in the beyond is applied the more technical term *aïdios*, denoting a strictly endless condition. Only life is explicitly declared to be eternal; death or ruin is "otherworldly," possibly "long-lasting," but not strictly "eternal."

In the New Testament, there are only two uses of the more philosophical term *aïdios*. The first (Rom 1:20) refers unproblematically to the power and divinity of God, which is eternal in the absolute sense. In the second occurrence, however (Jude 6), *aïdios* is employed in connection with divine punishment—not of human beings, but of evil angels, who are imprisoned in darkness "with eternal chains" (*desmois aïdiois*). But there is a qualification: "*until* the judgment of the great day." The angels, then, will remain chained up *until* judgment day—likewise in 2 Peter 2:4, evil angels are said to have been sent by God to Tartarus, "to be held for judgment." We are not informed of what will become of them afterwards. Why is *aïdios* used of these chains, instead of *aiōnios*, which is used in the next verse of the fire of which the punishments of the Sodomites is an example? Perhaps because they continue from the moment of the angels' incarceration, at the beginning of the world, or perhaps even before the world, until the judgment that signals the entry into the new *aiōn*: thus, the term indicates the uninterrupted continuity throughout all time in this world—this could not apply to human beings, who do not live through the entire duration of the present universe; to them applies rather the sequence of *aiōnes* or generations.

In the New Testament, as in the Old, death, punishment, and fire are described as *aiōnia*, pertaining to the world or *aiōn* to come, but *never* as *aïdia* or strictly eternal. This point, which I made for the first time in the above-mentioned monograph, had escaped scholars,[3] but it is so important that the Greek Fathers almost unanimously followed the biblical usage carefully, and therefore called death, punishment, and fire *aiōnia* or "otherworldly," or at most "long-lasting," but never *aïdia* or "everlasting, absolutely eternal." Some Latin theologians who, unlike Ambrose, Cassian, or Eriugena, did not know Greek, such as Augustine, relied on Latin translations of the Bible in which the rigorous differentiation of *aiōnios* and *aïdios* of the Greek Scriptures was completely blurred, since both adjectives were generally translated with *aeternus* or *sempiternus*. Thus, Augustine came to believe that in Scripture death, punishment, and fire in the other world are actually declared to be eternal,[4] and his perspective proved immensely influential in the Latin West, especially among those who did not know Greek. This, of course, bears enormously on the development of Western eschatology. It is significant that the Latin theologians who did know Greek, such as Marius Victorinus, St. Ambrose, St. Jerome, Rufinus, Cassian, and Eriugena, did not think that the Bible unequivocally proclaims eternal punishment, death, or fire, and Eriugena was even one of the most radical supporters of universal salvation.

Among the Greek fathers, the majority followed the biblical usage. Origen, who was an attentive biblical exegete and philologist, besides being one of the greatest patristic philosophers and theologians, also followed the linguistic usage of the Bible very closely, and this confirmed him in his argument that, "if life is eternal, death cannot possibly be eternal." In Origen, there are many passages that refer to the *aiōnios* life, in the formula characteristic of the New Testament: the emphasis seems to be not so much on eternity, that is, temporal infinity, as on the life in the next world or *aiōn* ("the life of the world to come," as the final clause of the Nicene-Constantinopolitan Creed, still recited today, has it).

3. Many universalists in the seventeenth, eighteenth, and nineteenth century also relativized the meaning of *aiōnios* in Scripture. Elhanan Winchester (1751–97), for instance, says that *aiōnios* only means eternal when applied to God, although he has no comparison with *aïdios* and no argument from how the fathers used *aiōnia* and *aïdia* in the same sense and with the same limitations as Scripture does. The second volume written by Robin Parry, also using much of my preparatory material, will explore the work of many of these universalists.

4. See my "Origen in Augustine: A Paradoxical Reception." Further work will be done on the presence of Origen (direct, indirect, known, unknown, or even paradoxical) in the various phases of Augustine's thought.

In Origen's Greek *Philocalia*, 1.30.21–23, the *aiōnios* life is defined as that which will occur in the future *aiōn*. God gave Scripture as a "body for those we existed before us [i.e., the Hebrews], soul for us, and spirit [*pneuma*] for those in the *aiōn* to come, who will obtain life *aiōnios*." So too, in the *Commentary on Matthew*, 15.25, the future life (*aiōnios*) is contrasted with that in the present (*proskairos*). Again, Origen in a series of passages opposes the ephemeral sensible entities of the present time (*proskaira*) to the invisible and lasting objects of the world to come (*aiōnia*). Consistent with the usage of the Septuagint and the New Testament, Origen also applies the adjective *aiōnios* to attributes of God. In one particularly illuminating passage, Origen speaks of the eternal God (*aiōnios*) and of the concealment of the mystery of Jesus over *aiōnioi* stretches of time (*khronois aiōniois*), where the sense is plainly "from time immemorial," and obviously not "eternal times." So too, Origen mentions the "days of the *aiōn*," and "*aiōnia* years" (*etē aiōnia*), that is, very long periods of time, and the phrase *eis tous aiōnas* here signifies, "for a very long time."

In Origen, *aïdios* occurs much less frequently than *aiōnios*, and when it is used, it is almost always in reference to God or his attributes, meaning "eternal" in the strict sense of limitless in time or beyond time. In *On First Principles* 3.3.5, Origen gives a clear sign that he understands *aiōn* in the sense of a succession of *aiōnes* prior to the final apokatastasis, at which point one arrives at the true eternity, that is, *aïdiotēs*. Eternity in the strict sense pertains, according to Origen, to God and the apokatastasis, not to the previous sequence of ages or *aiōnes*. So too, Origen explains that Christ "reigned without flesh prior to the ages, and reigned in the flesh in the ages" (*aiōniōs*, adverb).

Again, the "coming *aiōn*" indicates the next world (*ton mellonta aiōna*), where sinners will indeed be consigned to the *pyr aiōnion*, that is, the fire that pertains to the future world; it may well last for a long time, but it is not, for Origen, eternal. Origen, consistently with Scripture, calls the punishing/purifying fire *pyr aiōnion*, but never *pyr aïdion*. The explanation is that he does not consider this flame to be absolutely eternal: it is *aiōnion* because it belongs to the next world, as opposed to the fire we experience in this present world, and it lasts as long as the *aiōnes* do, in their succession. Similarly, Origen, exactly like Scripture, never speaks of *thanatos aïdios* ("eternal death"), or of *aïdia* punishments and torments and the like, although he does speak of *thanatos aiōnios* or death in the world to come, and *kolaseis aiōnioi*, i.e., punishment in the world to come.

For Origen, the biblical usage was further evidence for the doctrine of universal salvation. That Origen followed the Bible in never calling death, punishment, or fire "eternal," but only "otherworldly" or "long-lasting," is not surprising in the light of his own eschatological convictions: fire, punishment, and death imposed by God cannot be but remedial, and therefore they cannot be eternal. But what is striking is that, as emerges from *Terms for Eternity*, a number of other patristic thinkers closely followed this biblical usage. Among them there are, of course, all the supporters of apokatastasis, such as Didymus the Blind, St. Gregory of Nyssa, St. Evagrius Ponticus, Diodore of Tarsus, Theodore of Mopsuestia, etc. But there are also others who are usually not regarded as supporters of universal restoration, such as Eusebius, St. Athanasius, St. Basil the Great, St. Gregoy Nazianzen, Pseudo-Dionysius, and St. Maximus the Confessor. It is significant that—as I argued extensively in *The Christian Doctrine of Apokatastasis* and elsewhere, not only on the grounds of their linguistic use—all of these are in fact likely to have had a penchant for the theory of universal restoration.

APPENDIX II

A Reply to Michael McClymond's Review of
The Christian Doctrine of Apokatastasis[1]

I AM VERY GRATEFUL for the interest in my monograph, the fruit of sixteen years of research and work. I entitled it *The Christian Doctrine of Apokatastasis* not only to indicate that this is a doctrine that is Christian (and indeed it seems to have been supported by Christian, patristic authors for the first time; the later "pagan" Platonists who supported it, as well as Zoroastrian texts, embraced forms of apokatastasis knowing well already the Christian doctrine of apokatastasis),[2] but also and especially to distinguish its focus from non-Christian theories of *apokatastasis*, which will be the subject of a future monograph about "pagan" (pre-Christian and non-Christian) philosophical doctrines of *apokatastasis*. This will be the second volume of a trilogy, the third volume of which will be, God willing, an investigation into the historical, theological, political,

---

1. Michael McClymond published an article review of Ilaria Ramelli's *The Christian Doctrine of Apokatastasis* (Leiden: Brill, 2013) in *Theological Studies* 76.4 (2015), reprinted in Michael McClymond, *The Devil's Redemption* (Grand Rapids: Baker, 2018), 1089–1101. An extensive review of the Patristic section of this volume appears here in Appendix III. It was invited by a theological journal, the *International Journal of Systematic Theology*, which will also publish a shorter version. This appendix, reproduced here, is a reprint of Ilaria Ramelli's invited response to McClymond's review in *Theological Studies* 76.4 (2015) 827–35, with some updates. In the text above the words of McClymond are inserted in square brackets and minor characters, so that readers are able to better appreciate what I was asked to respond to.

2. See respectively my "Proclus of Constantinople and Apokatastasis" and "Christian Apokatastasis and Zoroastrian Frashegird," in addition to *The Christian Doctrine of Apokatastasis* and the two future works on philosophical apokatastasis and the rejection of apokatastasis announced in the main text.

and pastoral causes for the rejection of *apokatastasis* in late antiquity by the "Church of the Empire." An important role was played by the influence of Augustine's mature thought in the West, and of Justinian in the East. Thus, the thematic division of my trilogy is this: Christian *apokatastasis*, "pagan" philosophical *apokatastasis* (and its relation to patristic theories of *apokatastasis*), and the rejection of *apokatastasis*. Also, in my monograph's subtitle, "critical assessment (of)" means "scholarly investigation (into)," not necessarily "denigration (of)."

[McClymond: "Throughout her book, Ramelli reveals her ambition to vindicate the doctrine of apokatastasis as a Christian and Catholic teaching that does not violate either the teachings of Scripture or the decisions of the church councils. For this reason, one must take with a grain of salt her claim that 'the present study is not concerned primarily about "orthodoxy" and "heresy"' (2n3). Her book is more than a dispassionate analysis of ancient texts. On the very same page where she claims to disavow categories of 'orthodoxy' and 'heresy,' she argues for the salience of ancient discussions of universalism by appealing to pro-universalist statements by contemporary African-American Pentecostal bishop Carlton Pearson, by Christian Orthodox scholars such as Bishop Hilarion Alfeyev of Vienna and Bishop Kallistos Ware, and by the Roman Catholic archbishop of Westminster, Murphy O'Connor, and Pope John Paul II (2–3n6)."]

I am not interested in the categories of "orthodoxy" and "heresy" except from a historical perspective. I do not "appeal to" statements by Carlton Pearson, Hilarion Alfeyev, Kallistos Ware, Murphy O'Connor, or Pope John Paul II; I simply cite them in a footnote in the introduction as examples of the debate on soteriological universalism in the contemporary Christian panorama, to show how universalistic ideas are lively and discussed in various confessions. I do not cite Pearson "favorably" or unfavorably, nor do I subscribe to his views or condemn them; my critical enquiry focuses on patristic thinkers.

[McClymond: "From his own lifetime up through the past nineteen centuries, Origen's reputation was mixed. Later writers borrowed from Origen's exegesis, though the source of the ideas or quotations was usually not credited. The medieval author Peter Comestor (d. 1178) laid down the principle *"Non credas Origeni dogmatizanti"* (Do not trust Origen when he dogmatizes). . . . It was not Origen's exegesis so much as his 'dogmatizing'—and that of his followers—that stirred controversy for over a century and a half in the early church (390s–550s CE)."]

The dichotomy between Origen's exegesis (good) and his theology (bad) suggested by Comestor (and cited approvingly by Professor McClymond), comes from Jerome after his U-turn against Origen (*Epistle* 84.2). This dichotomy is the same as that which obtained in the reception of Evagrius. In both cases, the best recent scholarship is correcting the dichotomy.[3] In the case of Origen, the alleged dichotomy does not take into account his heuristic method, well known and overtly defended by the likes of Athanasius—who regarded (and quoted) Origen as an authority in support of the Nicene faith—and Gregory Nyssen and Gregory Nazianzen, who deemed Origen's "zetetic" method (i.e., philosophical investigation or *zetesis* applied to Christian exegesis and theology) the only one admissible in matters left unclarified by Scripture and tradition. Origen in *Peri archōn* is much more zetetic/heuristic than (as Jerome and Comestor would have it) "dogmatizing." A specific article will be devoted to this and a chapter of the future monograph on Origen will investigate Origen's zetetic approach to philosophical and theological issues and the exegesis of Scripture.

[McClymond: "The idea that Origen's universalism drew from earlier gnostic universalism—which existed in Alexandria prior to Origen's lifetime among the Carpocratians, Basilideans, and Valentinians—deserves more attention than the three pages Ramelli devotes to it (87–89). In her presentation, she ignores Holger Strutwolf's *Gnosis als System* (1993), which argues convincingly for continuities between Origen and second-century gnosticism. Because Ramelli defines 'gnosticism' in terms of soteriological elitism and determinism, she sees Origen's stress on free will and universal salvation as marking him as 'anti-gnostic.' Yet she overlooks the larger patterns, highlighted by Strutwolf, of the fall-and-restoration-of-souls motif as found among the Nag Hammadi community, the Valentinians, Plotinus and the Neoplatonists, and Origen's *Peri archōn*. Moreover, Ramelli's reduction of gnosticism to soteriological determinism is out of step with recent scholarship and does not take into account M. A. William's argument in *Rethinking 'Gnosticism'* (1996)."]

---

3. On Evagrius, see my "Evagrius and Gregory: Nazianzen or Nyssen?; Evagrius' *Kephalaia Gnostika*, monographic essay (vii–lxxxiv), new readings from the ms., translation, and full commentary; "Gregory Nyssen's and Evagrius' Biographical and Theological Relations"; "Origen to Evagrius"; "Mystical Eschatology in Gregory and Evagrius."

Origen certainly knew "gnostic ideas"—far from my being ignorant of it, I referred to Strutwolf's book in a separate essay twelve years ago[4]— and of course both Origen and most "gnostics" shared some (broadly conceived) Platonic ideas applied to Christianity. But Origen was professedly anti-gnostic, as is evident in all his extant writings, even in the recently discovered Munich homilies (see below). Origen spent his life refuting what he deemed gnostic tenets such as predestinationism, different natures among rational creatures, the separation between a superior God and an inferior—if not evil—demiurge, the severing of divine justice from divine goodness, Docetism, the notion of aeons as divine and the whole "gnostic" mythology, the refusal to interpret the OT spiritually and the NT historically, and more. Origen regarded "gnostic" Platonism as a bad Platonism, while he intended to construct an "orthodox" Christian Platonism, not only against other, non-Platonic philosophical schools, and "pagan" Platonism, but also against what he regarded as the unorthodox Christian Platonism of "gnosticism." I argued for this seminally in the chapter on Origen in the book under review, and will support this interpretive line further in the future monograph on Origen's philosophical theology.

On "gnostic" theories of *apokatastasis*, after my preliminary work in the *Journal of Coptic Studies*—to which I referred in my monograph under review (this is why I devoted only a few pages there to *apokatastasis* in "Gnosticism")—further investigation is underway, which will lead to a major study on the subject probably within the work on ancient philosophical theories of apokatastasis and their relations to Christian doctrines. I copiously cited and discussed Michael Williams' *Rethinking "Gnosticism": An Argument for Dismantling a Dubious Category*, not only in the above-mentioned essay in *Journal of Coptic Studies*, but also, e.g., in a review of Karen King's *What Is Gnosticism?* and in substantial articles on Gnosticism for the *Encyclopedia of Ancient Christianity* and the *Brill Encyclopedia of Early Christianity*.[5]

The pattern of "fall and restoration of souls" is common not only to Origen and the "gnostics," as McClymond suggests, but to *all* patristic Platonists, including the anti-Manichaean Augustine (who speaks of creatures' *deficere* and their restoration by God).[6] More broadly, it is

4. "Origen and the Stoic Allegorical Tradition" (2006).

5. See Ramelli, Review of Karen King, *What Is Gnosticism?*; Ramelli, "Gnosis-Gnosticism"; Ramelli, "Gnosis/Knowledge."

6. Analyzed in my "Origen in Augustine: A Paradoxical Reception."

common even to all Christians, who share the biblical story of creation and fall and believe in the restoration, the new creation, brought about by Christ.

If one objects that the difference between Origen's and the gnostics' "fall and restoration of souls" on the one side, and the "orthodox" Christians on the other, lies the resurrection of the body, included in the "orthodox" account but excluded by the "gnostics" and Origen, it must be observed that Origen sided more with "orthodox" Christians than with the "gnostics" regarding the resurrection. That Origen denied the resurrection of the body, as was often asserted in antiquity and sometimes still now, is a misconstruction—probably originating in his twofold conception of the resurrection, of body and soul, later developed by Evagrius— that cannot stand careful investigation, just as the supposition that he admitted of disembodied souls. Much can be argued against this.[7]

[McClymond: "Conspicuously missing from her expositions of Origen and Gregory are acknowledgements of differences between the two thinkers. ... Gregory deviated from Origen in basic ways and repudiated Origen's teaching on preexistent (or premortal) souls. Gregory also rejected the idea of the eschaton as the restoration of a primal condition of stasis. In Gregory's mature theological teaching, the final state is one of continuous change and development, a conception that contradicts Origen's *apokatastasis*."]

It can be argued that when Gregory Nyssen criticized the preexistence of disembodied souls, he was not targeting Origen, who did not in fact support it. Gregory's statement that his argument against preexistent souls had to do with "those before us who have written about principles" (*Hom. op.* 28.1) is, for many reasons,[8] not "an obvious reference to Origen," as is often assumed and as McClymond believes (fn. 23); I mention here only three of those reasons: (1) Gregory, in the aforementioned passage and in *De anima*, is attacking the preexistence of disembodied souls together with *metensomatosis* (the migration of a soul into various bodies), which Origen explicitly rejected; thus, Gregory's target could not have been Origen. (2) Among those who supported metensomatosis and the preexistence of disembodied souls were several Middle Platonists and

---

7. See some points in my "Origen."

8. Some of these I expounded in *Preexistence of Souls?* 167–226; I give further reasons in "Gregory of Nyssa's Purported Criticism of Origen's Purported Doctrine of the Preexistence of Souls."

Neoplatonists who wrote works entitled *Peri archōn*, including Porphyry, whom Gregory knew very well. (3) Moreover, Gregory does not say "one of us" Christians, but "one of those before us" (τις τῶν πρὸ ἡμῶν), a formula that he regularly uses to designate *non-Christians*, such as Philo.

Thus, it is true that Nyssen "rejected the idea of souls existing outside of mortal bodies," or better, he rejected the idea of souls existing outside of bodies *tout court*; but it is not really the case that, in McClymond's words, "he offered a teaching on *apokatastasis* no longer consonant with Origen's." In fact, Origen never affirmed the preexistence of disembodied souls, nor did Gregory ever state that the soul comes into existence together with the mortal body (Gregory was all too aware of the "perishability axiom"). Both Gregory's protology and eschatology are in fact in continuity with those of Origen.

Indeed, as for the distinctions between Origen and Nyssen that I allegedly blurred, my extensive research (supported by a research fellowship from Oxford and expected to be published in a future monograph, after a few articles) shows Nyssen's creative dependence on Origen's true thought in all fields. Misrepresentations of Origen's ideas clearly falsify the whole picture. The distinctions are between Origen's *alleged* thought—a misconstruction ultimately stemming from the Origenistic controversies—and Nyssen's, not between Origen's *actual* thought (as it emerges from his authentic texts) and Nyssen's. In fact, a painstaking critical assessment of Origen's genuine ideas allows for a reassessment of Origen's influence on many other patristic thinkers (from Nyssen to Augustine, Evagrius to Maximus, and Pseudo-Dionysius to Eriugena, not to speak of the *Dialogue of Adamantius*, which will hopefully make the object of an Oxford critical edition). Indeed, this brings about—borrowing McClymond's words—"a new paradigm for understanding the church's first millennium."

That Origen envisaged a "static afterlife," for instance, is questionable; and therefore it is debatable that "Gregory [Nyssen], Maximus Confessor, and Eriugena all rejected Origen's static afterlife," as McClymond alleges. I have extensively argued elsewhere that it is exactly in Origen that Gregory found inspiration for his doctrine of *epektasis*, which is the opposite of a static eschatology and is closely linked with *apokatastasis*.[9] Both Origen's and Gregory's eschatological ideas will make their way into Maximus the Confessor's ἀεικίνητος στάσις or "ever-moving rest."

---

9. "*Apokatastasis* and *Epektasis* in *Hom. in Cant.*"

Mateo-Seco (referenced by McClymond, n. 32) clearly acknowledges in Gregory the doctrine of universal restoration; Giulio Maspero's objections on this specific point are thoroughly refuted already in the monograph under review (pp. 433–36—but, apart from this, Maspero's work on Gregory is always insightful and very valuable, as my citations of it and our collaborations indicate), and a full response to Baghos' argument is included in the aforementioned research on Origen and Nyssen.

McClymond notes: "The vision of the eschaton in Evagrius' *Great Letter* . . . involved a pantheistic or pantheizing dissolution of the Creator-creature distinction." However, in his *Great Letter/Letter to Melania* Evagrius makes clear that there will be no confusion of *substance* between creatures and creator, but a concord of *will* (see pp. 474–75): "The one and the same nature and three Persons of God, and the one and the same nature and many persons of God's image, *will remain eternally*, as it was before the Inhumanation, and will be after the Inhumanation, thanks to the *concord of wills*."[10] Therefore, no pantheistic interpretation of Evagrius is tenable, and *Caelo volente* a future monograph on Evagrius will deepen this and other points. While Guillaumont offered an invaluable edition of Evagrius' *Kephalaia Gnostika* (which, apart from some new readings from the manuscript and emendations, I kept as a basis for my own commentary),[11] his view that Evagrius was a radical, "isochristic" Origenist whose ideas were the real target of the II Council of Constantinople needs reconsideration.[12]

Regarding Augustine, I have argued in my monograph that he embraced *apokatastasis* during his long anti-Manichaean phase, but not later—at least not overtly, and notably not in his anti-Pelagian phase. Contrary to what McClymond argues (i.e., "[Augustine's discussion of *De moribus* 2.7.9 in his *Retractiones* 1.6 is] a point Ramelli fails to mention," fn. 9), I *do* discuss *Retractationes* 1.6 (on p. 674, also mentioned in

10. Evagrius, *Letter to Melania* 23–25.

11. Ramelli, *Evagrius' Kephalaia Gnostika*.

12. Ramelli, "Evagrius Ponticus, the Origenian Ascetic (and not the Origenistic 'Heretic')." Reviewed by Doru Costache, *Phronema* Volume 31.2 (2016) 109–18, esp. 115–18: http://www.academia.edu/28714187/Orthodox_Monasticism_Past_and_Present_ed._John_A._McGuckin._Piscataway_NJ_Gorgias_Press_2015._588_pages._ISBN_978_1_4632_0530_0, and by Johannes van Oort, *Vigiliae Christianae* 70.5 (2016) 604.

my ancient authors index on p. 830), showing that Augustine was later embarrassed by his earlier adhesion to the *apokatastasis* doctrine, especially in *De moribus* 2.7.9. McClymond observes that in the latter passage I translated *ordinat* as "orders and leads," which he deems incorrect: "The verb is *ordinat*, which translates as 'orders' and not as 'orders and leads.' There is no second verb alongside of *ordinat*. Moreover, Augustine's statement that creatures are ordered toward restoration did not imply that all will attain it." Now, that *all* fallen creatures are ordered and guided by God's goodness *until* they are restored to the condition from which they had fallen ("Dei bonitas . . . omnia deficientia sic ordinat . . . donec ad id recurrant unde defecerunt") manifestly means that all are restored. *Ordinare* means both "to order, arrange," and "to marshal," "to manage, regulate, direct";[13] hence the double translation of *ordinat* as "orders and leads," the subject being God, and the object being rational creatures.

As to the (posthumous) condemnation of Eriugena's *Periphyseon* and its causes, to which McClymond refers in his review, I did analyze them on the first page of my treatment of Eriugena. I deem him the last patristic thinker in the West, obviously not in the confessional sense as canonized father, as suggested in the review, but because he relies so heavily on patristic authorities—from Origen to the Cappadocians, from Augustine to Pseudo-Dionysius—in all aspects of his philosophical theology. McClymond admits that Eriugena's notion of the *eschaton* involves a universal return of souls to God—and indeed Eriugena is unequivocal when he claims that, thanks to Christ's inhumanation, "every creature, in heaven and on earth, has been saved" (*Periphyseon* 5.24)—but he avers that "for Eriugena not all souls were happy in their final state with God." In fact, however, Eriugena is adamant that all rational creatures in their substances will be happy; no substantial nature can "be in unhappiness" (*Praed.* 16.1). All natures will enjoy "a wonderful joy" (*Praed.* 19.3). The evilness derived from sinners' perverted will perish in the other world; only their substance will remain (*substantia permansura, malitia peritura*), and this—their substance—will be happy (*Periphyseon* 5.931A).

McClymond is correct that according to Eriugena "all . . . shall return into Paradise, but not all shall enjoy the Tree of Life—or rather . . . not all equally," but this refers to the distinction between salvation and deification, and does not imply that not all will be saved. Sometimes Eriugena even suggests that deification itself will extend to all. For he postulates the

---

13. *Oxford Latin Dictionary*, 1266.

return of all to God, and transformation of all into God, through their primordial causes; at that point all will enjoy peace and eternal splendor: "When every sense-perceptible creature will be transformed into intelligible and every intelligible one into its causes/principles, and the causes into the cause of causes / principle of principles, who is God, they will enjoy eternal peace and will shine forth with ineffable glory and celebrate a perpetual feast" (*Quando omnis sensibilis creatura in intelligibilem et omnis intelligibilis in causas, et causae in causarum causam (quae Deus est) mutabuntur aeternaque requie gaudebunt ineffabilique claritate fulgebunt et sabbatizabunt, Periphyseon* 5.991C). At that point, it no longer even makes sense to speak of "a beatific vision not shared by all."

[McClymond: "Ramelli also states that Basil of Caesarea's statements on everlasting punishment are likewise not original but probably were interpolated into the texts (pp. 354–58). Her claims of interpolation are designed to uphold Origen's reputation and minimize disagreements between Origen and other ancient Christian authors."]

Let us come to Basil's problematic question-and-answer passage against *apokatastasis*, where he (if the passage is authentic) stated that his own brother, whom he appointed bishop, and his saintly sister, whom he greatly admired, are inspired by the devil. This seems, at very least, surprising. Here I hypothesize not only—as McClymond has it—an interpolation (and note that interpolations are demonstrably common in Basil's question-and-answer works; moreover, anti-Origenian interpolations and glosses are abundantly attested in the case of Nyssen in the manuscripts themselves), but also pastoral concerns. If that text were genuinely Basil's, in contradiction to his own linguistic usage and his knowledge of Origen's argument against what is claimed in that passage, this could still be explained in light of the intended monastic, not scholarly, audience of that oeuvre. For Basil shared Origen's own pastoral worries about the disclosure of the *apokatastasis* doctrine to simple or immature people. My hypothesis is furthermore supported by Orosius, who cannot be suspected of embracing *apokatastasis*, and who explicitly attributes this doctrine to Basil, as I argue in a separate article.[14] In Basil's commentary on Isaiah, then—whose authenticity finds more and more scholarly support—*apokatastasis* is simply obvious.

14. Ramelli, "Basil and *Apokatastasis*: New Findings." In addition to the chapter on Basil in *Apokatasisis*.

[McClymond writes concerning Rufinus, the ancient defender and translator of Origen who alleged that enemies of Origen deliberately interpolated theologically dubious material into his writings: "Ramelli commends 'the perspicacious Rufinus' (211) and writes that 'Rufinus was a faithful Origenian for the whole of his life' (656), who sought to 'show directly from the evidence of the texts Origen's greatness and his orthodoxy against his detractors' (636). Yet, it should be noted that Rufinus tampered with the textual evidence and saddled later scholars and readers with a skewed, inaccurate Latin rendering of *Peri archōn*."]

As for Rufinus, who never made any U-turn against Origen as Jerome did and shows to have understood well the reasons of the composition of *Peri archōn* (pointing to those that Origen himself indicated), scholars are progressively exposing his deep understanding of the aims of Origen's thought—entirely grounded in the concern for theodicy—as well as his overall reliability as a translator, who never altered but only abridged, simplified, and glossed Origen's texts. This is also confirmed by the newly discovered Greek homilies in the Munich codex,[15] which allow for further, fairly extensive comparison between Origen's Greek and Rufinus' translation.

McClymond writes:

> One indication of Origen's reputation as a heretic during late antiquity and the early medieval period is found in the wholesale destruction of most of his writings. If, as Ramelli suggests, the anathematizing of Origen—in the last place in Anathema 11—was not original, then the interpolation must have been added so quickly to the original text that no one recognized it as an interpolation. But then how is Ramelli—almost 1500 years later—able to identify an interpolation when no one before her seems to have done so?

Even setting aside that the interpolation was certainly not discovered by me, Photius in the ninth century could still read all of Origen's *Peri archōn* in Greek: thus, even Origen's most "dangerous" work was not yet destroyed by that time, over three centuries after Justinian and the supposed anathemas against Origen. On McClymond's hypothesis, this

---

15. Perrone, ed., *Origenes: Die neuen Psalmenhomilien*. These are often used in my future monograph on Origen and also confirm his life-long engagement against "gnostics" and Marcionites, against claims that this polemic was no longer vital in the last part of Origen's life.

should have been the first oeuvre of Origen to be burned, shortly after the Second Council of Constantinople. Moreover, the Latin translation of Rufinus—especially treacherous because it meant to present Origen as "orthodox"—should have been destroyed; yet, it survived up to Eriugena and the mediaeval monasteries, and has reached us in numerous manuscripts. Paradoxically, what has perished is not Rufinus' version, but Jerome's (after his volte-face), which was aimed at uncovering the allegedly heretical nature of Origen's work.

I am very glad that McClymond agrees that "*aiōnios* in ancient sources need not mean 'eternal' in the absolute, unqualified sense."[16] More precisely, it does not mean "eternal" beyond the strictly philosophical Platonic tradition (and certainly not in the Bible, where it has a number of other meanings, e.g., "remote," "ancient," "mundane," "future," "otherworldly," etc.).[17] Contrary to what McClymond claims, I comment on Jude 6 (which refers to the "*aidioi* chains" of the fallen angels) as the only biblical occurrence of *aidios* as describing punishment—but of fallen angels, not of fallen humans (*Christian Doctrine of Apokatastasis* 33). Aidios in Scripture never refers to punishment/death/fire in the other world for humans. Furthermore, what is "eternal" in Jude 6 are the *chains* that bind the angels (not the *punishment*), and those "eternal chains" are only said to bind the angels *until* the Judgment Day, at which point it might be that their punishment will be meted out. It is not said what will happen then, but the use of *aidios* may also be connected with the immortal life of angels.

[McClymond states that there is much untranslated Latin and many ancient languages in my monograph and adds: "one of the oddest aspects of this book is the attempt to clinch a biblical or exegetical argument by appealing to early translations, sometimes against the Hebrew or Greek texts. She appeals to the Vulgate when its rendering supports her scriptural interpretations (14, 23, 45, 47, 51n122). She also cites Syriac (12, 48) and Coptic (47–48) versions of the Bible."]

I cited Latin, Greek, Syriac, and Coptic, the original often being necessary for the language of restoration, but I always translated Syriac

---

16. For full analysis see Ramelli and Konstan, *Terms for Eternity: Aiōnios and Aïdios*; and Ramelli, *Tempo ed eternità in età antica e patristica*. See also here a very concise summary in Appendix I.

17. Full analysis in Ramelli and Konstan, *Terms for Eternity*, 37–70.

and Coptic, and Greek when the passages were long or difficult, e.g., in Dionysius the Areopagite. McClymond wonders why I reject the New Testament Greek text in favor of a Syriac translation of it. My occasional use of the Vetus Syra (anterior to the Peshitta) in NT criticism is amply justified, because it reflects a Greek *Vorlage* that is more ancient than all extant Greek manuscripts, apart from perhaps a couple of fragmentary papyri.[18] I referred to my previous works when necessary, to document what I was saying in my monograph. Otherwise, my assertions would have seemed mere opinions unsupported by arguments; or else, I would have needed to repeat the whole arguments, but this would have made the book (impossibly) longer.

Mine is a work of historical theology and patristic philosophy. As such, it does not aim at defending or refuting *apokatastasis*. I have rather argued—I hope forcefully and extremely carefully, for the first time in a comprehensive monograph, how the *apokatastasis* doctrine is biblically, philosophically, and especially Christologically grounded in its patristic supporters. This refutes views such as De Faye's, cited by McClymond, that "Origen made Christ all but irrelevant to the process of salvation." Brian Daley comes to conclusions on the Christology of Origen in his last book, *God Visible: Patristic Christology Reconsidered*,[19] which I support in my book on Origen, and Origen specialists such as Henryk Pietras and Panayiotis Tzamalikos agree.

I have painstakingly traced and disentangled the various strands of the doctrine of *apokatastasis*, and dismantled widespread assumptions about its opposition to the doctrine of freewill and its dependence on "pagan" philosophy more than on Scripture in the patristic era. Both Georgios Lekkas and Alfons Fürst and Christian Hengstermann in their last books on Origen agree with me in supporting the coexistence of *apokatastasis* and a strong support of freewill in Origen's thought. I have also demonstrated that the *apokatastasis* theory was present in more thinkers than is commonly assumed—even in Augustine for a while—and was in fact prominent in patristic thought, down to the last great Western patristic philosopher, Eriugena. Augustine himself, after rejecting *apokatastasis* (which he did support beforehand), and Basil attest that still late in the fourth and fifth centuries this doctrine was upheld by the vast

18. See, e.g., Brock, *The Bible in the Syriac Tradition*, 17, 19, 33–34, 111–14. See also my "Making the Bible 'World Literature.'"

19. Daly, *God Visible*, 83–93. My review is forthcoming in GNOMON.

majority of Christians—"indeed, very many" (*immo quam plurimi*, Aug. *Ench. ad Laur.* 29).

[McClymond: "The data that Daley[20] has carefully sifted shows sixty-eight authors and texts that clearly affirm the eternal punishment of the wicked, while seven authors are unclear, two teach something like eschatological pantheism, and perhaps four authors appear to be universalists in the Origenian sense. To summarize the early Christian data, the support for universalism is paltry in comparison with opposition to it. There is not much of a universalist tradition during the first centuries of the Christian church."]

Of course there were anti-universalists also in the ancient church, but scholars must be careful not to list among them—as is the case with the list of "the sixty-eight" anti-universalists, cited by McClymond on the basis of *The Hope of the Early Church*—an author just because he uses πῦρ αἰώνιον ("aionial" fire), κόλασις αἰώνιος ("aionial" punishment), θάνατος αἰώνιος ("aionial" death), or the like, since these biblical expressions do not necessarily refer to eternal damnation. Indeed, all universalists, from Origen to Gregory of Nyssa to Evagrius, used these phrases without problems,[21] for universalists understood these expressions as "otherworldly" or "long-lasting" fire, educative punishment, and death, and not "eternal" punishment, etc., which would have contrasted with their doctrine of *apokatastasis*. Thus, the mere presence of such phrases is not enough to conclude that a patristic thinker "affirmed the idea of everlasting punishment." *Didache* mentions the ways of life and death, but not *eternal* death or torment; Ignatius, as others among "the sixty-eight," never mentions eternal punishment. Ephrem does not speak of eternal damnation, but has many hints of healing and restoration, as I pointed out in the monograph and further in a detailed article in *Augustinianum*. For Theodore of Mopsuestia, another of "the sixty-eight," if one takes into account also the Syriac and Latin evidence, given that the Greek is mostly lost, it becomes impossible to list him among the anti-universalists. He

---

20. Daley, *The Hope of the Early Church*. This volume is a highly respected overview of eschatology in the early church, which I myself cited with support in many respects in my own works, along with Henryk Pietras' book on the eschatology of the early church.

21. For Origen, full analysis in my "Origene ed il lessico dell'eternità."

explicitly ruled out unending retributive punishment (*sine fine et sine correctione*).[22]

I have shown, indeed, that a few of "the sixty-eight" were not anti-universalist, and that the uncertain were often in fact universalists, e.g., Clement of Alexandria, *Apocalypse of Peter*, *Sibylline Oracles* (in one passage), Eusebius, Gregory Nazianzen, perhaps even Basil and Athanasius, Ambrose, Jerome before his change of mind, and Augustine in his anti-Manichaean years. Maximus too, another of "the sixty-eight," speaks only of punishment *aiōnios*, not *aïdios*, though living after Justinian he understandably talks about restoration only with circumspection, also using a *persona* to express the view. Torstein Tollefsen, Panayiotis Tzamalikos, and Maria Luisa Gatti, for instance, agree that Maximus affirmed *apokatastasis*.

It is not the case that "the support for universalism is paltry compared with opposition to it." Not only were "the sixty-eight" in fact fewer than sixty-eight, and not only did many of McClymond's "uncertain" in fact support *apokatastasis*, but the theologians who remain in the list of anti-universalists tend to be much less important. Look at the theological weight of Origen, the Cappadocians, Athanasius, or Maximus, for instance, on all of whom much of Christian doctrine and dogmas depends. Or think of the cultural significance of Eusebius, the spiritual impact of Evagrius or Isaac of Nineveh, or the philosophico-theological importance of Eriugena, the only author of a comprehensive treatise of systematic theology and theoretical philosophy between Origen's *Peri archōn* and Aquinas' *Summa theologiae*. Then compare, for instance, Barsanuphius, Victorinus of Pettau, Gaudentius of Brescia, Maximus of Turin, Tyconius, Evodius of Uzala, or Orientius, listed among "the sixty-eight" (and mostly ignorant of Greek). Furthermore, McClymond's statement, "there are no unambiguous cases of universalist teaching prior to Origen," should also be at least nuanced, in light of Bardaisan, Clement, the *Apocalypse of Peter*'s Rainer Fragment, parts of the *Sibylline Oracles*, and arguably of the NT itself, especially Paul's letters.

Certainly, "there was a diversity of views in the early church on the scope of final salvation." Tertullian, for instance, did not embrace *apokatastasis*. But my monograph is not on patristic eschatology or soteriology in general, but specifically on the doctrine of *apokatastasis*. Thus, I treated the theologians who supported it, and not others. It is illogical to criticize

22. From Marius Mercator, PL 48.232.

a monograph on patristic *apokatastasis* for not being a book on the diversity of early Christian eschatological teachings, as McClymond does; the latter already existed—for example, works by the aforementioned Brian Daley and Henryk Pietras, as I explain in my introduction. My monograph has a clearly different scope, methodology, focus, new research, and, inevitably, different conclusions. A review of a patristic book should be informed by fresh, direct reading (in the original languages) of the patristic theologians involved and of recent research into, and reassessment of, their thought. It should reflect a thorough study of the interactions of patristic philosophy and theology with ancient philosophy. It should not, in other words, limit itself to restating in 2015 the conclusions of another scholar's 1991 book.

APPENDIX III

Is Apokatastasis "Gnostic," Rather Than Christian?

A Review of Michael McClymond,
The Devil's Redemption[1][*]

INTRODUCTION

THE DEVIL'S REDEMPTION IS a thorough book, which must always be praised, especially in today's academic environment, which at times seems to encourage flashy subjects, research aimed at career or teaching relief, and inflamed *ad hominem* discussion (more attuned to social media than to academic scholarship), rather than life-long commitment to sustained research and systematic, important works. I concentrate here on McClymond's extensive patristics section, which traces the story from early Christianity to Eriugena. Concerning this section, my impression is that *what is good in this book is not really new*, and is present, in even more detail, in my own *Apokatastasis*,[2] Morwenna Ludlow's *Universal Salvation: Eschatology in Gregory of Nyssa and Karl Rahner* (Oxford: Oxford University Press, 2000), my essay on Zoroastrianism

---

1. Michael J. McClymond, *The Devil's Redemption: A New History and Interpretation of Christian Universalism* (Grand Rapids: Baker, 2018). A much shorter version of this review appears in the *International Journal of Systematic Theology* (forthcoming).

2. My response to McClymond's review of *Apokatastasis* appears as Appendix I in this book.

and apokatastasis,[3] and other treatments of patristic apokatastasis. Conversely, *what is new*, especially interpretations of universalistic arguments and critiques, *is mostly not very good*, in that it can easily find responses in the relevant fathers' own works, as on occasion I highlight below. As in all my works on patristic universalism, again, here I treat this subject entirely from the viewpoint of *historical* theology.

Most theologians in the first millennium were saints, as I often remind students and colleagues, and as Hans Urs von Balthasar remarked *e contrario*: "Since the great period of Scholasticism, there have been few theologians who were saints."[4] And a good number of these patristic theologians-saints supported universal restoration (as indicated in my *Apokatastasis*). However, McClymond maintains the "Gnostic, Kabbalistic, and esoteric roots of Christian universalism" (125). Now the Kabbala (Jewish mysticism) did influence some early modern Christian universalists (128), but certainly was posterior to the first systematizations of Christian universalism, from Origen onwards—just like Zoroastrian *Frashegird*, as is recognized in Appendix B and as I had thoroughly demonstrated in my article "Christian Apokatastasis and Zoroastrian Frashegird." Thus, purported Kabbalistic and Zoroastrian origins, just as mediaeval gnosis,[5] have no bearing on discussions of *patristic* apokatastasis. Our focus must be, instead, on McClymond's claims about "gnostic" origins.

"GNOSTIC" ORIGINS?

My View of the Matter

I think and have argued (in *Apokatastasis* and in this book, as well as in a chapter of a study on Origen in preparation) that patristic apokatastasis has both philosophical and, primarily, biblical and intertestamental origins; this is why Origen spoke of *"so-called* apokatastasis," referring to an earlier tradition, especially Scripture, the Petrine tradition, perhaps

---

3. Ramelli, "Christian Apokatastasis and Zoroastrian Frashegird."

4. Balthasar, "Theology and Sanctity," 181.

5. Treated on pp. 155–69 and from 170 respectively—including in Guillaume Postel (sixteenth century) and Sadhu Sundar Singh (nineteenth-twentieth centuries)—within a longer section on patristic thought that indeed continues (223) with a chapter on the much earlier Origen.

Clement, and philosophy (including Stoicism, though he vigorously refuted the Stoic version of apokatastasis).

Gnosticism, unlike most patristic supporters of apokatastasis, (1) had mostly no *holistic* doctrine of apokatastasis involving the restoration of both soul *and body*—such as the Carpocratians in Irenaeus' account, *AH* 1.25.4, who maintained that *only souls* will be saved, and moreover supported metensomatosis—and (2) in most cases supported not *universal* salvation, but salvation *only for a class of people* (the so-called *pneumatikoi* and part of the *psychikoi*),[6] although there may be some exceptions.[7]

McClymond's Use of "Gnostic" Texts

Let us consider McClymond's claims about "gnostic" origins for apokatastasis.[8] This will involve some considerations of specific "gnostic" texts. Unlike McClymond, I would not deem the eschatology of *On the Origin of the World* 126–27 to be "very optimistic" (146), since we read there that the imperfect "will never enter the kingless realm," and that "all must return to the place from where they come" and "their natures will be revealed," which means that, since there are different classes of people, they had different beginnings and will have *different ends*. Similarly, in the *Wisdom of Jesus Christ*, some know the Father perfectly, others defectively, and each will experience the rest appropriate to their group: again different ends, and perhaps those who do not know the Father will experience no rest at all. The *Apocryphon of John*, treated on p. 147, teaches both metensomatosis and eternal punishment (for at least the apostates and the blasphemers), both tenets rejected by Origen. The *Tripatite Tractate*[9] does promise the apokatastasis of the body of the church, but a whole class of humans, the "carnal" (*sarkikoi*), are excluded from it and will "perish" (118), as will a part of the *psychikoi*. So, this is also far from universal salvation, and farther from the patristic connection between

---

6. "Apokatastasis in Coptic Gnostic Texts from Nag Hammadi and Clement's and Origen's Apokatastasis."

7. Treated in a future monograph on philosophical doctrines of apokatastasis from antiquity to late antiquity and their relation to Christian doctrines.

8. There is no discussion of chronology in McClymond's treatment of "gnostic" treatises, which undercuts some of his work here.

9. On 147–48; analyzed in my "Apokatastasis in Gnostic Texts."

restoration and the resurrection of the body, since matter is declared to perish altogether. Galatians 3:28 is here projected onto eschatology.[10]

A parallel is drawn by McClymond between Valentinianism and Origen on universalism (153), but the evidence of total universalism without exclusions is very meagre in Valentinian texts, and different from that of Origen and followers: it generally excludes both the resurrection of the bodies as well as whole classes of humans. *Pistis Sophia* speaks of a "wise" fire, which discriminates between good and evil: this appears also not only in Origen (153; 271), and not only in *Hom.Luc.* 24 (271) but also in *Hom.Ier.* 2.3 and elsewhere, and also in Clement and in Gregory Nazianzen (e.g., *Or.* 39, PG36.356BC). Now Gregory cannot be labelled as influenced by Gnosticism, and yet has a penchant for apokatastasis, like Basil and, even more, like Nyssen.[11] It is true that there were influences of gnostic ideas on Origen, since he was well acquainted with such texts, but—like, and much more than, his colleague Plotinus—Origen devoted his life until his last works (such as *Against Celsus* and the recently discovered Munich homilies on the Psalms) to *refuting* the main gnostic tenets, especially the determinism coming from the division of humans into various natures, which we have encountered above. Indeed, it is mainly from this *refutation* of Gnosticism that Origen's grand theory of rational creatures, their fall, and their restoration stemmed.[12] Christian apokatastasis was, in part, an *anti*-gnostic move.

Metensomatosis (Transmigration of Souls)?

The account of preexistent, disembodied minds that fell into earthly bodies is certainly found in gnostic myths (248). However, unlike gnostics, most patristic supporters of apokatastasis, beginning with Origen and Nyssen, did *not* believe in metensomatosis (the transmigration of souls into bodies) and overtly refuted this doctrine.[13] Yet metensomatosis is

10. See my "Gal 3:28 and Aristotelian (and Jewish) Categories of Inferiority."

11. For Nazianzen: *Apokatastasis*, 440–61; Basil: *Apokatastasis*, 344–72; further "Origen the Christian Middle/Neoplatonist"; Nyssen: "Christian Soteriology and Christian Platonism"; *Apokatastasis*, 372–440; "Gregory of Nyssa on the Soul (and the Restoration): From Plato to Origen."

12. Demonstration in my "Origen, Bardaisan, and the Origin of Universal Salvation."

13. As I argue in "Origen" and "Gregory of Nyssa"; "Sôma"; "Ensomatosis vs. Metensomatosis."

mentioned by McClymond on 129 and 263 as an alleged core doctrine of patristic universalism, deriving from Gnosticism, where it was linked with the tenet of the preexistence of bare souls to any kind of bodies (141). However, the pre-existence of bodiless souls was a notion that both Origen and Nyssen—among the strongest supporters of apokatastasis—in fact *rejected*.[14] For instance, Origen declared: "The doctrine of the transmigration of souls is alien to the Church of God, since it neither has been transmitted by the apostles nor is supported in any place in Scriptures. . . . [T]he transmigration of souls will be absolutely useless if there is no end to correction, nor will ever come a time when the soul will no longer pass into new bodies. But if souls, due to their sins, must always return into ever new, different bodies, what end will there ever come to the world?" (*C.Matth.* 13.1–2; Pamph. *Apol.* 182–83). And even in the more ancient Commentary on John, the same argument appears: "If one supports metensomatosis, as a consequence one will have to maintain the incorruptibility of the world" (*C.Io.* 6.86), but this contradicts Scripture, he says.[15]

Likewise, Origen spoke only *metaphorically* of souls that can descend to the animal level, not literally within a context of transmigration of souls. Origen states: "Those who are alien to the Catholic faith think that souls migrate from human bodies into bodies of animals. . . . On the contrary, we maintain that human wisdom, if it becomes uncultivated and neglected due to much carelessness in life, becomes *like* an irrational animal [*efficitur uelut irrationabile pecus*] due to incompetence or neglectfulness, but *not by nature* [*per imperitiam uel per neglegentiam, non per naturam*]."[16] This issue was also at stake in the interpretation of Plato's mentions of animals: some took them as literal, others (such as Cronius, one of Origen's favorite readings in Porphyry *C.Chr.* F39) as metaphorical expressions of "becoming animal": "Some interpreters took 'wolves,' 'lions,' and 'asses' literally [*kyriōs*], but others deemed Plato to have been speaking metaphorically [*tropikōs*], using animals to represent characteristics of the soul. Indeed, Cronius in his work on palingenesis (i.e., metensomatosis) deems them all rational souls" (Nemesius *NH* 2.35).

14. Argument in my "Gregory of Nyssa's Purported Criticism of Origen's Purported Doctrine of the Preexistence of Souls."

15. *C.Matt.* 10.2; *C.Io.* 6.7; 85; 2.186. Further passages against metensomatosis in Tzamalikos, *Origen*, 48–53.

16. *C.Matth.* 11.17; *Apol.* 180.

Other "Gnostic" Motifs?

McClymond detects the notion of "Adamic androgyny" (223) in Gregory Nyssen and Eriugena—the notion that Adam had both genders together. One could note the presence of such ideas much earlier in Bardaisan of Edessa,[17] but in the case of Gregory and Eriugena one would better speak of a condition *above* gender, planned originally by God, then modified because of, or in prevision of, the fall, and restored again at apokatastasis.[18]

Likewise, the "return from exile" motif—described by McClymond as a "specifically cabalistic motif" (226), a comment that has no relevance to patristic theories apokatastasis, which long-predate Kabbalah—is deeply biblical. More than that, it is found in surely non-gnostic and non-Kabbalistic texts such as the Catholic prayer, *Salve regina* ("et Iesum [. . .] nobis, *post hoc exsilium, ostende*").

Similarly, "dematerialization" is described by McClymond as a gnostic-Kabbalistic motif he finds in patristic universalism (226), but in the early church such an idea was *rejected*, not embraced, by the main supporters of apokatastasis, such as Origen, Nyssen, and even Evagrius.[19]

Contrary to McClymond's claims, Origen's notion of theosis or deification is not pantheistic (266–67), resulting in an ontological absorption of a human into God's *substance*, but it is prevalently a union of *wills*: the wills of all rational creatures will be oriented towards God and they will live the divine life.[20]

AUGUSTINE'S THEOLOGICAL CRITIQUE OF ORIGEN

McClymond is correct to note that Augustine accused Origen of postulating an infinite series of restorations and falls, a critique that McClymond endorses on the basis of the eternal presence of freewill in rational creatures (265; 277). However, Augustine sometimes failed to grasp well

17. As analyzed in my *Bardaisan of Edessa: A Reassessment of the Evidence and a New Interpretation. Also in the Light of Origen and the Original Fragments from De India*, 107–26.

18. Demonstration in my "Body" and "Double Creation"; "Christian Platonists in Support of Gender Equality"; "Patristic Anthropology, the Issue of Gender, and its Relevance to Ecclesiastical Offices."

19. For Origen and Nyssen see "Origen" and "Gregory of Nyssa"; for Evagrius "Gregory Nyssen's and Evagrius' Biographical and Theological Relations." A future work on Evagrius' philosophical theology will include his eschatological views.

20. See my "Harmony"; further in the work on *Origen* in preparation, ch. 2.

Origen's thought, also being unable to access it perfectly in the original Greek. And it must be noted that originally, in his anti-Manichaean phase, Augustine seems to have embraced the doctrine of apokatastasis, using against dualistic Manichaeism Origen's monistic arguments, which had been devised against dualistic "gnostic" thought.[21] What is more, Origen argued precisely *against* the possibility of infinite restorations and falls in his *Peri archōn*, using a sentence by Paul, "love never falls," to demonstrate that, once in apokatastasis, perfect love is achieved, and in this state a rational creature will *never fall again*, even though it maintains its freewill—indeed, the first fall, of Satan, was due to his being unaware of God's love, which became manifest with Christ's incarnation and crucifixion: this is why his own love for God paled.[22] Origen posited apokatastasis at the *end of all aeons, once and forever*. So Augustine's critique misses the mark.

Augustine was aware, as all patristic Platonists were, of the "perishability axiom":[23] "nothing can be without any end of time, unless it has no beginning" (*nihil esse posse sine fine temporis, nisi quod initium non habet, CD* 10.31, quoted on p. 335). "Prior to Augustine, Gregory of Nyssa's arguments for the final extinction of evil and final salvation for all were likewise corollaries from Platonic assumptions" (335).[24] In fact, not only Gregory, but also Origen, Basil, Evagrius, and several other patristic authors used the perishability axiom; moreover, Gregory denied the preexistence of disembodied souls, though this axiom is the basis for the eternity of souls and of Good and for the perishability of evil in his thought.[25] Porphyry, as Augustine realized, "saw" that, for it to be happy, the soul must know that this happiness will be eternal, "and for this reason he asserted that the soul after purification returns to the Father, so that it may never be held back by the polluting contact of evil" (*CD*

21. Arguments, also about the way of Augustine's access to Origen, in my "Origen in Augustine: A Paradoxical Reception." Research into Origen's influence on Augustine in the various phases of his thought is needed and underway.

22. See my "Origen in Augustine"; *Apokatastasis*, 169–73.

23. On this axiom, see Elkaisy-Friemuth and Dillon, eds., *The Afterlife of the Platonic Soul*, and my review *Bryn Mawr Classical Review*, September 2010.

24. A survey of afterlife conceptions in Greco-Roman cultures includes Plato, but Plato was no universalist and seems to have taught the eternal punishment of very bad souls, as I demonstrated in 2013 (*Apokatastasis*, 153–54; further in an investigation into "pagan" philosophical theories of apokatastasis); this is correctly acknowledged by McClymond on pp. 136 and 272.

25. Demonstration in "Gregory's Purported Criticism."

10.30). Porphyry likely had learnt it from Origen, with whom, and whose works, he studied.[26]

ORIGEN'S THEOLOGICAL METHOD AND CASE

Origen offers many zetetic statements (259), especially in eschatology and other matters, while sometimes he is more assertive (259): this latter happens, I add, in matters defined by the Bible and tradition. A "permanent habituation into evil" and "ultimate impenitence" (262) are excluded by Origen, because this would lead to the annihilation of the sinning rational creature, since evil is non-being. But this would be a defeat of God's work of creation. This is why Origen insists that there cannot be a *substantialis interitus* of a bad soul, maybe even polemicizing against Philo's annihilationism.[27]

That Origen did not demonstrate the major premises of his doctrine of apokatastasis, as McClymond asserts (275), is debatable. The tenet that "the end is like the beginning" (275) is a tenet that Plotinus also supported (Origen's fellow-disciple at Ammonius Saccas') and, although he was one of the greatest philosophers, he also felt no need to demonstrate this point. Also, it is not the case that Origen never demonstrated that God's punishments are not retributive but ameliorating (275), for he often did so, mainly through Scripture, for instance in *Princ.* 2.5.3 and *Hom.Ier.* 1.15–16. Origen adduces, for example, 1 Peter 3:18ff. on the salvation of all sinners who perished in the deluge; Isaiah 47:14–15 on the ardent coals for the Chaldeans: sitting over these burning coals brings help to those sitting; and Psalm 77, according to whom God in the desert killed people in order to save them, etc. Similarly, the "primal equality among

---

26. Discussion in Ramelli, "Origen, Patristic Philosophy, and Christian Platonism"; Simmons, *Universal Salvation in Late Antiquity*, and my review in *The Classical Journal* 2017.05.02; "The Soul and Salvation in Origen and Porphyry."

On 247n.65, Porphyry's fragment on Origen, who was always reading Plato (*HE* 6.19), is represented by McClymond as the object of a debate whether it refers to Origen the Christian or another Origen. In fact, this passage surely refers to Origen the Christian, given that it mentions (and criticizes) his exegesis of Scripture. The scholarly debate mentioned concerns actually *another* passage of Porphyry, in *Vita Plotini*, and other testimonies from Hierocles, Proclus, etc., which I amply discuss elsewhere: "Origen, Patristic Philosophy"; "Origen the Christian Middle-Neoplatonist"; "Origen and the Platonic Tradition"; further in ongoing work.

27. Argument in my "Philo's Doctrine of Apokatastasis."

creatures" is not really undemonstrated (275), but it is argued through theodicy: otherwise, God would be culpable of injustice.[28]

The patristic argument that evil, as ontologically non-subsistent, must disappear is criticized by McClymond as ungrounded (286). However, both Origen and Gregory did ground it in Paul's assertion that God will be "all in all," which they take as a proof that there will be no evil left in apokatastasis, lest God be found in evil.[29] On the other hand, the identification of "the introducer of evil itself" with Satan (288) in Gregory's *Catechetical Oration* 16 is correct, which announces the eschatological purification from evil for both humans and the devil as a benefit of "the great Mystery of the divine Incarnation." Eriugena will remember this when teaching that thanks to the inhumanation of God's Son, every creature, angel, demon, or human, is saved: *Per inhumanationem Filii Dei omnis creatura, in caelo et in terra, salua facta est* (Eriugena, *Periph.* 5.24).[30]

I definitely agree with McClymond that "Origen's doctrine of universal salvation cannot be isolated from his other teachings on the nature of the soul, free will, the relation of human beings to angels and demons, divine providence, the possibility of multiple world-ages, God's reward according to merit," etc. (319). Indeed, I argued for this on several occasions.[31] Apokatastasis in Origen gains its power precisely from its "fit" within his coherent theological vision.

PURGATORY?

It is correct that Origen and Origen's followers equated universal eschatological submission and universal salvation on the basis of Philippians 2 (243) and, I would add, 1 Corinthians 15:24–28, often conflated.[32] It is also true that the doctrine of purgatory did not exist before the thirteenth century (270). Clement, Origen, and Nyssen laid the foundations for this notion (and actually many eschatological passages in Gregory were later

28. Argument in my "La coerenza della soteriologia origeniana," 661–88; received, e.g., by Battistini, *Bardesane di Edessa al crocevia dell'età e della cultura post-classica*, 136 and passim; *Apokatastasis*, section on Origen. Further arguments in the work on Origen in preparation.

29. Demonstration in my "Christian Soteriology."

30. Discussion in *Apokatastasis*, session on Eriugena.

31. *Apokatastasis*, section on Origen, and "Origen, Eusebius, and the Doctrine of Apokatastasis."

32. See my "Paul on Apokatastasis: 1 Cor 15:24–28 and the Use of Scripture."

interpreted as referring to purgatory), but, while purgatory was later distinguished from hell, what these patristic universalists taught is that *hell is in fact a purgatory.*

MCCLYMOND ON CONTEMPORARY ORIGEN SCHOLARSHIP

McClymond's chapter on Origen starts with a correct statement: there was no time when Origen was not controversial—it was normal to consider him theologically suspect (232).[33] And I agree that Nyssen, Evagrius, and Eriugena had their own versions of universalism (233), grounded in their own theologies. They all are very much indebted to Origen, as they show both explicitly and implicitly; Eriugena overtly cites Origen as his main authority on apokatastasis, and Nyssen even "copied" his arguments and scriptural quotations in support of it.[34] I agree too that Origen did not invent Christian universalism (234), but—and here is where we part company—he *didn't* appeal to gnostic teachings in support of his doctrine of apokatastasis (*contra* McClymond, 234), but rather, explicitly, to the Bible (OT and NT), inter-testamentary literature, and some philosophical (Platonic) tenets, such as the ontological non-subsistence of evil, which corresponds to the biblical teaching that evil was not created by God. At the same time, he combated gnostic ideas about freewill and soteriology all the time. The Bible, Jewish-Christian literature, the Petrine tradition, Bardaisan and Clement, and a Platonism consonant with Scripture, are the most likely sources of Origen's doctrine of apokatastasis.

In a brief history of the rehabilitation of Origen in recent decades, I am honored to see the account of my own work on Origen (237–38, close to the treatment of Henri Crouzel). This, like my book on Origen in preparation, is definitely no pre-constructed apologetics, but is based on a thorough study of all the texts of Origen, his antecedents in

33. Though Origen's year of death, 251, is debatable; it should be at least 254, and we could go until 255–56, as I argued in "Origen, Patristic Philosophy."

34. I indicated this thoroughly in *Apokatastasis*, sections on Nyssen, Evagrius, and Eriugena; "Christian Soteriology and Christian Platonism"; "Origen's Anti-Subordinationism and Its Heritage in the Nicene and Cappadocian Line"; a future work on Origen's influence on Gregory in all fields of his thought until his late life; *Evagrius' Kephalaia Gnostika*; "Gregory's and Evagrius' Relations," and my future monograph on Evagrius. For Eriugena, a future work on his debt to ancient and patristic Platonism (Origen in primis) is planned.

both Christian and "pagan" philosophical thought, his milieu, and his followers.

THE RUFINUS–JEROME DEBATE ON ORIGEN

Rufinus as a Good Interpreter of Origen

Part of the debate on the orthodoxy (or otherwise) of Origen relates to the defense of Origen provided by his follower Rufinus. Is Rufinus' orthodox Origen a faithful presentation of the real Origen or a whitewash to cover over his sub-orthodox ideas? McClymond dismisses Rufinus' pro-Origen works as an implausible attempt to make him palatable to the orthodox. However, scholars are progressively exposing Rufinus' deep understanding of the aims of Origen's thought—entirely grounded in the concern for theodicy—as well as his overall reliability as a translator, who abridged, simplified, and glossed Origen's texts, more than altering them. Sidonius Apollinaris highly praised the quality of Rufinus' versions: Rufinus grasped "both the letter and the sense" of Origen's oeuvre (*ad uerbum sententiamque, Ep.* 2.9.5) and translated Origen even better than Apuleius translated Plato, and Cicero Demosthenes. As Rufinus himself states in the epilogue to his translation of Origen's Commentary on Romans, in his versions of the Homilies on Joshua, Judges, and Psalms, he translated simply, without toiling to adapt Origen's text to the Latin public (*simpliciter ut inuenimus et non multo cum labore*). This is also confirmed by the newly discovered Greek homilies on Psalms in the Munich codex, which allow for further, fairly extensive comparison between Origen's Greek and Rufinus' translation, and confirms the latter's overall reliability.[35] Sometimes, Rufinus performs tiny adaptations and simplifications, for instance by dropping technical terms such as *epinoia* (*H.2Ps.*36.1, fol.42v), in reference to Christ's *epinoiai*, or ways of conceptualizing Christ-Logos-Wisdom. Rufinus' reliability is also confirmed by Edmon Gallagher: in general, Rufinus reflected faithfully Origen's NT canon.[36] In his preface

35. Prinzivalli, "L'originale e la traduzione di Rufino"; Prinzivalli, "Il Cod.Mon.Gr. 314, il traduttore ritrovato e l'imitatore"; earlier Crouzel, "Comparaisons précises"; Pace, *Ricerche sulla traduzione di Rufino del De Principiis*; Grappone, *Omelie origeniane nella traduzione di Rufino*, whose conclusions are deemed excessive by Perrone, *La preghiera secondo Origene*, 377, 412, 421, 426–27. John Behr, tr., *Origen: First Principles*, xxiv, agrees with me that Origen's works were indeed tampered with, and that Rufinus' translation is overall reliable.

36. Gallagher, "Origen via Rufinus on the New Testament Canon."

to his translation of *Princ.* 2, Rufinus claims that he was simply following Jerome's method: smoothing out "stumbling blocks" in Greek, that
Romans might find nothing "against our faith." Jerome admitted that he
had "emended what he wished" in his translation of *First Principles* (*Ep.*
84.7). *Pace* McClymond, it is not the case that Jerome translated faithfully, while Rufinus alone made Origen "more orthodox."[37] Hilary and
Victorinus paraphrased Origen's homilies;[38] Ambrose translated Origen's
Hexaëmeron, but made it look like Hippolytus and Basil (Jerome *Ep.*84.7).

According to McClymond, Origen's work was rejected by the church
as heretical. However, Photius in the ninth century could still read all
of Origen's *Peri archōn* in Greek: thus, even Origen's most "dangerous"
work was not yet destroyed by that time, not even in its original Greek,
over three centuries after Justinian and the supposed anathemas against
Origen. Moreover, the Latin translation of Origen's *Peri archōn* and other
speculative works of Origen, by Rufinus, who deemed and presented
Origen as "orthodox," should (on McClymond's account) have been destroyed; yet it survived up to Eriugena and the mediaeval monasteries,
and has reached us in numerous manuscripts. Paradoxically, what has
perished is not Rufinus' version, but Jerome's (after his volte-face), which
aimed at uncovering the allegedly "heretical" nature of Origen's work.

Was Origen's Work Interpolated?

Rufinus famously stated that Origen's manuscripts were tampered with,
which introduced questionable ideas not his own. This claim is declared
by McClymond to be an "implausible suggestion" (309), but in fact this
was what *Origen himself* lamented already in his earthly life.[39] It is, indeed,
what Origen denounced in a letter, containing Origen's self-fashioning as
a victim of misunderstandings and interpolations, reported by Rufinus
in *Adult.* 7, which, significantly, was placed by him at the very end of his

37. On 239n.25, Daniélou's correct observation is reported by McClymond that
Jerome's translation of Origen's homilies are faithful. However, this fidelity is not surprising, since homilies are not speculative treatises such as *First Principles*.

38. Hilary's case is exemplified in Image, *The Human Condition in Hilary of
Poitiers*; reviewed in *Reading Religion*, 21 February 2018: http://readingreligion.org/
books/human-condition-hilary-poitiers.

39. As I examined in "Decadence Denounced in the Controversy over Origen";
"Autobiographical Self-Fashioning in Origen"; further research in a future article on
reception and a work on Origen in preparation.

translation of Pamphilus' apology for Origen. This letter is Origen's famous letter to friends in Alexandria. After addressing the charge of supporting the salvation of the devil, Origen focuses on the interpolations in
his works and adduces three examples.[40] The first concerns a "heretic" and
promoter of "heresy" (*quidam auctor haereseos*) who, after having a public
debate with Origen in the presence of many people, "took the manuscript
from those who wrote it, and he added what he liked, cancelled what he
liked, and changed what seemed best to him, and then he circulated this
manuscript under my name!" (*accipiens ab his qui descripserant codicem,
quae uoluit addidit et quae uoluit abstulit et quae ei uisum est permutauit,
circumferens tamquam ex nomine nostro*). Some Christians in Palestine
then sent someone to Origen, who was in Athens, to receive the non-
interpolated copy of the debate from Origen himself. Origen at last found
it, not without difficulty, given its state of neglect.[41]

The second example adduced by Origen in his self-fashioning as a
victim of plagiarism and falsity is not even an interpolation, but a sheer
invention, coming from a lack of intellectual confrontation. A heretic
in Ephesus, as Origen recounts, first refused to have an open discussion with him: "Finally, in Ephesus, when a heretic saw me, he did not
want to have an encounter with me: he did not even want to open his
mouth with me, although I have no idea why he wanted to avoid that."[42]
After avoiding a discussion with Origen, this man invented a fictitious
debate and spread this false text in various places: then, he composed a
discussion between me and him in the way he liked, and transmitted it
to his disciples: those who were in Rome, but undoubtedly also to others
who live in other places" (*postea ex nomine meo et suo conscripsit qualem
uoluit disputationem et misit ad discipulos suos . . . ad eos qui Romae
erant, sed non dubito quod et ad alios qui per diuersa sunt*). Indeed, this
adversary of Origen spread this spurious text in Antioch, too: "He also
strolled around Antioch (and mocked at me), before I arrived there, so
that the above-mentioned written debate, which he brought with himself,
fell in the hands of many of our friends and followers" (*insultabat autem
et apud Antiochiam, priusquam ego illuc uenirem, ita ut et ad conplurimos
nostrorum perueniret ipsa disputatio quam portabat*).

40. Amacker-Junod, SC 464, 300–304.

41. *Quod ne relectum quidem uel recensitum a me antea fuerat, sed ita neglectum
iacebat ut uix inueniri potuerit.*

42. *Denique in Epheso cum me uidisset quidam haereticus et congredi noluisset
neque omnino os suum aperuisset apud me, sed nescio qua ex causa id facere deuitasset.*

When Origen finally met this opponent publicly, he asked him to produce that dialogue, in order to show that the parts ascribed to himself did not bear his own style and way of arguing: "But when I arrived and was there, I argued with him in the presence of many. Since he still continued, without any restraint, to maintain the false shamelessly, I asked that his book could be produced in the middle of us, that my style could be recognized by our brothers, who definitely know well which my arguments are in a discussion and what teaching I generally use."[43] The "heretic," however, refused to meet Origen's requests, having no courage to produce his falsified book, and was thereby convicted of forgery: "Now, this man dared not produce the book, so he was found guilty by all and was convicted of forgery, and therefore the brothers were persuaded not to pay attention to accusations."[44] Origen means specifically accusations against himself—which were abundant already during his life and increased after his death—and, by extension, charges against anyone.

The third example concerns a letter of Origen that was tampered with: "If anyone wants to believe me, since I am speaking under the eyes of God, let this person also believe me concerning the parts which in my letter are interpolated, that is, added afterwards (by someone else). If, instead, one does not want to believe, but simply wants to speak evil of me, he does not actually inflict any harm on me: rather, he himself will turn out to be a false witness against his neighbor before God, since he utters false testimony himself, or gives credit[45] to those who utter it."[46] Origen, therefore, represents himself not only as innocent and not responsible of all the tampering which has been done by others with his works, but even warns the interpolators and falsifiers that their action does not harm him, but rather themselves, since they turn out to be guilty of false testimony.

43. *Sed ubi adfui, multis eum praesentibus argui. Cumque iam sine ullo pudore pertenderet inpudenter adserere falsitatem, poposci ut liber deferretur in medium, stilus meus agnosceretur a fratribus, qui utique cognoscunt quae soleo disputare uel quali soleo uti doctrina.*

44. *Quique, cum ausus non esset proferre librum, conuictus ab omnibus et confutatus est falsitatis: et ita persuasum est fratribus ne aurem criminationibus praeberent.*

45. On this meaning of *credere*, see my "Alcune osservazioni su *credere*," and *Studi su Fides*; Morgan, *Roman Faith and Christian Faith*, 51–55, and my review in *Journal of Roman Studies* 107 (2017) 368–70.

46. *Si quis ergo uult credere mihi in conspectu dei loquenti, etiam de his quae in epistula mea conficta sunt et inserta credat. Sin autem quis non credit sed uult de me male loqui, mihi quidem nihil damni confert: erit autem ipse falsus testis apud deum aduersum proximum suum, falsum testimonium uel dicens uel dicentibus credens.*

This is a mortal sin, being against the Eighth Commandment (Exod 20:16), and God will punish it.

Origen denounced the same phenomenon of the adulteration of his works in another letter, also read by Rufinus: he adds this particular after reporting the letter of Origen I have analyzed above: "Origen himself, while he was still on earth, complained about the passages that he could personally discover as interpolations and falsifications in his own oeuvre. Actually, in another letter as well, I remember having read a similar complaint concerning the falsification of his writings. I have no copy of this letter now here with me, that I may add Origen's testimony to the others I have already adduced, testifying to their truth."[47]

For Rufinus

In the treatment of the Jerome-Rufinus debate over Origen,[48] McClymond suggests that "Rufinus tolerated Origen's errors because he did not understand them," since "his grasp of theological issues was rather weak" (310). However, another reason for his toleration of Origen may be that he knew that these were not errors (indeed, in many respects Origen grounded future orthodox tenets[49]). The "minimalist" definition of orthodoxy rightly individuated by Elizabeth Clark about Rufinus ("God the Creator, the Incarnation, the Trinity," with "freedom to discuss points that had not been so defined, such as the origin of the soul and the fate of the devil," cited on p. 310) indeed comes straight from the very same definition by Origen in the prologue of *Peri archōn*. Jerome's attack on Origen's apokatastasis (though only after his apparent U-turn against Origen) on the grounds that "it allowed no difference of rank in heaven" (315) refers merely to the very last stage of the process of restoration.

47. *Haec ipse adhuc superstes conqueritur, quae scilicet per semetipsum deprehendere potuit adulterata esse in libris suis atque falsata. Meminimus sane etiam in alia eius epistula similem nos de librorum suorum falsitate legisse querimoniam, cuius epistulae exemplar in praesenti non habui, ut etiam ipsius testimonium his pro fide ueritatis adiungerem (Adult. 8).*

48. I analyzed it in *Apokatastasis*, 627–58. It is here dealt with from p. 309 onwards. On p. 239, n. 25, Daniélou's correct observation is reported that Jerome's translations of Origen's homilies are faithful: this can be expected, since homilies are not speculative treatises such as First Principles. On this latter work, as on other speculstive works by Origen, the controversy was more enflamed.

49. See the last part of my "Ethos and Logos"; further in the monograph in preparation.

Origen, in fact, did postulate big postmortem differences, depending on merits and demerits, and these lay in the length and severity of purifying punishments.

CLEMENT, ORIGEN'S PRECURSOR

Regarding Clement, the precursor of Origen's doctrine of apokatastasis (together, I add, with Bardaisan), I agree with McClymond that he read and commented on the *Apocalypse of Peter* and was influenced by its penchant for universal salvation (240); indeed, I argued for this thesis in "Origen, Bardaisan,"[50] in *Apokatastasis*, 67–136, and further in "Stromateis VII and Clement's Hints of the Theory of Apokatastasis."[51] A fragment from the *Hypotyposeis*, in which it is declared that God "saves all," is rightly taken as evidence of Clement's teaching on universal salvation (242). Only, his teaching on apokatastasis, mainly based on the remedial nature of postmortem punishment, is not so systematic and widespread as in Origen. Lilla claimed that Clement intended to turn the Christian faith into a philosophical system (as we are reminded by McClymond on p. 240); but surely he wanted to defend Christianity from the accusation of irrationality and intended to support faith through the *logos,* as I have argued elsewhere.[52]

Photius' accusations to Clement (244) were studied by Piotr Ashwin,[53] who, as we are reminded on p. 245, thinks that the accusation of believing in metensomatosis finds no confirmation in Clement's oeuvre. This appears true, although new research is going on by Sami Yli-Karjanmaa, who has already written an interesting although somewhat controversial book, *Reincarnation in Philo of Alexandria* (Atlanta: SBL, 2015), and is extending the research to Clement.

Contra McClymond, the "interpretation of 'gnostic' in terms of soteriological elitism and soteriological determinism," an interpretation I endorse, is not my own (247), but rather Clement's and especially Origen's; on this basis Origen constructed his polemic, which led to his doctrine of apokatastasis. Interestingly, in many respects Origen's criticism

---

50. Cited on 230n.27.

51. In *The Seventh Book of the Stromateis*, ed. Havrda et al., 239–57.

52. In "Ethos and Logos"; "The Mysteries of Scripture."

53. Ashwin-Siejkowski, *Clement of Alexandria on Trial*; my review GNOMON 84 (2012) 393–97.

of "gnostic" ideas coincided with the criticism of his contemporary (and fellow-disciple at Ammonius') Plotinus against the "gnostic" worldview: he was interestingly criticizing "gnostics" who attended his school.[54] Of course, I am well aware that the writings from the Nag Hammadi Corpus differ from the accounts of the heresiologists.[55] It is worth noticing that Origen and Plotinus are more cautious and less schematic in their understanding of "gnostic" tenets, which they heard and knew *prima manu*.

GREGORY OF NYSSA AND ORIGEN

Gregory Draws on Origen

McClymond's short account of what I call Gregory of Nyssa's "theology of freedom" on p. 280 is well done. It must, however, be noticed that Gregory's account of freewill depends entirely on Origen, as I extensively argued elsewhere.[56] In this connection, Gregory's tenet that "evil exists only through the exercise of the creatures' will against God" (285) is exactly what Origen taught in his ontological monism. Nyssen's short treatise on 1 Corinthians 15:28, *In Illud: Tunc et Ipse Filius* (briefly examined on 285–86), depends entirely on Origen's exegesis and links anti-subordinationism (in reference to the Son) to the argument of apokatastasis, through the identification of the submission of all humanity—the body of Christ—to God as its salvation.[57]

McClymond is correct that for Gregory "free and deliberate choice by individual human beings is not in contradiction to corporate salvation but is integrated into it" (289). This held true for Origen as well, and I think it depends on the fact that they both embraced ethical intellectualism.[58] That the purifying fire may last *pros holon aiōna* refers to the future age *before apokatastasis*, according to Gregory, as well as according to

54. Parallels studied in the work on Origen in preparation; further in a future systematic comparison between Origen and Plotinus.

55. I discussed this in "Apokatastasis in Coptic Gnostic Texts" and "Origen, Bardaisan," and further in a work on philosophical notions of apokatastasis.

56. "Gregory Nyssen's Position in Late-Antique Debates on Slavery and Poverty and the Role of Ascetics"; *Social Justice*, ch. 4.

57. Arguments in my "*In Illud: Tunc et Ipse Filius* . . . (1Cor 15,27–28); "Origen's Anti-Subordinationism"; "The Father in the Son, the Son in the Father (John 10:38, 14:10, 17:21)."

58. Observations in my "Was Patristic Sin Different from Ancient Error?"

Origen.[59] Gregory's insistence on postmortem suffering (281) is rightly indicated: it is purifying and relates to the theology of the cross. Plato himself had insisted that evil can be removed only through suffering, something that struck both Origen and Gregory, although we are not sure that Plato was speaking of *vicarious* suffering. This, however, along with Scripture, was an important source for their conception of purifying suffering.

Gregory Did Not Reject Origen

McClymond rightly observes that Nyssen surely "rejected the doctrine of preexistent souls that fell from the love of God and then inhabited mortal bodies" (280), but neither did Origen endorse this theory. Gregory in *Op.hom.* 28, which links metensomatosis to the preexistence of souls theorized by people who wrote on protology, is not aimed at criticizing Origen (*contra* McClymond, 280n.183), as most people think, but likely "pagan" Neoplatonists such as Porphyry, who wrote *On First Principles*, or Manichaeans.[60] Nyssen, claims McClymond, "offered a version of universalism that omitted Origen's preexistent souls" (320): but as I have argued, this assertion, with regard to Origen, is very debatable.[61]

(Theophilus of Alexandria,[62] in the Festal Letter of 404, specified that the first humans were *not* "naked souls" (305–7). Who was he opposing? Origen? This idea of "naked souls" was certainly denied by Origen himself, who never postulated a preexistence of disembodied souls.[63] It may instead be Theophilus' response to his misunderstanding of Evagrius' notion of a "pure or naked Nous.")

---

59. Argument in "Αἰώνιος and αἰών in Origen and Gregory of Nyssa"; received by Boersma, "Overcoming Time and Space: Gregory of Nyssa's Anagogical Theology"; "Apokatastasis and Epektasis in *Hom. in Cant.*"

60. Argument in "Gregory's Purported Criticism."

61. I argued that Origen never supported the preexistence of bare souls in *"Preexistence of Souls"?* Further in "Origen."

62. Examined in *Apokatastasis*, 584–91; "Anthropomorphism."

63. Argument in my "Origen"; "Ensomatosis vs. Metensomatosis."

EVAGRIUS

On Physical Bodies

Evagrius was strongly influenced not only by Basil and Gregory Nazianzen (293), as commonly assumed, but also very much by Nyssen.[64] Concerning the two redactions of the *Kephalaia Gnostika*, it is noted that, unlike Casiday, Bundy does not assign S1 chronological priority over S2 (293n.230): I concur and explained some reasons in "Evagrius' Relations." Evagrius is often attributed the idea "that physical body or materiality will pass away" (294); however, this indicates not merely destruction, but subsumption into a higher reality: body into soul, soul into intellect, intellect into God.[65] This conception will be taken over and expanded by Eriugena. Evagrius' notion that "the movement is the cause of evil" (295) is taken from Origen, as well as his tenet that there was a time when evil was not and there will be one when it will no longer exist (295).[66]

On the Trinity

McClymond states that the idea that the Trinitarian distinctions will cease "could be inferred from Evagrius' *Great Letter*, but the point was not asserted in Evagrius as it was in Bar Sudhaili" (349)! Actually, this letter (*Letter to Melania*) explicitly *denies* a cessation of Trinitarian distinctions: the three hypostases, Father Son, and Spirit, will remain distinct in the eschaton.[67]

On Knowledge and Love

McClymond's contrast between Origen, who understood spiritual life in terms of knowledge, love, and will, and Evagrius, who understood it only

64. As I argued in "Evagrius and Gregory: Nazianzen or Nyssen?"; *Evagrius' Kephalaia Gnostika*, introduction and commentary; further in "Gregory Nyssen's and Evagrius' Biographical and Theological Relations."

65. "Gregory's and Evagrius' Relations" and "Evagrius Ponticus, the Origenian Ascetic (and not the Origenistic 'Heretic')."

66. On this important point and its ascendents, see my commentary in *Evagrius' Kephalaia Gnostika*.

67. I point this out in my monographic essay in *Evagrius' Kephalaia Gnostika*; further in a planned monograph on Evagrius, also dealing with his Christology.

in terms of knowledge (299), should be nuanced, given the equation that Evagrius draws between love and *apatheia*, and the importance given to both.[68]

On Christology

The question "whether Evagrius' Christology is orthodox in the Nicene sense" (299) should be answered in the positive.[69] KG 6.14 is one of the numerous statements in Evagrius' *Kephalaia Gnostika* and *Letter on Faith* that point in the opposite direction to "subordinationism": the Son is seen as wholly divine with the Father and the Spirit. Here I propose to read either the first sentence as that of an objector—which is attested elsewhere in Evagrius—or the whole *kephalaion* as an internal dialectics of thesis, antithesis, and discussion (what Evagrius repeatedly uses, in a "zetetic" fashion inherited from Origen). This is the only way to understand KG 6.14 in a non-contradictory manner, since it first states: "Christ is not consubstantial [*homoousios*] with the Trinity," and then: "Christ is consubstantial [*homoousios*] with the Father." The subject is always "Christ," in two sentences that form a contradiction in terms (*contradictio in adiecto*). If in KG 4.9 and 4.18 Evagrius distinguishes Christ from the Logos, in KG 6.14 he considers both together as a unity: "in union, Christ is *homoousios* with the Father" and "is the Lord" God. In KG 3.1, Christ is considered in his divine nature as Son, and thereby God: "The Father—only he—knows Christ, and the Son—only he—the Father." Christ and the Son occupy the same position in the equation: Father:Christ = Son:Father. This implies the identity between Son and Christ in his divine nature. Evagrius, like Origen, calls Christ sometimes the rational creature (*logikon*) alone, sometimes the union of this *logikon* with God's Logos/Son. In *Skemmata* 1, Evagrius treats Christ as a compound of creatural and divine nature, claiming that Christ qua Christ possesses the essential knowledge, that is, God, who constitutes his own divine nature. Consistently, Palladius in his biography of Evagrius depicts him as supporting, against 'heretics' such as "Arians" and Eunomians, the full divinity of Christ-Logos, God's Son, who also assumed a human body, soul, and

68. See my "Gregory's and Evagrius' Relations" and Tobon, *Apatheia and Anthropology in Evagrius of Pontus*.

69. See my Evagrius' *Kephalaia Gnostika*, the commentary sections on Christology; "Evagrius' Relations," and the work in preparation on Evagrius' philosophical theology.

nous. Thus, Christ is *both* God *and* a *logikon*. This hybridity of Christ was emphasized by Origen, whom Evagrius follows: see my "Atticus and Origen on the Soul of God the Creator: From the 'Pagan' to the Christian Side of Middle Platonism," *Jahrbuch für Religionsphilosophie* 10 (2011) 13–35, and my monograph on Origen in preparation.

Sometimes Evagrius is accused of supporting a dichotomic Christology, but this is the same that Nyssen had. This is unsurprising, as I think Gregory exerted more influence on Evagrius than is commonly assumed.[70] Evagrius is also charged with theorizing a Christology that does not point in the direction of Chalcedon—an accusation that views Evagrius from the perspective of posterior theological developments. Paradoxically enough, however, precisely in KG 6.14, the adverb "inseparably," in reference to Christ, who possesses "inseparably" the Essential Knowledge (God), is the same as the adverbs that at Chalcedon will describe the inseparability of Christ's two natures: *achōristōs, adiairetōs*. Indeed, "inseparable" is used here by Evagrius exactly to describe the union of Christ's divine and human natures: "Christ is the only one who always and inseparably possesses the Essential Knowledge in himself." "Always" might also be taken to anticipate Chalcedon's *atreptōs*, "without change over time." Thus, Christ is the only *logikon* who always and inseparably possesses God in himself. Christ is both a *logikon* and God. In sum, Evagrius was no Christological "heretic."

EPHREM

It is basically correct of McClymond to place Ephrem among the non-universalists, since he has no systematic treatment of apokatastasis, but he does show statements that open up the possibility of universal salvation, as I studied in an article and in my monograph on apokatastasis.[71] It is true that the wicked are said by him to have a different postmortem status than the righteous, but this is not said to be eternal. Origen himself maintained the same thing.

---

70. More on KG 6.14 and Evagrius' Christology is in my "Nyssen's and Evagrius' Relations"; further study, eventually, in a monograph on Evagrius.

71. "La centralità del Mistero di Cristo nell'escatologia di s. Efrem"; received by den Biesen, "A drop of salvation: Ephrem the Syrian on the Eucharist," 1139. Further proofs in my *Apokatastasis*, 331–44.

PSEUDO-DIONYSIUS

Pseudo-Dionysius, a Christian Neoplatonist, was admired and quoted by many, including Thomas Aquinas (about 1,700 times). It has been indeed advocated that Dionysius did *not* support the doctrine of apocatastasis (as McClymond reminds us on p. 342), since he speaks of apokatastasis in the present, and not in the future. In fact, Dionysius speaks of apoka-tastasis and reversal/conversion (*epistrophē*) in the present[72] not because he denies the eventual apokatastasis but because God, being atemporal, lives in an eternal present, as the co-eternal circle of the movements of love makes clear.[73]

BAR SUDHAILI

McClymond's treatment of Bar Sudhaili and his apokatastasis as pantheis-tic (and thus very different from that of Origen and Nyssen) is sound, just as the acceptance of Henri de Lubac's suggestion that what the Emperor Justinian famously condemned in the sixth century was not Origen's own thought, but that of Bar Sudhaili (347). Certainly, he did not condemn the *real* thought of Origen, least of all that of Gregory of Nyssa.[74]

MAXIMUS THE CONFESSOR

Maximus the Confessor's *Ambigua* offered, in McClymond's view, "a sys-tematic reinterpretation, or rather correction, of Origen and Evagrius" (364). Yet Maximus surely corrected a radicalized Origen*ism* and Evagri-an*ism*, more than Origen's own thought.[75] He transformed and developed Origen's ideas, rather than correcting them. Maximus did insist that "to be a creature is to be in movement" (365), but by doing so he was *follow-ing* Origen. *Pace* McClymond, Maximus was not "rejecting Origen's idea of an original state of ontologically static creatures," since Origen posited movement, in the primary sense of movement of the soul and an act of

72. "The Question of Origen's Conversion and His Philosophico-Theological Lexi-con of *Epistrophē*."

73. Argument in *Apokatastasis*, 694–721; "Origen, Evagrios, and Dionysios."

74. The correspondence of the almost contemporary Barsanuphius and John of Gaza about apokatastasis in Nyssen and about Evagrius' *Kephalaia Gnostika* is inter-esting; I analyzed it in *Apokatastasis*, 410; 725–28.

75. I argued for this in *Apokatastasis*, 738–57; further work in preparation.

will, as characteristic of all rational creatures and a gift from God (and the source of their fall or their adhesion to God).[76] When Maximus at the beginning of *Ambiguum* 7 criticizes those who posited an initial unity of rational beings "connatural with God" (*symphyeis theō*), this hardly could target Origen, who explicitly denied, against some "gnostics," that rational creatures could be connatural or *homoousioi* with God.[77] Shortly afterwards, when Maximus attacks those who thought that God imprisoned rational creatures to bodies as a result of their sin, he was not criticizing Origen's ideas, since Origen rather maintained that God created rational creatures with a spiritual body, which after the fall became heavy and mortal (for humans) and "ridiculous" (for demons).[78] Likewise, Maximus' objection to an endless series of falls and restorations, like that of Augustine, does not correspond to Origen's above-mentioned theory of a *finite* series of aeons followed by a restoration that will be definitive, the *telos*.

Maximus, as von Balthasar already suggested and as can be gathered from many more clues and further considerations, hinted at apokatastasis as a mystery to be honored by silence. The silence that Nyssen and others used in mystical apophaticism, with respect to God, Maximus seems to apply to apokatastasis and deification (*theōsis*), which is the culmination of apokatastasis.[79] Maximus significantly speaks of the eventual apokatastasis *per interpositam personam*, a nameless wise man who worked as a mouthpiece, out of prudence.

ISAAC THE SYRIAN

Isaac the Syrian (often referred to as Isaac of Nineveh) and Eriugena are the two last patristic supporters of apokatastasis the book deals with. Isaac posited that God's love is experienced differently in the other world and brings enjoyment to the good but torture to the wicked (372), although this torture will not be eternal but "will manifest some wonderful outcome" (*Second Part* 39). Isaac's idea is similar to that of Origen, who

76. See also my "Response to Giulio Maspero," in *Evagrius between Origen, the Cappadocians, and Neoplatonism*, 101–4.

77. Argument in my "Origen, Greek Philosophy, and the Birth of the Trinitarian Meaning of Hypostasis."

78. See my "Origen."

79. Discussion in my "Epopteia–Epoptics in Platonism, 'Pagan' and Christian, from Origen to Maximus," forthcoming.

asserted that the same God will be light for the just, but (purifying) fire for sinners: "God will become light without doubt for the just, and fire for sinners to consume in them any trace of corruptibility and fragility it will find in their soul."[80] All of Isaac's thought revolves around the notion of God's love and compassion, which never change, and God's immunity towards anger (a revisitation of the concept of the divine lack of passions, or *apatheia*).[81] God does not avenge evil, but he makes evil right and thereby *makes* justice: this is the notion of setting right (*diorthōsis*) of evil that Origen and the Origenian tradition, including Eusebius, upheld. Likewise, when Isaac specifies that in the end "all are going to exist in a single love, a single purpose, a single will, and a single perfect state of knowledge" (*Second Part* 40), he takes over Origen and Evagrius, who followed Origen in turn: the love of all rational creatures will be directed towards one object, God, the true Good, in a reorientation of all the dispersed wills of rational creatures, a unity of will and universal harmony (so much so that even demons will make no exception to this harmony).[82] Knowledge, in Evagrius' line, will be perfect in the eventual deification (*theōsis*), since this will be the *nous'* life in God, who is Essential Knowledge.

ERIUGENA

Eriugena's debt to Greek patristics is rightly acknowledged by McClymond (374), as well as his (Neoplatonist) *exitus-reditus* scheme (376), which dovetails with the creation–apokatastasis movement.[83] Indeed, he may be reckoned the last great patristic Platonist in the West. As such, it comes as no surprise that he admired Origen a great deal.[84] Against Augustine and his postlapsarian *non posse non peccare*, Eriugena "insisted

80. "Lux sine dubio iustis et ignis efficitur peccatoribus, ut consumet in iis omne quod in anima eorum corruptibilitatis et fragilitatis invenerit" (*Comm.Cant.* 2.2.21). See also my *Apokatastasis*, 758–66.

81. See my "Isacco di Ninive teologo della carità divina e fonte della perduta escatologia antiochena."

82. See my "Harmony between *arkhē* and *telos* in Patristic Platonism and the Imagery of Astronomical Harmony Applied to the Apokatastasis Theory."

83. *Apokatastasis*, 773–815; further, "From God to God: Eriugena's Protology and Eschatology against the Backdrop of His Patristic Sources."

84. See my "The Reception of Origen's Thought in Western Theological and Philosophical Traditions."

that human nature is essentially free" and "freedom remained after sin" (377). He followed Origen rather than Augustine in this respect.

Eriugena supported apokatastasis.[85] *Creatio ex nihilo* is rightly equated with *creatio ex Deo* in Eriugena's doctrine (378), in an apophatic perspective in which God becomes superabundant nothingness.[86] Regarding his notion that "purified souls will be absorbed into pure intellects" (379), I find it in line with the theory of Evagrius: the subsumption of body into soul, soul into "unified intellect [*nous*]," and this into God, at the stage of deification (*theōsis*) and unity—a theory indebted to Nyssen, and ultimately to Origen. Now, Eriugena was right to trace this theory precisely back to Nyssen: Gregory "builds up an addition: the transformation of the body into soul at the time of the resurrection, of the soul into intellect, and of the intellect into God."[87]

Eriugena's notion of deification appears somewhat different from that of Origen: while in Origen this was primarily a unity of will and life in God, Eriugena insisted that this will be a unity of substance or essence (*homo et Deus in unitatem unius substantiae adunati sunt, Hom.Prol.Io.* PL 122.296C). But it is awkward that one can question "whether the restoration of human nature carries with it the salvation of every human soul" (381, citing Gardner). Eriugena in fact is *crystal clear* that, thanks to Christ's inhumanation, "every creature, in heaven and on earth, has been saved" (*omnis creatura, in caelo et in terra, salva facta est, Periph.* 5.24). Eriugena is adamant that all rational creatures in their substances will be happy; no substantial nature can "be in unhappiness" (*Praed.* 16.1). All natures will enjoy "a wonderful joy" (*Praed.* 19.3). The evilness derived from sinners' perverted will shall perish in the other world; only their substance will remain (*substantia permansura, malitia in aeternum peritura*) and will be happy (*Periph.* 5.931A).

It is correct (381) that according to Eriugena "all . . . shall return into Paradise, but not all shall enjoy the Tree of Life—or rather . . . not all equally" (*Periph.* 1015A), but this refers to the distinction between salvation and deification, and does not imply that some will *not* be *saved*.

85. As I painstakingly show in *Apokatastasis*, 773–815 and "From God to God."

86. Idea examined by Theo Kobusch, "Creation out of Nothing—Creation out of God," lecture, Oxford workshop, *Eriugena's Christian Neoplatonism* (above), forthcoming.

87. "Gregorius . . . astruit mutationem corporis tempore resurrectionis in animam, animae in intellectum, intellectus in Deum" (*Periph.* 5.987C). See my "Gregory of Nyssa on the Soul (and the Restoration)."

Maybe some will not be *deified*. Though, sometimes Eriugena even suggests that deification itself will extend to all. For he postulates the return of all to God, and the transformation of all into God, through their primordial causes; at that point, all will enjoy peace and eternal splendor and joy: "*Quando omnis sensibilis creatura in intelligibilem et omnis intelligibilis in causas, et causae in causarum causam (quae Deus est) mutabuntur aeternaque requie gaudebunt ineffabilique claritate fulgebunt et sabbatizabunt*" (*Periph.* 5.991C). At that point, it no longer even makes sense to speak of a beatific vision not shared by all.

I hail with comfort and satisfaction a sustained academic book of the kind that costs a long time and concentration effort to be conceived, written, and read—the type that the current academic system and even some publishers sometimes seem to discourage nowadays. I look forward to reading also *That All Shall Be Saved: Heaven, Hell, and Universal Salvation*, by David Bentley Hart (Yale University Press, 2019).

Ilaria L. E. Ramelli
(Sacred Heart University; Angelicum;
Oxford; Durham; Erfurt MWK)

Ilaria Ramelli, FRHistS, is Professor of Theology and K. Britt Chair at the Graduate School of Theology, SHMS (Thomas Aquinas University "Angelicum"); the director of international research projects; senior visiting professor at major universities; *Humboldt-Forschungspreis* Fellow in Religion (Erfurt University, Max Weber Center); Fowler Hamilton Fellow (Oxford University, Christ Church) and Senior Research Fellow (Durham University, for the second time; Sacred Heart University, since 2003). She has been Professor of Roman History, Senior Research Fellow (Durham, for the first time; Oxford University, Corpus Christi; Princeton University, IAS, etc.), and senior visiting professor (Harvard, Columbia and other universities). She has taught courses and seminars and delivered invited lectures and main lectures in numerous leading universities and conferences in Europe, North America, and Israel. She received many academic awards and prizes and serves on directive and scientific boards of leading scholarly series and journals. She has authored numerous books, articles, and reviews in foremost scholarly journals and series, on ancient philosophy, patristic theology and philosophy, ancient Christianity, and the relationship between Christianity and classical culture.

Bibliography

Aelfric. *Aelfric's Catholic Homilies. Second Series.* Vol. 2. Edited by Malcom Godden. Oxford: Oxford University Press, 1979.

Ansell, Nik. "The Annihilation of Hell and the Perfection of Freedom." In *All Shall Be Well: Universal Salvation and Christian Theology from Origen to Moltmann*, edited by Gregory MacDonald, 417–39. Eugene, OR: Cascade, 2011.

Arnold, Johannes. *Der Wahre Logos des Kelsos: Eine Strukturanalyse.* Münster: Aschendorff Verlag, 2016.

Ashwin-Siejkowski, Piotr. *Clement of Alexandria on Trial: The Evidence of 'Heresy' from Photius' Bibliotheca.* Leiden: Brill, 2010.

Assemani, J. S. *Bibliotheca Orientalis Clementino–Vaticana*, III,I. Rome 1725. Reprint. Piscataway, NJ: Gorgias, 2004.

Ayroulet, E. *De l'image à l'image: Réflexions sur un concept clef de la doctrine de la divinisation de S. Maxime le Confesseur.* Rome: Augustinianum, 2013.

Baker, D.N. *Julian of Norwich. Showings: From Vision to Book.* Princeton: Princeton University Press, 1994.

Balthasar, Han Urs von. "Adrienne von Speyr: Über das Geheimnis des Karsamstages," *Internationale Katholische Zeitschrift Communio* 10 (1981) 32–39.

———. *Dare We Hope "That All Men Be Saved"? With a Short Discourse on Hell.* San Francisco: Ignatius, 1988.

———. *Kosmische Liturgie.* Einsiedeln, Switzerland: Johannes-Verlag, 1961.

———. "Theology and Sanctity." In *Explorations in Theology, I, The Word Made Flesh*, 181–86. ET. San Francisco: Ignatius, 1989.

Battistini, Luca. *Bardesane di Edessa al crocevia dell'età e della cultura post-classica.* Parma: University of Parma, 2017.

Bauckham, Richard. "The Apocalypse of Peter: A Jewish-Christian Apocalypse from the Time of Bar Kochba." *Apocrypha* 5 (1994) 7–111.

———. "Emerging Issues in Eschatology in the Twenty-First Century." In *The Oxford Handbook of Eschatology*, edited by Jerry L. Walls, 671–88. Oxford: Oxford University Press, 2007.

———. *The Fate of the Dead: Studies on the Jewish and Christian Apocalypses.* Leiden: Brill, 1998.

———, ed. *God Will Be All in All: The Eschatology of Jürgen Moltmann.* Edinburgh: T. & T. Clark, 1999.

———. "Universalism. A Historical Survey." *Themelios* 4.2 (1979) 48–54.

———. "Universalism. A Historical Survey." *Evangelical Review of Theology* 15 (1991) 22–35.

Bauckham, Richard, and Trevor Hart. *Hope Against Hope: Christian Eschatology at the Turn of the Millennium*. Grand Rapids: Eerdmans, 1999.

Bauckham, Richard, and Paolo Marassini. "Apocalypse de Pierre." In *Écrits apocryphes chrétiens I*, edited by François Bovon and Pierre Geoltrain, 745–74. Paris: Gallimard, 1997.

Beauchemin, Gerard. *Hope beyond Hell: The Righteous Purpose of God's Judgment*. 2nd ed. Olmito, TX: Malista, 2010.

Behr, John, tr. *Origen: First Principles*. Oxford: Oxford University Press, 2018.

Bell, Richard. *The Irrevocable Call of God: An Inquiry into Paul's Theology of Israel*. Tübingen: Mohr, 2003.

———. "The Myth of Adam and the Myth of Christ in Romans 5:12–21." In *Paul, Luke, and the Graeco-Roman World: Essays in Honour of Alexander J. M. Wedderburn*, edited by Jörg Frey et al., 21–36. Sheffield, UK: Sheffield Academic Press, 2002.

———. "Rom 5.18–19 and Universal Salvation." *New Testament Studies* 48 (2002) 417–32.

Bernstein, A. E. *The Formation of Hell: Death and Retribution in the Ancient and Early Christian Worlds*. Ithaca, NY: Cornell University Press, 1993.

Blowers, Paul M. *Maximus the Confessor: Jesus Christ and the Transfiguration of the World*. Oxford: Oxford University Press, 2016.

Boersma, Hans. "Overcoming Time and Space: Gregory of Nyssa's Anagogical Theology." *Journal of Early Christian Studies* 20.4 (2012) 575–612.

Boncour, Elisabeth. "Eckhart lecteur d'Origène." PhD diss., Paris, 2014.

Bouteneff, Peter. "Paradise." In *The Concise Encyclopedia of Orthodox Christianity*, edited by John McGuckin, 354–55. Malden-Oxford: Wiley-Blackell, 2014.

Bremmer, Jan. *The Rise and Fall of the Afterlife*. London: Routledge, 2002.

Bremmer, Jan, and Istvan Czachesz, eds. *The Apocalypse of Peter*. Leuven: Peeters, 2003.

Briggman, Anthony. "Literary and Rhetorical Theory in Irenaeus." *Vigiliae Christianae* 69 (2015) 500–27.

———. "Revisiting Irenaeus' Philosophical Acumen." *Vigiliae Christianae* 65.2 (2011) 115–24.

Brock, Sebastian P. *The Bible in the Syriac Tradition*. Piscataway, NJ: Gorgias, 2006.

———. "Four Excerpts from Isaac of Nineveh in Codex Syriacus Secundus." *Parole de l'Orient* 41 (2015) 101–14.

———. "Some Prominent Themes in the Writings of the Syrian Mystics of the 7th and 8th Century AD." In *Gotteserlebnis und Gotteslehre. Christliche und islamische Mystik im Orient*, edited by Martin Tamcke, 49–59. Wiesbaden: Göttinger Orientforschungen, 2010.

Brown, Sherri. "Prophetic Endurance and Eschatological Restoration: Exhortation and Conclusion in the Epistle of James." *Expository Times* online April 26, 2019. https://doi.org/10.1177/0014524619846399.

Buchan, Thomas. *Blessed Is He Who Has Brought Adam From Sheol*. Piscataway, NJ: Gorgias, 2004.

Buchholz, Dennis. *Your Eyes Will Be Opened: A Study of the Greek (Ethiopic) Apocalypse of Peter*. Atlanta: SBL, 1988.

Cameron, Michael. "Origen and Augustine." In *The Oxford Handbook of Origen*, edited by Ronald Heine and Karen Jo Torjesen. Oxford: Oxford University Press. Forthcoming.

Casiday, Augustine. *Evagrius Ponticus*. London: Routledge, 2006.

Chan, Michael. *The Wealth of Nations: A Tradition-Historical Study.* Tübingen: Mohr Siebeck, 2016.

Clark, Kelly James. "God is Great, God is Good: Medieval Conceptions of Divine Goodness and the Problem of Hell." *Religious Studies* 37 (2001) 15–31.

Clement. *The Seventh Book of the Stromateis.* Edited by Matyaš Havrda et al. Leiden, Brill, 2012.

Coakley, Sarah, and Charles Stang, eds. *Rethinking Dionysius the Areopagite.* Oxford: Wiley-Blackwell, 2009.

Cohn, N. *The Pursuit of the Millennium.* 2nd ed. London: Harper & Row, 1991.

Colledge, Edmund, and James Walsh. *A Book of Showings to Anchoress Julian of Norwich.* Toronto: Pontifical Institute of Mediaeval Studies, 1978.

Cranfield, Charles E. B. "The Interpretation of First Peter 3:19 and 4:6." *The Expository Times* 69 (1958) 369–72.

Crisp, Oliver. "Augustinian Universalism." *International Journal for Philosophy of Religion* 53 (2003) 127–45.

Cross, F. L., and Elizabeth A. Linvingstone, eds. *The Oxford Dictionary of the Christian Church.* 2nd ed. Oxford: Oxford University Press, 1983.

Crouzel, Henri. "Comparaisons précises." In *Origeniana*, 113–21. Bari: Università, 1975.

———. "Les condamnations subies par Origène et sa doctrine." *Origeniana Septima: Origens in den Auseinandersetzungen des 4. Jahrhunderts*, edited by W. A. Bienert and U. Kühneweg, 311–15. Leuven: Peeters, 1999.

———. *Une controverse sur Origène à la Renaissance.* Paris: Vrin, 1977.

———. "L'Hadès et la Géhenne selon Origène." *Gregorianum* 59.2 (1978) 291–331.

Cubitt, Catherine. "Apocalyptic and Eschatological Thought in England around the Year 1000," *Transactions of the Royal Historical Society* 25 (2015) 27–52.

Daley, Brian. "Apokatastasis and 'Honorable Silence' in the Eschatology of Maximus." In *Maximus Confessor*, edited by F. Heinzer and C. Schönborn, 309–39. Fribourg: Editions Universitaires, 1982.

———. *God Visible: Patristic Christology Reconsidered.* Oxford: Oxford University Press, 2018.

———. *The Hope of the Early Church.* Cambridge: Cambridge University Press, 1991.

———. *Leontius of Byzantium. Complete Works,* Oxford: Oxford University Press, 2017.

De Andia, Ysabel. "Irénée, théologien de l'unité." *La nouvelle revue théologique* 109 (1987) 31–48.

———, ed. *Denys l'Aréopagite et sa postérité en Orient et en Occident.* Paris: Institut d'Études Augustiniennes, 1997.

DeBoer, Martinus. *The Defeat of Death: Apocalyptic Eschatology in 1 Corinthians 15 and Romans 5.* Sheffield, UK: Sheffield Academic Press, 1988.

Delrosso, Jeana, Leigh Eicke, and Ana Kothe, eds. *Unruly Catholic Nuns,* eds Albany, NY: SUNY, 2017.

den Biesen, Kees. "A Drop of Salvation: Ephrem the Syrian on the Eucharist." In *Sacred Meal, Communal Meal, Table Fellowship, and the Eucharist Late Antiquity, Early Judaism, and Early Christianity*, edited by David Hellholm, 1121–42. Tübingen: Mohr Siebeck, 2017.

Dillon, John, and Sarah Klitenic Wear. *Dionysius the Areopagite and the Neoplatonist Tradition.* Aldershot, UK: Ashgate, 2007.

Doering, Lutz. "Urzeit–Endzeit Correlations in the Dead Sea Scrolls and Pseudepigrapha." In *Eschatologie–Eschatology: The Sixth Durham-Tübingen Research Symposium: Eschatology in the Old Testament, Ancient Judaism, and Early Christianity, Tübingen, September 2009*, edited by Hans-Joachim Eckstein, Christof Landmesser, and Hermann Lichtenberger, 19–58. Tübingen: Mohr Siebeck, 2011.

Dunavant, D. R. "Universalism." In *Evangelical Dictionary of World Missions*, edited by A. S. Moreau, 988–89. Grand Rapids: Eerdmans, 2000.

Dutton, Elisabeth. *Julian of Norwich: The Influence of Late-Medieval Devotional Compilations*. Cambridge: Cambridge University Press, 2008.

Edwards, Mark. *Aristotle and Early Christian Thought*. London: Routledge, 2019.

———. Review of *The Christian Doctrine of Apokatastasis* by Ilaria Ramelli. *Journal of Theological Studies* 65 (2014) 718–24. Excerpted at www.brill.com/christian-doctrine-apokatastasis.

Elkaisy-Friemuth, Maha, and John Dillon, eds. *The Afterlife of the Platonic Soul*. Leiden: Brill, 2009.

Eskola, Timo. *A Narrative Theology of the New Testament: Exploring the Metanarrative of Exile and Restoration*. Tübingen: Mohr Siebeck, 2015.

Evans, David. *Leontius of Byzantium: An Origenist Christology*. Washington, DC: Dumbarton Oaks, 1970.

———. "Leontius of Byzantium and Dionysius the Areopagite." *Byzantine Studies* 7 (1980) 1–34.

Field, Sean. *The Beguine, the Angel, and the Inquisitor: The Trials of Marguerite Porete and Guiard of Cressonessart*. South Bend, IN: University of Notre Dame Press, 2012.

Finney, Mark. *Resurrection, Hell and the Afterlife: Body and Soul in Antiquity, Judaism and Early Christianity*. London: Routledge, 2016.

Fiori, Emiliano. "The Impossibility of Apokatastasis in Dionysius the Areopagite." In *Origeniana Decima*, edited by Sylwia Kaczmarek and Henryk Pietras, 831–43. Leuven: Peeters 2011.

Flasch, Kurt. *Meister Eckhart: Philosopher of Christianity*. New Haven: Yale University Press, 2015.

Frey, Jörg. *Der Brief des Judas und der zweite Brief des Petrus*. Leipzig: Evangelische Verlagsanstalt, 2015.

Fudge, Edward W., and Robert A. Peterson. *Two Views of Hell: A Biblical and Theological Dialogue*. Downers Grove, IL: IVP, 2000.

Gallagher, Edmon. "Origen via Rufinus on the New Testament Canon." *New Testament Studies* 62 (2016) 461–76.

Gavrilyuk, Paul. "The Judgment of Love: The Ontological Universalism of Sergius Bulgakov." In *All Shall Be Well: Universal Salvation and Christian Theology from Origen to Moltmann*, edited by Gregory MacDonald, 280–304. Eugene, OR: Cascade, 2011.

Grappone, Aldo. *Omelie origeniane nella traduzione di Rufino*. Rome: Augustinianum, 2007.

Greer, Rowan. *One Path for All: Gregory of Nyssa on the Christian Life and Human Destiny*. Eugene, OR: Cascade, 2015.

Greggs, Tom. *Barth, Origen, and Universal Salvation: Restoring Particularity*. Oxford: Oxford University Press, 2009.

Grumel, V. "Maxime le Confesseur." In *Dictionnaire de théologie Catholique* Vol. 10.1, 448–59. Paris: Letouzey et Ané, 1928.

Grünstäudl, Wolfgang. *Petrus Alexandrinus: Studien zum historischen und theologischen Ort des zweiten Petrusbriefe*. Tübingen: Mohr Siebeck, 2013.

Hackett, Jeremiah, ed. *A Companion to Meister Eckhart*. Leiden: Brill, 2012.

Hall, Amy Laura. *Laughing at the Devil: Seeing the Wold with Julian of Norwich*. Durham, NC: Duke University, 2018.

Hansbury, Mary, trans. *Isaac the Syrian's Spiritual Works*. Texts from Christian Late Antiquity 45. Piscataway, NJ: Gorgias, 2016.

———, trans. *The Letters of John of Dalyatha*. Piscataway, NJ: Gorgias, 2006.

Harmon, Steven R. *Every Knee Should Bow: Biblical Rationales for Universal Salvation in Early Christian Thought*. Lanham, MD: Rowman & Littlefield, 2003.

———. "The Subjection of All Things in Christ: The Christocentric Universalism in Gregory of Nyssa (331/340–c.395)." In *All Shall Be Well: Universal Salvation and Christian Theology from Origen to Moltmann*, edited by Gregory MacDonald, 47–64. Eugene, OR: Cascade, 2011.

———. "The Work of Jesus Christ and the Universal Apokatastasis in the Theology of St. Gregory of Nyssa." In *Jesus Christ in the Theology of St. Gregory of Nyssa*, edited by Elias Moutsoulas, 225–43. Athens: Eptalophos, 2005.

Harrison, Nonna Verna. *Grace and Freedom according to St. Gregory of Nyssa*. Lewiston, NY: Mellen, 1992.

Hart, David Bentley. *That All Shall Be Saved: Heaven, Hell, and Universal Salvation*. New Haven: Yale University Press, 2019.

Heide, Daniel. "Ἀποκατάστασις: The Resolution of Good and Evil in Origen and Eriugena." *Dionysius* 3 (2015) 195–213.

Heil, Uta. "Orosius, Augustine, and the Origenist Controversy in the West." In *Origeniana Undecima: Origen and Origenism in the History of Western Thought*, edited by Anders-Christian Jacobsen, 525–44. Leuven: Peeters, 2016.

Hill, Carole. *Women and Religion in Late Mediaeval Norwich*. Woodbridge, UK: Boydell and Brewer, 2010.

Hill, T. "Universal Salvation and Its Literary Context in Piers Plowman B, XVIII 390." *Modern Philology* 69 (1972) 323–25.

Holliday, Lisa. "Will Satan Be Saved?" *Vigiliae Christianae* 63 (2009) 1–23.

Hübner, Reinhard. *Die Einheit des Leibes Christi bei Gregor von Nyssa*. Leiden: Brill, 1974.

Hull, M. F. *Baptism on Account of the Dead*. Atlanta: SBL, 2005.

Image, Isabella. *The Human Condition in Hilary of Poitiers*. Oxford: Oxford University Press, 2018.

Itter, Andrew. "The Restoration of the Elect." *StPatr* 41 (2006) 169–74.

Janowski, Johanna Christine. *Allerlösung*. Neukirchen: Neukirchener Verlag, 2000.

Jeauneau, Édouard. "La Métaphysique du Feu." In *Études Érigéniennes*, 299–318. Paris: Études Augustiniennes, 1987.

Johnson, Aaron. *Eusebius*. London: I. B. Tauris, 2014.

Johnson, Aaron, and Jeremy Schott, eds. *Eusebius of Caesarea: Traditions and Innovations*. Hellenic Studies 60. Cambridge: Center for Hellenic Studies Press (Harvard University Press), 2013.

Jukes, Andrew. *The Second Death and the Restitution of All Things*. Canyon County, CA: Concordant, 1976.

Karjanmaa, Sami-Yli. *Reincarnation in Philo of Alexandria*, Atlanta: SBL, 2015.

Kavvadas, Nestor. *Isaak von Ninive und seine Kephalaia Gnostika: Die Pneumatologie und ihr Kontext.* Leiden: Brill, 2015.

Kvanvig, Jonathan L. "Hell." In *The Oxford Handbook of Eschatology*, edited by Jerry L. Walls. Oxford: Oxford University Press, 2007. Online ed. 2009. DOI: 10.1093/oxfordhb/9780195170498.003.0024.

———. *The Problem of Hell.* Oxford: Oxford University Press 1993.

Larchet, Jean-Claude. *La divinisation de l'homme selon saint Maxime le Confesseur.* Paris: Cerf, 1996.

Le Boulluec, Alain. "Filiación y encarnación según Clemente de Alejandría." In *La filiación en Clemente de Alejandría: Actas de las XI y XII Jornadas de Estudio «La filiación en los inicios de la reflexión cristiana», Madrid 2013–2014*, edited by Andrés Sáez Gutiérrez, Guillermo Cano Gómez, and Clara Sanvito, 281–309. Madrid: Trotta, 2015.

Lenz, Christoph. "Apokatastasis." In *Reallexikon für Antike und Christentum*, vol. 1, 510–16. Stuttgart: Hiersemann, 1950.

Lincoln, Andrew. *Ephesians.* WBC. Waco, TX: Word, 1990.

———. *Paradise Now and Not Yet: Studies in the Role of the Heavenly Dimension in Paul's Thought, with Special Reference to His Eschatology.* Grand Rapids: Baker, 1991.

Lincoln, Andrew, and Alexander J. M. Wedderburn, *The Theology of the Later Pauline Letters.* Cambridge: Cambridge University Press, 1993.

Lloyd, Daniel. "Universalism in 3 Baruch." *Journal for the Study of Pseudepigrapha* 25.4 (2016) 299–325.

Louth, Andrew. *Denys the Areopagite.* London: Chapman, 1989.

———. "Eastern Orthodox Eschatology." In *The Oxford Handbook of Eschatology*, edited by Jerry L. Walls, 233–47. Oxford: Oxford University Press, 2007.

———. *The Origins of the Christian Mystical Tradition from Plato to Denys.* 2nd ed. Oxford: Oxford University Press, 2006.

Ludlow, Morwenna. *Gregory of Nyssa, Ancient and (Post)modern.* Oxford: Oxford University Press, 2007.

———. "Universalism in the History of Christianity." In *Universal Salvation? The Current Debate*, edited by Robin A. Parry and Christopher Partridge, 191–218. Carlisle, UK: Paternoster, 2003.

———. *Universal Salvation: Eschatology in Gregory of Nyssa and Karl Rahner.* Oxford: Oxford University Press, 2000.

———. "Why Was Hans Denck Thought to Be a Universalist?" *Journal of Ecclesiastical History* 55 (2004) 257–74.

MacDonald, Gregory, ed. *All Shall be Well: Explorations in Universal Salvation and Christian Theology, from Origen to Moltmann.* Eugene, OR: Cascade, 2011.

———. *The Evangelical Universalist.* 2nd ed. Eugene, OR: Cascade, 2012.

———. "Introduction." In *All Shall Be Well: Explorations in Universal Salvation and Christian Theology, from Origen to Moltmann*, edited by Gregory MacDonald, 1–25. Eugene, OR: Cascade, 2011.

Maftei, Eugen. *L'incarnation du Verbe: approche ontologique ou économie salvifique? Élements pour un débat soteriologique chez Athanase d'Alexandrie.* Paris: Cerf, 2014.

Mairey, A. "Pratiques de l'allégorie dans la poésie anglaise du XIVème siècle." In *Allégories des poètes, allégories des philosophes: études sur la poétique et l'herméneutique de l'allégorie de l'Antiquité à la Réforme*, edited by Gilbert Dahan and Richard Goulet, 266–88. Paris: Vrin, 2005.

Marshall, Christopher. *Beyond Retribution: A New Testament Vision for Justice, Crime, and Punishment*. Grand Rapids: Eerdmans, 2001.

Maspero, Giulio. *La Trinità e l'uomo. L'Ad Ablabium di Gregorio di Nissa*. Rome: Città Nuova, 2004.

———. *Trinity and Man. Gregory of Nyssa's Ad Ablabium*. Leiden: Brill, 2007.

McGinn, Bernard. *The Mystical Thought of Meister Eckhart: The Man from Whom God Hid Nothing*. New York: Herder & Herder, 2001.

———. "The Spiritual Heritage of Origen in the West: Aspects of the History of Origen's Influence in the Middle Ages." In *Origene maestro di vita spirituale*, edited by Luigi Pizzolato and Marco Rizzi, 263–89. Milan: Vita e Pensiero, 2001.

McGuckin, John A. "Eschatological Horizons in the Cappadocian Fathers." In *Apocalyptic Thought in Early Christianity*, edited by Robert J. Daly, 193–210. Grand Rapids: Eerdmans, 2009.

Méhat, André. "Apocatastase: Origène, Clément, Acts 3.21." *Vigiliae Christianae* 10 (1956) 196–214.

Michaud, E. "S. Maxime le Confesseur et l'apocatastase." *Revue internationale de théologie* 10 (1902) 257–72.

Mikhail, Maged S. A. *The Legacy of Demetrius of Alexandria 189–232 CE: The Form and Function of Hagiography in Late Antique and Islamic Egypt*. London: Routledge, 2016.

Moran, Dermot. *The Philosophy of John Scottus Eriugena: A Study of Idealism in the Middle Ages*. Cambridge: Cambridge University Press, 1989.

Moreschini, Claudio. *Storia della filosofia patristica*. Brescia: Morcelliana, 2004.

Morgan, Teresa. *Roman Faith and Christian Faith*. Oxford: Oxford University Press, 2015.

Murray, George R. Beasley. *Baptism in the New Testament*. London: Macmillan, 1962.

Murray, Michael. "Three Versions of Universalism." *Faith and Philosophy* 16 (1999) 55–68.

Nautin, Pierre. "Ignatius of Antioch." In *Nuovo Dizionario Patristico e di Antichità Cristiane*, vol. 2, edited by Angelo Di Berardino, 2514–16. Genoa: Marietti, 2007. English translation Downers Grove, IL: IVP, 2014.

———. *Origène. Sa vie et son oeuvre*. Paris: Beauchesne, 1977.

O'Leary, Joseph. *Christianisme et philosophie chez Origène*. Paris: Cerf, 2011.

Olson, Roger. *The Story of Christian Theology: Twenty Centuries of Tradition and Reform*. Downers Grove, IL: IVP, 1999.

Oxford Latin Dictionary. Oxford: Clarendon, 1968.

Pace, Nicola. *Ricerche sulla traduzione di Rufino del De Principiis*. Florence: Nuova Italia, 1990.

Panegyres, Konstantine. "The Rhetoric of Religious Conflict in Arnobius' *Adversus Nationes*." *Classical Quarterly*, online 22 April 2019. DOI: 10.1017/S0009838819000272.

Parker III, James. *The Concept of Apokatastasis in Acts*. Austin, TX: Schola, 1978.

Parry, Robin A., with Ilaria Ramelli. *A Larger Hope? Universal Salvation from the Reformation to the Nineteenth Century*. Vol. 2. Eugene, OR: Cascade, 2019.

Parry, Robin A., and Christopher H. Partridge, eds. *Universal Salvation? The Current Debate.* Carlisle, UK: Paternoster, 2003.

Perczel, István. "*Apocatastasis panton* in the Pseudo-Caesarius." In *Apocalypticism and Eschatology in the Abrahamic Religions (6th–8th Cent. CE),* edited by Hagit Amirav, Emmanouela Grypeou, and Guy Stroumsa. Leuven: Peeters, 2017.

———. "The Earliest Syriac Reception of Dionysius," in *Re-Thinking Dionysius the Areopagite,* edited by Sarah Coakley and Charles Stang, 27–41. Malden, MA: Wiley-Blackwell, 2009.

———. "God as Monad and Henad: Dionysius the Areopagite and the *Peri Archon.*" In *Origeniana VIII,* edited by Lorenzo Perrone, 1193–1209. Leuven: Peeters, 2003.

———. "St. Maximus on the Lord's Prayer." In *The Architecture of the Cosmos: St. Maximus the Confessor—New Perspectives,* edited by Antoine Lévy, et al., 221–278. Schriften der Luther-Agricola-Gesellschaft 69. Helsinki: Luther-Agricola-Society, 2015.

———. "Théologiens et magiciens dans le Corpus dionysien." *Adamantius* 7 (2001) 54–75.

Perrone, Lorenzo, ed., *Origenes: Die neuen Psalmenhomilien: Eine kritische Edition des Codex Monacensis Graecus 314.* GCS NF 19. Berlin: de Gruyter, 2015.

———. *La preghiera secondo Origene.* Brescia: Morcelliana, 2011.

Pettorelli, Jean-Pierre. "Vie latine d'Adam et d'Ève." *Archivum Latinitatis Medii Aevi* 57 (1999) 5–52.

Pietras, Henryk. *L'escatologia nei Padri della Chiesa. Dagli scritti giudaici fino al IV secolo.* Rome: Augustinianum, 2006.

Pinnock, Clark H. "Annihilationism." In *The Oxford Handbook of Eschatology,* edited by Jerry L. Walls. Oxford: Oxford University Press, 2007. Online edition 2009. DOI: 10.1093/oxfordhb/9780195170498.003.0027.

———. "The Finality of Jesus Christ in A World of Religions." In *Christian Faith and Practice in the Modern World,* edited by Mark Noll and David F. Wells, 152–68. Grand Rapids: Eerdmans, 1988.

Pollmann, Karla. "The Broken Perfume-Flask: Origen's Legacy in Two Case-Studies." Conference paper from *Origeniana XI,* Aarhus 26–31 August 2013.

Powys, David. *Hell: A Hard Look at a Hard Question: The Fate of the Unrighteous in New Testament Thought.* Carlisle, UK: Paternoster, 1997.

Prinzivalli, Emanuela. "Il Cod.Mon.Gr. 314, il traduttore ritrovato e l'imitatore." *Adamantius* 20 (2014) 194–216.

———. "L'originale e la traduzione di Rufino." In *Die Neuen Psalmenhomilien,* edited by Lorenzo Perrone, 35–55. Origenes XIII. Berlin: de Gruyter, 2015.

Ramelli, Ilaria. "1 Cor 15:24–26: Submission of Enemies and Annihilation of Evil and Death. A Case for a New Translation and a History of Interpretation." *Studi e Materiali di Storia delle Religioni* 74.2 (2008) 241–58.

———. "Αἰώνιος and Αἰών in Origen and Gregory of Nyssa." *Studia Patristica XLIV,* edited by Jane Baun, Averil Cameron, Mark Edwards, and Markus Vinzent, 57–62. Leuven: Peeters, 2010.

———. "Alcune osservazioni su *credere,*" *Maia* 51 (2000) 67–83.

———. "Alexander of Aphrodisias: A Source of Origen's Philosophy?" *Philosophie Antique* 14 (2014) 237–90: https://journals.openedition.org/philosant/807.

———. "Anthropomorphism." In *The Brill Encyclopedia of Early Christianity*, edited by Paul J. J. van Geest et al. Leiden, Brill, forthcoming. Online 2018 <http://dx.doi.org/10.1163/2589–7993_EECO_SIM_00000193>.

———. "Apokatastasis." In *Routledge Encyclopedia of Ancient Mediterranean Religions*, edited by Eric Orlin et al., 71. London: Routledge, 2016.

———. "Apokatastasis." In *Brill Encyclopedia of Early Christianity*, Leiden, Brill, forthcoming. Online https://referenceworks.brillonline.com/entries/brill-encyclopedia-of-early-christianity-online/apokatastasis-SIM_00000222.

———. "*Apokatastasis* and *Epektasis* in *Hom. in Cant.:* The Relation between Two Core Doctrines in Gregory and Roots in Origen." In *Proceedings of the XIII International Colloquium on Gregory of Nyssa, Rome, 17–20 September 2014*, edited by Giulio Maspero, 312–39. Leiden: Brill, 2018.

———. "Apokatastasis in Coptic Gnostic Texts from Nag Hammadi and Clement's and Origen's Apokatastasis: Toward an Assessment of the Origin of the Doctrine of Universal Restoration." *Journal of Coptic Studies* 14 (2012) 33–45.

———. "Apofatismo cristiano e relativismo pagano: un confronto tra filosofi platonici." In *Verità e mistero nel pluralismo culturale della tarda antichità*, edited by Angela Maria Mazzanti, 101–69. Bologna: Edizioni Studio Domenicano, 2009.

———. "Atticus and Origen on the Soul of God the Creator: From the "Pagan" to the Christian Side of Middle Platonism?" *Jahrbuch für Religionsphilosophie* 10 (2011) 13–35.

———. "Autobiographical Self-Fashioning in Origen," invited chapter in *Self, Self-Fashioning and Individuality in Late Antiquity: New Perspectives*, edited by Maren Niehoff and Joshua Levinson, ch. 13. Tübingen: Mohr Siebeck, 2019.

———. "Baptism in Gregory of Nyssa's Theology and Its Orientation to Eschatology." In *Ablution, Initiation, and Baptism. Late Antiquity, Early Judaism, and Early Christianity*, edited by David Hellholm, Tor Vegge, Oyvind Norderval, and Christer David Hellholm, 1205–32. Berlin: De Gruyter 2011.

———. *Bardaisan of Edessa: A Reassessment of the Evidence and a New Interpretation. Also in the Light of Origen and the Original Fragments from De India.* Eastern Christian Studies 22. Piscataway: Gorgias, 2009.

———. "Bardaisan: a Christian Middle Platonist from Edessa and his Reading of Scripture in the Light of Plato." In *Biblical & Qur'ānic Traditions in the Middle East*, eds Cornelia Horn and Sidney H. Griffith, 215–38. Warwick, RI: Abelian Academic, 2016.

———. "Bardaisan as a Christian Philosopher: A Reassessment of His Christology." In *Religion in the History of European Culture. Proceedings of the 9th EASR Conference and IAHR Special Conference, Messina 14–17 September 2009*, edited by Giulia Sfameni Gasparro et al., 873–88. Palermo: Officina di Studi Medievali, 2013.

———. "Bardaisan of Edessa, Origen, and Imperial Philosophy: A Middle Platonic Context?" *Aram* 30.1–2 (2018) 337–53.

———. *Bardaisan on Human Nature, Fate, and Free Will.* Tübingen: Mohr Siebeck, forthcoming.

———. "Basil and Apokatastasis: New Findings." *Journal of Early Christian History* 4.2 (2014) 116–36.

———. "The Beyond as an Educative Process in View of the Restoration: Christian Apokatastasis from Alexandria (and Edessa) to Antioch." In *Reading the Way to the Netherworld: Education and the Representations of the Beyond in Later Antiquity*, edited by Ilinca Tanaseanu-Döbler et al., 400–425. Göttingen: Vandenhoeck and Ruprecht, 2017.

———. "The Birth of the Rome-Alexandria Connection: The Early Sources on Mark and Philo, and the Petrine Tradition." *The Studia Philonica Annual* 23 (2011) 69–95.

———. "Body." In *The Brill Encyclopedia of Early Christianity*, edited by Paul J. J. van Geest et al. Leiden, Brill, forthcoming.

———. "Cappadocians." In *Brill Encyclopedia of Early Christianity*, Leiden, Brill, forthcoming. Online <http://dx.doi.org/10.1163/2589-7993_EECO_SIM_036679> First print edition: 20180827 https://referenceworks.brillonline.com/entries/brill-encyclopedia-of-early-christianity-online/cappadocians-SIM_036679.

———. "La centralità del Mistero di Cristo nell'escatologia di s. Efrem." *Augustinianum* 49 (2009) 371–406.

———. "Christian Apokatastasis and Zoroastrian *Frashegird*: The Birth of Eschatological Universalism." *Religion and Theology* 24 (2017) 350–406. DOI: 10.1163/15743012-02403007.

———. *The Christian Doctrine of Apokatastasis: A Critical Assessment from the New Testament to Eriugena.* Leiden: Brill, 2013. https://brill.com/view/title/16787

———. "Christian Platonists in Support of Gender Equality: Bardaisan, Clement, Origen, Gregory of Nyssa, and Eriugena." In *Otherwise Than the Binary: Towards Feminist Reading of Ancient Greek Philosophy, Magic, and Mystery Traditions*, edited by Danielle Layne and Jessica Elbert Decker, forthcoming.

———. "Christian Slavery in Theory and Practice," in *The Cambridge History of Ancient Christianity*, eds Bruce Longenecker and David Wilhite, Cambridge: CUP, forthcoming.

———. "Christian Soteriology and Christian Platonism: Origen, Gregory of Nyssa, and the Biblical and Philosophical Basis of the Doctrine of Apokatastasis." *Vigiliae Christianae* 61 (2007) 313–56.

———. "Christology 2. Third century." In *Brill Encyclopedia of Early Christianity*, Leiden, Brill, forthcoming. Online https://referenceworks.brillonline.com/entries/brill-encyclopedia-of-early-christianity-online/christology-02-third-century-ce-COM_037398?s.num=20.

———. "Clement's Notion of the Logos 'All Things as One': Its Alexandrian Background in Philo and Its Developments in Origen and Nyssen." In *Alexandrian Personae: Scholarly Culture and Religious Traditions in Ancient Alexandria (1st ct. BCE–4ct. CE)*, edited by Zlatko Plese. Tübingen: Mohr Siebeck, forthcoming.

———. "La coerenza della soteriologia origeniana: dalla polemica contro il determinismo gnostico all'universale restaurazione escatologica." In *Pagani e cristiani alla ricerca della salvezza. Atti del XXXIV Incontro di Studiosi dell'Antichità Cristiana, Roma, Istituto Patristico Augustinianum, 5–7 maggio 2005*, 661–88. Rome: Augustinianum, 2006.

———. *Companion to the Early Church.* Edited by Ilaria L. E. Ramelli, John A. McGuckin, and Piotr Ashwin Siejkowsky. London: T. & T. Clark Bloomsbury Academic, 2020.

———. "Constantinople II 553." In *Brill Encyclopedia of Early Christianity*, edited by Paul J. J. van Geest and Bert Jan Lietaert Peerbolte. Leiden: Brill, forthcoming.

———. "The Construction of the Professional Identity of Origen of Alexandria and the Question of Which Origen." In *Problems in Ancient Biography: The Construction of*

Professional Identity in Late Antiquity, edited by Elizabeth DePalma Digeser, Heidi Marx-Wolf, and Ilaria Ramelli. forthcoming.

———. "The Debate on Apokatastasis in Pagan and Christian Platonists (Martianus, Macrobius, Origen, Gregory of Nyssa, and Augustine)." *Illinois Classical Studies* 33–34 (2008) 197–230.

———. "Decadence Denounced in the Controversy over Origen: Giving Up Direct Reading of Sources and Counteractions." In *Décadence: 'Decline and Fall' or 'Other Antiquity'?* edited by Therese Fuhrer and Marco Formisano, 263–83. Heidelberg: Winter, 2014.

———. "The *Dialogue of Adamantius*: A Document of Origen's Thought? Part One." In *Studia Patristica LII*, edited by Allen Brent and Markus Vinzent, 71–98. Leuven: Peeters, 2012.

———. "The *Dialogue of Adamantius*: A Document of Origen's Thought? Part Two." In *Studia Patristica LVI*, edited by Markus Vinzent, 227–73. Leuven: Peeters, 2013.

———. *Dialogue of Adamantius*. Critical edition and commentary. In preparation.

———. "Dieu et la philosophie: le discours de Paul à Athènes dans trois 'actes apocryphes' et dans la philosophie patristique." *Gregorianum* 93 (2012) 75–91.

———. "Disability in Bardaisan and Origen. Between the Stoic Adiaphora and the Lord's Grace." In *Gestörte Lektüre. Disability als hermeneutische Leitkategorie biblischer Exegese*, edited by Wolfgang Grünstäudl, Markus Schiefer, 141–59. Stuttgart: Kohlhammer, 2012.

———. "The Divine as Inaccessible Object of Knowledge in Ancient Platonism: A Common Philosophical Pattern across Religious Traditions," *Journal of the History of Ideas* 75.2 (2014) 167–88.

———. "Divine Power in Origen of Alexandria: Sources and Aftermath." In *Divine Powers in Late Antiquity*, edited by Anna Marmodoro and Irini Fotini Viltanioti, 177–98. Oxford: Oxford University Press, 2017.

———. "La dottrina escatologica cristiana dell'apocatastasi tra mondo siriaco, greco, latino e copto." In *Costruzione e Percezione della Sfera del Post Mortem nel Mediterraneo Antico*, ed. Igor Baglioni, 2:221-238. Rome: Quasar, 2014.

———. "Double Creation." In *The Brill Encyclopedia of Early Christianity*, edited by Paul J. J. van Geest et al. Leiden, Brill, forthcoming.

———. *Early Christian and Jewish Narrative: The Role of Religion in Shaping Narrative Forms*, edited by Ilaria Ramelli and Judith Perkins, Tübingen: Mohr Siebeck, 2015. https://www.mohrsiebeck.com/en/book/early-christian-and-jewish-narrative-9783161520334.

———. "The Emmaus Disciples and the Kerygma of the Resurrection (Lk 24:34): A Greek Variant and the Old Syriac, Coptic, and Latin Traditions." *Zeitschrift für die neutestamentliche Wissenschaft* 105 (2014) 1-19.

———. "Epopteia, epoptics in Platonism, "pagan" and Christian." In *The language of inspiration or divine diction in the Platonic tradition*, ed. Harold Tarrant, Bream: Prometheus, 2019.

———. "Ensomatosis vs. Metensomatosis." In *Early Christian Mystagogy and the Body*, edited by Paul van Geest, ch. 5. Leuven: Peeters, forthcoming 2019.

———. "Escatologia filosofica nel Neoplatonismo Patristico." In *Filosofia ed Escatologia*, edited by Claudio Ciancio, Maurizio Pagano and Ezio Gamba, 131–54. Milan: Mimesis, 2017.

————. "Eriugena's Commentary on Martianus in the Framework of His Thought and the Philosophical Debate of His Time." In *Carolingian Scholarship and Martianus Capella*, edited by Sinead O'Sullivan and Mariken Teeuwen, 245–72. Turnhout: Brepols, 2012.

————. "Eternity." In *Encyclopedia of Ancient Christianity*, edited by Angelo Di Berardino, 1:841–44. Downers Grove, IL: InterVarsity 2014.

————. "Ethos and Logos: A Second-Century Apologetical Debate between 'Pagan' and Christian Philosophers." *Vigiliae Christianae* 69.2 (2015) 123–56: http://dx.doi.org/10.1163/15700720-12341205.

————. "The Eucharist in Gregory of Nyssa as Participation in Christ's Body and Preparation of the Restoration and Theōsis." In *The Eucharist: Its Origins and Contexts*, edited by David Hellholm and Dieter Sänger, 1165–84. Tübingen: Mohr Siebeck, 2017.

————. "Evagrius and Gregory: Nazianzen or Nyssen? A Remarkable Issue That Bears on the Cappadocian (and Origenian) Influence on Evagrius." *Greek, Roman, and Byzantine Studies* 53 (2013) 117–37.

————, ed. *Evagrius between Origen, the Cappadocians, and Neoplatonism. Studia Patristica* LXXXIV.10, Leuven: Peeters, 2017: http://oxfordpatristics.blogspot.com/2017/08/proceedings-of-xvii-international.html.

————, tr. *Evagrius' Kephalaia Gnostika*. Monographic essay (vii–lxxxiv), new readings from the ms., translation, and full commentary. Writings of the Greco-Roman World. Leiden-Atlanta: Brill-SBL, 2015. WGRW 38: https://secure.aidcvt.com/sbl/ProdDetails.asp?ID=061638P&PG=1&Type=BL&PCS=SBL.

————. "Evagrius Ponticus, the Origenian Ascetic (and Not the Origenistic 'Heretic')." In *Orthodox Monasticism, Past and Present*, edited by John McGuckin, 147–205. New York: Theotokos, 2014 (= Piscataway: Gorgias, 2015).

————. "Evil." In *Brill Encyclopedia of Early Christianity*, Leiden, Brill, forthcoming: https://referenceworks.brillonline.com/entries/brill-encyclopedia-of-early-christianity-online/evil-SIM_00001219.

————. *The Fear Option. An Investigation into the Rejection of the Theory of Apokatastasis*, in preparation.

————. "Forgiveness." In *Encyclopedia of Ancient Christianity*, ed. Angelo Di Berardino, Downers Grove, IL: InterVarsity 2014, 2:52–58.

————. "Freedom, Free Will." In *Encyclopedia of Ancient Christianity*, ed. Angelo Di Berardino, Downers Grove, IL: InterVarsity 2014, 2:66–69.

————. "Gal 3:28 and Aristotelian (and Jewish) Categories of Inferiority." *Eirene* 2019, forthcoming.

————. "The Father in the Son, the Son in the Father (John 10:38, 14:10, 17:21): Sources and Reception of Dynamic Unity in Middle and Neoplatonism, 'Pagan' and Christian." In *Die Quellen der Idee der dynamischen Einheit—der reziproken Ineinseins—im Iohannesevangelium*. Leuven: Peeters, forthcoming.

————. "Forgiveness. Christianity: Greek and Latin Patristics and Orthodox Churches." In *Encyclopedia of the Bible and Its Reception*, edited by H.-J. Klauck, B. McGinn, P. Mendes-Flohr et al., 9:450–52. Berlin: De Gruyter 2014.

————. "Forgiveness in Patristic Philosophy: The Importance of Repentance and the Centrality of Grace." In *Ancient Forgiveness: Classical, Judaic, and Christian Concepts*, edited by Charles Griswold and David Konstan, 195–215. Cambridge: Cambridge University Press, 2012.

————. "From God to God: Eriugena's Protology and Eschatology against the Backdrop of His Patristic Sources." Lecture, Oxford workshop, Eriugena's Christian Neoplatonism and Its Sources in Patristic Philosophy and Ancient Philosophy, directed by Ilaria Ramelli. Oxford University, August 2019, forthcoming.

————. "Gal 3:28 and Aristotelian (and Jewish) Categories of Inferiority." Forthcoming, *Eirene* 55 (2019).

————. "Gnosis-Gnosticism." In *The Encyclopedia of Ancient Christianity*, 3 vols., edited by Angelo DiBerardino, 2.139–47. Downers Grove, IL: InterVarsity, 2014.

————. "Gnosis/Knowledge." In *The Brill Encyclopedia of Early Christianity*, edited by Paul van Geest et al. Leiden: Brill, forthcoming.

————. "Good / Beauty." In *The Brill Dictionary of Gregory of Nyssa*, edited by Lucas Francisco Mateo-Seco and Giulio Maspero, 356–63. Leiden: Brill, 2010.

————. "Gregory and Evagrius." In *Mystical Eschatology in Gregory of Nyssa*, edited by Giulio Maspero. Leuven: Peeters, 2019, forthcoming.

————. *Gregorio di Nissa sull'anima e la resurrezione*. Milan: Bompiani–Catholic University of the Sacred Heart, 2007.

————. "Gregory Nyssen's and Evagrius's Biographical and Theological Relations: Origen's Heritage and Neoplatonism." In *Evagrius between Origen, the Cappadocians, and Neoplatonism*, edited by Ilaria Ramelli, in collaboration with Kevin Corrigan, Giulio Maspero, and Monica Tobon, 165–231. Leuven: Peeters, 2017.

————. "Gregory Nyssen's Position in Late-Antique Debates on Slavery and Poverty and the Role of Ascetics." *Journal of Late Antiquity* 5 (2012) 87–118.

————. "Gregory of Nyssa." In *A History of Mind and Body in Late Antiquity*, edited by Sophie Cartwright and Anna Marmodoro, 283–305. Cambridge: Cambridge University Press, 2018.

————. "Gregory of Nyssa on the Soul (and the Restoration): From Plato to Origen." In *Exploring Gregory of Nyssa: Historical and Philosophical Perspectives*, edited by Anna Marmodoro and Neil McLynn, 110–41. Oxford: Oxford University Press, 2018.

————. "Gregory of Nyssa's Purported Criticism of Origen's Purported Doctrine of the Preexistence of Souls." In *Lovers of the Soul and Lovers of the Body: Philosophical and Religious Perspectives in Late Antiquity*, edited by Svetla S. Griffin and Ilaria Ramelli, ch. 14. Cambridge: Harvard University, forthcoming 2019.

————. "Gregory of Nyssa's Trinitarian Theology in *In Illud: Tunc et ipse Filius*: His Polemic against 'Arian' Subordinationism and Apokatastasis." In *Gregory of Nyssa: The Minor Treatises on Trinitarian Theology and Apollinarism*. Proceedings of the 11th International Colloquium on Gregory of Nyssa (Tübingen 2008), edited by Volker Henning Drecoll and Margitta Berghaus, 445–78. Vigiliae Christianae Suppl. 106. Leiden: Brill, 2011.

————. "Harmony between *Arkhē* and *Telos* in Patristic Platonism and the Imagery of Astronomical Harmony Applied to Apokatastasis." *International Journal of the Platonic Tradition* 7.1 (2013) 1–49.

————. "Hebrews and Philo on Hypostasis: Intersecting Trajectories?" In *Pascha nostrum Christus. FS Raniero Cantalamessa*, edited by Pier Franco Beatrice and Bernard Pouderon, 27–49. Paris: Beauchesne, 2016.

————. *Hierocles the Stoic*. WGRW. Leiden, Brill, 2009.

————. ed. *Human and Divine Nous from Ancient to Renaissance Philosophy: Key Themes, Intersections, and Developments.* Leiden: Brill, in preparation.

————. Iamblichus, *De anima* 38 (66,12–15 Finamore-Dillon): A Resolving Conjecture." *Rheinisches Museum* 157 (2014) 106–11.

————. "Inequality and New Forms of Slavery: Late Antiquity and Contemporary Challenges." Oxford University Press Blog, 22 February 2017: https://blog.oup.com/2017/02/inequality-oppression-new-slavery/.

————. "*In Illud: Tunc et Ipse Filius* . . . (1 Cor 15,27–28): Gregory of Nyssa's Exegesis, Its Derivations from Origen, and Early Patristic Interpretations Related to Origen's." In *Studia Patristica XLIV*, edited by Jane Baun et al., 259–74. Leuven: Peeters, 2010.

————. "Institutionalisation of Religious Individualisation: The Case of Asceticism in Antiquity and Late Antiquity and the Rejection of Slavery and Social Injustice." In *Religious Individualization: Types and Cases. Historical and Crosscultural Explorations, 1: Facets of Institutionalization*, eds. Martin Fuchs, Bernd Otto, Rahul Parson, and Jörg Rüpke, 693-716. Berlin: De Gruyter, 2019.

————. "Isacco di Ninive teologo della carità divina e fonte della perduta escatologia antiochena." In *La teologia dal V all'VIII secolo tra sviluppo e crisi*, 749–68. SEA 140. Rome: Augustinianum, 2014.

————. *John 13–17.* Novum Testamentum Patristicum. Göttingen: Vandenhoeck and Ruprecht, in preparation.

————. "John the Evangelist's Work: An Overlooked *Redaktionsgeschichtliche* Theory from the Patristic Age." In *The Origins of John's Gospel*, edited by Stanley Porter and Hughson Ong, 30–52. JOST 2. Leiden: Brill, 2016. DOI: 10.1163/9789004303164_004.

————. "Late Antiquity and the Transmission of Educational Ideals and Methods." In *A Companion to Ancient Education*, edited by Martin Bloomer, 267–78. Oxford: Blackwell, 2015.

————. "The Legacy of Origen's Metaphysics of Freedom in Gregory of Nyssa's Theology of Freedom and Condemnation of Slavery and Social Injustice." In *Rethinking Origen*, special issue of *Modern Theology*, forthcoming.

————. "Il logos umano (anima razionale) in Origene e Gregorio di Nissa: il dibattito con il neoplatonismo 'pagano'". In *Il logos di Dio e il logos dell'uomo. Concezioni antropologiche nel mondo antico e riflessi contemporanei*, edited by Angela Maria Mazzanti, 247–74. Milan: Vita e Pensiero, 2014.

————. *Lovers of the Soul, Lovers of the Body: Philosophical and Religious Perspectives in Late Antiquity.* Edited by Svetla S. Griffin and Ilaria Ramelli. Hellenic Studies 88. Cambridge: Harvard University Press, 2019.

————. "Luke 16:16: The Good News of the Kingdom is Proclaimed and Everyone is Forced into It." *Journal of Biblical Literature* 127 (2008) 747–68.

————. "Luke 23:34a: A Case Against Its Athetesis." *Sileno* 36 (2010) 233–47.

————. "Macrobius: Astrological Descents, Ascents, and Restorations." *MHNH* 14 (2014) 197–214.

————. "Making the Bible World Literature: The Vulgate and Ancient Versions." In *Wiley-Blackwell Companion to World Literature, Volume One: To 600 CE*, edited by Wiebke Denecke and Ilaria Ramelli. Oxford: Wiley-Blackwell, forthcoming.

————. "Mansuetudine, grazia e salvezza negli *Acta Philippi*." *Invigilata Lucernis* 29 (2007) 215–28.

———. "Matt 17:11: 'Elijah Will Come, and All Beings Will Be Restored.' Philological, Linguistic, Syntactical and Exegetical Arguments for a New Interpretation." *Maia* 61 (2009) 107–26.

———. "The Mysteries of Scripture: Allegorical Exegesis and the Heritage of Stoicism, Philo, and Pantaenus." In *Clement's Biblical Exegesis*, edited by Judith Kovacs et al., 80–110. VCS 139. Leiden: Brill, 2016.

———. "Mystical Eschatology in Gregory and Evagrius." In *Mystical Eschatology in Gregory of Nyssa*, edited by Giulio Maspero. Leuven: Peeters, forthcoming 2019.

———. "Mystical Theology in Evagrius against the Backdrop of Gregory of Nyssa: Derivations and Inspirations." In *Reappraising Mystical Theology in Eastern Christianity: From the Early Church to Byzantium*. Essays in Honor of John Anthony McGuckin, edited by Matthew Pereira. Washington, DC: Catholic University of America, forthcoming.

———. "Mysticism and Love in Origen, Gregory Nyssen, and Dionysius." In *Dionysius Areopagita Christianus: Approaches to the Reception and Reconstruction of Christian "Tradition."* Leiden: Brill, forthcoming.

———. "Mysticism and Mystic Apophaticism in Middle and Neoplatonism across Judaism, 'Paganism' and Christianity." In *Constructions of Mysticism as a Universal. Roots and Interactions across the Borders*, edited by Annette Wilke. Studies in Oriental Religions. Wiesbaden: Harrassowitz, 2018.

———. Οἰκείωσις *in Gregory's Theology: Reconstructing His Creative Reception of Stoicism, in Gregory of Nyssa: Contra Eunomium III. An English Translation with Commentary and Supporting Studies. Proceedings of the 12th International Colloquium on Gregory of Nyssa (Leuven, 14-17 September 2010)*, ed. Johan Leemans & Matthieu Cassin, 643-659. Leiden: Brill, 2014, Vigiliae Christianae Suppl.124.

———. "Origen." In *A History of Mind and Body in Late Antiquity*, edited by Anna Marmodoro and Sophie Cartwright, 245–66. Cambridge: Cambridge University Press, 2018.

———. "Origen." In *The Neoplatonists and Their Heirs: Christian, Jewish, and Muslim*, edited by Ken Parry and Eva Anagnostou. Leiden: Brill, forthcoming.

———. "Origen and the Apokatastasis: A Reassessment." In *Origeniana Decima*, edited by Sylvia Kaczmarek and Henryk Pietras, 649–70. Leuven: Peeters, 2011.

———. "Origen's and Gregory Nyssen's Critical Reception of Aristotle." In *Aristotle in Byzantium*, edited by Mikonja Knezevic, 1–43. Alhambra, CA: Sebastian, 2019.

———. "Origen and Hypatia: Parallel Portraits of Platonists Educators." In *Reading and Teaching Ancient Fiction: Jewish, Christian, and Greco-Roman Narratives*, edited by Sara Johnson, Rubén René Dupertuis, and Chris Shea. 199–212. Atlanta: SBL, 2018.

———. "Origen and the Platonic Tradition." In *Plato and Christ: Platonism in Early Christian Theology*, special topics issue of *Religions*, edited by J. Warren Smith, 2017, 8(2), 21: doi:10.3390/rel8020021; http://www.mdpi.com/journal/religions/special_issues/Platonic_Influence.

———. "Origen and the Stoic Allegorical Tradition: Continuity and Innovation." *Invigilata Lucernis* 28 (2006) 195–226.

———. "Origen, Bardaisan, and the Origin of Universal Salvation." *Harvard Theological Rreview* 102 (2009) 135–68.

————. "Origen the Christian Middle/Neoplatonist." *Journal of Early Christian History* 22 (2011) 98–130.

————. "Origene ed il lessico dell'eternità." *Adamantius* 14 (2008) 100–129.

————. "Origen, Eusebius, and the Doctrine of Apokatastasis." In *Eusebius of Caesarea: Traditions and Innovations*, edited by Aaron Johnson and Jeremy Schott, 307–23. Cambridge: Center for Hellenic Studies Press (Harvard University Press), 2013.

————. "Origen, Evagrios, and Dionysios." In *The Oxford Handbook to Dionysius the Areopagite*, edited by Mark Edwards, ch. 5. Oxford: Oxford University Press, forthcoming 2019.

————. "Origen, Greek Philosophy, and the Birth of the Trinitarian Meaning of Hypostasis." *Harvard Theological Review* 105 (2012) 302–50.

————. "Origen in Augustine: A Paradoxical Reception." *Numen* 60 (2013) 280–307.

————. "Origen of Alexandria." In *Routledge Encyclopedia of Ancient Mediterranean Religions*, edited by Eric Orlin et al., 677. London: Routledge, Taylor & Francis, 2016.

————. *Origen of Alexandria as Philosopher and Theologian: A Chapter in the History of Platonism*. In preparation.

————. "Origen, Patristic Philosophy, and Christian Platonism: Re-Thinking the Christianization of Hellenism." *Vigiliae Christianae* 63 (2009) 217–63.

————. "Origen to Evagrius." In *Brill's Companion to the Reception of Plato in Antiquity*, edited by Harold Tarrant, Dirk Baltzly, Danielle A. Layne, and François Renaud, 271–91. Leiden: Brill, 2018: DOI: 10.1163/9789004355385_016.

————. "Origen's Allegoresis of Plato's and Scripture's Myths." In *Religious Competition in the Greco-Roman World*, edited by Nathaniel P. Desrosiers and Lily C. Vuong, 85–106. Atlanta: SBL, 2016.

————. "Origen's Anti-Subordinationism and Its Heritage in the Nicene and Cappadocian Line." *Vigiliae Christianae* 65 (2011) 21–49.

————. "Origen's Exegesis of Jeremiah: Resurrection Announced throughout the Bible and Its Twofold Conception." *Augustinianum* 48 (2008) 59–78.

————. "Origen to Evagrius." In *A Companion to the Reception of Plato in Antiquity*, edited by Harold Tarrant, Dirk Baltzly, Danielle A. Layne, and François Renaud, 271–91. Leiden: Brill, 2018.

————. *Origen's First Principles: The First Christian Treatise of Systematic Theology and Theoretical Philosophy*, in preparation.

————. "Origene ed il lessico dell'eternità." *Adamantius* 14 (2008) 100–129.

————. "Origene di fronte ai testi violenti dell'Apocalisse e il valore dell'allegoresi per far emergere significati 'degni di Dio'", in *Cristianesimo e violenza: Gli autori cristiani di fronte a testi biblici "scomodi."* Studia Ephemeridis Augustinianum 151, 141–54. Rome: Augustinianum, 2018.

————. "Origene: la Scrittura come incarnazione di Cristo-Logos e la sua interpretazione." In *Rivelazione e Storia: Pontificia Accademia delle Scienze*, edited by Ennio Innocenti and Salvatore Scuro, 154–72. Rome: 2014.

————. "Ousia, Hypostasis, and the Pneumatomachian Controversy: The Legacy of Origen (and the Cappadocians)." In *T. & T. Clark Companion to Creeds and Councils*. London: T. & T. Clark, forthcoming.

————. "Patristic Anthropology, the Issue of Gender, and Its Relevance to Ecclesiastical Offices." In *More than Female Disciples*, edited by Anelyia Barnes and Roberta Franchi. Turnhout: Brepols, forthcoming.

———. "Patristic Philosophy: A Critical Study." *The International Journal of the Platonic Tradition* 10.1 (2016) 95–108. Doi 10.1163/18725473–12341335.

———. "Paul on Apokatastasis: 1 Cor 15:24–28 and the Use of Scripture." In *Paul and Scripture*, edited by Stanley Porter and Christopher Land, 212–32. Leiden: Brill, 2019.

———. "Philo as One of the Main Inspirers of Early Christian Hermeneutics and Apophatic Theology." *Adamantius* 24 (2018), 276–92.

———. "Philo's Doctrine of Apokatastasis: Philosophical Sources, Exegetical Strategies, and Patristic Aftermath." *The Studia Philonica Annual* 26 (2014) 29–55.

———. "Philosophical Allegoresis of Scripture in Philo and Its Legacy in Gregory of Nyssa." *Studia Philonica Annual* 20 (2008) 55–99.

———. "The Philosophical Stance of Allegory in Stoicism and Its Reception in Platonism, 'Pagan' and Christian: Origen in Dialogue with the Stoics and Plato." *International Journal of the Classical Tradition* 18 (2011) 335–71. DOI: 10.1007/s12138-011-0264-1.

———. "Porphyry and the Motif of Christianity as παράνομος." In *Platonism and Its Legacy*, edited by John Finamore, 173–98. Bream: Prometheus, 2019.

———. *Preexistence of Souls? The Arkhe and Telos of Rational Creatures in Origen and Some Origenians*. Studia Patristica LVI, vol. 4. Leuven: Peeters, 2013.

———. "Proclus and Christian Neoplatonism: A Case Study." In *The Ways of Byzantine Philosophy*, edited by Mikonja Knežević, 37–70. Alhambra, CA: Sebastian-Kosovska Mitrovica: Faculty of Philosophy, 2015.

———. "Proclus of Constantinople and Apokatastasis." In *Proclus and His Legacy*, edited by David Butorac and Danielle Layne, 95–122. Millennium Studies 65. Berlin: de Gruyter, 2017.

———. "Prophecy in Origen: Between Scripture and Philosophy." *Journal of Early Christian History* 7.2 (2017) 17–39: http://dx.doi.org/10.1080/222258 2X.2017.1380504.

———. "The Question of Origen's Conversion and His Philosophico-Theological Lexicon of *Epistrophē*." In *Religious and Philosophical Conversion*, edited by Hermut Loehr and Athanasios Despotis. Leiden: Brill, forthcoming 2020.

———. "The Reception of Origen's Thought in Western Theological and Philosophical Traditions." Main lecture in *Origeniana Undecima: Origen and Origenism in the History of Western Thought, (Aarhus University, August 2013)*, edited by Anders-Christian Jacobsen, 443–67. Leuven: Peeters, 2016.

———. "The Rejection of the Epicurean Ideal of Pleasure in Late Antique Sources." *Mirabilia* 18 (2014) 6–21.

———. "The Relevance of Patristic Exegesis to Contemporary Biblical Hermeneutics." *Religion & Theology* 22 (2015) 100–132.

———. "Remission and Restoration between Luke and Acts." In *Bible, Qur'ān, and Their Interpretation*, edited by Cornelia Horn, 97–129. Warwick, RI: Abelian Academics, 2013.

———. "Reply to Professor Michael McClymond." *Theological Studies* 76.4 (2015) 827–835. DOI: 10.1177/0040563915605265.

———. Review of Anna Tzvetkova-Glaser, *Pentateuchauslegung bei Origenes und den frühen Rabbinen*. Frankfurt: Lang, 2010: *BMCR* 2011.05.50.

———. Review of Brian Daley, *God Visible*, 2018. *Gnomon*, forthcoming.

———. Review of David Konstan, *Before Forgiveness: The Origin of a Moral Idea*, Cambridge, Cambridge University Press, 2010: *Notre Dame Philosophical Reviews* 2011.03.21: http://ndpr.nd.edu/news/before-forgiveness-the-origin-of-a-moral-idea/.

———. Review of George Karamanolis, *The Philosophy of Early Christianity*, Durham: Acumen, 2013: *International Journal of the Platonic Tradition* 10.1 (2016) 95–108.

———. Review of Isabella Image, *The Human Condition in Hilary of Poitiers: The Will and Original Sin between Origen and Augustine*, Oxford: Oxford University Press, 2018: Reading Religion February 2018: http://readingreligion.org/books/human-condition-hilary-poitiers

———. Review of Jean-Marc Narbonne, *Plotinus in Dialogue with the Gnostics*. Leiden: Brill, 2011. *BMCR* 2011.10.25 http://www.bmcreview.org/2011/10/20111025.html.

———. Review of Joseph O'Leary, *Christianisme et philosophie chez Origène*, Paris: Cerf, 2011: *Gnomon* 84 (2012), 560–63.

———. Review of Karen King, *What Is Gnosticism? Invigilata Lucernis* 25 (2003) 331–34.

———. Review of Mark Edwards, *Religions of the Constantinian Empire*, Oxford: Oxford University Press, 2015: *Gnomon* 90 (2018) 57–61.

———. Review of Mark Edwards, 2019. *Journal of Theological Studies*, forthcoming.

———. Review of Paul M. Blowers, *Drama of the Divine Economy*. Oxford: Oxford University Press, 2012: *Zeitschrift für antikes Christentum* 19 (2015) 196–99.

———. Review of Paula Fredriksen, *Sin*. Princeton University 2012: *Gnomon* 85 (2013) 185–87.

———. Review of Piotr Ashwin-Siejkowski, *Clement of Alexandria on Trial*: *Gnomon* 84 (2012), 393–397.

———. Review of Bernard Pouderon and Anna Usacheva., eds. *Dire Dieu: Principes méthodologiques de l'écriture sur Dieu en patristique. Actes du colloque de Tours, 17–18 avril 2015*, Paris: Beauchesne, 2017: *Journal of Theological Studies* 69 (2018) 810–14.

———. Review of Teresa Morgan, *Roman Faith and Christian Faith*, Oxford: Oxford University Press, 2015: *Journal of Roman Studies* 107 (2017) 368–70.

———. "Riparte la filosofia patristica." Review article of Claudio Moreschini, *Storia della filosofia patristica*, Brescia 2004: *Rivista di Filosofia Neoscolastica* 97 (2005) 673–90.

———. "The Sentences of Sextus and the Christian Transformation of Pythagorean Asceticism." In *Pythagorean Knowledge from the Ancient to the Modern World*, edited by Almut-Barbara Renger & Alessandro Stavru, 151–62. Wiesbaden: Harrassowitz, 2016.

———. "Slavery and Religion in Late Antiquity: Their Relation to Asceticism and Justice in Christianity and Judaism." In *Slavery in the Late Antique World, 200–700 CE.*, edited by Chris L. De Wet, Maijastina Kahlos, and Ville Vuolanto, Cambridge: Cambridge University Press, 2020.

———. *Social Justice and the Legitimacy of Slavery: The Role of Philosophical Asceticism from Ancient Judaism to Late Antiquity*. Oxford: Oxford University Press, 2016.

———. "The Soul and Salvation in Origen and Porphyry." A lecture at the ISNS International Conference, *The Soul, Salvation, and Eschatology* Seminar, Ottawa, Dominican University, 2019, forthcoming.

———. "Soma (Σῶμα)," in *Das Reallexikon für Antike und Christentum*, edited by Georg Schöllgen. Stuttgart: Hiersemann, forthcoming.

———. "Soteriology." In *Brill Encyclopedia of Early Christianity*, Leiden, Brill, forthcoming; online <http://dx.doi.org/10.1163/2589-7993_EECO_SIM_0000 3236>https://referenceworks.brillonline.com/entries/brill-encyclopedia-of-early-christianity-online/soteriology-SIM_00003236.

———. "The Spirit as Paraclete in 3rd to 5th-Century Debates and the Use of John 14–17 in the Pneumatology of That Time." In *Receptions of the Fourth Gospel in Antiquity*, edited by Jörg Frey, Tobias Nicklas, and Joseph Verheyden, forthcoming.

———. "The Stoic Doctrine of Oikeiosis and its Transformation in Christian Platonism." *Apeiron* 47 (2014) 116–40. DOI: http://dx.doi.org/10.1515/apeiron-2012–0063.

———. *Stoici romani minori*. Milan, Bompiani, 2008.

———. "Stoicism and the Fathers." In *Brill Encyclopedia of Early Christianity*, edited by Paul J. J. van Geest, Bert Jan Lietaert Peerbolte, David Hunter, and Angelo DiBerardino. Leiden, Brill, forthcoming; online on 5 November 2018 https://referenceworks.brillonline.com/entries/brill-encyclopedia-of-early-christianity-online/stoicism-and-the-fathers-SIM_036681.

———. "*Stromateis* VII and Clement's Hints of the Theory of Apokatastasis." In *The Seventh Book of the Stromateis: Proceedings of the Colloquium on Clement of Alexandria (Olomouc, Oct 21–23, 2010)*, edited by Matyaš Havrda, Vit Hušek, and Jana Platova. 239–57. Leiden: Brill, 2012.

———. *Tempo ed eternità in età antica e patristica*. Assisi: Cittadella, 2015.

———. *Studi su Fides*, Madrid: Signifer Libros 2002, Graeco-Romanae Religionis Electa Collectio, 11.

———. "Tears of Pathos, Repentance, and Bliss: Crying and Salvation in Origen and Gregory of Nyssa." In *Tears in the Graeco-Roman World*, edited by Thorsten Fögen, 367–96. Berlin: De Gruyter, 2009.

———. "Time and Eternity," in *The Routledge Handbook of Early Christian Philosophy*, ed. Mark J. Edwards, London: Routledge, 2019.

———. "Transformations of the Household and Marriage Theory between Neo-Stoicism, Middle Platonism, and Early Christianity." *Rivista di Filosofia Neoscolastica* 100 (2008) 369–96.

———. "The Trinitarian Theology of Gregory of Nyssa in His *In Illud: Tunc et ipse Filius*: His Polemic against 'Arian' Subordinationism and Apokatastasis." In *Gregory of Nyssa: The Minor Treatises on Trinitarian Theology and Apollinarism. Proceedings of the 11th International Colloquium on Gregory of Nyssa (Tübingen, 17–20 September 2008)*, edited by Volker H. Drecoll and Margitta Berghaus, 445–78. Leiden: Brill, 2011.

———. *Tutti i commenti a Marziano Capella: Scoto Eriugena, Remigio di Auxerre, Bernardo Silvestre e anonimi*, Essays, improved editions, translations, commentaries, appendixes, bibliography. Milan, Bompiani–Istituto Italiano per gli Studi Filosofici, 2006.

———. "Unconditional Forgiveness in Christianity? Some Reflections on Ancient Christian Sources and Practices." In *The Ethics of Forgiveness. A Collection of Essays*, edited by Christel Fricke, 30–48. London: Routledge, 2011.

———. "The Universal and Eternal Validity of Jesus's High-Priestly Sacrifice." In *A Cloud of Witnesses: The Theology of Hebrews in Its Ancient Contexts*, edited by Richard J. Bauckham and others, 210–21. London: T. & T. Clark, 2008.

————. "Was Patristic Sin Different from Ancient Error? The Role of Ethical Intellectualism and the Invention of 'Original Sin.'" In *The Invention of Sin*, international conference, Paris, Institute of Advanced Studies, 13–14 April 2017, forthcoming.

————. "Valuing Antiquity in Antiquity by Means of Allegoresis." In *Valuing the Past in the Greco-Roman World. Proceedings of the Penn-Leiden Colloquium on Ancient Values VII, Leiden 14–16 June 2012*, edited by James Ker and Christoph Pieper, 485–507. Mnemosyne Supplements, Leiden: Brill, 2014.

————. "What Does Philosophy of Religion Offer to the Modern University?" *Philosophy of Religion: Big Question Philosophy for Scholars and Students*: http://www.PhilosophyOfReligion.org, 7 April 2016: http://philosophyofreligion.org/?p=476675.

————. "What Has the Violence of the Cross to Do with God's Omnipotence and Love? Responses from Gregory of Nyssa and Isaac of Nineveh." In *Violence, Trauma, and Identity in Early Christianity*, eds. Jennifer Otto and Katharina Waldner, Leuven: Peeters, forthcoming.

————. "What Norms or Values Define Excellent Philosophy of Religion?" *Philosophy of Religion: Big Question Philosophy for Scholars and Students*: http://www.PhilosophyOfReligion.org, 16 June 2018.

Ramelli, Ilaria, and David Konstan. *Terms for Eternity*. Piscataway, NJ: Gorgias, 2007 (new editions 2011; 2013).

Reimers, Adrian J. *Hell and the Mercy of God*. Washington, DC: Catholic University of America, 2017.

Richardson, Cyril C. "The Condemnation of Origen." *Church History* 6.1 (1937) 50–64. https://doi.org/10.2307/3160060.

Rolf, Veronica Mary. *An Explorer's Guide to Julian of Norwich*. Downers Grove, IL: IVP Academic, 2018.

Rosenau, Hartmut. *Allversöhnung*. Berlin: De Gruyter, 1993.

Rubino, Elisa. "*Ein grôz meister*: Eckhart e Origene." In *Studi sulle fonti di Meister Eckhart, II*, edited by Loris Sturlese, 141–65. Fribourg: Academic Press Fribourg, 2012.

Ruether, Rosemary Radford. *Sexism and God-Talk: Toward a Feminist Theology*. London: SCM, 1983.

Sachs, J. R. "Apocatastasis in Patristic Theology." *Theological Studies* 54 (1993) 617–40.

Schaefer, Christian. *The Philosophy of Dionysius the Areopagite*. Leiden: Brill, 2006.

Schär, Max. *Das Nachleben des Origenes im Zeitalter des Humanismus*. Basel-Stuttgart: Verlag Helbing, 1979.

Scully, Ellen. *Physicalist Soteriology in Hilary of Poitiers*. Leiden: Brill, 2015.

————. "Physicalism as the Soteriological Extension of Marius Victorinus' Cosmology." *Journal of Early Christian Studies* 26 (2018) 221–48.

Scully, Jason. *Isaac of Nineveh's Ascetical Eschatology*. Oxford: Oxford University Press, 2018.

Seppälä, Serafim. "Angelic Mysticism in John of Dalyatha." *Parole de l'Orient* 41 (2015) 425–33.

Sherwood, Polycarp. *The Earlier Ambigua of Saint Maximus the Confessor and His Refutation of Origenism*. Rome: Herder, 1955.

Silvas, Anna M. *Macrina the Younger, Philosopher of God*. Turnhout: Brepols, 2008.

Simkovich, Malka Z. "Echoes of Universalist Testament Literature in Christian and Rabbinic Texts." *Harvard Theological Review* 109 (2016) 1–32.

Simmons, Michael. *Universal Salvation in Late Antiquity: Porphyry of Tyre and the Pagan-Christian Debate*. Oxford: Oxford University Press, 2015.

Sinkewicz, Robert E. *Evagrius of Pontus: The Greek Ascetic Corpus*. Oxford: Oxford University Press, 2003.

Solomon of Basra. *The Book of the Bee*. Translated by E. A. Wallis Budge. Oxford: Clarendon, 1886.

Stauffer, Ethelbert. *New Testament Theology*. London: SCM, 1955.

Steenberg, Matthew. *Irenaeus on Creation*. Leiden: Brill, 2008.

Sterling, Gregory. Review of Karjanmaa 2015. *Review of Biblical Literature* 7 (2017).

Stroumsa, Guy G. *The Scriptural Universe of Ancient Christianity*. Cambridge: Harvard University Press, 2016.

Sweetman, Robert. "Sin Has Its Place, But All Shall Be Well. The Universalism of Hope of Julian of Norwich." In *All Shall Be Well: Explorations in Universal Salvation and Christian Theology, from Origen to Moltmann*, edited by Gregory MacDonald, 66–92. Eugene, OR: Cascade, 2011.

Talbott, Thomas. "Craig on the Possibility of Eternal Damnation." *Religious Studies* 28 (1992) 495–510.

———. "The Doctrine of Everlasting Punishment." *Faith and Philosophy* 7 (1990) 19–42.

———. "Freedom, Damnation, and the Power to Sin with Impunity." *Religious Studies* 37 (2001) 417–34.

———. "The Just Mercy of God: Universal Salvation in George MacDonald." In *All Shall Be Well: Explorations in Universal Salvation and Christian Theology, from Origen to Moltmann*, edited by Gregory MacDonald, 219–46. Eugene, OR: Cascade, 2011.

———. "Misery and Freedom: A Reply to Walls." *Religious Studies* 40 (2004) 217–24.

———. "Providence, Freedom, and Human Destiny." *Religious Studies* 26 (1990) 227–45.

———. "Universalism." In *The Oxford Handbook of Eschatology*, edited by Jerry L. Walls, 446–61. Oxford: Oxford University Press, 2007. Online edition 2009. DOI: 10.1093/oxfordhb/9780195170498.003.0026.

———. "Universalism and the Greater God: Reply to Gordon Knight." *Faith and Philosophy* 16 (1999) 102–5.

———. Universalism and the Supposed Oddity of Our Earthly Life: Reply to Michael Murray." *Faith & Philosophy* 18 (2001) 102–19.

Tamburr, Karl. *The Harrowing of Hell in Medieval England*. Cambridge: Brewer, 2007.

Tanner, Norman, SJ, ed. *Decrees of the Ecumenical Councils*. 2 vols. Washington, DC: Georgetown University Press, 1990.

Taranto, Salvatore. *Gregorio di Nissa: un contributo alla storia dell'interpretazione*. Brescia: Morcelliana, 2009.

Thomas, Arvind. *Piers Plowman and the Reinvention of Church Law in the Late Middle Ages*, Toronto: University of Toronto Press, 2019.

Timotin, Andrei. *La prière dans la tradition platonicienne, de Platon à Proclus*. Turnhout: Brepols, 2017.

Tobon, Monica. *Apatheia and Anthropology in Evagrius of Pontus*. London: Routledge, 2019.

Tollefsen, Torstein. *The Christocentric Cosmology of St. Maximus the Confessor*. Oxford: Oxford University Press, 2008.

Tsirpanlis, Constantine. "The Concept of Universal Salvation in Saint Gregory of Nyssa." In *Greek Patristic Theology I: Basic Doctrines in Eastern Church Fathers*, 41–56. New York: EO Press, 1979.

Tsironis, Niki. "Hades." In *The Concise Encyclopedia of Orthodox Christianity*, edited by John McGuckin, 235–36. Oxford: Wiley-Blackell, 2014.

Tzamalikos, Panayiotis. *Origen: Philosophy of History and Eschatology*. Leiden: Brill, 2007.

Tzamalikos, Panayiotis. *Anaxagoras, Origen, and Neoplatonism: The Legacy of Anaxagoras to Classical and Late Antiquity*, vols. 1–2, Berlin: DeGruyter, 2016.

Van Laak, Werner. *Allversöhnung. Die Lehre von der Apokatastasis, ihre Grundlegung durch Origenes und ihre Bewertung in der gegenwärtigen Theologie bei Karl Barth und Hans Urs von Balthasar*. Sinzig, Germany: Sankt-Ulrich, 1990.

Valentin Vesa. *Knowledge and Experience in the Writings of St. Isaac of Nineveh*, Piscataway: Gorgias, 2018, Eastern Christian Studies 51.

Vasilescu, Elena Ene-D. "Love Never Fails: Gregory of Nyssa on Theosis." In *Visions of God and Ideas on Deification in Patristic Thought*, edited by Mark Edwards, Elena Ene D-Vasilescu, ch. 3. Oxford: Routledge, 2016.

Vinzent, Markus. *Writing the History of Early Christianity: From Reception to Retrospection*, Cambridge: Cambridge University Press, 2009.

Volp, Ulrich. "For the Fashion of This World Passes Away: The *Apokritikos* by Makarios Magnes—An Origenist's Defence of Christian Eschatology?" In *Origeniana Decima*, edited by Sylvia Kaczmarek and Henryk Pietras, 873–89. Leuven: Peeters 2011.

Watson, Nicholas. "Visions of Inclusion: Universal Salvation and Vernacular Theology in Pre–Reformation England." *Journal of Medieval and Early Modern Studies* 27 (1997) 145–87.

Wayman, Benjamin. *Diodore the Theologian: Pronoia in his Commentary on Psalms 1–50*. Turnhout: Brepols, 2014.

Whealey, Alice. "The Greek Fragments Attributed to Eusebius of Caesarea's *Theophania*." *Vigiliae Christianae* 69 (2015) 18–29.

Whitehead, Christiania. "The Late Fourteenth-Century English Mystics." In *The Wiley-Blackwell Companion to Christian Mysticism*, edited by Julia Lamm, 357–71. Oxford: Wiley-Blackwell, 2013.

Wilberding, James. "Eternity in Ancient Philosophy." In *Eternity: A History*, edited by Yitzhak Melamed, 14–55. Oxford: Oxford University Press, 2016.

Williams, Duane. "Feminist Theology and Meister Eckhart's Transgendered Metaphor." *Feminist Theology* 24 (2016) 275–90.

Williams, George Huntston. *The Radical Reformation*. 3rd ed. Kirksville, MO: Truman State University Press, 2000.

Williams, Michael. *Rethinking "Gnosticism": An Argument for Dismantling a Dubious Category*. Princeton, NJ: Princeton University Press, 1999.

Windeatt, Barry. *Julian of Norwich, Revelations of Divine Love*. Oxford: Oxford University Press, 2016.

Woods OP, Richard. *Meister Eckhart: Master of Mystics*. London: Continuum, 2010.